REEL CHANGE:

The Changing Nature of Hollywood, Hollywood Movies, And the People Who Go To See Them

By Bill Mesce, Jr.

REEL CHANGE: The Changing Nature of Hollywood, Hollywood Movies, And the People Who Go To See Them
By Bill Mesce, Jr.
© 2014, Bill Mesce, Jr. All Rights Reserved.
No part of this book may be reproduced in any form or by any means, electronic, mechanical, digital, photocopying or recording, except for the inclusion in a review, without permission in writing from the publisher.

Published in the USA by:
BearManor Media
P O Box 71426
Albany, Georgia 31708
www.bearmanormedia.com

ISBN: 978-1-59393-763-8
Printed in the United States of America
Book design by Robbie Adkins

Front cover image © Riece | Dreamstime.com, back cover image © Krishnacreations | Dreamstime.com

CONTENTS:

Acknowledgments vii

Introduction ix

Walt Disney: The Original Master "Imagineer" 1

Armageddons on a B-Budget 6

Making of the West: Mythmakers and Truth-Tellers 12

Fiftieth Anniversary Thoughts: The Death of Marilyn Monroe,
  The Birth of James Bond 26

They're Blowin' This Town All to Hell! – Sam Peckinpah and *The
  Wild Bunch* 33

Happy Birthday, *A Clockwork Orange!* 41

A Conversation with Producer (and Legendary Cop) Sonny
  Grosso 44

Jeremiah Johnson: Hollywood's Most Beautiful—and Saddest—
  Western 50

Maria Schneider 59

Be-"Seiged": The Gordon Williams Novel v. Sam Peckinpah's
  Straw Dogs v. Rod Lurie's Remake 62

Super Chiefs and the Rise and Fall of the Hollywood Auteur 79

How the Blockbuster Ruined Hollywood 94

Titans: George Lucas v. Steven Spielberg 107

Pyromaniacs: Hollywood's Bad Boys 119

Bubbas, Chop-Sockies, Splatters and Sleaze—Oh My! 127

Right-Hand Man: Mike Elliott 135

On Corman's Front Line: Travis Rink 146

The Grindhouse That Wouldn't Die! 154

Guerilla Filmmaking 163

Neo-Noirist: John Dahl 182

Scorsese & Tarantino: Whose Streets Are Meaner? 190

Cinderella Man's Cinderella Man: Cliff Hollingsworth 202

The "Gray Ones" Fade to Black 209

The Life and Death of the "Passion Pits" 223
What Makes a Classic Movie Classic? 228
Comic-Con Prompts Thoughts on the Prospect of a Great
    Superhero Film... 231
An Uneasy Peace: The Disappearing War Film.....................................236
The Case of the Disappearing Private Eye 251
Raising Cain: The Work of James M. Cain 267
Max Allan Collins (*Road to Perdition*) on Carrying on Mickey
    Spillane's Legacy 275
Whatever the Size, Your TV Is Still Just a TV 284
The Bullying of "Bully," and Other Musings on Screen Violence .. 290
A Conversation with Reviewer Stephen Whitty.................................299
Why Can't an Oscar-Winner Look More Like a Hit? 309
The Artful Roger: A Thank You to Roger Ebert 318
CGI and the Banality of the Incredible 325
Is Motion Capture a Three-Legged Dog? 335
When "Great Leaps Forward" Aren't, or, the Art of Looking Bad 338
Will *The Hobbit's* New Tech Be Enough to Satisfy Audiences 344
We Live in a 3-D World—Or Do We? 347
The World's First Screenwriter: Aristotle 351
Taxman and the Box Office 354
The Piracy Wars: No White Hats Here 359
So Long, Luce: A Mother and Son at the Movies 375
References..382

To Luce, because it would have tickled her no end to see her name in print.

ACKNOWLEDGMENTS

It's a myth that writing is a solitary profession. Just because you sit at the keyboard alone, doesn't mean you're alone, and I would be remiss in the extreme, particularly in a work in which so many of the pieces involve shared experiences, if I didn't thank the many people who helped make this book happen.

First and foremost, I have to mention my colleagues at Sound on Sight, particularly site founder Ricky da Conceicao, the guy who invited me into the fold. Affectionate shout-outs to Kate, Simon, Josh, and Justine.

I have, over the years, been lucky enough to be mentored by some of the brightest guys in the business, but none means more to me than Bill Persky. Thanks, Pop.

And Bernie Dunlap. There was a quote he used to throw around from a director (sorry, Bernie, I can't remember the director's name): "My job is to make you see." Well, Bernie made me see.

I received no better education in the film and TV industry than the twenty-seven years I spent at Home Box Office where I had the good fortune to work for and with an incredible number of gifted and sharing people including Jeff Bewkes, Richard Plepler, Dave Pritchard, Jim Noonan, Dave Baldwin, Bob Conte, Bridget Potter, and many, many more.

Then there's the family that puts up with a lot of crap from me when I'm involved in these endeavors.

And a special acknowledgment to the guys I spent so many hours with in movie theaters, at drive-ins (when they still existed), and sometimes staying up late in front of someone's TV. It was never as much fun as that.

INTRODUCTION

In August of 2010, I'd been out of work almost exactly a year, which was plenty of time to find that all the bleak stories I'd been hearing since the 2007 financial meltdown about the lack of employability for ex-corporate staffers above a certain age who'd been on the street a certain amount of time were true. I was still trying to figure out what my Second Act was going to be when I answered an online ad looking for people to write about movies.

I'd had a couple of cinema books published through academic houses years before; in fact, I had some backlogged material, which had had to be cut from those books. Maybe what this ad was offering was a chance for me to get some mileage out of those pieces. My initial interest didn't go much beyond that.

I submitted a test piece and, based on that, I was invited to contribute to Sound on Sight; a website then only a few years old dedicated to looking at film and TV (and later branching out into comic books).

This wasn't the dry academic formalism I'd had to write within on my previous work. This was writing with a passion along with other passionate lovers of film *for* passionate lovers of film. It reminded me of the old days, back in my college dorm, up late with the other film geeks and talking about this new guy Scorsese and how the latest Woody Allen had us practically peeing in our pants, and Kubrick, well, there was a guy whose head didn't work like anybody else's, and on and on and on. I hadn't realized how much I'd missed those dorm room squawk sessions.

Writing for Sound on Sight brought that back to me, and I soon went past those backlogged pieces to pour that revived energy into new posts, as I grappled with the changing face of a medium and an industry that had meant so much to me for so many years, both professionally and personally.

At about the same time, I found my Second Act; I began teaching as an adjunct instructor at several colleges and universities in New Jersey. But when the work was sparse, or paid badly (as it almost always did), or when my students had me reaching for the aspirin, I could turn to Sound on Sight, and when I wasn't losing myself in the fun of writing my own pieces, I could lose myself in the fun of reading the pieces by my new colleagues... and yes, my new friends.

I never met them (and still haven't), and maybe the connection I felt was no more than the connection of people who share an interest. That made it no less real for me, and in the years that I've contributed to Sound on Sight, they've come to mean a great deal to me. Maybe that's because without them and without the site, a hard time in my life would've been a whole lot harder.

The pieces here are not arranged in the order they were posted, but roughly follow a motion picture industry chronology from the post-World War II period up to the present day, tracing the changing face of movies, the movie industry, and the collective mindset of the people who go to movies. I hope you enjoy reading them at least half as much as I enjoyed writing them.

Walt Disney: The Original Master "Imagineer"
(posted 8/1/12)

Full disclosure: when I was a kid, I didn't like Disney cartoons. My family took me to all of them—new and the regularly rereleased: *Pinocchio* (1940), *Bambi* (1942), *Snow White and the Seven Dwarfs* (1937), *Lady and the Tramp* (1955). And we went to see the live-action Disney flicks too: *20,000 Leagues Under the Sea* (1954), *The Shaggy Dog* (1959), *The Absent-Minded Professor* (1961). I watched Disney's short cartoons on his Sunday night showcase, *Walt Disney's Wonderful World of Color*, and on reruns of *The Mickey Mouse Club*. Yeah, I saw it all... but I didn't particularly like a lot of it.

Disney—the brand, not the man—was cute. It was nice. It was sweet. So much so, it made my cavities hurt.

When it came to cartoons, even as a kid, I preferred the classic Warners shorts from the 1930s-1950s. They were made for less money and on shorter schedules than the Disney cartoons, but they weren't interested in being cute. In fact, according to Chuck Jones, one of Warners' best animators, they knew they couldn't match the adorability of Disney's stuff, so they didn't even try. Instead, they went another way. They went for *funny*. And not nice funny, but funny in a kind of sharp-edged, street-savvy, wise-ass way that really clicked with a kid growing up in Newark.

Even later, as a film student, while my appreciation had grown for what Disney had accomplished with animation—elevating it from a novelty to an art and big-money business—I still didn't like his stuff much. And because of that, I never gave the man the credit he deserved, not as an animator (although he deservedly stands as one of the giants in the field) or for, well, you'd have to say his vision.

That's a word that gets tossed around a lot in the movie business: vision. Spielberg's vision, Lucas's vision, Kubrick's vision. You hear it a lot. But when it comes to the—as Bush #1 infamously put it—"the vision thing," Walt Disney saw further, and in more shades and dimensions than anyone else in the history of modern entertainment. To use a word he coined for his guys who helped put together Disneyland, he was truly and completely an Imagineer.

Intellectually, I'd long come to understand that. George Lucas gets credit for redesigning the movie business by, through his example, pushing the industry toward vertically integrated entertainment combines with the various arms feeding—and feeding off of—each other. But Lucas based his game plan on something Disney, by the time of *Star Wars* (1977), had had in place for decades.

As early as the 1950s, Disney had expanded from moviemaking into television, music, merchandising, and, with the 1955 opening of Disneyland, amusement parks, using each as a platform to promote and support the others. His TV shows kept Disney fans abreast of all the latest goings-on during the five years it took to develop Disneyland, pumping up their curiosity and anticipation. When the park opened, there were rides and merchandise keying off Disney TV shows and movies. Each new Disney film provided more TV spin-off and/or promotional opportunities as well as merchandise, which was hawked at Disneyland and so on and so forth in an endless cycle of constant cross-promotion.

But I don't think I appreciated the breadth of Walt Disney's vision at a visceral level until a recent vacation I took with my family to Orlando. The brilliance of the guy sunk in when, on our first night in Orlando, we took the kids to the Magic Kingdom to watch the nightly fireworks display which goes off over the Cinderella Castle: the park's centerpiece.

When you enter either Disneyland or Disney World, you start at the head of Main Street USA: a boulevard designed to look like straw-hat era, smog-free, horse-drawn carriage America. Framed at the far end of Main Street is Cinderella's Castle. In anticipation of the fireworks, the lights are dimmed, then the sky fills with flaming bursts choreographed to music, and the picture is complete.

It's not a random assemblage, and the architects didn't just get lucky. There's not another major amusement park in the United States designed with such attention to how it'll look from certain vantage points: not the Six Flags parks, not MGM/Universal, not King's Dominion, not Colonial Williamsburg.

And that's no accident.

That's the magic of Disney. That's the master Imagineer at work.

*****

When Walt Disney broke ground for Disneyland on 160 flat, unsculpted acres of what had been orange and walnut groves near Anaheim, California, his charge to his Imagineers was, "I just want it to look like nothing else in the world."

Disney wasn't after just another amusement park. It was a grander concept than that.

"Disneyland is a show," he said. "Disneyland is the star, everything else is in the supporting role." He wanted to create a total, unified, engulfing environment—*that* was the attraction, not the rides and exhibits. "I want (people) to feel like they're in another world."

Well, they did... and they didn't. Disneyland wasn't another world, but an idealized, dreamy version of *this* world. America, anyway. The kind of rural, not-too-over-developed, still simple but forward-looking America you see in those *Twilight Zone* episodes about a harried business exec yearning for a simpler time of band concerts on the village green. Disneyland was, by Disney's own edict, "... dedicated to the ideals, the dreams, and the hard facts that have created America..." It is, in effect, a 3-D presentation on unbridled optimism. With the arguable exception of its roller coasters, there aren't even any scary rides at Disneyland.

OK, you could argue this kind of thesis made the place a little overly nationalistic, maybe even oppressively patriotic (Uncle Walt was, after all, the guy who branded the animators who tried to unionize his shop as Commies and destroyed a career or two when he testified in front of the House Un-American Activities Committee), and certainly a bit kitschy and sentimental... but damned if it doesn't work.

It certainly worked in 1955. People had been telling Disney—who had tied up every nickel he had in building the park—it would be a disaster. It was expected to be a come-and-go novelty that would ultimately leave a big smoking crater where Disney's company had been.

I think you know how that played out.

But even after the immediate and overwhelming success of Disneyland, its creator remained committed to seeing what else he could do, how much further he could push.

By the end of the decade, commercial jet travel was turning the whole country into one, big, family vacation opportunity. Florida had been a get-away spot for the moneyed set back to the late nineteenth century, but cheap flights put it in reach of anyone, everyone. That spurred Uncle Walt to see something out there in the empty swamps around Orlando: a family haven even bigger and more spectacular than Disneyland.

The Magic Kingdom would be the draw, but his passion was the Experimental Prototype City—EPCOT: a vision of the future turned real (the EPCOT that now stands, built years after Disney's death, is substantially different than what he had envisioned, although he no doubt would have appreciated its expansion of his concept of enveloping visitors in foreign environments).

Disney never saw Disney World realized. He died in 1966, one year before construction began, but it was every bit his Disney World. Yeah, it was bigger, fancier than Disneyland, but it shared the same branding imagery, the same upbeat, all-American, it-just-feels-so-damned-good-to-be-here atmosphere, the same completely immersive experience of being in a cohesive, complete someplace else, yet a place always and easily recognizable as eminently Disneyesque.

No entertainment entrepreneur ever invested as much effort and imagination into branding as Disney did. Mickey Mouse became more than a character: he became an internationally recognized icon. Stick those two, round ears on something—*anything*—and everybody knows it signifies Mickey/Disney.

Or take the Cinderella Castle. It's as much a real-world logo as an amusement park attraction. Its silhouette at the beginning of Disney flicks immediately communicates almost a century's worth of meaning in a way the Warners WB shield or 20th Century Fox's fanfare doesn't. Those are just company logos; that castle and the name "Disney" *mean* something.

I understood—I mean I really got what Disney had pulled off—some years ago when I was still working at HBO. It wasn't long after our parent, Time Inc., had merged with Warner Communications in 1989 to form Time Warner. Warner held a part ownership in the Six Flags string of amusement parks. Part of the goal of the merger was to vertically integrate the various businesses of Time and Warner, and one of the strategies mentioned was to get Warners' cartoon characters out there into the Six Flags parks à la Disney.

And they did. But it didn't really create much of a spark. Kids took their pictures with Bugs and Daffy, but it was more of a, Yeah, they're cute, but so what?

Even when the parks introduced the Batman ride, I doubt few park patrons made the connection that the park and Batman and Batman's movie home at Warner Bros., and his literary home at D.C. Comics all lived under the same Time Warner roof. It didn't all cohere the way all those similar kinds of parts did at Disney, because at Time

Warner, it was an after-the-fact plan. For Disney, that had been his plan from the get-go; he didn't create characters and settings, he nursed his creations into icons. Disney's greatest creation wasn't any one thing: it was that Disney universe.

I still don't like Disney's classic cartoons, and, as entrancing as the parks are, I'm still a parent who gets pains shooting up and down his left arm when he sees what things there cost. Uncle Walt may have made a lot of noises about doing things for more reasons than money, but family lunch at a sit-down restaurant in one of his parks costs about as much as a kidney transplant (or at least it feels that way).

Still...

As I stood out in front of Cinderella's Castle that night, oohing and ahhing right along with my kids, I got it. I saw what Walt Disney had done, and saw that no one else had ever—and probably never would—come close.

I knew that castle long before I'd ever stood in front of it because I'd seen it a thousand times in movies and TV shows over the course of my entire life. Bathed in colored lights and the flashes of fireworks, it looked exactly the way I thought it would, because Uncle Walt had designed it to look that way.

Armageddons on a B-Budget
(posted 10/14/10)

Science-fiction, horror, monsters on the loose—they've been a part of the movies almost since the beginning of the medium. Georges Méliès famously turned out a vaudeville-flavored adaptation of Jules Verne's *From the Earth to the Moon* in 1904, the Edison company produced the first of a nearly century-long parade of film (and later TV) adaptations of Mary Shelley's *Frankenstein* in 1910, and early special effects wizard Willis O'Brien sent a stop-motion animated dinosaur rampaging through the streets of London in a 1925 version of *The Lost World*, paving the way for future generations of similarly marauding giant apes, resurrected dinosaurs, and oversized insects. Still—on a purely quantitative basis—the collective output in genres of the fantastic and macabre throughout cinema's early years was dwarfed by a massive explosion in their popularity following the Second World War.

It was the beginning of the Atomic Age, the Space Age, and the Cold War. At the same time, the movie business was growing increasingly dependent on a young audience with leisure time, disposable income, and which also—due to the events of the day—possessed a sense of great and horrible scientific possibility as well as the ever-present threat of nuclear annihilation. Throughout the 1950s, the youth audience's appetite for the sensational and fantastic was fed with a steady diet of, for the most part, cheaply made, shabbily produced, blatantly juvenile sci-fi thrillers and monster movies heavy on action and short on credibility, yet often still managing to touch on the conscious and subliminal fears of the time, particularly the only half-understood effects of atomic weapons, and the Cold War possibilities of invasion, subversion, and wholesale destruction.

There were massive alien onslaughts (*The War of the Worlds*, 1953), and less conspicuous extraterrestrial infiltrations (*Invaders from Mars*, 1953); any number of prehistoric beasts resurrected from their hibernations (*The Deadly Mantis*, 1957) or discovered in remote, unevolved corners of the world (*The Land Unknown*, 1957); monster-creating experiments gone awry (*The Killer Shrews*, 1959) and accidental mutations (*Beginning of the End*, 1957); the odd end-of-the-world scenario (*Day the World Ended*, 1955).

Even by the standards of the day, many of these entries were embarrassingly bad. In *Invaders from Mars,* the dorsal zippers on the costumes of the alien "mu-tants" are painfully obvious; the overgrown *Killer Shrews* are clearly dogs in shaggy coats; the army of giant grasshoppers overrunning Chicago in *Beginning of the End* are too evidently *not* scaling the side of a downtown newspaper building, but crawling along a 2-D photograph of same.

Still, among the massive amounts of dross, a few golden nuggets did emerge. Many of the more memorable sci-fiers from the period share several characteristics. For one, they were often the successful, more attentively made prototype from which cheaper, sillier clones glutting the market were derived. For another, their elevated quality owes no small debt to the fact they were often turned out by storytellers with a stronger grounding in mainstream drama than in sci-fi and fantasy. For many of these moviemakers, such work had less to do with an interest in aliens or the usual trappings of movie science-fiction than in the dramatic promise of the material, and these directors and producers creatively connected with their stories in fashions no different or any less serious than they did with any other property.

Howard Hawks was already an established director of high reputation with films like *His Girl Friday* (1940), *The Big Sleep* (1946), and *Red River* (1948) to his credit when he produced his only sci-fi effort—and a classic 1950s sci-fier—*The Thing from Another World* (1951). Director Robert Wise—whose later films included the classic musical *West Side Story* (1961), insightful historical epic *The Sand Pebbles* (1966), and the science "factual" *The Andromeda Strain* (1971)—had begun his career as an editor at RKO working on prestigious films like *Citizen Kane* (1941) and *The Magnificent Ambersons* (1942), then served his directorial apprenticeship in RKO's B-unit, helming superior if small-scale efforts like gothic horror *The Body Snatcher* (1945), and the dramatically full-bodied Western, *Blood on the Moon* (1948), before turning to *The Day the Earth Stood Still* (1951), another piece of memorable 1950s sci-fi. Cambridge-educated Don Siegel—who, twenty years later, would begin a fruitful collaboration with Clint Eastwood on a string of films including *Dirty Harry* (1971) and *Escape from Alcatraz* (1979)—had come out of Warner Bros.' shorts department to direct several tough, smart B-pictures like *The Big Steal* (1949) and *Riot in Cell Block 11* (1954) before turning out his only sci-fi movie—yet another celebrated tale of the fantastic from the period, *Invasion of the Body Snatchers* (1956).

Still other sci-fiers which, perhaps, don't deserve to be labeled classics, are nevertheless worthwhile and remain entertaining today thanks to the non-fantasist pedigree of their makers. Eugène Lourié, who launched the revived-dinosaur-on-the-loose trend with *The Beast from 20,000 Fathoms* (1953), was not even a director by trade, but a respected art director who had worked with director Jean Renoir in his native France before coming to the U.S. in the 1940s. It was no doubt Lourié's designer's eye that helped him camouflage the thinness of his $250,000 budget with a visual stylist's flair and a penchant for mood. Only able to afford having his creature—brought to life by the dean of stop-motion animation, Ray Harryhausen—on-screen for just a few minutes of his movie's eighty-minute running time, Lourié hoards that precious footage, often showing the beast only in brief, tantalizing glimpses, or keeping it cloaked in darkness.

To cite one particularly illustrative moment: the beast has come ashore in lower Manhattan. That night, the city is under blackout orders with citizens ordered to stay in their home—a dramatically valid and clever device for keeping the streets of Warner Bros.' back lot set dark and depopulated. As the animal prowls among the shadowy downtown canyons, it comes in contact with an electrical barrier set up by the military. In lightning flashes, the beast is seen roaring and rearing in pain as it touches the hot wires. Blackout. Then, fade up on silent files of soldiers moving slowly along the blacked-out avenues tracking the blood spoor from the wounded creature, the only sound their boots on the pavement.

Lourié's precise and restrained handling of *The Beast* becomes more impressive when compared to the similarly plotted, but more opulently produced, 1998 remake of *Godzilla* (estimated budget: $130 million). Where Lourié's lean and focused plot tantalizes and tries to treat its fantastic premise with a measure of intelligence, *Godzilla* is a loud, busy, often ridiculous and bloated construction, trading mood and mystery for overwhelming spectacle and numbing action.

Gordon Douglas was a solid journeyman director with a full, well-rounded resumé (his filmography includes everything from Hal Roach comedies to the gritty Frank Sinatra vehicle *The Detective* [1968]) who brought a craftsman's touch to his one sci-fi title, the movie that launched the giant bug cycle: *Them!*, a fast-paced yet disciplined story about giant ants which, in the film's action-packed climax, nest in the storm sewers of Los Angeles. The mechanical ants may seem laughable compared to present-day CGI creations, but Douglas's handling of such fantastic material—presenting his incredible tale with a low-key, almost *Dragnet*-like proceduralism—gives the film a deliciously slow build and sense of mystery typically lacking in today's more extravagantly produced, hyperkinetic effects-fests.

*****

While so much downscale sci-fi product from the 1950s was turned out by producers and directors whose chief talent seemed to be no more than an ability to bring their movies in on time and within their scanty budgets, there were a few genre specialists who managed—even within their budget constraints—to deliver tales of the incredible with a recognized intelligence, and more than a little flair and style.

Producer George Pal is often credited with launching the 1950s science-fiction boom with such early successes as *Destination Moon* (1950), *When Worlds Collide* (1951), and *The War of the Worlds*. Pal's movies typically benefited from more upscale production values than most 1950s sci-fi fare, with a good deal of his budgets going into what were then remarkable special effects giving his movies—still small by major studio standards—a grand-scale feel.

One of Pal's favorite directors was Byron Haskin. A one-time newsreel cameraman, cinematographer, and special effects technician, Haskin brought a sense of visual style missing in so much 1950s sci-fi to Pal's fantasies. Looking at *The War of the Worlds*, one is struck by Haskin's carefully orchestrated visual plan; gliding, extended, scene-setting crane shots, contrasting with sharp static diagonals and increasingly frantic, fragmenting cutting in his action sequences.

Haskin's films for Pal were well above the 1950s sci-fi norm thanks to Pal's ambition to position his projects as serious, major efforts. Most sci-fi directors of the time, however, plied their trade at an unmistakably B level (or lower).

Of those who regularly worked in the genre, only one seemed able to routinely and sure-footedly walk the line between creative cinema and commercial necessity: Jack Arnold.

Arnold directed a series of modestly budgeted sci-fi films for Universal through the mid-1950s, stretching the genre as far as imagination and his limited budgets allowed. He successfully added the first new creature to the Universal horror ranks (think Frankenstein, the Wolf Man, the Mummy, Dracula, and the Invisible Man) in over two decades, with his three pictures featuring the Creature from the Black Lagoon. His movies set in the California desert are respected by genre aficionados for his ability to exploit the barren terrain's sense of isolation and threat.

Best of the desert series, *It Came from Outer Space* (1953), shows Arnold's skill at creating a sense of foreboding without resorting to budget-busting effects or gimmickry. The story of a crash-landed alien vessel whose inhabitants take human form in a benign but misinterpreted effort to repair their ship and be on their way, Arnold wisely avoids showing the aliens as much as possible. Instead, their presence is depicted in the subtle giveaways in their human guises: a woman unfazed by a chill desert wind, a man staring unblinkingly into the blinding sun.

Arnold's acknowledged masterwork is the self-described *The Incredible Shrinking Man* (1957). What could have been a simple gimmick movie gradually becomes an essay on the value of every individual's existence. The movie is, for the time, surprisingly downbeat: there is no cure, no rescue for the protagonist (Grant Williams). The story moves from visceral excitement—a doll-sized Williams stalked by a housecat—to a grim, brutal battle for survival between a still-smaller Williams and a spider in the shadowy basement of his abandoned house.

On the verge of turning completely dour as Williams helplessly shrinks to the microscopic, Richard Matheson's script (adapted from his own novel) instead takes a turn toward the inspirational. Looking up at the star-filled night sky, size, Williams muses, has nothing to do with worth: "So close—the infinitesimal and the infinite." As Arnold's camera pulls up and away from the dwindling Williams, and Elliot Lawrence's score swells as images of mammoth galaxies float by, Williams realizes no life—however small—is meaningless. And his last voiceover lines are a defiant: "To God, there is no zero! I still exist!"

True, these were the exceptions rather than the norm. Most of the sci-fi and fantasy that played across 1950s movie screens was nothing more than cheaply produced, forgettable matinee fodder; movies with no more ambition than to divert the young folk on a weekend afternoon.

But, on occasion, a sharp director, an ambitious producer, a keen writer was able to turn a little into a lot... in contrast to the situation today, when so many with so much manage to accomplish so little.

Making Of The West: Mythmakers and Truth-Tellers
(posted 11/4/10)

The "adult" Western—as it would come to be called – was a long time coming. A Hollywood staple since the days of *The Great Train Robbery* (1903), the Western offered spectacle and action set against the uniquely American milieu of the Old West—a historical period which, at the dawn of the motion picture industry, was still fresh in the nation's memory. What the genre rarely offered was dramatic substance.

Early Westerns often adopted the same traditions of the popular Wild West literature and dime novels of the nineteenth and early twentieth centuries producing, as a consequence, highly romantic, almost purely mythic portraits the Old West. Through the early decades of the motion picture industry, the genre went through several creative cycles, alternately tilting from fanciful to realistic and back again. By the early sound era, and despite such serious efforts as *The Big Trail* (1930) and *The Virginian* (1929), Hollywood Westerns were, by and large, downscale offerings, usually cheaply made bottom-of-the-bill fodder with a distinctly juvenile flavor. By the end of the decade, however, the major studios had begun to upgrade their Westerns, and, more frequently, they were A-caliber productions with major stars in front of the camera and top-ranked talent behind it.

Yet the heart of the improved Western, while it had become less childish, hadn't grown all that much more sophisticated. The movies were better produced, the storytelling more polished, but entries still tended to stress action and adventure over drama, and their collective image of the West remained sanitized and idealized, still rooted not in history, but in the kind of dime fiction tropes popularized by pulp novelists like Ned Buntline.

Change for the Western came with World War II. During the war years—and more markedly, in the postwar period—moviemakers began to explore the potential of the Western to deal with themes, stories, and characters with a dramatic heft equal to any other genre e.g. *The Ox-Bow Incident* (1943), a brooding, adamant indictment of vigilante justice; *The Gunfighter* (1950), a ruminative portrait of a gunman haunted by his bloody past; *High Noon* (1952) and its allegorical story of social responsibility and collective cowardice.

As the genre grew more popular and dramatically promising, any number and variety of directors assayed the Western: William Wyler turned out the epic-scaled *The Big Country* (1958), Edward Dmytryk gave the so-called "psychological Western" a try with *Warlock* (1959), as did Arthur Penn with his introspective spin on the Billy the Kid legend, *The Left-Handed Gun* (1958), and George Stevens delivered one of the most revered and referenced titles of the early adult Western period with *Shane* (1953). While many other noteworthy Westerns also came from one-time visitors to the genre, some of the most significant contributions to the adult Western came from a handful of moviemakers for whom the form was their frequent touchstone.

The directors who demonstrated an affinity for the Western tended to fall into two, not always completely separate schools, one of which were the romantics, its promulgators in love with the mythic Old West. The poet laureate of the romantics, and a director whose name would become synonymous with the Western, and who may have been more responsible than any other moviemaker of the time for the artistic and commercial elevation of the genre, was John Ford.

Though his filmography contains everything from broad comedy *(Donovan's Reef,* 1963), to war stories *(They Were Expendable,* 1945), to a classic story of loyalty and betrayal during the Irish "troubles" *(The Informer,* 1935), Westerns were his first love. He once claimed that, given a choice, they were "... all I would make."

Born in Maine of Irish immigrants, with no personal knowledge of the frontier, Ford unabashedly embraced a romanticized vision of the West. His sense of the mythic and the imagined showed in nearly every frame. His favorite setting was Monument Valley, though it would've been impossible for the pioneers and ranchers he often idyllically pictured there to have eked out even the barest living from such a wasteland. His stories played out in openly sentimental broad strokes. His heroes were as majestic and outsized as the spires of Monument Valley, and as pure of heart and chivalric in their conduct as Round Table knights. His villains were despicably villainous; his Indians either ruthless or noble savages; his comic relief broad; male relationships were characterized by a sense of frat house high-jinx-leavened camaraderie; and it seemed a virtual mandate for his cavalry features to include a burly, hard-drinking career sergeant, and one or two bumbling junior officers. His female characters were often his weakest: tittering old biddies, stoic pioneer or soldiers' wives, and pretty young things waiting patiently for the obligatory romantic subplot to resolve itself. Ford preferred action and plain-speaking men to sexual intrigue, and his on-screen male/female relationships avoided strong passion, resembling, instead, awkward high school romances.

If Ford's West and its Westerners are fables, they are nonetheless fables with heart, set in an imaginary land, peopled by characters who may not be realistic but are nonetheless idealized reflections of human concerns, foibles, and aspirations. The flesh-and-blood heft of Ford's fables comes from his gift for texture, the *feel* of a story more important to him than the story itself. The pace of his pictures—like that of his characters—is unrushed, and his stories, his settings, and his people are given ample breathing room to come alive.

All these elements fit together snugly in what is usually considered his best movie, *The Searchers* (1956). John Wayne, one of Ford's favorite leading men, embarks on an epic years-long quest to find his niece taken by the Indians who slaughtered her family. Accompanied by a naifish Jeffrey Hunter, for whom Vera Miles endlessly waits back home with marriage in mind, Wayne's Ethan is an Ahab-like obsessive, his hatred of Indians so bone-deep he slaughters passing buffalo on the chance they might provide the despised Comanche with food. It becomes a nagging question as to whether or not Ethan will actually save his niece (Natalie Wood), or find her so corrupted by life among her captors that he'll write her off as one of the tribe and kill her. The ending is Ford's sentimental side wielded at his expert best: Wayne corners Wood, grabs her small frame and holds her high as if to dash her down, but, instead, brings her down in an embrace; family survives all, good reclaims the damaged part of the heart. He returns her to her relatives where she is welcomed warmly, and then Ethan, perhaps too long on his quest to know anything but the pursuit, awkwardly turns his back on the off-screen reunion, and, framed by the dark doorway of the family home, heads back out into the glaring white sands of Monument Valley.

The tenor of Ford's movies would change through the 1950s, becoming tinged with darker, more unsettling and less reassuring sentiments. In *The Searchers*, Natalie Wood is taken back into white civilization without pause, but by the time of Ford's *Two Rode Together* (1961), returned white captives are ostracized and looked down upon; Ford's frontier settlers are no longer icons of decency but carriers of suspicion and prejudice.

These gloomier themes made a poor fit with Ford's poetic touch. In *Sergeant Rutledge* (1960), the story of a black cavalryman tried for the rape/murder of a little girl, the bird-like old ladies in the gallery, the thundering Judge Advocate, the ennobled accused, the hysterical breakdown of the real perpetrator on the stand all have the over-the-top flavor of Victorian melodrama; his Civil War tale *The Horse Soldiers* (1959) builds to an apocalyptic battle Ford cannot deliver; *Cheyenne Autumn* (1964), his most concerted attempt to sympathetically tell the Native American side of the conquest of the West, falters from an inability to truly understand the character of the people he is trying to ennoble.

Even in the best of his later works, Ford's sentimental streak collided with the brutal reality he seemed to be striving for. *The Man Who Shot Liberty Valance* (1962) has James Stewart as an idealistic lawyer from the east come to practice on the frontier. He becomes a favorite target of abuse by sadistic gunman Valance (Lee Marvin), and competes for the affections of Vera Miles with rough-hewn rancher John Wayne. Shot in a *noir*-ish black-and-white, there's an apprehensive sense of tragedy and violence waiting to break through the movie's shadowy surface at any moment, and a brutality Ford rarely displayed. (His fictional version of the Custer massacre in *Fort Apache* [1948] took place cloaked in a swirl of dust.) Ultimately, Stewart and Marvin face-off, the inept Stewart miraculously kills Marvin, and then is shamed when the fame of the killing carries him to political prominence. Later, Wayne confesses to Stewart it was really Wayne who killed Marvin, shooting him from the shadows as Stewart fired. Recognizing, as Ford heroes often do, a greater good at stake and a greater need at hand, Wayne pushes Stewart on his political path for the betterment of the territory, and steps out of his rival's way re: Ms. Miles. Wayne becomes the Old West obligingly lying down to die so the new, civilized West can take its place.

The Fordian romantic touch plagues the movie with contrivances: Wayne is such a take-no-guff character one constantly wonders why he doesn't dispatch Marvin from the outset; the local law is the ludicrous, quaking Andy Devine, an incredible choice for a town terrorized by the likes of Liberty Valance. Stewart and Miles are too old for their socially awkward roles—especially Stewart—Ford ignoring their seasoned visages and seeing them, instead, in the kinds of roles they had played years (in Stewart's case, a generation) before.

Ford was the best of the romantics, but hardly the only one. Prominent among the others stands Howard Hawks. Hawks did not visit the Western as much as Ford, but, like Ford, he favored manly tales, and his Westerns carry much the same flavor as his other actioners such as *Hatari!* (1962), *Air Force* (1943), and *Only Angels Have Wings* (1939).

Hawks believed in a harder, more violent set of myths than Ford, but which had just as little connection to the historical West. Hawks's Western ethos reflected, rather, his own Hemingwayesque background as a hard-drinking outdoorsman, combined with a simple moviemaking agenda of entertaining an audience. He defined the Western simply as "… gunplay and horses."

His on-screen world was generally male, and the alphas among them were unequivocal men of action solving a problem with a quick draw rather than fast talk, and who could hit what they aimed at. His heroes were not common men taking up arms to defend themselves; Hawks sanctified, instead, the skilled professional, a thesis most clearly expressed in one of his best movies, *Rio Bravo* (1959, a story Hawks returned to in the de facto remakes *El Dorado* [1967] and *Rio Lobo* [1970]). John Wayne plays a sheriff backed by rehabilitated town drunk *cum* top gun hand Dean Martin, fast-on-the-draw Ricky Nelson, and cackling deputy Walter Brennan. Wayne arrests a land-grabbing rancher on a murder charge. The remaining running time consists of Wayne and company fending off various attempts by the bad guy rancher's henchmen to free him. The Hawks villain is often superfluous, consigned, in *Rio Bravo* (and its remakes), to a jail cell and ignored for much of the movie, serving mainly only to spark the action. The good townspeople are both helpless and hapless, their well-meaning volunteerism shooed aside by the professionals who warn them they'll only get in the way.

Like Ford, Hawks seemed more comfortable with men than women in his action movies. His on-screen romances have the same adolescent awkwardness as Ford's, and though Hawks gives his women an independence and outspokenness not often apparent in Ford's work, his model of the ideal woman for his action heroes became, over the course of the 1950s and into the 1960s, that of a tomboy able to smoke, drink (and, on occasion, pick up a gun) as well as a man... only wrapped in a voluptuous and available package.

Ford sold legends: Hawks provided entertainment. In opposition to both was, in the 1950s, an expanding school of Western directors attempting to inject the genre with a greater historical accuracy and/or dramatic honesty, looking for a successful blending of the audience-stirring mythic and the revelatory realistic. Though none of these moviemakers ever achieved the stature of Ford or Hawks, some of their work remains among the best in the genre.

The trademark of the Westerns helmed by Delmer Daves was a legitimately come by authenticity. Unlike the eastern-raised Ford, Daves was the grandson of pioneers who had crossed the West by covered wagon. His grandfather had been a Pony Express rider, and Daves had spent periods of his youth among Hopi and Navajo tribes. Whereas Ford had wanted to picture the West as he thought it should be, Daves wanted to capture the West as he *knew* it to be. His sympathies for Native Americans came through in *Broken Arrow* (1950), and his feel for the grittiness of the West showed itself in his depictions of ranch life in *Jubal* (1955), and particularly his harsh portrait of the cattle trail in *Cowboy* (1958). His acknowledged best work is the tense, psychologically dense *3:10 to Yuma* (1957), its script by Halsted Welles seemingly designed to deliberately refute *High Noon*'s earnest lessons in social responsibility, and the Hawks myth of the gunman-as-knight-errant *à la Rio Bravo*.

Van Heflin is an impoverished farmer who takes the job of safeguarding outlaw Glenn Ford until a train can arrive to carry Ford to prison. Where *Rio Bravo*—and its loose remakes—ran on action, with Good Guys and Bad Guys engaging in a series of gun-blazing moves and countermoves, *3:10* is nearly all dramatic suspense. The duel here is a mental one, with Ford working on Van Heflin's increasingly fraying nerves. Oozing the same purring charisma he'd used on women earlier in the movie, Ford tries to seduce the farmer with bribes, alert him to the certainty of death, worry him with images of his wife as a widow and his son left fatherless. At some point, the psychology tips the other way, and Ford, coming to identify with the plight of the farmer, ultimately helps him escape his outlaw band and get on the train to Yuma Prison.

Howard Hawks despised and misconstrued *3:10 to Yuma* for the very elements that make it such a unique and exceptional Western.

In the Hawks universe, the "sheriff"—as Hawks mis-identified Van Heflin—would have said, "You better hope your friends *don't* catch up with you because you'll be the first man to die." But Van Heflin is no lawman nor any kind of professional gunslinger. The strength of the movie is in his resounding ordinariness. He's afraid, he hesitates, and he's reluctant to use a gun. He has taken the job out of economic necessity only to find himself in an unexpected life-and-death situation he neither wishes nor has any taste for.

Budd Boetticher had spent a number of years in Mexico, some as a professional bullfighter, and, like Delmer Daves, preferred his Westerns with a rougher edge than Ford's, and less glamorized than Hawks's. Boetticher was one of a number of directors who worked in the B-movie realm but gave their work an A-caliber dignity. He imbued his modestly budgeted pictures with an emotional and psychological undercoat he considered essential. Though he would make a variety of movies throughout his career, ranging from *The Bullfighter and the Lady* (1950) to the stylish gangster bio *The Rise and Fall of Legs Diamond* (1960), Boetticher would become particularly noted for a series of tough-hided little Westerns he made in partnership with actor Randolph Scott: *Seven Men from Now* (1956), *The Tall T* (1957), *Decision at Sundown* (1957), *Buchanan Rides Alone* (1958), *Ride Lonesome* (1959), *Westbound* (1959), and *Comanche Station* (1960).

By Boetticher's own admission, the plots of most of his Westerns— often written by Burt Kennedy—were only variations on the same general storyline: the hero is on a quest to find his wife's murderer. Where Boetticher excelled was in the nuance and depth he could build into these simple, repetitive plots.

According to Boetticher, one dramatic line he enjoyed exploring was the parallel between a Good Guy with his vengeance-distorted values, and a Bad Guy trying to break with his villainous past. He eschewed the sentimentality of Ford, or the macho swagger of Hawks, opting instead for a sharp-edged but underplayed quality. Unlike Hawks's heroes, the protagonists invariably played by Randolph Scott are not professional gunmen and rarely win through superior gunplay. Scott's heroes are average men driven to obsessive quests by trauma, sometimes to the point of self-destructiveness. Or, in another variation, they are pulled, by chance, into another character's predicament that resonates with his own. As important as Scott's combat with the Bad Guys in Boetticher's Westerns, is Scott's inner fight to avoid being utterly consumed by his monomania.

In contrast to Hawks's perfunctory villains, Boetticher's Bad Guys are usually the most interesting characters in his movies. These are fully realized characters, not always completely reprehensible, sometimes seeing in Scott—as in *The Tall T*— the kind of man they could have been barring a bad turn or two. The standard Good-Guy-chasing-Bad-Guy form became, in Boetticher's hands, a moral debate between the hero and his articulate doppelganger who had "... 'crossed over' into the world of crime..." Boetticher compounded the gravitas given his villains by his scripts with shrewd casting, displaying a fine eye for rising talent: Lee Marvin, Richard Boone, James Best, L.Q. Jones, Claude Akins, Henry Silva, Pernell Roberts, Lee Van Cleef, and James Coburn all spent time facing off against Scott.

Instead of pioneer ancestors or an adventure-filled biography, Anthony Mann came to the movies from the New York stage where he'd been an actor and director. He may not have had Daves's and Boetticher's innate sense of the authentic, but his Westerns are more dramatically dense and marked by a sometimes disturbing psychological intensity.

Mann first made his mark as the director of several impressive B-*noirs*, and he brought that same bleak sensibility and visual flair to a series of more upscale Westerns he made over the course of the 1950s, most memorable of which were several featuring James Stewart. Even compared to realists like Daves and Boetticher, Mann's movies are striking in their consistent tough-mindedness, cruel violence, and disconsolate mood. Mann's Westerns may be among the most disturbing and violent of the 1950s.

Like Boetticher's heroes, Mann's protagonists are obsessed, but where Randolph Scott was the epitome of stoicism, Stewart—under Mann's direction—plays average men energized to extreme violence, showing flashes of barely repressed psychotic fury in stories usually stemming from a past wrong. Mann's West is a place with no moral compass; each man sets his scale of right and wrong and attempts to balance it. It is this almost complete lack of moral restraint—even in pursuing a moral cause—which brands Mann's Westerns so uniquely, and gives them their unremitting emotional brutality along with a fair measure of physical cruelty. In *The Man from Laramie* (1955), Stewart is dragged through a fire, then, while several of the chief Bad Guy's henchmen hold him outstretched, he is shot through his gun hand; in *The Far Country* (1955), he's shot and thrown in a river; in *Man of the West* (1958), Julie London, taken by a barbaric outlaw band, is forced to perform a striptease for the Neanderthalish desperados.

Also striking are the plot constructions of Mann's strongest efforts. He often seemed discontented telling a simple, linear story, and sometimes juggled several storylines of near equal importance. In *The Man from Laramie*, Stewart has his hands full, looking to avenge his brother's death, and to get even for his own slights suffered at the hands of the callow, brutal son of a powerful rancher. Having introduced the Stewart story, Mann also begins to amplify the *King Lear*-like situation at Alex Nicol's spread as the rancher is torn between his disappointing son (the one who tortured Stewart), and the son he'd wished he'd had in Arthur Kennedy's loyal foreman. In *Winchester '73* (1950), Stewart has been chasing after Stephen McNally for killing his father*, meets up with him at a sharp-shooting competition where Stewart wins a prized Winchester rifle, and loses it to McNally in a fight. Thereafter, the movie becomes a roundelay, the rifle passing from one set of hands to another, the exchanges introducing us to a series of parallel storylines that eventually intertwine and finally collide in the movie's climax. (*We find out in the last minutes of the movie McNally is actually Stewart's brother.)

Mann had a feel for locations giving a visual power to his stories and themes; not in the sometimes sun-burnished sometimes elegiac golden and amber hues of John Ford's West, but in images as stark and inhospitable as his characters. The climax of *Winchester '73* follows the two feuding brothers about a boulder-strewn mountain, their positions becoming ever more precarious as they scramble higher, the feeling being of a hunt taken to the edge of the world; the town of Lassoo, in *Man of the West*, with its supposedly cash-laden bank, is talked about throughout the movie as a kind of El Dorado, but it turns out to be a crumbling ghost town, the eerie setting for a final gunfight in which bandits die along with their dreams of riches, and sham loyalties finally betray themselves.

John Sturges never developed the critical standing of a Boetticher or Mann (let alone a Ford or Hawks), and was usually considered a competent but unexceptional craftsman who benefited from treating the Western with the seriousness of any other dramatic form. In some ways, his movies do seem less like originals than riffs on the work of more acknowledged directors: *The Gunfight at the OK Corral* (1957) has a grand, romantic Fordian tone; *Last Train from Gun Hill* (1959) owes much to Daves' similarly constructed *3:10 to Yuma*; and *The Law and Jake Wade* (1958) is equally akin to Mann's *Man of the West*. But, in those syntheses, one sees the coming together of the various developing elements of the adult Western even as Sturges own cinematic voice was still evolving, and, throughout the 1950s, he made of those components a body of suspenseful, compelling, dramatically substantive Westerns. His best work, however—*The Magnificent Seven* (1960)—and fittingly the first one on which he acted as his own producer, stands among the classics of the genre, and is possibly one of the most imitated action models in movies. With *Seven*, the moviemaker's predilections finally came together in a recognized Sturgian manner. One of the most important action movies of the 1960s, *Seven* is both the culmination of the trends of 1950s Westerns, and the template for generations of action thrillers that followed.

Sturges shared Ford's penchant for deliberate pacing as well as his clean, unencumbered visual sense. Like Ford, he let his characters share the frame, let the audience watch relationships breathe, only rarely breaking up dramatic scenes with close-ups. But where Ford's characters often wore their sentiments on their sleeves, Sturges preferred a more low-key, subdued, hard-edged style. As he grew more successful and independent, he turned away from the open-faced emotion of the more typical Hollywood stars of his early Westerns (William Holden in *Escape from Fort Bravo* (1953); Burt Lancaster and Kirk Douglas in *Gunfight at the OK Corral*; Robert Taylor in *The Law and Jake Wade*) for a new kind of actor, a younger generation of physically economical performers who understood the big screen's ability to convey as much with the right look as with dialogue e.g. Steve McQueen, James Coburn, Charles Bronson. James Coburn's role as a Zen-flavored knife-wielding hired gun in *The Magnificent Seven* stands as the epitome of Sturges's tight-lipped style; a major character established through weight of presence rather than the less than 100 words of dialogue he's given throughout the picture.

Unlike most action directors of the time—including Ford, Hawks, and Mann—Sturges resisted obligatory romances, understanding the manly appeal of his movies. As his production independence grew, he increasingly refused to compromise that appeal, minimizing intrusive romantic elements (in *The Magnificent Seven*, the chore is delegated to a secondary character) or eliminating it altogether.

Where Ford found majesty and grandeur in a setting like Monument Valley, Sturges—in *Escape from Fort Bravo* and *The Law and Jake Wade*—took similar terrain and saw it as a scabrous, lethal place. Ford's frontier forts are the first colonies of a taming civilization; Fort Bravo, on the other hand, is a far-off island in a hostile sea of desert and raiding Mescaleros to which settlers, Union soldiers, and Confederate prisoners desperately cling for safety. The ghost town at the climax of *Jake Wade*, picked over by Indians, shows colonization not as an assured process, but a tentative one easily undone by the elements, native hostiles, and weakness of will.

In Hawks' fashion, Sturges' protagonists are professionals: William Holden's harshly self-disciplined cavalry officer in *Fort Bravo*; Burt Lancaster, Kirk Douglas, Robert Taylor are supremely dedicated lawmen in *OK Corral*, *Last Train from Gun Hill*, and *Jake Wade*, respectively; the guns-for-hire of *The Magnificent Seven*. But, instead of the smooth-operating machines of Hawks, these emotionally compelling—and often flawed—characters are more akin to those of Boetticher and Mann: driven, obsessive, psychologically fractured, and/or incomplete. One thinks of Holden's Captain Roper, sadistically towing a bound, bedraggled Confederate escapee back to Fort Bravo behind his horse, explaining himself to the outraged rebel commander (John Forsythe) saying the man had escaped in despicable fashion, riding his horse to death: "If he'd run like a man, I'd 've brought him back like a man." There's Kirk Douglas' marshal in *Last Train from Gun Hill*, barely restraining himself from strangling the man who raped and murdered his wife, contenting himself with mentally torturing the young man, talking him through the step-by-step process of dying by hanging: "Your Adam's apple turns to mush... Your brain begins to boil..." *The Magnificent Seven*—a deft transposition by William Roberts and an uncredited Walter Brown Newman of Akira Kurosawa's classic of feudal Japan, *The Seven Samurai* (1954)—seems designed to reject both Kurosawa's subtext of social responsibility as well as the Hawksian model of the knight errant gunfighter. These are desperate, down-at-the-heels types, dinosaurs in a West where "... people are all settled down-like," no longer having need of their lethal trade. Emblematic of their plight, one gunman (Charles Bronson) is found chopping wood for his breakfast, recalling the exorbitant sums he's been paid in the past. "You cost a lot," he's told. "That's right," he responds curtly; "I cost a lot." When he's told the offer is a miniscule twenty dollars for six weeks, he nearly drops his axe. Then, "Twenty dollars? Right now, that's a lot." Another gunfighter (Robert Vaughn) is on the run and has lost his nerve. He takes the job as "The final supreme idiocy: the deserter hiding out in the middle of a battlefield." At the story's second act climax, having been run out of the farming village by bandits, one by one the Seven decide to return for a final fight, but even then their motives are mixed. Says James Coburn, "Nobody throws me my own guns and says 'Run.' Nobody."

Sturges also had a Hawksian ear for sharp dialogue, though where Hawks looked for the entertainment value in a witty line, Sturges looked for the laconic barb cutting to the emotional bone. At the end of *Jake Wade*, Robert Taylor—Richard Widmark's prisoner throughout most of the movie—has turned the tables on his old outlaw riding partner and asks if, when the time had come, Widmark had intended to give him a gun or kill him in cold blood. Widmark replies he'd intended to give Taylor a gun. Taylor responds by handing Widmark his gun belt, but then tosses his pistol to the far end of the street. "I was going to hand you yours!" Widmark snaps. "Well," says Taylor dryly, "You like me more than I like you." In an early scene in *The Magnificent Seven*, Good Samaritan traveling salesman Val Avery, trying to provide a burial for an old Indian who had fallen dead in the street, is told by undertaker Whit Bissell that the ceremony is off due to objections from the townspeople. Stunned the Indian will not be allowed interment even among the derelicts of Boot Hill, Avery asks, "How long's this been going on?" "Ever since the town got 'civilized,'" says Bissell. Avery presses, Bissell responds his hearse driver has quit. "He's prejudiced, too?" "Well, when it comes to getting his head blown off, he's downright bigoted!"

Like Mann and Boetticher, Sturges' villains are full-bodied creations. Bandit leader Calvera (Eli Wallach) in *The Magnificent Seven* bemoans the fact that neither the Mexican farmers on whom he preys nor the gunmen hired to drive him off sympathize with his paternal obligation to his men. During his first confrontation with the Seven, he's confounded by his American counterparts' loyalty to their *campesino* employers. He asks if "... men of our profession..." can afford that kind of thinking: "It might even be sacrilegious!"

Often, Sturges' movies lack a defined villain at all. In *Escape from Fort Bravo*, there are no Good Guys or Bad Guys: just two honorable forces in opposition—Holden and Forsythe—joining forces at the end of the movie in a desperate defense against an attack by the Mescaleros. In *Last Train from Gun Hill*, Douglas' opposition is not the man who killed his wife, but the killer's father (Anthony Quinn), an old friend torn between the son he knows is a failure (and whom he's failed as a father), and the friend for whom he'd do anything except the one thing he demands: giving up his son for the hangman.

The one aspect where Sturges' cinematic voice was always clear from early on was in his use and understanding of violence. Ford doled it out sparingly, but almost always found the glory and grandeur in dedicated men fighting and dying for a cause, even if the dying—as in the case of *Fort Apache*—was unnecessary. For Hawks, on the other hand, violence was simply action: choreographed and played for antiseptic entertainment value, ladled out in strong, regularly applied doses. Sturges was as sparing as Ford in his use of violence; for a moviemaker characterized as an "action director," it's surprising how little physical action there actually is in his movies. Sturges himself once said, in self-appraisal, "I've no objection to being called an action director... but I don't think people realize how much they're laughing, how many lumps in the throat there are in my films." In his most imitated (and often poorly so) picture, *The Magnificent Seven*, there are less than fifteen minutes of action over the course of a 126-minute running time, nearly all of it in the first major combat between Calvera's band and the Seven over halfway into the picture, and in the third act climax. Instead of regular action installments, screen time is invested in a meticulous foundation-laying of character and plot so that Sturges' climactic fights can be as emotionally compelling as they are viscerally exciting, and exciting they are.

Not even Boetticher and Mann, nor even Hawks at his best, could surpass Sturges's ability to choreograph an action sequence. Where Ford hid the last stand of a cavalry troop in *Fort Apache* discretely behind a cloud of dust and consummated the massacre in a few minutes, Sturges took the barest of physical elements at the end of *Fort Bravo*—a handful of people huddled in a shallow depression in the middle of a desert plain—and made their stand his entire third act. The climax of *OK Corral*, however woefully inaccurate it may be in relation to the historical event (the real gunfight at the OK Corral was over in about thirty seconds while Sturges' version ran about five minutes and took four days to film), is the best thing in the film. In his 1967 effort, *Hour of the Gun,* a movie that attempted a more historically factual rendering of the Wyatt Earp saga, Sturges staged a more accurate—and even more brutal—depiction of the famed shoot-out.

In Sturges' movies, violence is about emotional as well as physical pain; there is loss, and resolution without triumph. There is no glory in victory, even for the just cause. Sturges's protagonists are never immune to the wastefulness and tragic nature of what they are compelled to do. At the end of *Gun Hill,* Douglas is forced to kill Quinn but can only feel sorrow; throughout the finale of *Fort Bravo,* the sentiment is one of sadness as, one-by-one, the Confederate escapees now fighting alongside Holden are killed.

Sturges is also aware of the "hidden costs" of a life of violence, a point of introspection, which never occurs to Hawks' glib killing machines. In *The Magnificent Seven,* after Seven leader Yul Brynner's Chris punctures the glory balloon of young, aspiring *pistolero* Chico (Horst Bucholz) saying, "It's just a matter of knowing how to shoot a gun. Nothing big about that," Chico responds disbelievingly, "How can you say that? Your gun has got you everything." The veterans in the Seven begin toting up the rather empty value of that "everything:" "Wife: none. Children: none. Prospects: zero." The youthful Chico misunderstands: "That's the kind of arithmetic I like." "So did I at your age," says Chris ruefully.

At the end of the movie, after Calvera is killed, his outlaw band defeated, and despite early talk about settling down and perhaps putting their guns away, the three survivors of the Seven—Chris, Chico, and Steve McQueen's Vin—prepare to ride out. One of the village elders says of the farmers, "They would not be sorry to see you stay." To which the insightful Chris answers, "They won't be sorry to see us go, either." The trio stop on a rise just outside the village, Chico turns back to rejoin his fellow *campesinos.* Chris regards the farmers working their fields, Chico hanging up his gun to join them, and, in what might be the epitaph for every man of the West who opted for a life of the gun, says to Vin, "Only the farmers won. We lost. We'll always lose."

Fiftieth Anniversary Thoughts: The Death of Marilyn Monroe, The Birth of James Bond
(posted 11/1/12)

Fifty years ago this month, Marilyn Monroe passed away from a suspected accidental drug overdose—although conspiracy geeks love to contemplate more nefarious scenarios. The commemoratives are already showing up on magazine and newspaper entertainment pages, and cable channels have announced their Marilyn film fests and documentary tributes. There's little of worth I can add, either in academic consideration or aesthetic appreciation to all the testimonials as well as to the previous fifty years of ruminating in print and on film re: the lasting appeal of La Monroe. I can only wonder, with a sort of melancholic amazement, over the fact we're still talking about her all these years later.

That persistent hold she has on popular culture is a fascinating study in itself. Her career had already been faltering when she died, and she's been gone a half-century, yet there are people who carry her image on T-shirts and purses, and God knows what else, while barely knowing who she was. Somehow, she's still with us in all her bleached-blonde, ruby-lipped, pneumatically curved glory. One recent *USA Today* story pointed out she's made the cover of *Vanity Fair* three times since 2008. Not bad for a ghost.

Part of the attraction, I suppose, is certainly her tragic end, and with it the tantalizing pondering of what a life unlived might have been like. Perhaps it's that death memorialized her as a beauty. She was only thirty-six, still attractive—hell, she was still gorgeous—when she left us. We've seen countless contemporary celluloid beauties try to put up a faltering bulwark of Botox and botched cosmetic surgery against the onslaught of time; Marilyn was spared that, and so is our memory of her.

Most appreciations touch on her vulnerability: something of the real Norma Jean Baker— damaged in childhood, unsure, wanting to be respected as much as liked, all of which came through on screen.

Consider her in comparison to some of the contemporaries she worked with. Jane Russell, who co-starred with Monroe in *Gentlemen Prefer Blondes* (1953), never looked vulnerable; she looked like if you'd made an unwanted pass, you were going home to put your crushed *cojones* on ice. And there was Betty Grable and Lauren Bacall in *How* to *Marry a Millionaire* (1953); Grable had a next-door-neighbor wholesome kind of sexiness (I get the paradox, but it's there nevertheless), while Bacall had a cool, almost patrician quality, but neither had that please-like-me-please-be-nice-to-me quality Monroe had. When the chips were down, both could turn on a kiss-my-ass-buster toughness.

But Monroe was never hard—it wasn't in her. Even in her few dramatic roles—like *The Misfits* (1961), *Don't Bother to Knock* (1952), or her small early-career part in *The Asphalt Jungle* (1950)—there was a soft, bruised quality to her screen persona. If a guy was interested in Jane Russell, she was the kind of captain-of-her-own-ship who would say, "Well, maybe, if I like you, and maybe not even then." Monroe, on the other hand, wanted to meet the man of her dreams, hungered for it, but would surrender to the wrong guy out of fear the right guy wasn't ever going to show up.

Or maybe… Maybe it was because she was accessible. I don't mean that she came off as easy, but most of Monroe's characters were not exceptional women. She didn't play high society queens, she didn't play hard-driven, ambitious career women, and even when she played a show biz type—a showgirl in *Gentlemen Prefer Blondes*, a tipsy ukulele player in an all-girl orchestra in the classic *Some Like It Hot* (1959)—she was no star, but a rank-and-file chorine. Marilyn was working class—for all her voluptuousness and breathy wet-dream sexiness, she was blue collar. She was one of *us*.

And maybe, in the end, that's what she had over the other sex idols of her generation: she was believable, a believable dream, something maybe not probable, but certainly possible. You put that together with that inherent fragility of hers she could never quite conceal, and it made her real; someone any of us could know.

If she had lived… Well, as horrible as it sounds to say it, she may have passed at the right time. Although she didn't die until 1962, she was a model out of the 1950s, an age of wide lapels, puffy poodle skirts, and big cars with big fins and big chrome bumper "tits" (sorry, that's what we called them). Twiggy and a generation of sexy sylphs—Faye Dunaway, Julie Christie, Susannah York, Goldie Hawn, Mia Farrow, Jacqueline Bisset, and Ali MacGraw—were right around the corner. If she had lived, Marilyn would've looked like an aging '59 Caddy parked next to a fresh-off-the-production-line '64 Mustang.

So, there are no embarrassing, eroding later years, no soft-focus camouflage to cover a slow fade to old age. How we remember her is how she was: a sunny smile; baby-faced, part cherub, part Botticelli Venus; tousled bleached-blonde hair tumbling down across sleepy blue eyes that asked, with more hope than expectation, for us to "Be nice."

*****

Two months or so after Marilyn Monroe died, *Dr. No*—the first big screen adaptation of Ian Fleming's literary creation, James Bond—premiered in the United Kingdom (because elements of the film echoed the Cuban Missile Crisis, the film's U.S. premiere was put off until the following May). One legend ended, another was born.

Rest easy. While I'm (painfully) aware a number of my posts tend to have a grumpy, "Ya know, young feller, back in my day..." attitude, I'm not here to declare Sean Connery was The Bond Bomb and it's all been downhill ever since. In fact, I think the Daniel Craig Bonds are the best thing to happen to the series since Connery's heyday in the role, and I'm even open to the idea they—and Craig—may even be better.

With Craig, for the first time, Bond seems identifiably human (well, a bit). Connery's Bond was always something of a fantasy; the kind of man who fantasizing men could never be, and the kind of man fantasizing women could never have. Craig is a bit more life-sized, and, as spectacular as the action in his Bond films has been, so is the world he moves in. Connery's world was always a bit, well, comic booky.

But as good as they are, there's one thing the Craig Bonds can never replicate, that no amount of money can buy or special effects magic can conjure, and that's something the Connery Bonds will have, forever and always. It doesn't make them better or worse, but it is what distinguishes them from the seventeen Bond-quels that followed (and, yeah, that includes Connery's two returns to the role after he did the first five).

How to describe it?

Well, it's like the nuns used to tell the girls back in Catholic school: you can only lose your virginity once.

In an era that's long been steeped in big-action spectacles, it's hard to remember that when the James Bond films first came on the scene in the early 1960s, there was nothing like them. Never had been. And it would be a long time before anything could match them.

In their casual sexuality, their equally casual violence, their ever-growing spectacle, and in their supreme jet-age '60s coolness, they were unique. And so was Bond, a hybrid between Mickey Spillane's brutal, carnal Mike Hammer, and a comic book superhero, maybe the movies' first top-end superhero (Batman and Superman had been filmed before, but in cheapie serials).

I had missed the first two Bonds: *Dr. No* and *From Russia with Love* (1963). They hadn't been overly spectacular performers and had skipped my neighborhood theater. But then came *Goldfinger* (1964) and Bond-O-Mania exploded. (I would finally get to see *No* and *Russia* when they were rereleased after *Goldfinger* to capitalize on the Bond explosion.) *Goldfinger* was the breakout flick, the critical mass. After *Goldfinger*, it seemed like, overnight, kids on the block had James Bond lunch boxes, coloring books, bubblegum cards, Aston Martin DB5 models, and Bond toys that keyed off all that nifty it-looks-like-this-but-it's-really-that hardware of the movies. (I had a toy camera that turned into a pistol; a friend of mine had what looked like a portable radio that turned into a submachine gun.)

Up until then, spy movies—gritty, life-sized, and laced with Cold War paranoia and desperation—for the most part, had been grim affairs about grim men doing a dirty job playing by dirty rules, like *Pickup on South Street* (1953) and *Night People* (1954).

But the Bonds were glitzier, shinier, a complete break with what had come before. From the opening bars of John Barry's brassy theme—Bwaaaa-WAAAAA—and Shirley Bassey belting out the movie's theme song—"His name was Gold-feen-gah!"—and the opening credits sliding by over gold-painted bikini babes, we knew we were being taken to some place the movies hadn't taken us before. No back alleys here; this was a world of cool cars and swanky hotels. Commercial jet travel was only a few years old and the idea of some suave, well-dressed guy flitting around the globe to hang out in Miami Beach one day and Switzerland the next was impressive in its own right. The gizmos were oh-wow impressive: that gimmick-packed Aston Martin, Goldfinger's laser (the first in a commercial movie). There were Ken Adam's space-agey, chrome-laced sets. Like I said: unique, novel, cutting edge (at the time)—ultimate coolness.

And as if all that wasn't enough, the bad guy was going to knock over Fort Knox. Fort Knox! And what a Fort Knox! Wholly created out of the imagination of Ken Adam, the bullion vault with its chrome bars, Florsheim-glossy floor, and gold bars piled stories high was just what a nine-year-old thought Fort Knox would look like.

Again: ultimate coolness.

And then, at the end, that tantalizing credit: "James Bond will return in..."

There was gonna be *more?*

The Encore pay-TV channel has been celebrating the superspy's anniversary with a festival of James Bond flicks. Catching a few of the early Bonds, it hit me—maybe for the first time—that while *Goldfinger* was my first Bond, it's not the one I think of when I remember that fresh flush of excitement I had for the series in the early years. No, the one that signifies what was so damned entrancing about the Bonds for me then was actually #5 in the series: *You Only Live Twice* (1967).

Goldfinger had come on like an assault. It shook you up, a cultural earthquake to tell you cinema's tectonic plates were shifting. But by *Live Twice*, the change had already taken place. We knew Bond's world, so now the job was to take us further.

Goldfinger came at you—like the opening theme—brassy and hard, but *You Only Live Twice* was a seduction, opening with the gently cascading violins of the opening theme and Nancy Sinatra purring instead of Shirley Bassey blasting. Even today, when I hear those opening strings, the feeling I had the first time I saw the movie comes back to me so vividly I can feel the damp cool air of the Royal Theater and smell the faint mustiness of the old upholstery on the seats.

I was twelve. It was summer. I'd hit the Royal for a weekday matinee. Couldn't have been more than two dozen people scattered around the seats. The movie opens in Hong Kong, Bond's in bed—surprise!—with a Chinese cutie setting him up for an assassination. Goons bust in, there's a burst of submachine gun fire, and then Bond lying dead (but not really), the camera zooms in on the crimson blood splattered across the white sheets that segue slickly into the spinning Oriental patterns of Maurice Binder's credit sequence rolling across that incredibly wide screen of the Royal.

Dr. No had been filmed in Jamaica: ocean and beaches. We had that ocean and beaches in Jersey. *From Russia with Love?* Much of it took place on a train. Most of *Goldfinger* was set in Kentucky (I'd missed 1965's *Thunderball*). But *You Only Live Twice* was filmed in Japan, and director Lewis Gilbert so deftly captured a sense of the place that he brought a new component to the Bonds: a sense of the exotic. This wasn't back lot Japan, this wasn't back projection Japan: this was *Japan*.

One of my favorite scenes in the film is a rooftop chase along the Kobe docks. Gilbert does all the things in shooting the bit that you're not supposed to do with an action sequence. For one thing, it's filmed in long shot—extreme long shot, actually, from a helicopter, no less—and the camera pulls still further away as the scene progresses. The chase is a single, long take—no cuts. An extended, uninterrupted take in long shot: by conventional wisdom, all elements to play down the dynamics of the action.

But what Gilbert does in that shot as the camera pulls further back is something you rarely see in an action sequence. That long, wide shot frames the action squarely against the Kobe waterfront. This isn't a set, this isn't a penny-pinching production trying to pass off Vancouver as a more alluring locale. That's James Bond fighting it out with real Japanese guys on the real Kobe waterfront.

What Gilbert managed to do with sequences like this, which were rarely matched in the other Bonds (or many other action thrillers for that matter), was to do what we always want movies to do: take us someplace else.

As whisked away as I was at twelve by *You Only Live Twice*, there's an aspect of that movie I only came to appreciate—I mean *really* appreciate—years later.

The action climax of the movie takes place in the villain's lair in a hollowed-out volcano. In those pre-CGI days, you could sometimes pull this off with miniatures, matte paintings, but they were techniques that wouldn't let the set "live." If you wanted a set to *do* something, your only option, then, was to actually build it 1:1.

The volcano set Ken Adam built was one of the largest ever constructed up to that time, and supposedly was visible up to three miles away. It had a usable, movable helipad, a moving rocket gantry with a full-sized rocket that could actually spit smoke and look like it was lifting off, a working monorail, and a retractable roof. And then James Bond and an army of Ninjas break in and blow the hell out of it.

It's awesome. I don't mean that in the contemporary, hey-dude tossed-off sense of the word, but in the classical definition sense: the massive scale and the effort it represented still fill me with awe.

And that, I'm afraid, will never—can never—happen again.

A kid growing up today is swamped by the spectacular from the day he/she is born. It's a world of CGI-filled movies and videogames populated by wizards and zombies and aliens in hyperkinetic big-action scenarios where over-the-top has become the new normal. In that context, the new James Bonds may fit right in, but they don't stand out. They may be good—maybe even great—but they're not unique anymore.

The series is fifty years old—that's inevitable. And as one of the most successful movie series ever, it's been constantly copied, cloned, ripped off and parodied (Mike Myers's *Austin Powers* movies are a salute to/parody of the Bonds, and Christopher Nolan has several times admitted the influence of the Connery era Bonds in his films, with that influence particularly clear in the mountaintop fortress sequence in *Inception* [2010]). That constant Xeroxing of the original can't help but take some of the freshness away.

That's the thing I miss most, I guess: going to see the newest James Bond movie, knowing I was going to be dazzled and awed by something I'd never seen before and wouldn't see anywhere else.

You may be able to live twice, but things can only be new once.

They're Blowin' This Town All to Hell! — Sam Peckinpah and *The Wild Bunch*
(posted 4/24/11)

Curiously, with all the bold, ambitious, fresh talent storming into Hollywood in the 1960s/1970s—directors who'd cut their teeth in TV like Sidney Lumet and John Frankenheimer; imports like Roman Polanski and Peter Yates; the first wave of film school "film brats" like Francis Ford Coppola and Martin Scorsese—one of the most popular genres during the period was one of Old Hollywood's most traditional: the Western. But the Western often wrought at the hands of that new generation of moviemakers was rarely traditional.

During the Old Hollywood era, Westerns typically had been B-caliber productions, most of them favoring gunfights and barroom brawls over dramatic substance, and nearly all adhering to Western tropes that ran back to the pre-cinema days of dime novelist Ned Buntline. With the 1960s, however, the genre began to change; or, more accurately, expand, twist, and even invert.

To be sure, there would still be Westerns revolving around familiar Western myths, with some Old Hollywood directors—energized by the upscale refurbishing New Hollywood was giving the genre—turning in some of their most entertaining work, e.g. Howard Hawks and *El Dorado* (1966), and Henry Hathaway with *The Sons of Katie Elder* (1965) and *True Grit* (1969). There were also somewhat younger directors—like Burt Kennedy and Andrew V. McLaglen—who followed in their elders' footsteps, finding there was still plenty of box office mileage left in the traditionalist iconography of a swaggering John Wayne—albeit one bloated and craggy with middle age—duking it out with sneery Bad Guys in the likes of *The War Wagon* (1967), *The Undefeated* (1969), and *Chisum* (1970).

But among the new blood coming into the industry, there were those who saw in the venerable old form the potential to expand its dramatic reach and heft (George Roy Hill's *Butch Cassidy and the Sundance Kid*, 1969), to inject an unprecedented level of realism and honesty (Sydney Pollack's *Jeremiah Johnson*, 1972), to peel back the myths and find the less-than-legendary underside of the legendary Old West (Arthur Penn's *Little Big Man*, 1970). They discovered in the Western a pliability allowing the use of the mythic setting of the American frontier as a vehicle to comment on such contemporary subjects as racism (Pollack's *The Scalphunters*, 1968), war (Robert Aldrich's *Ulzana's Raid*, 1972), the dehumanizing corporatization of the American spirit (Robert Altman's *McCabe & Mrs. Miller*, 1971).

In the vanguard of those who reenergized the Western by utterly revamping it stood Sam Peckinpah. Although he would essay other genres over the course of his career, his most potent vehicles were usually Westerns, and his most monumental contribution: *The Wild Bunch* (1969).

Born in Fresno in 1925, Peckinpah had often spent time on his grandfather's ranch, and grew up hearing stories about his family's forays into lumber, ranching, hauling borax, and wagon-making during what was then a not-too-distant era when northern California had still been very much a vestigial part of the Old West. Peckinpah would draw on those stories and that upbringing to give his Westerns—even at their most romantic—a sense of authenticity and a flavor few other Western moviemakers have matched. At the same time, Peckinpah's Westerns—among the genre's finest—cast often controversial reflections of a troubled present day, with a recurring theme throughout his Westerns, both period and contemporary, being that of, according to critic Kathleen Murphy, "... the American Dream profaned... going, gone rotten..."

Peckinpah first made a name for himself as a *maestro* of the genre in 1950s television, first by writing and directing for such popular series as *Gunsmoke*, *Have Gun Will Travel*, and *Zane Grey Theater*, then by creating the hit series *The Rifleman*, followed by the critically lauded—if short-lived—*The Westerner*. He moved to features with the little-noticed *The Deadly Companions* (1961), but followed with one of the acknowledged classics of Western cinema: *Ride the High Country* (1962).

Peckinpah did significant but uncredited rewriting of N. B. Stone, Jr.'s original *High Country* script, infusing it with his own sense of the West, and an eye for unique details as in a bizarre horse vs. camel race early in the movie, but most especially in his portrait of the rowdy, slapdash mining town of Coarsegold, a muddy tent city whose only permanent structure is the saloon/brothel. Peckinpah's touch is also in the rustic yet graceful dialogue ("I just want to go into my house justified," says aging lawman Joel McCrea ruminating on his encroaching mortality), and the poignant little human moments like McCrea excusing himself from a room so no one can see him pull on spectacles to read a letter. Still, the invigorating rough patina Peckinpah brought to the movie braced what was essentially a gentle and respectful core story; *High Country* was not an overturning of Western traditions, but a salute to their passing.

Peckinpah began to show a more openly revisionist hand with his flawed but nevertheless intriguing *Major Dundee* (1964), cowritten with Harry Julian Fink and Oscar Saul. Charlton Heston is a Union cavalry officer guilty of some unspecified misstep on the Civil War battlefields in the east, now punitively assigned to the lowly job of overseeing a prisoner of war camp amid the New Mexico wastelands. To redeem himself, Heston assembles a motley collection of volunteers, including several of his Confederate prisoners, for an unauthorized pursuit into Mexico after an Apache raider.

Dundee is a complete inversion of the quietly dignified cavalrymen of John Ford's West of a generation before. Dundee is an arrogant, condescending, hubristic, inflexible, unforgiving egotist, a man Peckinpah conceived as one who "... kept failing in what he was doing" in a self-aggrandizing, self-destructive quest the director likened to that of Ahab chasing his white whale.

The Wild Bunch would provide Peckinpah with his breakout commercial success, and also push him to the fore as one of the most controversial directors of the time. With *The Wild Bunch*, cowritten with Walon Green from a story by Green and Roy N. Sickner, Peckinpah severed all ties with the Westerns of old, and created a period piece that—as much as any other movie of the time—captured the moral chaos and dislocation of the late 1960s.

It is the early 1900s, a time of transition for the West. Men on horseback carrying six-guns stand side-by-side with "horseless carriages" and heavy machine guns. Under the beginning credits, a squad of soldiers commanded by William Holden rides into a Texas border town heading for the railroad office. On the surrounding roofs, a scruffy, rotten-toothed gang of ambushers wait. The credit sequence ends with a tight close-up of Holden's half-lit, weathered face as he turns to his men lining up the office staff and customers at shotgun point. "If they move," he snaps icily, "kill 'em!" Freeze frame, the deep thrum of the final note of Jerry Fielding's title music, the credit "Directed by Sam Peckinpah," and the moral compass of the movie takes the first of many freewheeling spins with this revelation that the "soldiers" are a band of notorious outlaws in disguise, and the repellent bushwhackers actually represent the law; a posse commissioned by the railroad.

A temperance march comes down the street in front of the railroad office. Tipped to the ambush by the clumsiness of the posse, the Bunch intends to use the passing parade to cover their escape. Peckinpah builds to the coming detonation with brilliant skill: the music of the temperance band—"Shall We Gather at the River"—grows louder as the marchers near; on the rooftops, the posse waits in almost pre-orgasmic expectation, grinning, embracing and kissing their rifles; in the railroad office, weapons are cocked, eyes narrow, as the Bunch wait for the right moment. On the soundtrack, underneath the growing volume of the temperance band, Fielding's score introduces an almost imperceptible swell, and then comes the sound of a heartbeat, growing faster as the crucial instant comes. The marchers pass by the office, Holden shoves out a hostage to draw fire, a flash cut to two of the band members turning at the noise, and then one of the most violent action sequences in commercial cinema ensues.

As the town's Main Street sinks into a chaotic mix of gunfire, running bodies, dust and spurting blood, any doubt about who the Good Guys might be is removed: there aren't any. There are only two forces in opposition with the innocent townspeople caught in the crossfire between them.

Throughout the remainder of the movie, Peckinpah challenges the audience to sympathize with his group of violent outlaws, making no attempt to soften their edges or make them more ingratiating: they kill without compunction, steal with little thought as to whom they're stealing from, and they quarrel amongst themselves sometimes to an almost lethal extent. One moment bringing their utter self-interest into bold relief comes when, having been contracted by a thief-in-uniform Mexican general to steal American Army rifles for a fee of $10,000, a Mexican member of Holden's Bunch—a Villa sympathizer (Jaime Sanchez)—balks at going along, protesting, "Would you steal guns to kill your mother or your father?" Holden replies drolly: "Ten thousand cuts an awful lot of family ties."

Yet, in spite of themselves, the Bunch does gain the viewer's sympathy. Outlaws they may be, but they are also the last vestiges of an American West which, however brutal and lawless it may have been, was also a place of a kind of left-handed honor, of frontier independence, of undoubted courage. There's an undeniable poignancy to their plight; last of the Old West outlaw bands, they are like gasping fish floundering from one puddle to another at the bottom of a drying pond as their world evaporates around them.

Even in their violence—ruthless, merciless, and cold-blooded—there is an odd strain of honorability. They kill out of necessity, as opposed to the bounty-lusting posse hunting them who seem to relish the spilling of blood… *any* blood. Following the opening shoot-out, the bounty hunters pick over the dead for boots and valuables and quarrel over credit for kills, while one of their number squeals, "This is better than a hog-killin'!" When two of them (Strother Martin and L. Q. Jones) squabble over possession of a corpse, Martin dares Jones to dig the bullet out of the body "… and see if it ain't my ought-six."

The Bunch stands apart from the Mexican general Mapache (Emilio Fernandez) and his little army as well. The *federales* are no more than *banditos* in uniform who have stripped the countryside clean and spend their time engaged in constant debauchery when not indulging in the entertainment of torture. When Holden jokingly compares Mapache's thievery to the Bunch's own, one of the Bunch—an insulted Ernest Borgnine—repudiates the connection: "Not so's you'd know it, Mr. Bishop, but we ain't *nothin'* like him! We don't *hang* nobody!"

It was, however, not such dramatic subtleties, nor the inversions and overturnings of Western tropes that drew the most attention from the critical community at the time of *The Wild Bunch*'s release.

The debate about the growing quantity and quality of movie violence had grown more vociferous and heated as on-screen acts had grown more brazen and graphic. *Psycho*, in 1960, had offered up the butchering of a nude Janet Leigh, while 1964's *The Killers* had ended with Lee Marvin coldly gunning down Angie Dickinson, and *Point Blank* three years later had Marvin tossing a nude John Vernon to his death from a penthouse terrace. There had been *The Dirty Dozen* (1967) and its story of twelve felons trained by the Army to be more efficient killers before being unleashed to carry out a massacre of high-ranking German officers and their mistresses. *Bonnie and Clyde* (1967) had featured a succession of increasingly brutal gun battles climaxing with the slow motion death ballet of the titular couple falling beneath a hail of machine gun fire. *The Wild Bunch* took screen violence—and the debate over it—to still another level.

From the outset of the *Bunch* shoot, Peckinpah—ever a *provocateur*—had bragged, "We're going to bury *Bonnie and Clyde!*" By the end of the first day's shooting of the opening massacre, he had exhausted the company's stock of blank ammunition and fake blood. When the "squibs" used to blow out the windows on the railroad office failed to sufficiently impress him, dynamite charges were used instead. Equally dissatisfied with the squibs used to simulate bullet impacts on his actors, Peckinpah demonstrated the effect he wanted by shooting a real gun at a mock-up human target. Thereafter, the special effects crew experimented with larger-caliber squibs loaded with blood and small pieces of meat. Peckinpah had the effects crew squib his actors front and back to give the impression—a first in movie violence—of bullets completely piercing a human body.

He was motivated by more than indulgent morbidity, his personal experience here again coming to bear on what he was trying to attain on-screen. There was an image he'd never forgotten from his youth hunting deer in the Sierra Nevada foothills, a memory of his first kill and the erupting spray of blood on white snow.

Escalating the visual impact still more was his decision to film these most brutal acts in slow motion. It was not a new device; the great Japanese director Akira Kurosawa had used slow motion as long ago as his 1954 classic *Seven Samurai* to extend and solemnize the exquisite horror of a mortally struck swordsman momentarily wavering on his feet before collapsing in death. A fan of *Samurai*, Walon Green had hoped to recapture that same, frozen moment of entrancing horror by incorporating the concept into his initial solo draft of *The Wild Bunch* screenplay. However, the effective mix of real-time and slow-motion in the film was worked out between Peckinpah and chief editor Lou Lombardo.

For some critics, Peckinpah's perceived obsession with taking screen violence to a new extreme was the creative freedom of 1960s cinema pushed to an indulgent, repugnant extreme.

But others saw hypocrisy—or denial—in such a stand. Over the course of *Bunch*'s nearly three-month shoot, both Martin Luther King, Jr. and Robert Kennedy were assassinated, there were race riots in several cities, and outside the Chicago convention hall where the 1968 Democratic convention was taking place, club-wielding policemen waded into ranks of anti-war protesters while the Vietnam War ground bloodily on. Said *Bonnie and Clyde* director Arthur Penn,

"You had to be an ostrich with a neck two miles long buried in the sand not to see we were living in a violent time…"

In 1994, Warner Bros. decided on a limited rerelease of *The Wild Bunch* to commemorate the film's twenty-fifth anniversary. As the studio was issuing a new director's cut of the film, *Bunch* had to be resubmitted to the MPAA for a new rating. Though it had originally been released with an R-rating in 1969, after reviewing the new print, the MPAA slapped the film with an X (Warners would opt for releasing the new print without a rating).

Superficially, nothing about the new rating made sense. Time was supposed to ameliorate the impact of controversial films, not amplify them. Released in 1969 with an X-rating, *Midnight Cowboy*, for example, would be rerated R in 1971. Stanley Kubrick's *A Clockwork Orange* (1971) was also originally released with an X, which was later stepped down to an R.

Certainly, more graphically violent and gorier movies had been released since 1969, from a torrent of R-rated slasher flicks and gorefests like the *Friday the 13th* and various *Living Dead* films to such upscale mainstream releases as *Die Hard 2* (1990; Bruce Willis stabs a villain through the eye with an icicle), *Total Recall* (1991; Michael Ironside plummets to his death after an elevator severs both his arms), and *Silence of the Lambs* (1991; featuring a disembodied head in a jar, a partially skinned female corpse, a grotesque posing of an eviscerated policeman, and serial killer Anthony Hopkins escaping detention by wearing the sliced-away face of one of his guards—the movie would win the Best Picture Oscar, and Hopkins take the Best Actor prize for his performance as serial killer "Hannibal the Cannibal").

So, if not for Peckinpah's elaborately choreographed mayhem, why the X? It could only have been for the movie's *power*, its dramatic gravitas still intact after twenty-five years; that all the shooting and bloodletting wasn't just empty action, but actually *meant* something—a rarity by the 1990s, and even more rare today.

In a 2004 documentary on Peckinpah, critic Elvis Mitchell remarked on the rerating business and *The Wild Bunch*'s ability to disturb and provoke decades after its debut, saying this very quality made it everything a movie should be, "… something that contains the weight and the cultural resonance of its time. It's supposed to be a statement, a signature."

In retrospect, one can see how lucky Peckinpah had been. He had come along at just the right time, able to make one of the most provocative movies ever released into American cinema's commercial mainstream at a time when studios were up for such gambles, and the mass audience was hungry for movies that told them something—even unpalatable, disturbing somethings—about themselves and the world they lived in.

It says something about how we, the audience, have changed since then. Immersed in numbing escapism, we sit with fingers in our ears, stretching our necks—as Arthur Penn had said—to bury our heads deep in the sand, rearing up mightily offended when unpleasant real-world truths leak through.

Happy Birthday, *A Clockwork Orange*!
(posted 1/7/11)

It is a mark of how jaded and inured to screen violence we've become that the "ultra-violence" of Stanley Kubrick's 1971 portrait of a not-too-distant future dystopia, *A Clockwork Orange*—considered so shocking at the time it brought death threats by the bushel to the director and caused him to withdraw the movie from distribution in the UK—barely raises an eyebrow today. Forty years of slasher flicks, horror grotesques, and torture porn have left the movie's stylized beatings and assaults looking surprisingly tame... and that's a "shame on us."

It is also a mark of how flyweight mainstream moviemaking has become that while the movie's violence doesn't seem like so much, *Clockwork* remains a disturbing, resonating movie that burrows into the brain much like the film's eye-bulging "Ludovico Treatment." And that is why the violence, for all its relative toothlessness, still impacts—because it *means* something. Made today, *Clockwork* would undoubtedly have come from a small company and be put in limited release on the art house circuit because it would be believed—with fair reason—there'd be no mass audience for it. Again, shame on us.

For Kubrick, *Clockwork* was the crest of an incredible professional ascension. He'd started in the early '50s on small, independently produced films, breaking through to the big time in 1960 with *Spartacus*, arguably the best and most intelligent of the sword-and-sandal epics of the '50s-'60s. The blockbuster success of *Spartacus* bought him the license to chart his own course in Hollywood, one in which he never played safe, instead pursuing ever more adventuresome projects. He followed *Spartacus* with the (for its time) sexually brazen *Lolita* (1962), and then *Dr. Strangelove or: How I Learned to Stop Worrying and Love the Bomb* (1964), a movie that turned the threat of nuclear apocalypse into fuel for the darkest—and funniest—of black comedies. Thereafter came his sci-fi tone poem, *2001: A Space Odyssey* (1968), an audacious non-narrative epic, which remains one of the most unconventional big budget mainstream films ever released by a major studio.

Kubrick's ability to find commercial success with such seemingly non-commercial material led Warner Bros. production chief John Calley to offer the filmmaker a permanent home at Warners, free to pursue whatever projects he chose, and to take as long to develop them as he needed. It was an unprecedented—and remains unmatched—offer of Hollywood studio largesse. *A Clockwork Orange* would be the first of five features Kubrick would make at Warners, which remained his production base until his death in 1999.

Reacting against the monstrously elaborate production that had marked *2001*, Kubrick shot *Clockwork* with uncharacteristic economy. Nearly all of the film was shot on available locations (supposedly, only one set was built for the production), using a minimal lighting kit and the then new wireless microphones to provide natural sound. From the beginning of production to release was a span of about a year—for the usually snail-paced Kubrick, practically a land speed record.

Yet the film looks as meticulously crafted as any of his films, and – with the exception of a few bits of electronic hardware—wonderfully undated. Kubrick wanted to depict a future just slightly ahead of the present day, and the blocky, characterless new apartment flats and sleek Ikea-esque furnishings mixed with the decaying edifices of yesteryear do the job just as well today as they did forty years ago.

It remains an aesthetically daring and challenging film as well: think of Kubrick's long, static, but meticulously composed shots, his willingness not to dilute the gang argot from the original Anthony Burgess novel, an uncompromising portrayal of its malevolent central character, and its morally ambiguous, ultimately downbeat stance.

Despite its modest futuristic trappings, Kubrick was not talking about the future. *Clockwork* was just the mildest extrapolation of contemporary dysfunctions, and there's little in the movie audiences in 1971—and, sadly, in 2011—couldn't recognize: family breakdowns, lawless youth gangs in the streets, overwhelmed and ineffective law enforcement, politicians and interest groups desperate to glom on to any espoused cure-all to curry favor with the public. *Clockwork* is less about the future than it is a funhouse mirror rendering of the present.

Its moral ambiguity—so characteristic of American '60s/'70s cinema—might be its most challenging aspect in an age dominated by superhero movies and their moral hyperclarity. *Clockwork* pits the value of free will—even a corrupted, depraved free will—against forced obedience. Convicted felon Alex DeLarge (Malcolm McDowell in an amazing debut performance), to gain early release from prison, volunteers to take "the Ludovico treatment," a sort of Pavlovian conditioning the new administration touts as a cure for the rising violent crime rate. But the treatment is no more than a set of chemical handcuffs. It does not cure Alex of his affinity or taste for violence, he develops no guilt, no conscience, and it does not release the better angels of his nature. He is still the same impulsive sociopath, only now, whenever he considers turning to violence, he suffers crippling nausea. He's no more truly cured than handcuffing a wife beater cures him of wife beating.

Worse, the treatment turns Alex from victimizer to victim, which is what happens when Alex is "cured" without curing the violent, morally anarchic culture that created him; his doctors have cured the symptom, not the disease. Unable to resort to his talent for "the old ultra-violence," Alex is now at the mercy of a society that remains brutal and vindictive, and here Kubrick manages the trick of turning Alex—a thieving, sadistic, rape murderer—sympathetic. The only "happy" ending—and face-saving turn left for the government that had de-fanged Alex before turning him loose among a fanged public—is to turn him back into the uninhibited, gleefully malevolent little shit he was before. And so they do.

There are no simple solutions in *Clockwork*, because there are no simple problems. That hasn't changed in the last 40 years or the last 140 years. It's entirely probable future film aficionados will be looking at the eightieth anniversary rerelease of *A Clockwork Orange* remarking on how sadly relevant the movie continues to be, and marveling that at one time people lined up around the block to see such a movie.

A Conversation with Producer (and Legendary Cop) Sonny Grosso
(posted 2/20/11)

"I grew up in a world where Edward G. Robinson, Humphrey Bogart, James Cagney... these were the heroes. Not the cops. Cops were the bad guys. Or they were stumbling around, couldn't find their asses with both hands."

So says Sonny Grosso, and it is a screen iconography he has worked hard to change. Grosso-Jacobson Communications has produced over 750 hours of programming for network and premium and basic cable television in its thirty-odd years. Though its output has run from *Pee Wee's Playhouse* to adventure fare like *Counterstrike*, the most acclaimed of the company's offerings have been true-life *policier* TV movies like *Out of the Darkness* (1985), the story of the breaking of the "Son of Sam" case; *Trackdown: Finding the Goodbar Killer* (1983); and *A Question of Honor* (1982), based on Grosso's book *Point Blank* (Grosset & Dunlap, 1978), about mishaps and tragedy in a police corruption investigation gone bad. "I try to show in movies what a cop's life is all about."

His commitment is understandable once you know that before getting into television, Sonny Grosso spent twenty years with the New York City Police Department. He reached the rank of first grade detective after just three and a half years in the bureau—faster than anyone in the history of the Department. Along with partner Eddie Egan, he broke one of the biggest narcotics smuggling rings in the annals of American law enforcement in the early 1960s. The case would come to national attention with author Robin Moore's 1969 bestselling account of the case, *The French Connection*.

When movie rights were acquired by 20th Century Fox, Grosso and Egan were both hired on as consultants to the project. Though the movie would be a fictionalized telling of the story, both detectives saw it as their job to exact a level of authenticity from the filmmakers.

The movies, according to Grosso, have only rarely gotten the picture of cops right. After those early days when the hoods were the sympathetic characters, there followed a more positive image in the 1950s which Grosso credits to Jack Webb. Webb had had a supporting role in a 1948 thriller, *He Walked By Night,* and been quite taken by the picture's semi-documentary approach and its attempt to realistically render a police investigation and the professionals who carried it out (thanks to director Alfred L. Werker and an uncredited Anthony Mann, and screenwriters Crane Wilbur, John C. Higgins, and Harry Essex). Many of the stylistic tropes of the movie—the flat, narrating voiceover, realistic plot based on a true-life case, clipped dialogue, accurate depiction of police procedure and techniques—all found their way into Webb's consequent creation, *Dragnet*, a series which first premiered on radio, then found huge success on television.

"That 'Just the facts, Ma'am,' kind of thing, I liked it," says Grosso. "I liked *Dragnet*. But everybody I knew said, '*I* don't know any cops like that!'"

Dragnet may have rehabilitated the image of the policemen Grosso had grown up with, but it was a sanitized portrait nonetheless. When Grosso met with the young tyro who'd landed the job of directing the movie version of *The French Connection*—William Friedkin—Grosso gave him his mandate. "I told Billy, 'If you can show what cops are like below the surface, you don't have to make them pretty or nice, as long as you get across *why* we do what we do.'" The detective said something similar to Gene Hackman who was playing Popeye Doyle, the character based on Eddie Egan: "Get to the honesty of it."

To that end, Grosso and Egan had regular input into Ernest Tidyman's developing screenplay, and also spent three weeks with Hackman and Roy Scheider (who, in an Oscar-nominated turn, would play the character based on Grosso). When Hackman and Scheider had been told they would be meeting with the detectives, they'd assumed they'd be sitting with them while the cops talked about their jobs. Instead, Grosso and Egan took the two actors out on the street with them, executing searches and rousts, experiencing the day-in/day-out of being a narcotics detective in Harlem.

Grosso talks about one of the movie's most famous set-pieces, a scene where Doyle storms into a bar that's a hangout for low-level dope peddlers. "Eddie must've done the thing in the bar a dozen times in those three weeks (we were with the actors). I'd seen him do it a *thousand* times before." According to Grosso, during the first week, the actors would stand outside the bar while he and Egan went inside; the second week, the actors would be inside with the detectives while they rousted the bar. "The third week, we waited outside while Gene and Roy did it!"

"It's like a set of railroad tracks," says Grosso. "One rail is the experience of the cops; the other rail is the perception of civilians." When the rails are too far apart or too close, explains Grosso, the train can't run. "In *French Connection*, the balance was just right."

While Grosso credits much of the movie's success to Friedkin ("Billy's a genius," he says unabashedly), he is also aware of the collaborative network of which Friedkin was a part. The commitment to make *The French Connection* something different and more real than previous cop stories ran all the way to the executive suite at 20th Century Fox and Richard Zanuck who was running the studio at the time. When it came to casting the film, Friedkin allows that Gene Hackman "… wasn't our first choice… he wasn't our *tenth* choice." But Zanuck's direction was to eschew the Hollywood A-list: "I'm not looking for big stars. I'm looking for reality," he told the *Connection* production staff.

Grosso particularly notes the contributions of producer Phil D'Antoni. D'Antoni had started in radio and television producing specials like *An Evening with Elizabeth Taylor in London;* hardly the fare to indicate his qualities as a producer of the hardest of the hard-boiled classic cop thrillers. But in 1968, D'Antoni had delivered the lean, terse *Bullitt*, a movie that had successfully combined Hollywood entertainment with a sense of authenticity. *Bullitt* star Steve McQueen had gone as far as to do "ride-alongs" in patrol cars to help ground his portrayal of a sharp, veteran San Francisco PD detective. Having feared a typical Hollywood shoot-'em-up, San Francisco city officials had been quite pleased with the finished picture. D'Antoni hoped to repeat the accomplishment with *The French Connection*.

However, where director Peter Yates and cinematographer William Fraker had played to *Bullitt*'s sense of toughness with a sun-burnished hardness befitting the West Coast setting, D'Antoni wanted a different look for the New York-set *The French Connection*. He'd seen a few TV documentaries made by Friedkin, thought that was the look the film needed, and though Friedkin had done little feature work, decided, "He felt right." Helping Friedkin get the sooty, winter-in-New York drabness was another relative newcomer to features, cinematographer Owen Roizman, who, at the time, had only one previous feature credit (Roizman would be nominated for an Oscar for his work on *Connection*).

"Billy had a partner in D'Antoni," explains Grosso. Though producer and director would tussle over competing visions throughout the production ("Fox threatened to fire Billy many times on *French Connection,*" reports Grosso) it was their collaboration that brought together the elements that made the film a classic.

For example, the famed car chase was not a part of the true story, nor was it initially part of Tidyman's adaptation. D'Antoni had explicitly stated he wanted a chase to outdo the one in *Bullitt,* but Friedkin kept putting off dealing with the sequence. "We did have a chase," says Grosso, "but it was completely different." According to Grosso, there was to be a scene where one of the drug suspects boards a subway shuttle and loses Hackman and Scheider. The pair then run back up to the street to race across town and head off the shuttle. Grosso says it was D'Antoni's idea to move the entire chase above ground.

In *The French Connection 30th Anniversary Special,* Friedkin explains how the sequence was actually developed to be shoehorned into the narrative. In a long conversation with D'Antoni, director and producer pieced the sequence together in reverse order. First, they needed the bad guy on the train, which meant Hackman would be in the car, which meant he would have to commandeer the car, etc.

Grosso was not always satisfied with the creative decisions that were made. "I asked Billy not to have Hackman shoot that guy in the back," he says, referring to the climax of the chase when an exhausted Hackman calls to the Frenchman (Marcel Bozzuffi) who's tried to kill him, then shoots him when the killer turns to run. "I was so pissed off at him for doing that!" But even Grosso admits that when he saw the finished film, "it worked. The audience cheered like hell! He was right."

As with *Bullitt,* the authenticity of so much of *The French Connection* made even such Hollywood prerequisites as the car chase and shootings appear as credible as anything else in the film. Made for $1.8 million (a modest sum even then), *The French Connection,* released in 1971, was both a critical and commercial hit, nominated for eight Oscars, winning five, and earning nearly $52 million at the US box office ("That picture bailed out Fox," Grosso says).

Grosso would go on to act as a consultant and technical advisor (and occasional bit player) on a number of other movies, including *The Godfather* (1972), *Report to the Commissioner* (1975), *Cruising*

(1980), and *The Brinks Job* (1978) (these last two also directed by Friedkin), as well as write the story for *The Seven-Ups* (1973), which Phil D'Antoni would direct. Grosso also advised on several TV series including *Kojak*, *The Rockford Files*, and *Baretta*. After retiring from the NYPD, it almost seemed a natural step for Grosso to begin his own production company, partnering with TV producer Larry Jacobson.

Looking back over several generations of movie cops, Grosso describes the evolutionary line: "We went from a time when the cops were the bad guys to, 'Just the facts, Ma'am,' then the cops were the good guys but real people, and now the cops are superheroes." These days, he says, "Each movie tries to outdo the others."

While he rues the change, it doesn't surprise him. The movies are "... a copycat world. If you have a car chase where the car goes sixty miles an hour, then in the next movie it's going to go eighty, then the next one it goes ninety and everybody's got a car chase in their movie... Now, it's all everything blowing up, cars going over bridges... out-stunting each other." He shakes his head. "Where would Frank Capra fit into Hollywood today?"

Part of it, he concedes, is a reflection of the "excessive world we live in." He points out that, "You've got bad guys today who can take out the World Trade Center. What do the good guys have to do to fight that? So, you see a lot of heavy technology, a lot of heavy firepower. When was the last time you saw a detective in a movie use a magnifying glass?"

But just as much behind the change is a Hollywood mindset targeting young audiences. "They're not even worrying about whether or not old viewers are going to come any more," he sighs. "They're addressing movies to younger and younger audiences." The growing action quotient in the latest generation of thrillers moved Grosso to once ask Bruce Willis, "If it keeps on like this, how many people are you gonna kill in the next movie?"

It is not so much the violence Grosso takes issue with as how it is trivialized. "This is a violent country we live in, a violent world. My only problem with violence is you don't show the results of violence." He mentions fist fights and brawls where eyes don't get blackened and teeth remain firmly fixed in jaws. "The first time you shoot a guy, you're not right for a long time after that. It disturbed me for months. You don't feel or see that in the movies."

He felt his series *Night Heat* was an attempt to get back to a "Just the facts, Ma'am" kind of cop storytelling. "TV still keeps it life-size," he judges, "even if a lot of it is a simplistic, problem-of-the-week kind of thing." But even TV cops have gone down a path that doesn't exactly enamor Grosso. "*Kojak* looked like they kept him in a box until the next episode. You didn't even know he had a penis. Then you look at *NYPD Blue*. That's *exactly* what it was: a blue version of the old *N.Y.P.D.* (a 1960s series from producer David Susskind) that was less about crime than everybody's personal problems."

He is pessimistic about the possibility of a swing back to the more realistic cop thrillers of the 1960s and 1970s. "I know people who're waiting for a change, but I don't think it's gonna happen... As long as young audiences like it, it'll stay the way it is. Is it interesting? It's *all* interesting. I went to these pictures when they first started coming out. But it's all the same thing now... If I had the money, I would make them the way they used to." He reflects on the decision-making behind *The French Connection*, from Fox's acquiring the property on through the production: no focus groups, no audience research, and no talk of demographics. "In those days, they were still making decisions on guts.

"I find it sad that you and I have a conversation where I say, 'Where's the place for a Capra?' and you say maybe we couldn't even get *The French Connection* made today." He shrugs. "Maybe you *could* make it today. But Popeye'd have to be way better looking. And they'd give him a girlfriend. And there'd have to be more action. *Lots* more action.

"Right now, everybody's looking for something *different*. They should be more concerned about just doing it *well*." He considers something said to him about the modern-day movie-making process: the input from marketers as well as development people, the parade of rewrite men, the demands of stars pulling a project one way while a director pulls another. "Somebody said to me, is the problem that there's too many cooks spoiling the broth?" He shakes his head. "The problem is, there's too many people in the kitchen who can't cook."

Jeremiah Johnson: Hollywood's Most Beautiful—and Saddest—Western
(posted 1/6/13)

Directed by Sydney Pollack
Written by Edward Anhalt and John Milius
1972

The Western, at its creative and commercial peak—the late 1960s to early 1970s—proved itself an astoundingly pliable genre. It could be molded to deal with topical subject matter like racism (*Skin Game*, 1971), feminism (*The Ballad of Josie*, 1967), the excesses of capitalism (*Oklahoma Crude*, 1973). It could be bent into religious allegories (*High Plains Drifter*, 1973), or an equally allegorical address of the country's most controversial war (*Ulzana's Raid*, 1972). Westerns could be used to deconstruct America's most self-congratulatory myths (*Doc*, 1971), and address historical slights and omissions (*Little Big Man*, 1970). They could provide heady social commentary (*Hombre*, 1967), or simple adventure and excitement (*The Professionals*, 1966). They could be funny (*The Hallelujah Trail*, 1965), unremittingly grim (*Hour of the Gun*, 1967), surreal (*Greaser's Palace*, 1972), even be stretched into the shape of rock musical (*Zachariah*, 1971) or monster movie (*Valley of Gwangi*, 1969).

But what Westerns were rarely about was The West.

Oh, there were—and always have been—Western movies about the pioneers pushing West, settling the wilderness, turning the open range into the tilled land that would feed a nation, taming the lawless frontier—all the familiar tropes.

But The West itself... *The West*...

That strange, tugging, magical hold it had that pulled on a people, on a nation, hypnotizing it into a march that stopped only where the Pacific began. That part of the West—that thing that made The West *The West*—rarely found its way onto the screen.

And that was no surprise. The Indians, the deserts and plains, the buffalo, the masked Bad Men and badged Good Guys, the ranches, the farms... those were easily identifiable, concrete things. But those were only the accoutrements of The West. None of them explained the West and those ineffable, intangible qualities that kept it a vital part of the American psyche almost into the twenty-first century.

Why did we revere it so for so long? Why did generations of little boys fantasize about it? Why did storytellers as disparate as Sam Peckinpah and John Ford, Edward Abbey and Cormac McCarthy mourn its passing?

Jeremiah Johnson (1972) is as close as I've ever seen a film come to portraying the ferocious, entrancing majesty of that nineteenth century place beyond American civilization's outermost borders often marked on maps of the time as simply, bluntly, "Unexplored."

*****

Robert Redford is Johnson, a disaffected soldier who's bailed on the carnage of the Mexican War (which sets the movie in the mid-1840s) for the life of a mountain man. He steps off a barge into a rustic settlement—the demarcation line between cultivated America and wilderness—equips himself, and sets off following the instruction, "Ride due west as the sun sets. Turn left at the Rocky Mountains."

But the Rockies have little tolerance for brave fools, and Johnson comes close to freezing and/or starving to death, saved only by the sage Bear Claw (Will Geer), an old timer who makes his living "huntin' grizz" (grizzly bears). Under Bear Claw's tutelage, Johnson finally develops a mountain man's savvy, although at times it seems Bear Claw's form of teaching is as dangerous as the Rockies. One night, Johnson follows Bear Claw's example of sleeping on a bed of warm coals covered by a layer of earth to keep warm through the mountain night. It's not long before Johnson is dancing around the camp in pain, beating at his smoldering clothes. "Didn't bury 'em deep enough," says Bear Claw matter-of-factly as he rolls over to go back to sleep. "Seen it right off."

Eventually, Johnson rides off to find his own way. In a small hollow, he finds a woman (Allyn Ann McLerie) driven insane by the massacre of her family by Indians. Her husband has disappeared, and the only other survivor is a young boy (Josh Albee), struck mute by the killing. The woman is clearly suicidal, so Johnson takes the boy with him, christening him Caleb.

They come across the colorful and loquacious trapper Del Gue (Stefan Gierasch), and cross paths with a tribe of Flathead Indians. Johnson's misstep of offering the Flathead chief a grand peace-making gift puts the chief in the position of having to provide an even greater gift: his daughter Swan (Delle Bolton) as a wife.

With a wife and son he'd never wanted, Johnson leads his ad hoc family into the wilds and finds a suitable place to set up a permanent home. Working together building their cabin, hunting and playing together, the three become a true, loving family.

But the idyll is broken when Johnson reluctantly agrees to lead a cavalry patrol to rescue a wagon train bogged down in snow in one of the high passes. To get there, the troop violates a Crow taboo by cutting through a tribal burial ground. By the time Johnson returns to his cabin, the Crow have taken their revenge; Johnson finds Swan and Caleb murdered.

Johnson tracks down the Crow raiding party and kills them all but one, leaving the last survivor to sing his death song. Thereafter, Crow braves singly track Johnson down, but Johnson always emerges the victor. He drifts back through the hollow where he'd found the crazy woman, her cabin now taken over by the settler Qualen (Matt Clark) and his family. There, the Crow have created what Qualen describes as something akin to "a monument"—a tribute to the Crow's great enemy, Johnson. "Some say you're dead 'cause of this," says Qualen, meaning the tribute. "Some say you never will be 'cause of this."

Johnson drifts on, and finally, at a distance, faces a Crow brave he'd met when he was still a floundering, half-frozen mountain novice—Paints His Shirt Red (Joaquin Martinez). Johnson begins to reach for his rifle, but holds as Paints His Shirt Red raises his hand in peace. Johnson reaches his own hand out as if to touch the brave. It seems the war is finally over.

*****

The screenplay for *Jeremiah Johnson* violates any number of taboos set down by today's screenwriting gurus. We learn very little about Johnson. We never learn where he's from, or why he's come to the frontier. He's simply introduced in the opening scene by Tim McIntire's earthy, gravelly voiceover:

> *His name was Jeremiah Johnson, and they say he wanted to be a mountain man. The story goes that he was a man of proper wit and adventurous spirit, suited to the mountains. Nobody knows whereabouts he come from and don't seem to matter much. He was a young man and ghosty stories about the tall hills didn't scare him none... Bought him a good horse, and traps, and*

other truck that went with being a mountain man, and said goodbye to whatever life was down there below.

We get clues, hints. There's the Army uniform he wears when he shows up at the outpost, and his near-total disinterest in life "down there below." Later in the film, as he leads the cavalry troop on their rescue mission, he asks the troop commander about the war with Mexico. When told it's over, he asks, without any real interest, "Who won?"

And still later, after witnessing Johnson fend off yet another Crow attack, when Del Gue suggests it might be better if Johnson went down to the safety of a town, Johnson replies quietly, "I've seen a town, Del." Redford gives the line a weight that says more than the words; that says for all the grief and pain Johnson has suffered, and, at the hands of the Crow, will continue to suffer, the piney mountains are still more of a home to him than the civilization he left behind.

There is no great, driving thrust to the story. Johnson is not on a quest, there is no one thing he is after. Even through the film's later section, as he fends off one Crow attack after another, there's no build to some single, culminating fight, no "If I just beat the chief…" cathartic climax. There is simply a quiet, unspoken agreement between Johnson and Paints His Shirt Red that the duel is over. There's no explanation why: impasse, acknowledged defeat, respect, the tired recognition that enough blood has been shed—it could be any or all of them, yet that understated, opaque coda still seems part of the film's natural order of things.

The film is episodic (another supposed screenwriting taboo), with an amiable, ambling drift, not unlike the travels of its title character. Rather than a conventional narrative arc, it offers a portrait of a man who, for his own, unshared reasons, detaches himself from "down there below" to recreate himself—chapter by chapter—amidst the wilds of the high country.

And in so doing, without ever overtly stating it, the film suggests the arc of the opening and closing of the West. At first, the country is virgin to Johnson, and every new episode expands the film's vision of the boundless, unmapped expanse of the frontier and the endless variety of beings who inhabit it. But after the death of Swan and Caleb, the territory begins to feel played out; there are no more firsts. Johnson recrosses paths with Del Gue, Bear Claw,

Paints His Shirt Red. Johnson and Del Gue talk about country in Canada that entices because it's land "no man has ever seen." Bear Claw laments that "There's no more grizz…" Johnson wanders back to the hollow and the cabin where he'd first found Caleb and his grief-crazed mother. The woman is dead, her cabin now occupied by Qualen and his family. When Qualen tells Johnson he's a settler, the word registers with Johnson: the coming of settlers is the beginning of the end for the territory as mountain man country.

*****

The two screenwriters who developed *Jeremiah Johnson* were polar opposites in temperament and sensibility. (The screenplay would also pass through the uncredited hands of David Rayfiel, Pollack's go-to script doctor whose strength was in dialogue and character.)

John Milius was—and remains—one of Hollywood's great macho posturers. A self-professed gun nut and militarist, Milius's films—either as a screenwriter or writer/director (e.g. *The Wind and the Lion* [1975], *Conan the Barbarian* [1982], *Red Dawn* [1984], *Flight of the Intruder* [1991])—are bathed in a romanticized, violence-laced machismo, throwbacks to a-man's-gotta-do-what-a-man's-gotta-do ethic played against an often simple-minded, black-and-white moral terrain. Think of the testosterone fest that's *Conan*, the atavistic flag-waving of *Red Dawn* and *Flight of the Intruder*. Milius's is a world that recognizes little in the way of moral complexity, and is peopled by stoic heroes willing to cut through the bull with a sword-swipe or a well-placed bullet or bomb. Milius would often later voice his unhappiness over the finished *Johnson*. At one point, Sam Peckinpah was considered to direct and Clint Eastwood star as Johnson, and no doubt that would have produced a more visceral tale than the one that evolved and that would probably have been more to Milius's taste.

After Warner Bros. bought Milius's original script as a vehicle for Robert Redford, Edward Anhalt took over the screenplay chores. A veteran screenwriter at the time, Anhalt had always been a more reflective, more nuanced, headier writer. He shared an Oscar (with his wife) for the story for Elia Kazan's gritty *Panic in the Streets* (1950), and his films ranged from the very un-Milius sprawling antiwar saga *The Young Lions* (1958) to the medieval drama of *Becket* (1964). *The Boston Strangler* (1968) is a surprisingly thoughtful treatment of the sensational serial murder case from the 1960s; *Hour of the Gun* a ruminative revisionist take on the Gunfight at the OK Corral and its aftermath. Even when Anhalt was doing a straight-ahead thriller, like *The Satan Bug* (1965), he wrote with intelligence, preferring real-world weight to overstated myth and Hollywoody histrionics.

Yet somehow these two conflicting sensibilities (drawing on Vardis Fisher's novel *Mountain Man*, and Raymond W. Thorp and Robert Bunker's non-fiction account, *Crow Killer*, about the real-life inspiration for *Jeremiah Johnson*; John "Liver Eating" Jonstone, a mountain man who went on a revenge spree after a Crow party murdered his pregnant wife) come together in a seamless, elegant balance between a rugged and often brutal authenticity, and a rustic poetry.

Death is a constant factor in *Johnson*, even long before the titular character's drawn-out fight with the Crow. Bone-chilling cold, lack of food and shelter, bears, wolves—death is everywhere. Simply staying alive is an accomplishment; there's the authenticity.

And it rides comfortably alongside the poetry. One of Johnson's most lyrical moments comes after the death of Swan and Caleb and Johnson has met up again with the scoundrel with a poet's heart, Del Gue. As they part company, Del Gue rides off across open ground toward the jagged wall of the Rockies in the distance. Inspired by the unspoiled beauty of the high country, Del Gue indulges in what could be taken as the evangel of mountain men, the thing that has drawn them all into this place to which, despite its rigors and punishments, they all come to find themselves bound. As Del Gue recedes into the distance, his voice rises hoarsely in rabid devotion, as if he's proclaiming his love for the land as much to the universe as to the man he's left behind:

> *Ain't this somethin'? I told my pap and mam I was going to be a mountain man. Acted like they was gut-shot. 'Make your life go here, son. Here's where the peoples is. Them mountains is for Indians and wild men.' 'Mother Gue,' I says, 'the Rocky Mountains is the marrow of the world,' and by God, I was right... I ain't never seen 'em, but my common sense tells me the Andes is foothills, and the Alps is for children to climb!... These here is God's finest sculpturings! And there ain't no laws for the brave ones! And there ain't no asylums for the crazy ones! And there ain't no churches except for this right here! And there ain't no priests*

excepting the birds! By God, I are a mountain man, and I'll live 'til an arrow or a bullet finds me!...

I remember a reviewer once saying of Robert Redford that his often overlooked strength wasn't that he was an actor, but an excellent re-actor in the way that the events and people around him were reflected in his face. In his best roles, Redford worked with a precise economy. He could be as charming as any other leading man (think of him in *The Sting*, 1973), but he was even better as the man who holds it in, someone who only hinted at the roiling feelings inside. Other than George Roy Hill—who directed Redford in *Butch Cassidy and the Sundance Kid* (1969), *The Sting*, and *The Great Waldo Pepper* (1975)—no director knew better how to exploit Redford's particular reflective gifts than Sydney Pollack.

Pollack had an edge over other directors who worked with Redford. Pollack had started his career as an actor, having studied with the legendary Sanford Meisner, and he and Redford met as fellow actors cast in the low-budget war movie, *War Hunt* (1960). They became friends on the shoot, and the friendship lasted until Pollack's death in 2008. All told, he and Redford would make seven films together, including the hits *The Way We Were* (1973), *Three Days of the Condor* (1975), and *Out of Africa* (1985).

Throughout his career, Pollack was always considered an actor-friendly director, and he had a knack for blending commercially appealing properties with a more sensitive, intelligent, even artistic sensibility. It was a winning combination that, along with his share of box office winners, racked up forty-eight Oscar nominations including eleven wins for everything from performances to one win as Best Director.

Pollack understood the camera, and he understood Redford, and knew the latter didn't have to do much for it to have an impact on the former. Redford's lean style gives the simplest of lines the greatest of weight: "I've seen a town, Del." Or in the same conversation, when Del Gue seems surprised that Redford had stayed with Swan rather than—as Del had suggested—sell her off, Redford answers simply, "She weren't no trouble." And that seems to say it all.

I couldn't even tell you how he does it, what to look for, but somehow over the running time of the movie, Redford's Johnson goes from clueless naïf to melancholy drifter, and you can almost see the weight of his accumulating scars dragging at him in some internal way.

That low-key style gives Redford's few explosive moments all that much more effect. After yet another attack by a Crow warrior, the battered Redford stands, his usual stoicism shatters as he shouts to the skies, to the witnessing mountains that rebound his yell—a mixture of defiance and rage, exasperation and grief.

But Redford's best moment—and equally the best example of Pollack's understanding of the actor—is on his return to his cabin to find Swan and Caleb dead. In the shadowy interior of the cabin, Redford sits with the bodies of his loved ones for a day, a night, into the next day. With the smallest of adjustments, Redford's face goes from pained grief, to a duller, more lingering ache, and then resignation. He's stirred back to connecting with the outside world by the restless shifting of his horse. He goes to the horse, cradles its head as it nuzzles him; a warm, friendly touch such as he'll never know again from the family behind him. Then he sets Swan and Caleb together in bed and sets fire to the cabin.

There is no breast-beating, no hysterical sobs, no bellowing of "Nooooo!" to the skies. And because of that, the moment is all the more poignant.

*****

Though Pollack is rarely referred to as the most conspicuously visual of directors, in the works where it mattered, he had a keen understanding of the importance of place; that the setting of a movie not only could be a character, but be one of a story's most important characters. Think of the medieval castle at the center of *Castle Keep* (1969), the glorious vistas of *Out of Africa*, and it is particularly true of *Jeremiah Johnson*.

Cinematographer Duke Callaghan and Second Unit Director Mike Moder do more than take pretty pictures. The terrain forges men like Johnson and Bear Claw and Del Gue into the scrappy, tough-hided, prosaic survivors they are. The mountains—sometimes bathed in bright sunshine, sometimes cloaked in brilliantly white snow, other times wreathed in ominous clouds—entice, threaten, stand in witness. Like the sirens of Greek legend, they beckon adventurers onward, often to their doom. It is the rare man who can make a life there. The mountains are never conquered; one either learns to respect them, or die through any number of ways the mountains can kill.

And for the man who does find his life in the mountains, "down below" becomes a distant, alien place. Late in the movie, when Johnson and Bear Claw meet up in snowy woods and share a bite to eat, Johnson asks, "You wouldn't happen to know what month of the year it is?"

Bear Claw doesn't know either.

The mountains, for them, are a world not governed by the calendar but by the passing of the snows, the coming and going of the animals. Time doesn't exist.

And so it seems perfectly reasonable—even believable—when the film ends freezing on the image of Johnson reaching out in peace toward Paints His Shirt Red, and Tim McIntire's rough-edged voice sings, "And some folks think... he's up there still..."

Maria Schneider
(posted 2/5/11)

Sometimes things come together in and around a movie in such a way—like an alignment of the planets—that the gravitational pull it exerts on the collective cultural consciousness is out of all proportion to its actual mass. *Last Tango in Paris* (1972) was that kind of movie—of its time, at just the right time. And in that, it made and possibly damned its leading lady, Maria Schneider, who died at age fifty-eight earlier this month, reportedly from cancer.

Throughout the 1960s and into the 1970s, mainstream moviemaking had become more daring, more experimental, pushing at—and sometimes punching through—the boundaries that just a few years earlier had protected those aspects of the human experience supposedly too sacred, too sensitive and intimate, too taboo to put on film. This was the time of *Midnight Cowboy* (1969), *Deliverance* (1972), *The Killing of Sister George* (1968), *Reflections in a Golden Eye* (1968), *The Sergeant* (1968), *Straw Dogs* (1971), *Bob & Carol & Ted & Alice* (1969). Even today—maybe *especially* today when the multiplex is dominated, both on-screen and in the auditorium seats, by an adolescent mentality fixated on toilet humor and pyrotechnics—there's still a militantly adult vibrancy to these films, an air to them of the committed, angry revolutionary screaming to be heard above the din of banality. They were all part of a strain of surprisingly commercial moviemaking (*Tango* would go on to gross nearly $100 million worldwide; approximately $550 million in today's currency without accounting for differences in ticket prices), which felt like a grasping for some grand, ultimate *something* about the connection between heart and mind and body. With all its flaws (the movie certainly has them), *Last Tango* seemed to be some sort of cathartic culmination, going further than any of the others visually and thematically in the dark eroticism it was trying to plumb.

Perfectly in synch with *Tango*'s still audacious yet very 1970s exploration of human connection, love, sex, manipulation, and emotional violence was Maria Schneider. She seems so of the film, so of its time, it's hard to picture her in any other context. Or maybe the unhappy magic of the film is it makes us see her that way.

Again, that alignment of the planets... Everything conspired to make Schneider a legend, from the tragic brevity of her film career to the tragic brevity of her life. Though she had made some films before *Tango*, and others afterward, she remained, in popular perception, a one-hit wonder, defined and forever identified with this one unforgettable film. To the international audiences who came to know her through *Tango*, she seemed to come from nowhere, and just as abruptly disappear. The answers to "Hey, whatever happened to... ?" only enhanced her mystique: 1972's quintessential sexual icon coming out two years later as a bisexual, problems with drugs and alcohol, suicide attempts, walking off the set of *Penthouse*-produced sex epic *Caligula* in 1979 to sign herself into a Rome mental hospital.

Always in the air around her, with each revelation, this most tantalizing wondering: Had she always been too fragile for the movies? Were her problems the result of the stresses and strains of an always cruel and demanding—and sexist—business working their way on fault lines already there? Or had it been *Tango*?

She had only been nineteen when director/cowriter Bernardo Bertolucci had cast her as Jeanne, a young Parisian who falls into a torrid, anonymous sexual tryst with middle-aged widower Paul (Marlon Brando). Bertolucci had gotten the idea for the movie from his own sexual fantasies, and whatever else *Tango* did—or didn't—accomplish artistically, it hit a resonating chord in the minds of a generation of young men with Schneider as a tantalizingly attainable-seeming fantasy.

Schneider wasn't Hollywood beautiful. She still had a teen's round face framed in a cascade of hippy-dippy hair, an un-Hollywood-like fullness to her body—like an earth motherish commune-living version of Marilyn Monroe. In her bell bottoms and long scarves and floppy hats she would've looked at home on any college campus of the time. That real-worldness of her made her tangible, possible, and her free, comfortable sexuality filled in the idea of her as a flower child's wet dream.

Maybe it was her own inexperience, maybe the fact she was constantly having to respond to Brando's improvisations, but there was an unpolished, natural, honest quality to her performance. She would later say the film's most (in)famous scene—"Go, get the butter"—was unscripted, spontaneously inflicted on her by Brando, and that the tears she shed on-screen during the scene were real. She didn't seem like she was acting because often she *wasn't* acting, and it was at those moments when her fragility came through that she seemed all the more real, all the more touchable, and because of that, when she seemed most hurt she seemed most alluring.

Afterward, she would say both Bertolucci and Brando had exploited her, that in her 19-year-old naiveté she hadn't been able to divine just what a mindfuck the movie was. And perhaps it was, and that was why the drugs and alcohol and the psychological problems. Or perhaps the problems were already there and that's what had made the experience such a mindfuck for her.

She would never get out from under that cloud; she would always be the girl from *Last Tango in Paris*. It was a mantle she hated, possibly doomed her subsequent career, and she never forgave Bertolucci for what she felt he'd put her through.

Whatever the truth of the matter—whether she had been a problemed girl going in, or a problemed girl coming out—and despite the undeniable sadness and tragedy of the course of her life, the impression she made on-screen thirty-nine years ago remains indelible, captured on film forever young, forever enrapturing, eternally desirable.

Be-"Seiged": The Gordon Williams Novel v. Sam Peckinpah's *Straw Dogs* v. Rod Lurie's Remake
(posted 8/7/11)

Heaven and earth are ruthless
And treat the myriad creatures as straw dogs;
The sage is ruthless
And treats the people as straw dogs

The *Cahiers du Cinema* called it "the furious springtime of world cinema," and nowhere was it more furious than in the United States.

From the 1960s through the 1970s, a confluence of events sociological and cultural combined with sea changes in the motion picture industry to ignite one of the most creatively combustive periods in American commercial filmmaking. All the shouldn'ts, and couldn'ts, can'ts and don'ts of studio moviemaking established over decades by the Hollywood establishment were now being bent, twisted, and inverted when not being plainly shoved aside or steam rollered. What had been taboo had now become the backbone of the trade, and there was hardly a social hot button of the time—sexuality, homosexuality, the division between young and old, Vietnam, government malfeasance, ageism, feminism, racism, the nuclear threat, etc.—that didn't, sooner or later, find itself thrown on the big screen and often tackled with a brutal frankness. This was the era of *Dr. Strangelove, or: How I Learned to Stop Worrying and Love the Bomb* (1964), *Little Big Man* (1970), *Dog Day Afternoon* (1975), *One Flew Over the Cuckoo's Nest* (1975), *A Clockwork Orange* (1971), *Being There* (1979), *Badlands* (1973), *Raging Bull* (1980), *The Conversation* (1974), *The Killing of Sister George* (1968), *Joe* (1969), *Bonnie and Clyde* (1967), *M*A*S*H* (1972), *Midnight Cowboy* (1969), *Reflections in a Golden Eye* (1967), *Point Blank* (1967), *2001: A Space Odyssey* (1968), *Apocalypse Now* (1979), *Taxi Driver* (1976), *Network* (1976), *The Godfather* (1972), *Nashville* (1975), *Last Tango in Paris* (1972), *Deliverance* (1972), *Chinatown* (1974)... The list of memorable and landmark movies from the time goes on and on, staggering in both its length and breadth.

Notable among the notable was 1971's *Straw Dogs*. Appropriately enough, one of the most provocative movies from that time was directed and cowritten by one of the most controversial filmmakers of that time: Sam Peckinpah.

Peckinpah had already single-handedly escalated the then ever-growing, ever more heated debate over film violence with his blood-drenched 1969 revisionist Western, *The Wild Bunch*. *Straw Dogs* would become an even more polarizing film... and also the director's biggest commercial success up to that time.

The film's screenplay was adapted from a 1969 novel by Scottish author Gordon Williams: *The Siege of Trencher's Farm*. It says something about the impact of the movie—and the way it continues to reverberate among serious cineastes—that the most recent reprint from Titan Books, published this year to capitalize on a remake of Peckinpah's film to be released this fall, is billed as (in small print), *The Siege of Trencher's Farm: The Novel that Inspired* (in print twice as big) *Straw Dogs.*

While Williams no doubt appreciates how the endless notoriety of the film has brought him years of continued royalties on a book that most probably would have disappeared—as most do—within a few years of its first publication, the fact is Williams hated Peckinpah's film. *Hated* it. Called it "horrific" at the time of its release, claiming he would "... .never again sell one of my books to an American." According to one 2003 interview conducted in conjunction with the UK video release of *Straw Dogs,* it seemed Williams *still* hated the movie thirty years later, flatly declaring it "crap."

And from the few peeks so far offered of writer/director/producer Rod Lurie's upcoming remake, it's a good bet Williams will hate that film too. *Hate* it.

*****

Born in Paisley, Scotland, in 1934, Gordon Williams had bounced around the provinces for some years as a journalist, but by the late 1960s, he was shaping up as a rising figure on the UK literary scene. Paramount had paid him big money for his novel, *The Man Who Had Power Over Women* (released in 1970 starring Rod Taylor), and his next book, the 1968 work, *From Scenes Like These,* a grim picture of working class life in late 1950s rural Scotland, had been shortlisted for the inaugural awarding of the Booker Prize the following year (P. H. Newby's *Something to Answer For* would ultimately receive the prize).

The Paramount money underwrote a move by Williams and his family to Devon, a largely rural county in southwest England. Devon also happened to be home to the famed Dartmoor Prison. Williams put the brooding presence of Dartmoor together with stories about escaped British gangland killer and certified psycho Frank "The Mad Axeman" Mitchell (it was later learned Mitchell hadn't escaped but been kidnapped and murdered by some of his underworld associates), and started coming up with the cornerstone elements of his next novel: an escaped lunatic, a band of vigilantes, an isolated farmhouse, and the idea of turning "... a group of ordinary people... into murderers by eight o'clock tomorrow morning."

According to Williams's 2003 interview for *The Guardian*, he intended the book as nothing more than "... a hit-and-run cheap paperback," banging it out in a startlingly short nine days.

The resultant work—*The Seige of Trencher's Farm*—is a consequently schizophrenic work, showing, at times, the same strong, lyrical prose that had earned Williams a contender's spot for the Booker bumping up against the kind of awkward storytelling one might expect from a quickly ground out potboiler hung on an intriguing hook but an undercooked narrative. It is a novel both overly complicated yet simplistic; by turns sluggish and pulse-pounding; at times hot-blooded, yet clumsily contrived, sometimes to the point of corny melodrama.

George Magruder is an American academic working on a book about nineteenth century English literary footnote Branksheer. His homesick English-born wife of nine years, Louise, has persuaded him to spend his writing sabbatical back in her home country. Along with their daughter Karen, they take a house in the rural west country of England.

This is a marriage already in trouble. Back in the States, faced with George's disciplined emotions and growing sexual inattention, Louise had drifted into a fling with a visiting English poet, a sore spot George does not hesitate to poke during their frequent squabbles. Too many years together and now cooped up in their rented farmhouse, having only modest contact with the insular villagers nearby, the quirks and minor irritations they had once tolerated in each other now set off regular shouting matches. Here on her native soil, Louise has come to realize just how out of place she had been back in the States—and how George is even more out of place in England.

Driving home through a blowing snowstorm from a church-sponsored Christmas party for the parish children one night, George accidentally hits a figure wandering across the road. It turns out to be Henry Niles, a mental patient escaped from an ambulance when the vehicle crashed on the icy roads. Although years of imprisonment and illness have left Niles a hapless figure, he remains the village boogey man, always spoken of with a mix of fear and distaste having been locked up in the nearby asylum for molesting and killing three children.

George takes the injured Niles home unaware that, at that moment, the villagers are looking for a missing young girl, some of them positive she's fallen victim to the escaped Niles. When word reaches the girl's father that Magruder has Niles at his house, he and some of his less than savory pub mates trek out to the Magruder house and demand George turn over Niles. Already resenting the Magruders as outsiders, and—by the village's threadbare standards—for their affluence, their liquor-stoked vigilantism leaves them in no mood for reasoned argument. The stakes tragically escalate to all-or-nothing when one of George's well-meaning neighbors is accidentally killed by one of the men while trying to talk them into going home.

Cut off from escape by the snow, their phone line severed by the small mob outside, George realizes—as do the men—that the vigilantes' only option for avoiding punishment for the killing is to murder the family of witnesses inside the house. At first, George's defense of the house is an analytical process of problem-solving, but as the mob begins to get inside his walls, the fighting becomes increasingly brutal and mindlessly savage. By daybreak, George stands triumphant, having beaten three of the invaders senseless, caused another to inadvertently shoot off his own toes, and gouging out the eyes of the last:

> *He had won! That mattered, nothing else... He felt tired. And proud. The greatest feeling in the world... To know you could stand up to anything in the world. To know you were a man, to be able to feel it in your guts.*

Louise, who had reached a point in their marriage where she'd come to think little of her husband as a man, and had wanted him to give Niles up, now recants her disparagements, her affair, her disappointments: "I don't deserve you, George, it's true, I don't, I don't..." And with that, the family is, again, whole.

The feeling one gets reading *The Siege of Trencher's Farm* is of Williams having this terrific idea of the eponymous siege (which takes up well over half the novel) and of turning his innocuous villagers and bookish academic "... into murderers by eight o'clock tomorrow morning," but then of having to quickly slap together some kind of functional set-up in order to get to the good stuff. It almost feels as if he worked backward, starting with the siege and then figuring, "Well, to end up there, this has to happen; and to get *there*, *this* has to happen," and continuing on back to the beginning, giving the story more of an obviously constructed (or contrived, depending on how ungenerous you feel) vibe rather than that of a naturally flowing arc.

Even the idea of the Magruders coming to this far-off bit of England is a forced construct. Louise's feeling of homesickness makes sense, but why this cosmopolitan Londoner already suffering marital doubts would push to settle in such an isolated, impoverished part of the country far from everything she knows—including her own family—hardly seems the solution to her problems. The couple fight because Williams needs them to fight; because they can't make up at the end of the book unless they fight; and so they claw and spit at each other at the slightest provocation, each fight quickly going nuclear.

Too much of the book is built around such has-tos. Niles's escape hangs on the hoariest of clichés; a distracted driver in a rush, a snowstorm, slippery roads. And later, during the siege, while George still has a working phone, the ill-fated good neighbor calls about stopping by but it never occurs to George to use the phone to tell the police there's an angry mob outside his house looking to lynch Henry Niles. Things happen because Williams *needs* them to happen to ignite his rousing third act; not because they would naturally happen, or because they even make sense.

Williams sets the events of the story within what should be a pressure cooker of a twenty-four-hour framework, but until the siege begins, the story never works up much momentum. Instead, the compressed time frame forces Williams to keep interrupting the forward flow of the plot to make regular installments of backstory to justify the actions of not only George and Louise, but nearly every integral character in the book—as well as a good number of peripheral characters (the minister putting together the Christmas children's party; the bartender at the local inn; the cops trekking overland through the snowstorm to bring in Niles etc.).

That kind of omniscient, ensemble approach probably worked fine for a portraiture like *From Scenes Like This*, but here, for much of *Seige*'s first act, it leaves the book feeling unfocused, inchoate, the stop-start-stop-start rhythm of the plot regularly halting for more backstory turning the first ninety pages into a slog.

It doesn't help that Williams's dialogue is flat and colorless and often heavy-handedly expository, even when the characters are at their most heated (nor does George's "Americanese" sound particularly American). Consider this spat between George and Louise early in the book. Christmas is coming up and Louise asks George to put his work aside to join in with Karen and herself wrapping gifts. George says no, Louise presses, and soon the argument starts sounding like bad soap opera dialogue. After Louise refers to George as a "so-called professor," George immediately sends off his nukes:

"A so-called professor! That's better than being a so-called poet. I suppose you're just eating your heart out for that fat slob."

"Are you referring to Patrick Ryman? If so, I—"

"Who else would I be referring to? That's why you wanted us to come to this precious little country of yours, isn't it? Romantic fantasy. Did you think he'd come riding up the lane and carry you off? Come to England, I want to show you *my* country! Horseshit! All you wanted was to indulge some sordid little romantic daydream."

"Oh, clever, clever. You found another word for fantasy, you're improving."

When we meet George and Louise at the beginning of the book, Williams doesn't give us much to connect with. They're already sniping at each other, there's no sense of some happier past, and there's little more to them than Louise being something of an unhappy bitch and George a spiteful tight-ass.

But if Williams seems to stumble through the book's first act, the book does begin to jell once the siege begins, gaining intensity with its narrowing focus, and accelerating as the fight for the house becomes more desperate. By the climax of the siege, with George in a frantic hand-to-hand grapple with one of the home invaders, the book is in a roaring third gear and almost glowing with the heat of animal rage.

It is times like that—and they happen off and on throughout the book—when one sees the novel *The Siege of Trencher's Farm* might have been; reminded, then, that it was not for nothing Williams had been a Booker contender. One of the best sections of the novel is the opening chapter, which today's editors, mindful of an ADD just-get-on-with-it audience sensibility, would probably have told Williams to cut. It doesn't serve the plot, it doesn't serve the characters. And yet, it is the book's keystone, making so much of what follows understandable (and much of Williams's later exposition redundant):

"In the same year that Man first flew to the Moon and the last American soldier left Vietnam there were still corners of England where lived men and women who had never travelled more than fifteen miles from their own homes. They had spent all their lives on the same land that had supported their fathers and grandfathers and great-grandfathers and unknown generations before that."

For the next several pages, Williams paints a bleakly lyrical picture of this insular, impoverished, inward-turned rural backwater, a place isolated as much by ignorance and suspicion of outsiders and their world as by the surrounding hills and easily choked off narrow unpaved roads. It is a place tragically mired in its own dark history, with a longstanding, long instilled sense of ritual loyalty to "our own" trumping any moral judgment or transgression. For those few pages, Williams seems on the verge of pulling off an English version of James Dickey's *Deliverance* (published two years later). But he only comes close to Dickey's eloquence intermittently, and never attains the same haunting soulfulness. Where Dickey lets his more existential themes bubble along as subtext, Williams clubs the reader with the obvious in case it was somehow missed among all the eye-gougings and beatings: "Now he knew the truth. All that nonsense about thresholds and civilization."

Williams delivers a book that is ultimately cathartically entertaining, but not particularly compelling or insightful.

Unlike Williams, Sam Peckinpah had more on his mind than a "hit-and-run" quickie thriller. But then he almost always did.

*****

As happened on disturbingly regular occasions, Sam Peckinpah's career was—yet again—at a problematic point at the beginning of the 1970s.

In 1961, Peckinpah had graduated from a successful TV career to the big screen directing the neatly done but little noticed Western *The Deadly Companions*. He followed this in 1962, with what was instantly declared a newly minted Western classic, *Ride the High Country*. In 1964, Peckinpah tackled the more epic-scaled cavalry adventure, *Major Dundee*, but the film fell victim to last minute budget cuts, clashes between Peckinpah and his producers, and arguably Peckinpah's own limitations in handling his first grand scale production. *Dundee* was an expensive commercial and critical flop, and after being fired from his next project—*The Cincinnati Kid*—just a few days into shooting, Peckinpah was tacitly blacklisted as a feature director (Norman Jewison would complete the 1965 feature).

In his few short years as a feature director, Peckinpah had well earned a reputation for being combative, rebellious, paranoid, regularly stoking his demons with constant heavy drinking. He had fought bitterly with his producers on all of his feature film projects. Those years had left him labeled with that most toxic of Hollywood descriptives—"difficult"—and he was considered unemployable.

But Peckinpah came back, first in a 1966 return to TV to write and adapt an award-winning version of Katherine Porter's short story, "Noon Wine," for producer Daniel Melnick. Peckinpah's big screen resurrection came in 1969, with another Western classic and one of the seminal films of the 1960s/1970s, the apocalyptic *The Wild Bunch*. Trying to demonstrate he was more than just an action director, Peckinpah followed *Bunch* with the elegiac *The Ballad of Cable Hogue* (1970), but even before the film was finished, Peckinpah was fighting with the very same Warner Bros. execs of whom he'd been so complimentary during the production of *Bunch*. The blowback was that while *Hogue* was a critic's darling, Warners gave the film only the most minimal release and it quickly disappeared.

Marshall Fine, in his biography *Bloody Sam: The Life and Films of Sam Peckinpah*, tells of Peckinpah casting about after *Hogue* for an opportunity to break out of the action/Western director mold he felt he was being funneled into, but having little luck generating any studio interest in his non-Western/non-actioner projects (ironically, one project Peckinpah had wanted in on was the film adaptation of *Deliverance* that went to John Boorman). Then his old "Noon Wine" associate, Daniel Melnick, making his first stab at producing a feature, called Peckinpah about a project he'd been developing with his partner, David Susskind, based on a novel Susskind had bought called, *The Siege of Trencher's Farm*.

According to Fine, Peckinpah had been playing around for years with ideas inspired by his reading of sociological anthropologist Robert Ardrey's books on the instinctive violence he saw still residing somewhere within civilized men. In *Siege*, Peckinpah saw a vehicle to put those concepts into play. Though the story climaxed with the brutal farmhouse battle, much of the story was drama-driven and would thus stand apart from his previous work. The project also provided Peckinpah with his first feature opportunity to demonstrate his skill with contemporary material set far away from the Old West with which he had come to be identified.

By the time Peckinpah was brought on, the project had already been through the hands of several screenwriters with no success at nailing down Williams's story for the screen. Melnick hired screenwriter David Zelag Goodman (previous credits included cult Western *Monte Walsh*, and bittersweet rom-com *Lovers and Other Strangers* [both 1970]), and he and Peckinpah would continue to work on the script all the way through production (although other writers would also contribute to the screenplay, Goodman and Peckinpah are the credited writers).

One of the numerous changes they made to Williams' novel was replacing his long-winded title. Walter Kelley, an acquaintance from Peckinpah's TV days who would become one of the director's regular uncredited collaborators, gave Peckinpah a quote by the Chinese philosopher Lao-tse, which would provide the new title: *Straw Dogs*. It was possibly the only change in the source material Williams liked, the author telling e-zine *iofilm* in the early 2000s, "It's obviously memorable."

Whereas Williams had produced a plot complicated in its construction but simplistic in its dramatic heft, Peckinpah, Goodman, et al greatly simplified the construction to produce a more dramatically complex narrative. The screenplay does away with Williams' twenty-four-hour framework, giving the story the breathing room to gradually open up over a much more extensive period without having to jam in a lot of justifying backstory. The film starts with the couple—childless and now renamed David and Amy Sumner—having only recently moved into Trencher's farm. Unlike the novel, they begin as a reasonably happy couple, their relationship only deteriorating bit by bit over time as the dramatic stresses of the story slowly ratchet up.

Key to the film's set-up—and a vast improvement over the book—is awarding both Amy and David compelling reasons for settling in the English backcountry. For Amy (Susan George)—presented here as both younger and, one senses, more attractive than Louise—this is a triumphant return home. It's not hard to see that, back in the States, Amy must have been considered something of a trophy wife for the bespectacled, dweebish David (Dustin Hoffman). By the same token, David is a trophy husband, socially and intellectually head and shoulders above the boorish, ignorant villagers. Amy is here with David in tow to showboat how far she's come since leaving her little backward hometown.

Her return comes with a complication: old boyfriend Charlie Venner (Del Henney). It's clear from the outset that while Amy has somewhat boastfully moved on, the feelings on Venner's end are more unresolved. Or perhaps, following through on Robert Ardrey's theses, Venner's feelings are more primal, territorial; Amy was mine and that makes her mine always.

David is not a literary researcher, but something even more arcane: an astromathematician, someone with his mind literally in the clouds, which only emphasizes how inept he is at handling terrestrial affairs. David's reasons for the move to England are anchored in a subtext that probably eludes contemporary audiences, but which viewers in 1971 well understood.

From the late 1960s on, American college campuses had become something of a social battleground. Student protests—some of them violent—over the Vietnam War, and subsequently other social issues as well, had become a regular feature on the nightly news. Students clashed with police and with older blue collar counter-protestors, ROTC buildings were burned and bombed, administration buildings were occupied and campuses shut down. Student unrest reached an emotional peak in May 1970, with the killing of four students and wounding of nine others by National Guardsmen called in to break up a protest on Ohio's Kent State University campus sparked by the expansion of the war into Cambodia.

Williams's book is criminally oblivious to the state of campus affairs at the time, but it's critical to the film's David. He has come to this empty corner of the world—Amy at one point accuses him—"because there's no place left to hide." Later in the film, as he and Amy begin to go at each other, she calls him out on this very point when he tries to hide behind his work, telling him he'd come to England not to noodle formulae in peace, but "... because you didn't want to take a stand!"

This, then, becomes the foundation on which the rest of the film's narrative is built; a marriage probably built less on true love than on passion and ego, one not-quite-mature partner coming home to display her catch, the other to hide from a society demanding commitment and confrontation. In her notes for a Peckinpah film festival sponsored by Lincoln Center, critic Kathleen Murphy nails the character of the Sumners as that of "... children playing at life."

Showing he's a good sport, David hires Venner and his pub cronies to repair the roof on his garage. When Amy complains about some of the comments the men make as she passes by, the confrontation-avoidant David blows it off as good-natured wise-cracking. The men grow more lackadaisical in their work, their opinion of the mousey American dwindling by the day.

In the book, George finds the family cat strangled out on the grounds, Williams portraying the killing as a simple act of random violence; part of the dark nature of the country. In *Straw Dogs*, David and Amy find their cat strangled and hanging in their bedroom closet, nothing random about it. Amy wants David to confront the men working on the garage, certain one of them is responsible. David waffles, claiming they can't know that for sure, and, besides, why would they do it?

"To prove to you that they could get into your bedroom!"

Easily the most controversial change the film makes from the book – and one of the elements Williams most despised—was the rape of Amy. Williams was outraged, and feminists and some critics—and particularly feminist critics like Molly Haskell—declared Peckinpah a misogynist indulging in the macho fantasy that women enjoy rape.

The oblivious David takes Venner and his mates up on their invitation to join them on a "snipe hunt." Leaving David abandoned on the moor, Venner sneaks back to the farmhouse to—in Ardrey fashion—take back what's his: Amy. When he tries to force himself on her, she resists and Venner strikes her a blow that floors her. She only surrenders herself when Venner threatens a second blow. But what at first begins as a violation begins to change and at a certain point Amy begins to respond. She has grown apart from her husband, old feelings of communion are stirred up by her ex, and just as Venner and his mates have judged David not up to their primal standards of masculinity, so too Amy has come to the same view.

Now, how much true-to-life psychological validity this has is certainly up for debate, but within the context of the film's narrative, it makes a sad sense.

But the scene doesn't end there, and what follows should have (but didn't) put a stake through the breastbone of the macho-rape-fantasy view. Afterward, Venner looks up to see one of his mates—Scutt (Ken Hutchison)—holding a shotgun on him, beckoning him to move away from Amy so he can take his turn. Venner shakes his head, but the muzzle of the shotgun wins the argument. Amy doesn't know what's happening until Scutt turns her round to take her from behind. Venner—in a warped display of tribal male loyalty—holds Amy down for Scutt, even though his distaste is obvious.

This time, there is no transformation of the act from violation to revived passion. It's a brutal, animalistic act leaving Amy emotionally scarred.

She cannot confess the true rape to David without confessing the not-quite-rape by her onetime lover, and so David returns from the moor seeming all the more petty in his pissing and moaning about "your (Amy's) friends," completely insensitive to the obvious fact something's amiss with his wife. Besides, by this time Amy has come to view David as a coward: what could he possibly do about it?

Later, at the church talent show, Amy is tormented by the leering looks from Scutt and the mates with whom he's no doubt shared the story of his triumph. The trauma of his attack comes back to her in disturbing flash cuts. She asks David to take her home and that's when David strikes Henry Niles (David Warner) with his car.

Henry Niles' part in the film has also been streamlined from the novel. He's a simple-minded fellow—think *Of Mice and Men*'s Lenny—living with his brother in the village, and though some allusion is made to past acts and warnings are made to Niles's brother to keep Henry away from the local children, he is no murderer, and there is no melodramatic escape from his asylum keepers.

Williams goes into the siege portion of the novel having laid out clear moral divisions between attackers and defenders, and by the end of the book he's kinda/sorta cheated to keep them that way. Williams' Niles has killed in the past, but this time he's innocent, the missing child having simply wandered off and become lost in the snowstorm (and later found). Williams even adds the unnecessary wrinkle that George and Louise had participated in an anti-death penalty protest years earlier to save Niles from hanging during the last days of England's capital punishment. George's defense of his house first begins on the elevated principal of protecting the helpless and innocent Niles. Then later, when it becomes a more primal matter of survival, there's still a heroic quality to George's stand since it's not only his and his wife's life he's trying to preserve, but also that of his eight-year-old daughter. And, despite the brutality George falls back on to fend off the invaders, none of them die at his hands, preserving George's position on the moral high ground.

But Peckinpah was a filmmaker who gloried in moral ambivalence. The hero of *Major Dundee* is a soldier with an Ahab-sized obsession who nearly destroys his command trying to justify his own opinion of himself by chasing after an Apache raider; the men of *The Wild Bunch* are ruthless, robbing killers who gain our sympathy only because they are less reprehensible than the ragtag posse chasing after them.

In *Straw Dogs*, no young, mentally afflicted girl wanders off into the storm and is later found alive. Instead, she is an older, sexually curious teen (early in the film she had spied on David and Amy's lovemaking) who lures Niles away from the Christmas show for some necking in a barn. When Niles hears his brother calling for him, he panics and accidentally strangles the girl.

Niles, then, is guilty—after a fashion. But the mob that comes chasing after him doesn't know about the dead girl, nor does David just as he doesn't know about his wife's rape. David, the man who number crunches the paths of planets, hasn't a clue what's happening in his own house. Consequently, when the siege begins, unlike the book's George, David is unknowingly protecting a killer (albeit an accidental one).

In a bit of common sense lacking in the book, David calls on the local lawman and it is he—not an interceding neighbor—who is killed outside David's house. At that point, the fight – for David—goes beyond mere survival. Niles becomes irrelevant, there is no daughter to protect, and what little is left of his marriage is quickly coming apart under the blows of the mob at his front door.

Amy refuses to help David, tries to respond to Venner's entreaties to let him in, and even attempts to leave. David slaps her, pulls her away from the door by her hair and tells her, "Do as you're told. If you don't, I'll break your neck."

This is more than a "worm turns" story. This is David, à la Ardrey, defending his property—and that includes his woman; one alpha male (though a latently developed one) fighting off a rival pack. "This is where I live," he declares to Amy, "This is me. I will not allow violence against this house."

Despite Peckinpah's reputation as a master of mayhem, and even with the film's body count in mind, the filmed siege is more restrained than the one in Williams' pages. On film, the third act battle takes up about eighteen minutes in the 118-minute film, while it takes up over half the novel. Many of the more brutal acts are taken straight from the book: throwing boiling cooking oil (in the book its boiling water) at the invaders, one of the mob shooting off his foot (though in the book, this only cripples), beatings with a fireplace poker (in the book, it's a baseball bat). Peckinah foregoes the eye-gouging.

Which brings up another sharp departure from the book. David wins not by disabling, but by killing. Standing in his shattered sitting room surrounded by bodies, he say, in a mix of quiet triumph and disbelief, "Jesus... I got them all." While detractors indicted Peckinpah for equating manliness with violence, there is nothing in the portrayal that either salutes or slams David's victory; it's an adamant expression of a plain fact: "We're violent by nature," Peckinpah told *The New York Times* in defending his film, "It's one of the greatest brainwashes of all times to say we're not." Open to interpretation, David's "win" can equally be taken as disturbing as much as some sort of triumph. In a pure expression of Peckinpah-esque moral ambivalence and ambiguity, David salutes himself for killing five men in defense of a killer and a wife who no longer loves him.

In the novel, come the next day, George is saluted as a hero and becomes the media's story of the day. His wife, impressed at his manly defense of his family, paints herself unworthy and recommits to him.

Peckinpah and his collaborators struggled to come up with an ending more appropriate to their story all the way through filming. There is no day after, no media salute, no congratulations from the constabulary. David leaves both his house and his marriage in shambles, takes Niles to the car and proceeds to drive him back to the village. Out of a few minutes improvisation in the car between Dustin Hoffman and David Warner, Peckinpah finally came up with what screenwriters refer to as "the button."

"I don't know my way home," Niles says.

"That's ok," says David with a small, self-amused smile. "I don't either."

Like most of Peckinpah's protagonists, David has won... at the cost of everything.

Peckinpah did not throw out Gordon Williams' book. Though re-plotted, the essence of Williams's story is there. Peckinpah just took it a step further. George's climactic sense of "I *am* a man!" now becomes something darker, more primordial, and a less comforting accomplishment. It's as if Peckinpah took Williams' seat at the card table, played the same hand, but wagered far more aggressively, raising the stakes and taking the game to another level.

Williams told the story of an emotionally repressed academic who defends his family by falling back on the primal violence within. Peckinpah expanded the thesis, taking out the nobility of defense of family to find the animalistic sense of territoriality and blood lust presumably within every man, ready and waiting to be unlocked under the right combination of circumstances.

The natural argument is, which is better? But that does a disservice to each work; each artist was after something different. Williams' thriller was primarily looking to thrill, and ultimately it does.

But next to Williams' nine-day quickie, Peckinpah's film is clearly the more ambitious, the dynamic between David and Amy easily more dramatically dense than the soapy sniping between George and Louise, and the film has certainly resonated over time much more strongly than *The Siege of Trencher's Farm*, coming to be considered one of the director's best films; some argue perhaps even his most accomplished.

Which certainly presents a hell of a challenge to any filmmaker daring/foolhardy enough to remake it... making Rod Lurie either one of the most daring filmmakers on the scene today, or an incredible fool.

*****

Judging a movie only by its trailers is like judging the quality of a restaurant by reading the menu: it hardly compares to actually tasting the food.

Still, if the menu offers nothing but hash and grits, one's expectations can't help but be low, and the aroma from Rod Lurie's kitchen so far doesn't bespeak of a Gordon Ramsay hard at work.

From his filmography, it's clear Lurie, a one-time film critic whose loose, instigatory style got him banned from any number of critics' screenings, is a seriously intentioned filmmaker. But only with his 2000 effort—the political drama *The Contender*—has his execution come close to matching his ambitions. Most of his feature credits are nobly intended misfires like *Deterrence* (1999), *The Last Castle* (2001), and *Nothing but the Truth* (2008). Even with *The Contender*—easily one of the best big screen political dramas of the 2000s—Lurie copped out with a third act *deux ex machina*, which dumped all over the two hours of taut, adult, halls-of-power drama that had come before. Nor has he ever been able to connect with the mass audience; *The Contender*, his best performing film, returned just over $22 million worldwide on a $20 million budget.

The question with *any* remake is, of course, why do it? The power of Peckinpah's *Straw Dogs* is that it continues to speak to viewers about the deep-rooted propensity for violence in the human animal, but, at the same time, the original's plot is firmly anchored in the social turmoil of its time. For all the economic-bred dissatisfactions and disillusionments of today, it's hard to find a similarly trenchant counterpart to that '60s/'70s subtext.

Lurie's acknowledged plan is to not go back to the Gordon Williams source novel. It is Peckinpah's movie he is remaking, his view being the original is a strong but a "... very imperfect movie... murky..." with room for improvement. Lurie guarantees his remake will be every bit as disturbing and controversial as the 1971 film. But, like relocating the story to the American south, the trailer suggests Lurie may only be making cosmetic changes (and, in true twenty-first century fashion, amping up the action) while generally staying close to the narrative line of Peckinpah's film.

It's still childless David and Amy (only now David is a screenwriter), it's still a return to Amy's old hometown, David still hires Amy's ex and his cronies to repair his garage, et al. In fact, what gives the trailer now in circulation such an unsettling feeling to those who know the original film is just how many of the original's key points—including specific lines ("I will not allow violence against this house"), images (the impregnable fieldstone farmhouse looking a bit strange in backwoods Louisiana), and actions (the boiling oil; wrestling with a mantrap) are packed into the 2:32 clip. Even the current one-sheet for the movie closely apes the striking image of the 1972 poster.

While Lurie, to his credit, likes emotionally charged adult situations and grand themes, he's never shown any flair for the kind of moral fog that was Peckinpah's specialty. Even in *The Contender*, Lurie's best work thus far, the bad guys are *clearly* the bad guys and bad for venal, petty reasons, while the good guys are good because they're pledged to a higher, greater good. That's a moral clarity that would have made the Sam Peckinpah of *Major Dundee*, *The Wild Bunch*, *Straw Dogs*, *Bring Me the Head of Alfredo Garcia* (1974), *Pat Garrett & Billy the Kid* (1973) gag, and makes Rod Lurie an odd choice to try to re-bottle Peckinpah's unique brand of cinematic lightning.

Last year, the Coen Brothers managed the paradox of a remake—in *True Grit*—which felt fresh and original. They went back to Charles Portis' source novel to find the flavors, the voices, the textures the 1969 original film missed. But the early indications are Lurie's *Straw Dogs* may be more like another Peckinpah remake: Roger Donaldson's 1994 second take on Peckinpah's *The Getaway* (1972). Donaldson didn't go back to the Jim Thompson novel, but, instead, executed a suffocatingly close redo of Peckinpah's film, lifting some scenes and dialogue directly from the original, which only made Donaldson's movie look all the more stale and unnecessary.

For Gordon Williams, this is a no-win game. Even if Lurie out-Peckinpahs Peckinpah—or at least comes close to some kind of parity - it's re-presenting a take on *The Siege of Trencher's Farm* Williams has long been unhappy with. One can only imagine how much unhappier he'll be if Lurie bobbles the ball and turns out only a pallid version of a story Williams already hates.

But that would be a finale Peckinpah would have appreciated; that even when you win... you lose.

Super Chiefs and the Rise and Fall of the Hollywood Auteur
(posted in two parts on 11/17/10 and 11/21/10)

From the 1960s into the 1980s, one by one, the legendary studios of old – MGM, United Artists, Warner Bros., Paramount, Columbia, 20th Century Fox—were gobbled up by conglomerates, some of which had had almost no previous interests in the entertainment business, such as Paramount's acquirer, Gulf + Western (a motley collection of properties ranging from Caribbean sugar companies to auto parts), and Kinney National Service (a hodgepodge of funeral homes and parking lots that had bought up Warner Bros.). This corporatization of the major studios—the once mighty fiefdoms of the old moguls subjugated by invaders with little or no practical or emotional affinity for movies—is often viewed disparagingly as a sea change signaling the end of the grand Old Hollywood; the Hollywood of Gable and Garland, of *Casablanca* (1942) and *Gone with the Wind* (1939).

Factually, however, that Hollywood had been dying for years. Nearly all of the major studios were in desperate financial shape by the 1960s having been losing audience steadily since the end of World War II. In 1945, weekly attendance had stood at 80 million, but by 1950 – when there were less than 4 million U.S. TV households to cannibalize movie-going—the weekly numbers had already plummeted to 55 million. By the mid-60s, weekly attendance had fallen below 20 million (attendance would not bottom out until 1971 at 16 million). Though swelling TV ownership would later accelerate the erosion of attendance numbers, the underlying problem was the legendary movie moguls – MGM's Louie Mayer, Columbia's Harry Cohn, Warner's Jack Warner, et al—who'd been running the majors for two generations or more, were growing older and increasingly out of touch with a movie-going audience growing significantly younger.

The relentlessly southbound numbers had forced the studios to sell off their back lots for their real estate value, cut loose their vast pools of salaried talent and craftsmen, MGM had famously auctioned off the contents of its property and wardrobe departments including such treasured and iconic items as Judy Garland's ruby shoes from *The Wizard of Oz* (1939), and finished one major—RKO—as a production entity. By the 1960s, most of the moguls had either been shown the door or sidelined within their own organizations. All that in mind, the studio buy-ups, in retrospect, seem less a desecration than a form of corporate Darwinism sweeping away the sclerotic remnants of Old Hollywood.

In its stead, with the new owners came a remarkable collection of production executives at nearly every one of the major movie companies. As a class, the new production chiefs were young, ambitious, as naturally inclined by their own tastes as the dire situation of their respective studios to take risks on new talents and provocative material. Most notable and representative of the breed were John Calley at Warner Bros., Paramount's Robert Evans, and Richard Zanuck at 20th Century Fox.

*****

Calley had been a movie producer *(The Americanization of Emily* [1964], *The Cincinnati Kid* [1965] among others) before being offered the top production job at Warner in 1969. He was a radical change from the prior generation of studio exec: laid back, informal, with an art house aesthete's taste for movies from the likes of Akira Kurosawa, Francois Trauffaut, and Federico Fellini. Before Calley, moviemaking at the studio had been a producer-driven affair, but Calley re-directed Warner along a more *auteurist* path favoring directors, particularly those with a break-from-the-pack storytelling style.

Among Calley's strengths was an ability to understand and recognize the commercial needs of the business while still providing the opportunity for creatively ambitious moviemakers to deliver a more personalized form of mainstream cinema. As an example of the former, Calley was not above pumping out a string of undistinguished, modestly budgeted sequels to Warner's 1971 hit *Dirty Harry*; a cost-efficient formula all but guaranteeing the studio a return. He also moved the studio into the post-*Star Wars* (1977) big-budget movie franchise game with the first—and still one of the best—comic-book inspired blockbusters, *Superman: The Movie* (1978).

At the same time, Calley also offered one of commercial cinema's few true *auteurs*—Stanley Kubrick—an incredibly liberal production arrangement, giving Kubrick a studio home, license to pursue whatever projects he chose at his own pace, and complete control over every aspect of his films including marketing. Kubrick's arrangement with Warner—which extended through *A Clockwork Orange* (1971), *Barry Lyndon* (1975), *The Shining* (1980), *Full Metal Jacket* (1987), and

Eyes Wide Shut (1999)—became the envy of both mainstream and art house directors everywhere.

Under Calley, Warner turned out an admirable and successful blend of the popular *(The Towering Inferno* [1974], *Hooper* [1978]), the disturbing *(Deliverance* [1972]), the lyrical *(Jeremiah Johnson* [1972], *Barry Lyndon)*, the provocative *(Dirty Harry, A Clockwork Orange)*, the artistically daring *(Mean Streets* [1973], *McCabe & Mrs. Miller* [1971], *THX 1138* [1971]), and the prestigious *(All the President's Men* [1976]). It was also under Calley that the studio saw its biggest hit up to that time with the screen adaptation of William Peter Blatty's 1971 best-selling supernatural thriller novel, *The Exorcist* (1973), which turned in rentals of a then-astounding $88.5 million on a $10 million budget.

*****

Robert Evans, who took over production at Paramount in 1966, offered a striking contrast to Calley. Flashy and self-promoting, there is little to say about Evans he hasn't already said himself in his 1994 autobiography, *The Kid Stays in the Picture*, as well as in the 2002 documentary of the same name.

Evans had made his money in sportswear, his only background in the motion picture industry having been a short, unsuccessful stint as an actor in the 1950s. However, like Calley, he was passionate about movies, and showed himself to be a canny executive with an uncanny gut instinct for the box office. Evans managed to completely reverse Paramount's faltering fortunes with a mix of the commercially popular and aesthetically impressive, among them *Love Story* (1970), *The Odd Couple* (1968), *Rosemary's Baby* (1968), *Romeo and Juliet* (1968), *Goodbye Columbus* (1969), and *The Godfather Parts I & II* (1972 & 1974).

*****

As the son of the legendary Darryl Zanuck, Richard Zanuck had been raised in the movie industry. When his father—who'd quit 20th Century Fox in 1956 after twenty-three years as the studio's top exec—resumed charge of Fox in 1962, Zanuck the elder hired Zanuck the younger as head of production (Dick Zanuck would later be elevated to the office of company president).

Neither an art house aficionado like Calley, nor a self-promoting seat-of-the-pants exec like Evans, Zanuck was something of a hybrid, a blend of Old and New Hollywood sensibilities. Richard Zanuck's

Fox was just as likely to turn out a piece of Old Hollywood treacle like *The Sound of Music* (1965) as it was a counter-culture classic like the marijuana-flavored anti-war black comedy *M*A*S*H* (1972), or the tongue-in-cheek convention-busting Western *Butch Cassidy and the Sundance Kid* (1969), or high-risk gamble *Planet of the Apes* (1968). And, as one might expect from a production exec standing between Hollywood's two creative poles, there were also those projects that blended the two sensibilities. If Zanuck's Fox was going to make a grand scale period epic, then it would be in the shape of an allusion to the country's then current embroilment in Southeast Asia in *The Sand Pebbles* (1966); if it was going to turn out a rather simply plotted police procedural, it would do so after injecting an unprecedented near-documentary warts-and-all authenticity into *The French Connection* (1971).

*****

One of the salient characteristics of that generation of production chiefs was their willingness to open their respective studios to promising though relatively unproven talent. Martin Scorsese had only directed one low-budget thriller for B-movie king Roger Corman before John Calley acquired Scorsese's independently produced *Mean Streets* and hired him to direct *Alice Doesn't Live Here Anymore* (1974); with the exception of his Oscar-winning screenplay for *Patton* (1970), Francis Ford Coppola's box office track record as both a writer and director could only be judged underwhelming prior to Robert Evans's tapping him to work both chores on *The Godfather;* TV director Franklin J. Schaffner had directed just one underperforming feature before tackling *Planet of the Apes* for Richard Zanuck.

The flood of new talent that came into the industry under the aegis of the new studio chiefs wasn't limited to young directorial tyros. Along with them came an equally significant collection of writers, craftsmen, and actors who helped change the substance, look, and even the sound of movies for a generation.

Among the screenwriters were Stirling Silliphant who'd served his apprenticeship as a TV writer and producer before winning an Oscar for the screenplay of *In the Heat of the Night* (1967); novelist-cum-screenwriter William Goldman who won Oscars for his work on *Butch Cassidy and the Sundance Kid* and *All the President's Men;* and Robert Towne, another Corman graduate, who turned out such 1970s classics as *Chinatown* (1974) and *The Last Detail* (1973). There were cinematographers like Conrad Hall *(Butch Cassidy)*, William Fraker *(Bullitt,* 1968)), Haskell Wexler *(American Graffiti,* 1973), John Alonzo *(Chinatown)*, master of the New York milieu Owen Roizman who was nominated for an Oscar on only his second feature *(The French Connection)*, and the legendary Gordon Willis whose work on *Klute* (1971), *The Parallax View* (1974), and *The Godfather* movies did for the color thriller what Nicholas Musuraca had done for black-and-white *noirs* a generation earlier. There were editors like Lou Lombardo who shattered acts of violence into a hundred jarring fragments *(The Wild Bunch,* 1969), and Scorsese's editorial right hand Thelma Schoonmaker *(Raging Bull,* 1980); and sound designer Walter Murch who turned intricately interlaced layers of distorted audio into an encrypted murder conspiracy in *The Conversation* (1974), and a form of *musique concrete* during the classic helicopter attack sequence in Francis Coppola's Vietnam War epic, *Apocalypse Now* (1979).

Even the music of the movies changed with the jazz flavors of Lalo Schifrin *(Bullitt, Dirty Harry)* and Dave Grusin *(Three Days of the Condor,* 1975), minimalist Michael Small *(The Parallax View, Marathon Man* [1976]), and the premier composer of the 1960s/1970s, Jerry Goldsmith, whose work included the all-percussion score for *Seven Days in May* (1964), the lush, soaring *The Blue Max* (1966), the haunting trumpet voluntaries of *Patton* (1970), and the breakthrough atonalities of *Planet of the Apes*.

The performing ranks changed too. There was still room for the square-jawed good looks of a Robert Redford and a Paul Newman, but the new directors, in their search for a grittier, more realistic look sanctioned by the new production chiefs, opened leading roles to the kind of faces which, a generation earlier, might have been relegated to supporting character roles, e.g. Robert De Niro, Gene Hackman, Dustin Hoffman, Richard Dreyfuss, Robert Duvall, Elliott Gould, Roy Scheider, et al. The rebelliousness and discontent of the young audience was simpatico with the self-possessed, subversive spirit of an impish Jack Nicholson, or a hip, cool, anti-hero like James Coburn. There were still other actors striking a fresh, minimalist chord, their clean, low-key performances demonstrating an understanding of how little it took to fill the big screen, and which fit neatly into an evolving genre of lean, stark thrillers, e.g. Charles Bronson, Clint Eastwood, Lee Marvin, and, for a time, one of the most successful of the bunch, Steve McQueen. McQueen could very well have been the poster boy for the breed, flipping through a script and judging, "Too many words, too many words. I'll give you a close-up that'll say a thousand words."

Within the welcoming and protective arms of the new production chiefs, this unique blend of above- and below-the-line talent was responsible for one of the most creatively daring and artistically productive periods in American commercial cinema. Look at any roster of memorable American films—the National Film Registry, the American Film Institute's "100 Best" lists, "The A List: 100 Essential Films" compiled by the National Society of Film Critics, etc.—and one of the largest blocks, if not *the* largest, is typically comprised of films from the 1960s-1970s.

But streaks, by definition, end. Early triumphs earned this generation of filmmakers increasing creative license and, along with it, bigger budgets to spend on their personal visions. But, total freedom and blank checks fostered a lethal combination of hubris and indulgence, and, one after another, the *wunderkind* began turning out expensive flops. The execs who had brought them into the studio fold and had greenlit those pocket-draining failures were held to account.

By the late 1970s, the age of the Hollywood *auteur*—as well as their production chief patrons—was coming to an end. The tremendous creative license the major studios under a new generation of production chiefs had granted the young tyros of the 1960s—Coppola, Scorsese, et al—had expired as each managed to deliver at least one, major, back-breaking flop. For Scorsese, it had been the grim musical *New York, New York* (1977, $13.8 million U.S. vs. a budget of $14 million); Peter Bogdanovich turned out a streak of losers including period piece *Daisy Miller* (1974), comedy *Nickelodeon* (1976), and another disastrous musical, *At Long Last Love* (1975, $1.5 million U.S./$6 million cost); after the back-to-back hits of *The French Connection* and *The Exorcist*, William Friedkin delivered *Sorcerer* (1977, $6 million U.S. against a crushing $22 million cost); and Francis Coppola, after a string of commercial and/or critical home runs including *The Godfather* (1972), *The Conversation* (1974), *The Godfather Part II* (1974), and *Apocalypse Now* (1979), turned out *One from the Heart* (1982, an abysmal box office take of less than $500,000 against a bank-busting $26 million cost).

But perhaps the most emblematic failure of the *auteur*-centric trend of the period was *Heaven's Gate* (1980), an ambitious epic Western written and directed by a Michael Cimino just coming off the triumph of *The Deer Hunter* (1978), a commercial hit that had won him Best Picture and Best Director Oscars. The critically drubbed *Heaven's Gate* cost a whopping (for the time) $35 million, grossed a mere $3.5 million U.S., permanently derailed Cimino's career, and is widely considered responsible for sinking United Artists.

The director-friendly production chiefs of the 1960s/1970s were, for one reason or another, gone by the 1980s. The major studios, under a new generation of more bottom line-oriented bosses, subsequently reasserted their authority over creative development and pointed their companies increasingly toward expensive, action/effects-driven spectacles trying to ape the success of movies like *Star Wars* (1977) and *Jaws* (1975). As big-budget thrillers became more prevalent in studio release slates, the real *auteur* signature became, more often than not, that of the producer.

*****

Five producers who exemplify the trend—and who have probably done the most to define the blockbuster form—are Steven Spielberg, Joel Silver, the team of Mario Kassar and Andy Vajna, and Jerry Bruckheimer.

After years of toiling in TV, and with one respected but commercially disappointing feature to his credit, it was a summer blockbuster—*Jaws*—that put Steven Spielberg's career into high orbit. Spielberg seemed to instantly grasp the commercial dynamic of the summer blockbuster. As both director and producer (through his personal production company Amblin Entertainment, and, later, his DreamWorks SKG partnership formed in 1996 with Jeffrey Katzenberg and David Geffen), he has grown from pioneer to master of the form.

Over two-thirds of the movies Spielberg produced and/or directed between 1974's *The Sugarland Express* and 1998's *Saving Private Ryan* opened during the summer months to a collective domestic gross in the neighborhood of $5 billion, with his productions fueling his expansion into the whole gamut of blockbuster ancillaries including video games, merchandising, theme park rides, TV production, etc. Amblin/DreamWorks releases over the years include *Poltergeist* (1982 with sequels in 1986 and 1988), *Gremlins* (1984 with a sequel in 1990), *The Goonies* (1985), *Back to the Future* (1985 with sequels in 1989 and 1990), *Harry and the Hendersons* (1987), *Innerspace* (1987), **Batteries Not Included* (1987), *Arachnophobia*

(1990), *The Flintstones* (1994), *Casper* (1996), *Twister* (1996), *Small Soldiers* (1998), *The Mask of Zorro* (1998 with a sequel in 2005), *Galaxy Quest* (1999), *The Haunting* (1999), *Gladiator* (2000), *Shrek* (2001 with sequels in 2005, 2007, and 2010), *Seabiscuit* (2003), *House of Sand and Fog* (2003), *Flags of Our Fathers* and *Letters from Iwo Jima* (both 2006), and *Transformers* (2007 with a sequel in 2009 and a third installment in the works).

Most of the action thrillers Spielberg or his production entities have turned out share a broad-stroked version of the moviemaker's own sensibility; a mix of pop culture, B-movie nostalgia, Huckleberry Finnish juvenile adventure, and more than a small dose of Spielberg's own middle class suburban outlook. Spielberg productions often "quote" the movies and TV shows Spielberg and his generation of directors experienced as youths, sometimes overtly (big screen versions of *The Flintstones*, The Little Rascals, Casper the Friendly Ghost, remakes of 1963's *The Haunting* [in 1999] and 1960's *The Time Machine* [in 2002], *The Mask of Zorro*'s hearkening back to the swashbucklers of Old Hollywood, *Gladiator*'s resurrection of the sword-and-sandal epic), sometimes obliquely (the torrent of Hollywood inside jokes in *Who Framed Roger Rabbit?* [1988] and *Gremlins*, *Galaxy Quest*'s affectionate, thinly veiled lampooning of the original *Star Trek* TV series). They have also usually been built around a storytelling form Spielberg worked out with producer George Lucas on *Raiders of the Lost Ark* (1981), one in which the peaks and valleys of classic cinema drama have been replaced with a non-stop succession of ever greater climaxes—a template now *de rigueur* for the typical summer blockbuster.

Despite a few notable exceptions, much of Spielberg's production output has been thrillers, often constructed with an eye toward the valuable audience of young males, avoiding real violence and indulging in a cloying, contrived sentimentality. Despite occasional gems like *Men in Black* (1997) and *Poltergeist*, a goodly number of films put out under his banners have been dramatically flimsy projects that seem inspired by commerce more than a creative spark, often coming across as watered-down versions of Spielberg's own work, e.g. *The Goonies* as a juvenile transposition of the Indiana Jones adventures by way of The Little Rascals; there's more than a little bit of *E.T.: The Extra-Terrestrial* (1982) in *Batteries Not Included*.

Movies like *Twister* (1996), *Deep Impact* (1998), and remakes *The Haunting* and *The Time Machine* demonstrate all of Spielberg's interest in state-of-the-art movie-making technology, but little of his storytelling heart, being pictures heavy on special effects, light on characterization and credible plot, and often falling back on arbitrary plot devices to move a story along, e.g. the competing storm chasers in *Twister*. Until recently, Spielberg productions regularly reflected his own long-held aversion—one he seemed unable to overcome until such latter works as *Schindler's List* and *Saving Private Ryan*—to dark and/or adult themes.

Upbeat, action-heavy, sentimental, youth-directed, effects-driven, and typically disposable are often the trademarks of "Spielbergian" presentations.

*****

"I make action movies," Joel Silver once flatly declared, "that's what I do." In his first twenty-three years as a producer, Silver produced thirty movies—most of them action thrillers—with an accumulated domestic gross of $2.5 billion. If Spielberg-produced movies lean toward sweetness and light, Silver's pull toward the tart and dark. Silver productions have included *Commando* (1985), *Jumpin' Jack Flash* (1986), *Predator* (1987, with a sequel in 1990), *The Last Boy Scout* (1991), *Demolition Man* (1993), *Assassins* (1995), *Executive Decision* (1996), *Conspiracy Theory* (1997), the remake *House on Haunted Hill* (1999), *Swordfish* (2001), the remake *Thir13een ghosts* (2001), *Ghost Ship* (2002), and *Gothika* (2003), but his signature products have been the *Lethal Weapon, Die Hard,* and *Matrix* franchises.

Unlike Spielberg, Silver rarely caters to the youngest viewers. His movies are male adolescent, testosterone-addled, blood-spattered, shoot-'em-up/hack-'em-up fantasies, with plots that rarely make much sense and are engineered primarily to get a movie from one pyrotechnic set piece to the next. Spielberg likes amazing effects; Silver goes for old-fashioned gunplay, but ladled on thickly. "Automatic weapons have always been important in movies," Silver has said, outlining his simple philosophy. "Audiences want to see guys with more firepower." It's a credo evident in such never-miss gun-blazers as *Lethal Weapon*'s LAPD detective—and one-time government assassin—Riggs (Mel Gibson), master-of-all-firearms NYPD detective John McClane (Bruce Willis) of the *Die Hards,* Arnold Schwarzenegger's one-man army in *Commando,* Keanu Reeves and his downloaded weapons/hand-to-hand expertise in *The Matrix* films, and the behind-the-lines strike team in *Predator*—small as a squad but armed with a battalion's worth of firepower.

Silver heroes are bigger than life, muscled macho men who can outshoot, outfight, and often out-bleed anyone else in the movie. Think of muscle-bound Schwarzenegger in *Predator* heading one of the most sinewy casts in action movies: Carl Weathers, Jesse Ventura, and Sonny Landham. There's Sylvester Stallone in *Demolition Man* squaring off against an equally steroidal Wesley Snipes, a pumped-up Bruce Willis in the *Die Hards,* and lion-maned Mel Gibson in the *Lethal Weapons.* Even Silver's version of *Sherlock Holmes* (2009) featured a more buff version of the deductive detective than had graced any previous rendering of Sir Arthur Conan Doyle's intellectual hero.

If Spielberg's productions often dollop out maudlin sentiment, there's little room for sentiment, romance, or even sex in a Silver actioner. Such elements might slow the action, or show the hero in a vulnerable state, both of which are intolerable in a Joel Silver thriller. Early in the 1990s, Silver proclaimed the only practical role for women on-screen was "... either naked or dead."

On the few occasions when a Silver thriller has had a female principal—Julia Roberts's D.A. in *Conspiracy Theory,* Halle Berry's terrorized mental patient in *Gothika,* brassy Whoopi Goldberg in *Jumpin' Jack Flash,* Juliann Margulies salvage ship First Mate in *Ghost Ship,* Renee Russo's kick-boxing cop in *Lethal Weapons 3* (1992) and *4* (1998)—there's something tomboyish about them. They're the kind of tough-hided, one-of-the-boys women who never threaten the macho posturing of the heroes (but rather support it), and can participate as equals in all the adolescent mayhem.

Fast, loud, bloody, and not for children—these are Joel Silver's trademarks.

*****

Mario Kassar and Andy Vajna, who built their production company Carolco into a veritable blockbuster factory in the 1980s-1990s, set the still-standing standard for big-scale, star-powered, action-heavy, big-budget thrillers having produced—according to one entertainment writer—"... just about every big, dumb, loud, profitable action movie in town." Over its thirteen years in business, Carolco released twenty-nine titles with a cumulative domestic gross of $1.1 billion.

Though it's little remembered, Carolco turned out a wide variety of releases, ranging from Holocaust drama *Music Box* (1989), to biopic *Chaplin* (1992), the Steve Martin comedy *L.A. Story* (1991), and Mel Gibson's production of *Hamlet* (1990). Still, the company's fortunes rose and fell with its thrillers, and it was Carolco's actioners that have had a lasting impact on the blockbuster form through pictures like *First Blood* (1982 with sequels *Rambo: First Blood, Part 2* in 1985, and *Rambo III* in 1988), *Red Heat* (1988), *Total Recall* (1990), *Air America* (1990), *Terminator 2: Judgment Day* (1991), *Basic Instinct* (1992), *Universal Soldier* (1992), *Cliffhanger* (1993), *Stargate* (1994), *Cutthroat Island* (1995).

The larger-than-life sensibility rife throughout Carolco's filmography was illustrated by the company's preference for such over-sized leads as Sylvester Stallone (the *Rambo* and *Cliffhanger* movies), Arnold Schwarzenegger (the *Terminator* movies as well as *Red Heat* and *Total Recall)*, and junior league musclemen like Jean-Claude Van Damme and Dolph Lundgren *(Universal Soldier)*. It was also evident in the company's penchant for directors more notable for their flair for grand scale action than for their dramatic prowess. One Carolco veteran remembers the company having, at one time, a fleet of such directors simultaneously at work in the company's "... very testosterone-charged..." offices including Renny Harlin *(Cliffhanger)*, James Cameron *(Terminator 2)*, Paul Verhoeven *(Basic Instinct, Total Recall)*, and the writing/directing/producing team of Roland Emmerich and Dean Devlin *(Universal Soldier, Stargate)*.

Fueled by the breakout success of their first hit—the aptly titled *First Blood*—Carolco went on a buying binge of talent, kicking off the age of inflated performer's salaries and skyrocketing budgets. Kassnar and Vajna were committed believers in the big-budget actioner and in beating the competition on-screen in much the same way as they'd beat it in talent acquisition: by outspending. Most Carolco thrillers were opulently produced movies little remembered for their dialogue or often inane plots, but marked with frequent jaw-dropping action set pieces.

Carolco was also one of the first companies to fully exploit blockbuster merchandising possibilities. *First Blood* sequel *Rambo: First Blood, Part 2*, for example, set the stage for a wave of title-related merchandise including Rambo action figures, Rambo bed sheets, and even a Saturday-morning Rambo cartoon series.

But in the 1990s, the company went bankrupt, tripped up by its own free-spending habits and some abysmally bad choices (e.g. *Cutthroat Island* that cost over $100 million but grossed only $10 million U.S; and *Showgirls*, 1995, with a gross of $20.3 million against a budget of $45 million). Still, the company's template—expensive stars in costly, large-scale, action-heavy adventures—remains a standard blockbuster formula today.

*****

Perhaps only Steven Spielberg's and George Lucas's name have as much value on a marquee as that of producer Jerry Bruckheimer. Twenty-five percent of those buying a ticket to a Bruckheimer movie do so because of the producer's name over the title—remarkable drawing power for a behind-the-scenes operator. He may very well be the current crown prince of the blockbuster, having started with nothing a little over forty years ago, but now ruling over one of the most successful production companies in Hollywood. Even those who question the quality of Bruckheimer's efforts—and they are legion—acknowledge his nose for hits. In his 2002 memoir, *What Happened? Bitter Hollywood Tales from the Front Line*, producer Art Linson writes that the prime responsibility of any film executive is to have a handle on "… what the audience wants. Unfortunately, no one except Jerry Bruckheimer seems to know what that is."

Bruckheimer's explanation for his success is simple. "I'm one of 'them," he told Charlie Rose in a 2003 interview, referring to the general public. A self-professed populist, he told Rose with neither humility nor braggadocio, "I'm in synch with the audience." The validity of Bruckheimer's self-analysis is his box office track record. In a winning streak extending back from his 2003 Charlie Rose interview to the 1980s, Bruckheimer's fifty-odd productions to that point—produced first with partner Don Simpson, and then solo after Simpson's 1995 death—had collectively earned $12.5 billion. Better than eighty percent of Bruckheimer's productions have been thrillers, among them *Days of Thunder* (1990), *Bad Boys* (1995 with a sequel in 2003), *Crimson Tide* (1995), *Enemy of the State* (1998), *Pearl Harbor* (2001), *Kangaroo Jack* (2003), *National Treasure* (2004 with a sequel in 2007), and such signature offerings as *Beverly Hills Cop* (1984 with a sequel in 1987), *Top Gun* (1986), *Con Air* (1997), *Black Hawk Down* (2001), and *Pirates of the Caribbean: The Curse of the Black Pearl*

(2003, with sequels in 2006 and 2007, and a fourth entry currently in the works).

A Bruckheimer blockbuster typically has a dose of Spielbergian gratuitous sentiment (convict Nicolas Cage protecting the doll intended for his daughter in *Con Air*; convict Sean Connery's concern for his barely scene daughter in *The Rock* [1996]; Bruce Willis's self-sacrifice so daughter Liv Tyler can live to marry protégé Ben Affleck in *Armageddon* [1998]), an inflating injection of Carolco-like scale (the average budget of a Bruckheimer thriller 1990-2007 was $108.4 million), a Joel Silver-sized body-count (one- and two-man armies triumph against overwhelming odds in *Con Air, Top Gun, The Rock, Pearl Harbor*, and both *Bad Boys* movies), and, of course, heavy doses of action.

Still, there are ways in which Bruckheimer's thrillers are unique and distinctive even as they amalgamate the successful traits of other blockbuster strains. More than any of his big-movie colleagues, Bruckheimer has been less committed to specific formulas and has shown an astoundingly acute sense of the affinities of the mainstream audience. Mixed among the quip-laced, over-the-top action of *The Rock, Gone in 60 Seconds* (2000), *Armageddon, Con Air*, and the *Bad Boys* and *Beverly Hills Cop* movies are releases like the more brutally realistic *Black Hawk Down*, the family adventure *Kangaroo Jack*, a revamping of medieval legend in *King Arthur* (2004), the wry mix of camp and fantasy in the *Pirates of the Caribbean* series, as well as such non-thriller successes as the music-driven *Flashdance* (1983) and the true sports story *Remember the Titans* (2000).

Along with Bruckheimer's willingness to maneuver so freely within the thriller category goes an adventurousness in casting against type for his action heroes. At the time Tom Cruise starred in *Top Gun*, his biggest previous success had been the teen comedy *Risky Business* (1983), and his only action hero role had been in the fantasy flop *Legend* (1985); prior to starring in the cop thriller *Bad Boys*, one-time stand-up comedian Martin Lawrence's biggest credit had been as the lead in the TV sitcom *Martin*, and co-star Will Smith's previous credits included rap recording, starring in the sitcom *Fresh Prince of Bel-Air*, and the lead in the screen adaptation of John Guare's stage drama, *Six Degrees of Separation* (1993); both Nicolas Cage and Johnny Depp had been actors with checkered box office records and associations with quirky comedies and heavy, sometimes bizarre dramas (such as Cage's *Leaving Las Vegas* [1995], *Wild at Heart* [1990], and *Moonstruck* [1987]; and Depp's *Donnie Brasco* [1997], *Ed Wood* [1994], and *What's Eating Gilbert Grape?* [1993]) before Bruckheimer turned them into action thriller icons with Cage in *The Rock, Con Air,* remake *Gone in 60 Seconds,* and *National Treasure,* and Depp in the *Pirates of the Caribbean* series.

But Bruckheimer thrillers do have their standard features, most visibly the heavy troweling on of action and violence. In the standard Bruckheimer action thriller, character and drama are secondary. The producer's usual development process pushes writers through several drafts before turning the screenplay over to "hired guns" to punch up specific scenes or to create particular pieces of action even if it means that, as a result, characters act inconsistently or speak with a different "voice" from one scene to the next, or that elements of the plot cease to make much sense. The story for *Crimson Tide,* for example, was first drummed up by screenwriter Michael Schiffer and novelist Richard P. Henrick before it passed through the rewriting hands of Quentin Tarantino, Robert Towne, and Steve Zaillian.

One of the more egregious examples of the failings of the Bruckheimer process is in *The Rock*. Government officials agree to a press blackout of the crisis at hand (renegade U.S. soldiers hold hostages on Alcatraz Island while threatening to launch biochemical weapons at the city) even though Sean Connery has already left an impossible-to-miss tornado-like path of destruction through the city during a completely gratuitous car chase.

With so much physical action, dramatic lines and characters become, unsurprisingly, simple-minded. Bruckheimer is a devout disciple of clear, unambivalent Good Guy vs. Bad Guy storytelling as he explained to *The New York Times* while promoting his 2004 summer entry, *King Arthur:* "It's heroism, camaraderie, brotherhood. (The knights) are fighting... for the moral high ground—all the kinds of themes I love." These Bruckheimer-treasured themes reach flag-waving peaks in the "pretty-boy jingoism" and "synthetic apple pie" of his military-themed projects: *Top Gun, Crimson Tide, Pearl Harbor,* and *Black Hawk Down.*

More than the blockbusters of his big-budget peers, Bruckheimer's thrillers also favor a similar visual look of quick edits and eye-entrancing cinematography, a look some have compared to being that of "... essentially MTV videos at feature film length." Bruckheimer has gravitated toward directors who share the same, strong, visual sense he himself developed first as a youngster interested in photography, and then during his first professional incarnation as a maker of TV commercials. Bruckheimer's most commercially successful collaborations have been with directors Tony Scott and Michael Bay (both began their careers in commercials and, in Bay's case, music videos as well) who, between them, account for nine Bruckheimer-produced hits; the largest single block in the producer's filmography.

Some consider Michael Bay the directorial yin to Bruckheimer's producer's yang. Bruckheimer provided Bay with his big screen directorial debut with *Bad Boys* and produced all of the director's subsequent features until 2005's *The Island*. With Bay's hyperkinetic visuals and a near-dismissive attitude toward character and plot, he seemed perfectly at home amid the action-drenched sci-fi nonsense of *Armageddon* and the atavistic *Pearl Harbor*. The box office scoreboard of their relationship testifies as to how in synch Bay's and Bruckheimer's sensibilities were with each other and with the international action thriller audience: with his five Bruckheimer-produced features, Michael Bay became the youngest director to reach the $1 billion mark in cumulative worldwide grosses.

There are still filmmakers who hearken back to that creatively audacious age of two generations ago. Scorsese has managed to survive and turn out some of his most popular work, and there are a handful of new tyros—like Christopher Nolan—who have managed to turn the blockbuster spectacle on its ear and produce something both spectacular as well as unique and personalized.

But, for the most part, the true cinema artist—the *auteur*—has been pushed out of the mainstream, relegated to the ever-dwindling art house circuit. It was a perfect storm of circumstances that brought auteurism and the mass audience together for one of the most memorable eras in American commercial cinema; circumstances that, like an alignment of the planets, is not likely to happen again.

How The Blockbuster Ruined Hollywood
(posted 5/1/11)

The big-budget (usually summer) blockbuster is the financial cornerstone of the American motion picture industry, and has been for much of the last thirty-five years or so. In all its forms—action/adventure, suspense, Western, war story, horror, science-fiction, fantasy, et al—the big budget thriller's earning power is unmatched by any other movie form. Romantic comedies like *The Proposal* (2009), slapstick and teen comedies like *The Hangover* (2009) and *Little Fockers* (2010), are sometimes capable of blockbuster-caliber domestic earnings, but rarely match those of the thriller, nor can they rival its attraction overseas. The performances of more adult-themed dramas and comedies—even those considered financial successes—are often weaker still. The reliance of most major thriller releases today on action-driven plots is a form of cinematic Esperanto, transcending barriers of language and cultural nuance. The blockbuster thriller is as accessible to Asian audiences as it is to Latin American audiences as it is to U.S. ticket-buyers, even more so in some cases. Consider the comparative domestic/worldwide earnings of the top five live-action thrillers of 2010 vs. the top five live-action non-thrillers.

U.S./Worldwide (in millions)

Alice in Wonderland	$334.2 / 1063.2
The Twilight Saga: Eclipse	300.5 / 698.5
Iron Man 2	312.4 / 622.1
Harry Potter & the Deathly Hollows Pt. 1	295 / 954.5
Inception	292.6 / 825.5

Vs.

The Karate Kid	176.6 / 359.1
Grown Ups	162 / 271.4
Little Fockers	148.4 / 309.5
The King's Speech	135.5 / 398.5
Sex and the City 2	95.3 / 288.3

Each year, the blockbuster thriller dominates box office charts here and abroad, tends to comprise the single largest block of the year's top twenty earners, and normally produces the industry's single biggest block of box office revenue. In 2009, for example, out of a year's total output of 522 titles, live-action thrillers comprised six of the year's top ten earners, turning in domestic receipts of $2.2 billion out of a total box office for the year of $10.6 billion; in other words, the year's top six thrillers alone accounted for over twenty percent of the American movie industry's *total* theatrical gross for the year. In 2010, out of 531 releases, five of the top ten were thrillers collectively earning $1.5 billion of the year's $10.6 billion take.

The box office dominance of the big-budget thriller is overwhelming. As at the end of 2010, of the twenty all-time box office champions, sixteen are thrillers, only two of which were released earlier than 1993. Of the top 100 biggest earners, almost two-thirds are thrillers, the majority of which were released after 1990.

The earning muscle of the thriller doesn't stop at the box office. The strongest theatrical earners also tend to be the strongest performers in ancillary markets like DVD sales and rentals, sales to television, and in overseas theatrical and ancillary markets. The successful blockbuster is often a platform for launching a (hoped-for) long-running series of movies: a franchise. The franchise is a brand name cutting through the marketing clutter of a crowded theatrical marketplace, with a name value capable of being spun off into related products: film sequels and spin-offs, TV programs, Internet attractions, recorded music, publishing, toys, video games, Halloween costumes, collectibles, and so on. Today, Hollywood earns less than eighteen percent of its revenues from the domestic box office, the bulk coming, instead, from overseas, ancillaries, and merchandising. Unsurprisingly, then, this upcoming summer will see the release of sequels *Pirates of the Caribbean: On Stranger Tides, Transformers: Dark of the Moon, Harry Potter and the Deathly Hollows—Part 2, Spy Kids 4: All the Time in the World, Final Destination 5,* and prequels *X-Men: First Class* and *Rise of the Planet of the Apes,* as well as hoped-for franchise launches *Thor, Priest, Green Lantern,* and *Captain America: The First Avenger.* The year has already seen the release of sequels *Scream 4, Fast 5,* and attempted franchise launch *The Green Hornet.*

Hollywood's blockbuster mentality has now been in place so long that to a young generation of moviegoers it must seem as if this is how things have always been. Actually, in terms of the industry's 100+ year history, it is a fairly recent phenomenon.

The Hollywood studio system established during the 1920s-30s arose from the need to feed an insatiable public demand for movie entertainment. Even with a rollback in audience in the early years of The Depression, weekly movie attendance throughout the 1930s averaged almost 69 million, and increased during the World War II years peaking at 84 million in 1943 and 1944.

The studio system, with its salaried rolls of performers, behind-the-camera talent, and craftsmen, and its enormous physical assets (back lots, standing sets, manufacturing shops, recording studios, etc.), gave studios the ability to pump out a constant stream of A- and B-features, animated and live-action shorts, newsreels and adventure serials on a timely and cost-efficient basis. While many today tend to think of the studio era as represented by evergreen classics like *Casablanca* (1942) and *Gone with the Wind* (1939), such timeless works were the exceptions more than the rule. Studio output at the time generally tended toward quantity over quality. A film only had to amuse audiences for a week or so, just long enough for the next feature off the studio production line to take its place. Some genres were more popular than others, but none were particularly critical to the financial health of the studio.

The dynamics of the movie industry began changing with the end of World War II. The business received a financial body blow with the resolution of a long-running anti-monopoly case initiated by the Federal government in the 1930s. Most of the studios had owned their own chains of theaters, or were owned—in fact, had been set up—by exhibition companies to provide their screens with a steady flow of product, a construct the government viewed as monopolistic. The case was resolved in 1948, when the studios agreed to divest themselves of their theaters.

There was, of course, an immediate financial consequence as each affected studio now had to split box office revenues with an outside exhibitor.

Perhaps more worrisome for studio chiefs, however, was that studios no longer had a guaranteed exhibition platform for their product. Each release would now have to compete head to head with every other film in distribution for screen space turning what had prior been a somewhat predictable business into one marked by tremendous volatility.

Then there was the cannibalizing effect of television. Although only a few hundred thousand U.S. households owned TV sets in the late 1940s, sets were in ninety percent of American homes by 1962.

As TV ownership became more universal, movie theater attendance—already sliding since 1945—nosedived. TV programming evolved away from the high-brow live dramas considered the hallmark of the so-called Golden Age of TV of the early 1950s toward more widely popular forms, and by the end of the '50s, prime time airwaves were glutted with game shows and action-driven fare like Westerns and police shows—the kind of B-type pulp which had once comprised so much of Hollywood's output. Legendary movie producer Sam Goldwyn looked at the shoot-'em-ups on TV and the sagging theatrical box office concluding, "It's a certainty that people will be unwilling to pay to see poor pictures when they can stay home and see something which is at least no worse."

By the mid-1960s, with costs soaring and attendance beginning a third decade of steady decline (not bottoming out until the 1970s with a weekly attendance of just 16 million), the industry seemed on the verge of collapse. The financially-bleeding studios had been forced to sell off their physical assets including back lots and props, do away with their salaried pools of talent, and shrink production slates. It was a sign of their growing enfeeblement that, from the 1960s through the 1980s, most of the major studios were absorbed by conglomerates: Paramount by Gulf + Western Industries, and Warner Bros. by The Kinney Group for example.

Paradoxically, the apparent near-collapse of the industry provided just the right circumstances for its creative resurgence.

A new, younger, more daring breed of production executive began to come to power in the industry in the 1960s and 1970s, some of the more noteworthy being John Calley at Warner Bros., and the legendary Robert Evans at Paramount. Calley, Evans, et al had an earnest passion for movies and found themselves in tune with a new generation of young movie-goers who loved them too.

In the 1960s and 1970s, movies became part of the youth culture in a way that went well beyond their role as entertainment. In a proliferating number of college classes and degree programs, young people studied films and filmmaking, learning to appreciate the range of cinema from the classics of the American studio era to the more visually stylish and dramatically opaque films of the European *nouvelle vogue*. This new, young, cinematically literate audience came to theaters with a hunger for the provocative and unconventional, and for material reflecting one of the most turbulent times in American social history.

Dissatisfaction with the war in Vietnam, and a sense of disillusionment following a series of political assassinations and revelations of misconduct at the highest levels of government were fueling a widespread sense of social dislocation and questioning of the status quo. The magazine *Life* would go as far as to describe the time as one of the greatest periods of social upheaval in the U.S. since the Civil War.

In the same period, there came an infusion of fresh storytelling talent into the industry in tune with this rising young audience, and artistically equipped to tell new, brave kinds of film stories reflecting, in some manner or another, the angsty ethos of the era in new, brave ways. Graduating from television were directors like Sidney Lumet (*Fail-Safe*, 1964), John Frankenheimer (*The Manchurian Candidate*, 1962), Franklin J. Schaffner (*Planet of the Apes*, 1968), Robert Altman (*M*A*S*H*, 1970), William Friedkin (*The French Connection*, 1971), Robert Mulligan (*To Kill a Mockingbird*, 1962), Martin Ritt (*Hud*, 1963), Arthur Penn (*Bonnie and Clyde*, 1967), Sydney Pollack (*They Shoot Horses, Don't They?*, 1969), and Sam Peckinpah (*The Wild Bunch*, 1969). Another group of directors who had been working at the fringes of the industry—some for quite a few years—were brought into the mainstream where they would do some of their most notable work such as Stanley Kubrick (*2001: A Space Odyssey*, 1968), Robert Aldrich (*The Dirty Dozen*, 1967), and Don Siegel (*Dirty Harry*, 1971). The new, open-minded production chiefs also welcomed a generation of artistically daring European filmmakers, raising them up from the art house circuit and bringing them into the circle of commercial majors, e.g. Roman Polanski (*Chinatown*, 1974), John Schlesinger (*Midnight Cowboy*, 1969), Karel Reisz (*The Gambler*, 1974), John Boorman (*Point Blank*, 1967), Ulu Grosbard (*Straight Time*, 1978), Nicholas Roeg (*Don't Look Now*, 1973), and Peter Yates (*Bullitt*, 1968).

But perhaps the most notable group of Hollywood newcomers were the so-called "film brats," a generation of directors unlike any which had come before. They were young, had studied film in heralded cinema programs at the likes of USC and NYU, were influenced by both the highly visual styles of the European *nouvelle vogue* and the storytelling of classic American mogul-era Hollywood. Their names would become synonymous with 1960s/1970s cinema, among them: Francis Ford Coppola (*The Godfather*, 1972), Brian DePalma

(Carrie, 1976), Robert Benton *(Kramer vs. Kramer,* 1979), Peter Bogdanovich *(The Last Picture Show,* 1971), Terry Malick *(Badlands,* 1973), Steven Spielberg *(Jaws,* 1975), Paul Schrader *(American Gigolo,* 1980), George Lucas *(Star Wars,* 1977), and Martin Scorsese *(Mean Streets,* 1973).

It was a "perfect storm" of circumstances combining to produce one of the most creatively fertile periods in American commercial movie-making: a new breed of production chiefs trying to save their faltering studios by gambling on an incoming generation of artistically ambitious talent, and a receptive audience hungry for the dramatically provocative, thematically relevant, and stylistically daring, all happening within the context of a society gripped in a painful period of self-questioning and reexamination.

With a pool of audacious filmmakers constantly testing the limits of the commercial mainstream and regularly challenging the movie-going audience, films of the time were dizzying in their variety of visual style, approach, and in the material they attempted to address. They ranged from near-documentary realism *(The French Connection; McCabe & Mrs. Miller* [1971]; *Dog Day Afternoon* [1975]) to the surreal *(Point Blank; Castle Keep* [1969]); from the poetic and lyrical *(Jeremiah Johnson* [1972] *Badlands)* to the consciously abrasive and confrontational *(The Wild Bunch; A Clockwork Orange* [1971]); from the straightforward *(Bullitt; Dirty Harry)* to the opaque and elliptical *(The Conversation* [1974]; *The Parallax View* [1974]; *THX 1138* [1971]). Some seemed like street-corner poetry *(Mean Streets; The Friends of Eddie Coyle* [1973]), while others had a near-operatic majesty *(The Godfather Parts I & II* [1974]) or a sense of Shakespearean tragedy *(Chinatown).* Filmmakers' concerns might be timely and topical (racism in *In the Heat of the Night* [1967]; the Watergate scandal in *All the President's Men* [1976]; the ecological threat of nuclear power in *The China Syndrome* [1979]; Cold War tensions in *Dr. Strangelove or: How I Learned to Stop Worrying and Love the Bomb* [1964]; the Vietnam War in *Apocalypse Now* [1979]), or something more universal and timeless (the animal nature of man in *Straw Dogs* [1972]; dehumanization in the modern day in *Point Blank;* unmoored youth in *The Graduate* [1967]; social dislocation in *Joe* [1970]), or even aspire to the existential *(Night Moves* [1975]; *2001: A Space Odyssey; Last Tango in Paris* [1972]). They confronted the fallacy of cherished American myths *(Little Big Man* [1970]; *Pat*

Garrett & Billy the Kid [1973]), inverted typical Hollywood conventions *(The Flight of the Phoenix* [1965]; *The Dirty Dozen; The Wild Bunch)*, and found a terrible beauty and sympathy for those living at society's fringes *(Taxi Driver* [1976]; *Bonnie and Clyde; Midnight Cowboy; Scarecrow*[1973]; *Hardcore* [1979]; *Bring Me the Head of Alfredo Garcia* [1974]; *Klute* [1971]; *Hard Times* [1975]).

It appeared no subject matter was beyond consideration, no approach too daunting, with the best of the crop intelligently and artfully capturing all the moral confusion, ambivalence and ambiguity of the time, the period's sense of self-doubt and dislocation, the true-to-life idea that right was not always clearly identifiable from wrong, and even when it was, doing the right thing did not necessarily guarantee a happy ending. It was, in retrospect, one of the most explosively and liberated creative periods in commercial moviemaking, a part of a worldwide binge in expansive cinematic artistry aptly described by the French film journal *Cahiers du Cinema* as, "the furious springtime of world cinema."

But just two movies would change the creative direction of Hollywood forever.

In summer of 1975, Universal rolled out *Jaws*, the movie adaptation of Peter Benchley's bestselling first novel. Every major aspect of the release ran contrary to then conventional industry wisdom:

Typically, summer was a time for cheap juvenilia the studios served up to summer-idled youngsters, yet Universal rolled out this major release in June;

The standard release protocol at the time called for putting a movie into upscale cinemas in major markets around the country, then touring the title through secondary markets and cycling it down through first-, second-, and third-run venues. Wide releasing was reserved for expected failures, a way to mine some kind of quick return on a title a studio suspected would die as soon as negative word-of-mouth spread. But, looking at the success Paramount had had pioneering wide releases for major titles with *Love Story* (1970) and *The Godfather*, Universal chose to roll out *Jaws* in a nationwide "break" of over 400 theaters;

While national TV ad buys had never made sense during the days of limited release with movies generally supported by local print advertising, Universal promoted its wide release by supplementing its print ads with a national TV promo campaign.

Despite having defied all the major conventions of the day—or rather *because* of these contraventions—*Jaws* powerhoused its way through the summer of 1975 to become the biggest—and fastest—earner in Hollywood history, being the first movie to ever earn more than $100 million in rentals; the mark that would thereafter define the "blockbuster." *Jaws* would ultimately gross $260 million in the U.S., and ring up another $210.6 million overseas, an incredible tally for the time.

Any idea the extraordinary success of *Jaws* might be what the industry sometimes dismisses as a "nonrecurring phenomenon" was dispelled two years later when 20th Century Fox released *Star Wars*, written and directed by another young directorial *wunderkind*, George Lucas. In its initial release, *Star Wars* earned a staggering domestic gross of $322.7 million and another $191 million overseas.

Along with out-earning *Jaws*, Lucas took the blockbuster concept several steps further. For one thing, he had shrewdly retained the merchandising rights for *Star Wars*, and turned his hit film into a wildly successful merchandising platform, with Lucas ultimately earning more from merchandising than the films themselves earned.

For another, he had also retained the sequel rights. Historically, Hollywood had considered sequels a purely mercenary effort. Normally produced quickly and for less than the original, often with lesser talent both in front of and behind the camera, a sequel was deemed a success if it grossed 40% of the original. But, when Lucas produced *The Empire Strikes Back* three years later, he upped the budget from the original—$18 million v. $13 million—to turn out a bigger, more spectacular follow-up justifying the effort with a domestic gross of $209.4 million and overseas earnings of $247.9 million making it, at the time, the second highest-grossing movie of all time behind the original *Star Wars*. He only reconfirmed the concept of nurturing a franchise—rather than cheaply exploiting it—in 1983 when *Revenge of the Jedi*, made for $32.5 million, returned $263.7 million at the U.S. box office and another $128.1 million overseas.

However, even before *Jedi*, the idea of the blockbuster thriller as a replicable phenomenon had been taking root. Between *Jaws* and *Jedi* had come such near-blockbuster and blockbuster hits as *The Omen* (1976), *Rocky* (1976), *Close Encounters of the Third Kind* (1977), *Smokey and the Bandit* (1977), *Superman: The Movie, Star Trek: The Motion Picture* (1979), *Alien* (1979), *The Amityville Horror* (1979), *The*

Cannonball Run (1981), *Raiders of the Lost Ark* (1981), *48 Hours* (1982), *E.T.: The Extra-Terrestrial* (1982), *Poltergeist* (1982), and *First Blood* (1982). Most of these titles would be followed by sequels, and, in a number of cases (e.g. *The Omen, Rocky, Superman, Star Trek, Alien, Poltergeist, First Blood, Raiders*) lead to long-running film series and TV spinoffs some of which continue to this day.

It is not difficult to extrapolate from that point to the current environment in which Hollywood pumps out a parade of hoped-for blockbusters throughout the year, with the competition among them reaching a fever pitch during the summer months when the studios can best target the audience most critical to the blockbuster: the young males who not only are attracted to the kind of action-driven fare which is the blockbuster's forte, but are willing to go back to a thriller they like two, three or more times as well as buy affiliated merchandise.

In the late 1970s and early 1980s, the blockbuster was still a singular event; *Jaws* had the summer of 1975 to itself. Today, the summer season sees a major studio picture roll out in wide release nearly every weekend. Looking at just the top releases for the upcoming summer for example:

May 6 Thor
May 13 Priest
May 20 Pirates of the Caribbean: On Stranger Tides
May 26 The Hangover Part II / Kung Fu Panda 2
June 3 X-Men: First Class
June 10 Super 8
June 17 Green Lantern
June 24 Cars 2
July 1 Transformers: Dark of the Moon
July 15 Harry Potter and the Deathly Hallows—Part 2
July 22 Captain America: The First Avenger
July 29 Cowboys & Aliens
August 5 Rise of the Planet of the Apes
August 19 Conan the Barbarian / Fright Night / Spy Kids 4: All the Time in the World
August 26 Final Destination 5

The summer glut means that, in contrast to the days of *Jaws* and *Star Wars* where an uncontested blockbuster could rule the summer, even the biggest present day hits typically experience significant drop-offs in business just by the second week as each subsequent week's big releases draw audience away from earlier releases. The difference between a success and a flop is the rate of that decline and the size of a given movie's opening box office tally (as a rule, even top earning hits earn as much as seventy-five percent of their domestic take in just their first three weeks of release), thus today's obsession with opening weekend grosses.

In an attempt to insure that prerequisite big-earning opening weekend, summer thrillers roll out in wide breaks sometimes numbering *thousands* of screens, supported by relentlessly cross-promoting multimedia ad campaigns beginning weeks, maybe months, sometimes as much as a year in advance in the hope of stoking audience anticipation. Toward the end of the 1990s, the cost of promoting a movie in an increasingly crowded marketplace was growing at twice the rate of actually *making* a movie. Marketing expenses for any wide release now run somewhere between $30-40 million, and those for big-budget summer thrillers even higher.

The competitive pressure among blockbusters has sent production budgets soaring. The cost of the average major release today runs $60-70 million, but those of summer blockbusters often considerably higher. The thrillers in the slate listed above were produced for a cumulative outlay of almost $2 billion (not counting marketing costs), with budgets ranging from a low of *Fright Night*'s $17 million to a high of *Transformers: Dark of the Moon*'s $250-300 million, for a per-picture average of somewhere close to $130 million (again, minus marketing).

In the 1960s/1970s, the studios—with nothing to lose – had been willing to gamble modest budgets on the iconoclastic and unconventional, but by the 1980s, having regained a measure of attendance stability, and finding among young ticket-buyers an audience almost predictably attracted to a narrow range of often expensive material, major movie companies became increasingly risk-averse. As the potential risks—and rewards—grew to unprecedented heights, creative development among the studios trended conservative. Big budgets became the province of franchise launches and sequels and clones of previous major hits, of remakes and big screen adaptations of TV shows with their presumed name recognition value, of adaptations of comic books and video games which appealed to the same demographic the studios were trying hardest to reach. Projects came to be selected by studio committees which not only included creative executives, but marketing and merchandising officers, with one eye on the American audience and another on the overseas box office. The summer of 2011 illustrates the strategy *in extremis;* of the eighteen major releases listed above, ten are sequels, two are remakes, seven are based on comic books, and one is an adaptation of a 1970s TV cartoon series which, in turn, was based on a set of toys. In fact, only one—the relatively modestly budgeted ($45 million) *Super 8*—has no ties to comics, isn't a sequel, or is intended as a franchise launch.

While critics often decry the apparent creative poverty of an industry addicted to remakes, rehashes, and sequels, and even some in the industry bemoan an era in which it seems marketability counts for more than a project's dramatic qualities, and some industry gadflies—like *Variety* editor and one-time production chief Peter Bart—go as far as to declare studios have an "obligation" to produce movies for a wider variety of audiences than has become the status quo, box office scores regularly make such points academic.

Just as impressive as box office scores is the fact that so many blockbusters turn in strong earnings despite tepid to strongly negative reviews, e.g. 2010's *Alice in Wonderland,* ($1.024 million worldwide), *The Twilight Saga: Eclipse* ($698 million w/w), *Iron Man 2* ($622 million), *Clash of the Titans* ($493 million), *The Chronicles of Narnia: The Voyage of the Dawn Treader* ($415 million), *Tron Legacy* ($399 million), *Prince of Persia: The Sands of Time* ($335), *Robin Hood* ($322 million), *The Last Airbender* ($320 million), and *Resident Evil: Afterlife* ($296 million). That such undistinguished fare consistently scores at the box office, and that it seems often to be review-proof, says as much about the blockbuster audience as it does the mercenary attitudes of studio production execs.

As was the case in the 1960s/1970s, young moviegoers remain the major driver of the contemporary box office, but in the case of the blockbuster thriller, the audience skews much younger than it did a generation or two ago with the under-eighteen crowd now more important to the success of big budget releases. An R-rating can translate into twenty to thirty percent fewer potential ticket-buyers, a lethal drop in the case of movies costing $100-200 million or better. As a consequence, producers of costly action/effects-driven fare tamp down—or completely avoid—strong sexual or violent elements as well as adult themes, developing, instead, material incorporating elements with a strong juvenile appeal. By way of measuring the shift, during the first six years after the institution of the Motion Picture Association of America's (MPAA) rating system in 1967, over a third of theatrical releases were R-rated, including twenty-five percent of the top-performing thrillers of the time. In comparison, in the years 2000-2005, only eleven of the top sixty live-action thrillers were R-rated.

More than a simple shifting of the demographic has been at work. The studios now deal with a markedly different audience mindset then faced them in the 1960s/1970s. Today's young consumers are incredibly technologically adept and immersed, yet, paradoxically, despite their near-addictive use of the Internet, studies show them to have limited interest in or knowledge about the world around them.

The generational visual sensibility has changed as well. Today's youngsters grow up in households with access to dozens of cable TV channels, Internet access to hundreds of websites, and with an enormous affinity for video games, with young males particularly attracted to fast-paced and action-driven gaming scenarios. Cruising the cable or Internet spectrums and a regular diet of frenetic videogames has cultivated a penchant in the young audience for non-stop pacing and over-the-top action which has, not coincidentally, become the standard thriller construct.

On this growing "addiction" to a lifestyle of high-tech multitasking, particularly prominent among the young, psychologist David Greenfield observed that the priority seems to be about "... distraction, numbing oneself... There is no self-reflection, no sitting still"; style characteristics common in most of today's big-budget thrillers.

Today's mainstream commercial thriller—and especially the big-budget blockbuster—has come full circle; as escapist and disposable as the movies of the 1930s, but overblown with outscale action and special effects. At a time when advances in special effects technology—particularly in the field of Computer Generated Imagery (CGI)—have given moviemakers the ability to put on film anything they can conjure in their imaginations, paradoxically thrillers have become less dramatically imaginative than ever before.

The life-sized, resonant movies of the 1960s/1970s have been replaced with a steady output of live-action comic books, drowned in the fantastic if not outright fantasy, and richly shaded life-sized heroes replaced by pure-of-heart superheroes or similarly larger-than-life protagonists. With their breathless pace and non-stop action, there is little room for character, texture, or layered plotting. In fact, such hyper-energized constructs force plotting and characterization toward easily and quickly digestible clichés and predictable forms. Commitment to projects is based not on a passion for the material, but on a calculation of how many toys might it sell; how well it might play in Japan; how easily it can be condensed into a catchy 30-second TV ad. The cinema of ideas, Peter Bart once mourned in his weekly *Sunday Morning Shootout* TV series, is long dead and gone.

In a review of the 2007 thriller *Rendition*, *Entertainment Weekly* reviewer Owen Gleiberman wondered if "... America... has checked out on the promise of movies that delve into the issues of our time," a proposition seemingly borne out by the across-the-board underperformance of a raft of issue-inspired and/or drama-driven films released in the fall of that year along with *Rendition: The Kingdom, Michael Clayton, In the Valley of Elah, The Assassination of Jesse James by the Coward Robert Ford, We Own the Night,* and *3:10 to Yuma.*

In fact, what had once been the selling points of the 1960s/1970s classics are now looked at as debits: complexity, moral ambiguity, topical relevance, dramatic resonance, and a willingness to upset expectations and challenge the audience. Instead, rampant imitation, predictability, an adherence to an extremely narrow range of story forms, and total escapist irrelevance are the order of the day along with a dependence on spectacle and effects gimmickry.

Bigger, costlier, more physically impressive than ever before, the studio thriller of today is also typically forgettable and disposable, with one big budget opus looking much like another. For all their scale, so said director *provocateur* Oliver Stone in a TV profile, movies today are, in the dramatic sense, "growing smaller," and all the surfeit of large scale action set-pieces and eye-dazzling effects cannot mask the fact that Hollywood's movies have "lost (their) magic."

Titans: Spielberg and Lucas
(Posted 1/17/11)

George Lucas and Steven Spielberg. Three and a half decades after their breakout successes, they remain arguably two of the most potent brand names in American entertainment and understandably so. Probably more than any other two individuals, they have been—for good or for ill—responsible for a massive reconfiguration of media entertainment, expanding from film into TV, merchandising, and new media, constantly exploring the ability to cross-pollinate all these strains, and sparking a rethinking of the kinds of movies Hollywood makes and the way they're made.

Lucas and Spielberg are credited—and sometimes blamed—for launching, expanding, and perfecting the concept of the synergistic, merchandisable blockbuster franchise. After their commercial breakouts in the late 1970s, their movies regularly dominated the all-time best box office performers list for most of the following decades, and even today, after such recent additions as *Avatar* (2009), *Titanic* (1997), *The Passion of the Christ* (2004), the *Spider-Man, Pirates of the Caribbean,* and *The Lord of the Rings* trilogies, and the *Harry Potter* series, as directors and/or producers, Lucas's and Spielberg's names are still attached to almost one-quarter of the all-time top 100 box office hits (even after adjusting for inflation, Lucas/Spielberg still account for twenty of the top 100 earners).

Even this does not adequately measure their respective commercial muscle, omitting, as it does, the lesser but nevertheless notable movies associated with their respective production arms, as well as their expansions into animation, TV production, computer and interactive on-line games, and a variety of merchandising lines. After over three decades at the top of the industry's commercial pyramid, Lucas and Spielberg remain classic archetypes of the era, and the acknowledged *maestros* of the blockbuster game.

George Lucas and Steven Spielberg. It's nearly impossible to think of one without the other and, again, understandably so. Colleagues, friends, sometimes collaborators, they are close in age, broke big about the same time, share a somewhat similar sensibility. They are both "children of television," much of the work they've directed and/or produced being inspired by—if not displaying an outright nostalgic affection for—the monster, science-fiction, and war movies, the vintage serials, the cartoons and TV programs they viewed for hours on end as youngsters. *Star Wars* (1977), *Jaws* (1975), *Close Encounters of the Third Kind* (1977), *Twilight Zone: The Movie* (1983), *Poltergeist* (1982), *1941* (1979), the *Indiana Jones* films, just to name a few, all have their roots in the Saturday morning TV viewing of Lucas and Spielberg. Their handle on popular culture has given them a preternatural instinct for material which will play for the mass audience, as well as the best way to portray that material.

A youthful passion for movies and moviemaking manifested itself as a technical proficiency impressive even at the start of their careers, and which has grown into a technical mastery few current moviemakers can match. From their earliest days, they have pushed at the limits of moviemaking technology, looking for any new device or technique which can bring their imaginings to credible life on-screen, whether it's shooting *Jaws* on location in the open waters off Martha's Vineyard with an animatronic shark, resurrecting dinosaurs through the magic of CGI (*Jurassic Park*, 1993), or injecting actors into a wholly alien universe composed almost entirely of computer-generated imagery, and performing side-by-side with an equally unreal computer-manifested co-star (Jar-Jar Binks in *Star Wars: Episode 1—The Phantom Menace*, 1999).

They continue to get the kind of media attention few other directors and producers do, and have retained their marquee value longer than most on-screen stars in the business today. Last year saw announcements for 2011 projects which will continue to demonstrate their on-going commercial potency. Lucas announced yet another rerelease of his *Star Wars* films, this time all six released in sequence with the—literally—added dimension of having been reformatted for 3-D. As for Spielberg, two theatrical features will be released within weeks of each other—*War Horse* and *The Adventures of Tintin: The Secret of the Unicorn*—and the year will also see the debut of two Spielberg-produced TV series, *Terra Nova* and *Falling Skies*.

Yet, for all their commonalities, the announcements of their respective 2011 plans illustrate their vast, polar-opposite differences. For all they share, their careers have followed two distinct, increasingly disparate arcs: one that of a filmmaker who built on his early successes, and the other that of one seemingly trapped by his.

Lucas, for example, has been strikingly spare in his output. The final installment in the *Star Wars* saga—*Star Wars: Episode*

III—Revenge of the Sith (2005), marked only Lucas's sixth directorial credit, four of them *Star Wars* episodes. As a producer, Lucas's name has been attached to only twenty theatrical titles in thirty years, with most of them—other than the *Star Wars* and *Indiana Jones* films—box office flops. When Lucas received the American Film Institute's Lifetime Achievement Award in 2005, in light of his slim body of work, the recognition was generally considered to be for Lucas's technological contributions to moviemaking, and the impact of the *Star Wars* series.

Spielberg, on the other hand, seems to barely finish one project before he's on to the next, having directed twenty-five features between 1974 and the present, and acted in some sort of producer's role on several dozen more. His production entities—Amblin and Dreamworks SKG—have turned out still more pictures on which he served no direct role, a wildly eclectic canon including the *Shrek* movies, *Who Framed Roger Rabbit?* (1988), the *Back to the Future* series, *The Bridges of Madison County* (1995), *American Beauty* (1999), *Gladiator* (2000), *Cast Away* (2002), *Road to Perdition* (2002), and *House of Sand and Fog* (2003).

The difference between the filmographies of the two men is not only the striking one of quantity, or even quality, but of breadth, and therein, perhaps, is the true measure of the creative difference between them.

*****

George Lucas attended the film program at the University of Southern California with the goal of becoming "… a documentary filmmaker, cameraman, and editor…" He was not interested in mainstream commercial cinema, wanting, instead, to concentrate on more abstract fare while professing little concern for making money in the business. He came under the mentoring wing of Francis Ford Coppola who engineered Lucas's first professional directorial assignment, an expansion of an award-winning short Lucas had shot at USC which would evolve into the feature *THX 1138* (1971), a film which, in every frame, reflected the serious, near-abstract art house work Lucas had explored as a student. Set in a dehumanizing, emotionally constrained future, *THX 1138* is deliberately opaque, brooding, constructed more poetically than along linear dramatic lines. It is also as emotionally aloof as its striking, icy, white-on-white visuals, and, unsurprisingly, failed to connect with the mainstream audience.

The commercial failure of *THX 1138* pushed Lucas to look for a more accessible, and, hopefully, commercial project. He drew on his own teenage experiences to come up with *American Graffiti* (1973). As warm-hearted as *THX 1138* is cold, as bubbly with youthful experience as *THX* is deliberate and restrained, *Graffiti* easily connected with a young audience who, after years of Vietnam and Watergate, eagerly lapped up its loving portrait of a more innocent time, and simpler pleasures and pains. *Graffiti* became a huge hit ($21.3 million domestic against a budget of $775,000), kicked off a national craze for 1950s nostalgia, and opened the door to Lucas for his first major production: *Star Wars* (later redubbed, *Star Wars: Episode IV—A New Hope*).

A record-breaking hit at the time ($215.5 million domestic against a $13 million budget), *Star Wars* not only cemented Lucas's entrée into Hollywood's major leagues, but his profits from the movie and the merchandising (for which he'd shrewdly retained control) bought him complete independence from Hollywood. He self-financed *The Empire Strikes Back* (1980, although he turned the directorial chores over to Irvin Kershner), and afterward built a full-service, state-of-the-art production facility—dubbed Skywalker Ranch—far removed from Hollywood in northern California, set up his own production company (Lucasfilm), as well as Industrial Light and Magic, a special effects house which remains one of the premier movie technology laboratories today. But, having done so, Lucas seemed at a loss of what to do with his newfound independence.

He walked away from directing claiming, "I'm never going to direct another establishment-type movie again," although the one-time aspiring experimental filmmaker now found himself presiding over a production facility which seemed expressly designed for just that kind of work. As a producer, he has, occasionally, husbanded the kind of serious moviemaking he aspired to as a student: he acted as executive producer for the American release of Akira Kurosawa's samurai epic *Kagemusha* (1980), as well as for the collage-like documentary *Powaqqatsi* (1988), and was also an uncredited producer on the *noir* homage *Body Heat* (1981) which marked the directorial debut of Lawrence Kasdan who had worked on the screenplays for Lucas's *The Empire Strikes Back* and *Raiders of the Lost Ark* (1981). But, other than the *Star Wars* and *Indiana Jones* titles, much of Lucasfilm's scanty producer's filmography consists of misfires like *Willow* (1988), *Howard the Duck* (1986), and *The Radioland Murders*

(1994), along with mushy children's fare like *Twice Upon a Time* (1983) and *The Land Before Time* (1988).

When Lucas did return to directing, after an absence of twenty-one years, it was not to helm some against-the-commercial-grain individualistic effort, but yet another "establishment-type movie"—in fact, a series of them as he began turning out the second *Star Wars* trilogy. Despite impressive box office, critics—and many fans of the original trilogy—considered them an artistic disappointment.

Lucas has often seemed uncomfortable with the more human elements of cinema, preferring, evidently, to immerse himself in the wonders of moviemaking technology, going as far as to remark, at times, that "actors are irrelevant." On the original *Star Wars*, the joke among the cast was how Lucas's direction rarely went beyond, "Faster and more intense!" To that point, critics generally consider *The Empire Strikes Back* as the most dramatically rewarding of the original three movies; a movie which Lucas neither directed nor wrote. Even on the character-driven *American Graffiti*, Lucas seemed at a loss as to how to deal with his large ensemble cast, hiring a dialogue coach to work with the performers while he busied himself with camera set-ups. When the second *Star Wars* trilogy began to hit screens, beginning with *Star Wars: Episode I—The Phantom Menace* (1999), it appeared that all of his penchants—weakness with character and drama, technical mastery—had grown only more entrenched. *The New York Times*'s A. O. Scott shared a common reviewers' opinion in its judgment of *Episode II—Attack of the Clones* (2002) as a feature-length "action-figure commercial," and that it was "... not really much of a movie at all, if by movie you mean a work of visual storytelling about the dramatic actions of a group of interesting characters."

Attack of the Clones, while one of the top box office earners of 2002, would be the first *Star Wars* entry not to take the box office crown during its theatrical release, that honor going to the better reviewed, comparatively more flesh-and-blood *Spider-Man*.

Many of Lucas's ancillary works are marked by an incessant recycling and merchandising of his limited core of films, e.g. two TV movies and a series featuring the Ewoks— the cuddle-toy cute creatures introduced in *Star Wars: Episode VI—Return of the Jedi* (1983)—two TV series based around a young Indiana Jones, *Star Wars*-based videogames, a long-running animated series—*Star Wars:*

The Clone Wars—and the constant rereleasing—in theaters and in various home entertainment formats—of the movie series.

*****

Steven Spielberg, on the other hand, for all his technical flash and embrace of effects technology, has always been a more humanistic filmmaker.

Spielberg had been attending California State College at Long Beach in the late 1960s when Sidney Sheinberg, then head of Universal's television division, saw a short Spielberg had made and offered the twenty-one-year-old student a directing contract. The following year, Spielberg made his directing debut with the middle segment of a *Twilight Zone*-ish TV movie triptych penned by Rod Serling: *Night Gallery* (1969).

In this, his maiden professional effort, Spielberg's immediately recognizable visual fluency is every bit equaled by his ability to give emotional heat to the performance *pas de deux* between two veterans of mogul-era Hollywood which comprises the bulk of the piece: Joan Crawford's bitterly vindictive and selfish blind magnate willing to stop at nothing for the chance of a few hours sight, and noble but defeated Barry Sullivan, the doctor she blackmails into performing an illicit eye operation.

As Spielberg's career advanced and his directorial projects became more elaborate and their settings more fantastic, Spielberg never let his technological mastery eclipse the human elements in his movies. On *Jaws*, he had the original screenplay by the novel's author Peter Benchley run through one set of rewriter's hands after another for the major purpose of enriching the characters. He tangled with screenwriter Paul Schrader over the first draft of the script which would evolve into *Close Encounters of the Third Kind* for the same reason, looking to see his sci-fi fantasy populated with recognizably everyday characters.

Spielberg also knew how to get those carefully etched characters off the page and onto the screen: nine performers have received Oscar nominations for their work in Spielberg's movies as of this writing (vs. Lucas's one).

And, where all but one title in Lucas's slim filmography is set in a Never-Never Land of futuristic fantasy, much of Spielberg's work—*including* his fantasies—is grounded in an amiable, recognizable, middle-class suburbia much like the neighborhoods in which the filmmaker spent his childhood. Some of his most effective early works—*Close Encounters, E.T.: The Extra-Terrestrial* (1982), and *Poltergeist* (which he produced but did not direct)—gain their power from cross-pollinating childhood fantasies of ghosts under the bed and alien visitors with equally vivid recreations of a comfortably familiar and banal suburban milieu.

Like Lucas, much of Spielberg's work references the TV shows and movies he saw as a youngster, but where Lucas had spent several years in the intellectual hothouse of USC's film program, Spielberg had, in essence, gone straight from watching TV to *making* TV. Though he had ambitions of wanting to do "serious" film work, he was not the aspiring anti-establishment maverick—as Lucas initially was—trying to find a way to work outside the system, but rather proved to be very much at home *within* the Hollywood system. At the Universal shop, that system provided Spielberg the opportunity to learn and perfect his craft through years of directing episodes for major network series like *Marcus Welby, M.D.* and *Columbo*, as well as the experience of working with the studio's veteran craftsmen. He graduated to made-for-TV movies and gained his first major acclaim for *Duel* (1971), an artfully creepy bit of suspense about a traveling businessman (Dennis Weaver) who finds himself in a fight for his life with the never-seen driver of a tanker truck. Spielberg made several more TV features, but it was *Duel*, in which he displayed his knack for action without letting the picture devolve into empty chase mechanics, which led to his first theatrical feature: *The Sugarland Express* (1973).

Sugarland represented a significant increase in complexity for Spielberg over his TV work both logistically and creatively. Most of *Duel* had consisted of one truck, one car, a lonely stretch of road in the California desert, and one principal actor. On his series work, major characters had long been established by the respective series' stars, and the shows were shot on the studio back lot. *Sugarland*, however, had action sequences involving dozens of police cars and helicopters, locations spread all across Texas, four principals and a host of supporting parts, and a challenging storyline gradually changing from the gently comic to the heartbreakingly tragic, and in which the most sympathetic characters—a young, married pair of minor felons on a cross-Texas quest to regain their son from foster care—are also the story's "villains." Though the movie failed commercially (possibly suffering from being one of a glut of couples-on-the-run stories all opening over the same period e.g. *The Getaway* [1972], *Badlands* [1973], *Thieves Like Us* [1974]), reviewers enthusiastically agreed Spielberg had made an auspicious theatrical debut.

The Sugarland Express had been produced by one-time 20th Century Fox chief Richard Zanuck and his partner, David Brown. When the duo acquired the rights to the novel *Jaws*, Spielberg asked on as director. The unprecedented success of *Jaws* ($260m US v $8m budget) would do for Spielberg what *Star Wars* would do for Lucas two years later; buy him creative independence in Hollywood.

Soon after *Jaws*, Spielberg set up Amblin Entertainment, his own production company, so he could more easily initiate and maintain creative control over projects. Amblin was a much different entity than Lucasfilm and the Skywalker Ranch. Spielberg did not remove himself from Hollywood; his company was based in Los Angeles, and Spielberg kept strong ties with the company which had nurtured him through the early part of his career—Universal—and later with Warner Bros. where he forged a strong, personal relationship with Steve Ross, the then chief of Warners' parent company, Warner Communications (later Time Warner).

Almost immediately, Spielberg became as prolific a producer as a director, spinning off projects of interest in which he had neither the time nor inclination to direct himself, and providing major breaks for new or up-and-coming directors like Robert Zemeckis (who cut his directorial teeth on *I Wanna Hold Your Hand* [1978] and *Used Cars* [1980] for Amblin), Joe Dante (*Gremlins*, 1984), and Barry Levinson (*Young Sherlock Holmes*, 1985). By the mid-1980s, Spielberg was producing as many movies as he was directing. Within eleven years after making *The Sugarland Express*, Spielberg had directed nine theatrical features (more than George Lucas has directed to date), and had produced *another* nine just since 1978.

The 1980s saw Spielberg creatively stumble. His work seemed to waffle between a desire to move up to more adult themes (with the exception of *The Sugarland Success*, all of his movies prior to 1985 had been some sort of adventure or fantasy), and a fear of alienating the mass audience with stories darker and more troubling than the fare with which he'd come to be associated.

It was, in fact, a chronic fear. On *Sugarland*, producer and director had reversed stereotypical roles in a debate over the tone of the movie with Spielberg pushing to compromise the picture with a more upbeat finish while Richard Zanuck argued to protect the integrity of the original tragic finale. On *Jaws*, while Spielberg admirably wanted the principal characters to have more dimension, he also wanted them to be universally likeable, so both the obsessive shark hunter Quint (Robert Shaw) and snobby oceanographer Hooper (Richard Dreyfuss) were softened from their book versions. And, while Spielberg may have enjoyed spinning out his fantasies in familiar milieus, he seemed uncomfortable with the more drab aspects of everyday existence.

With films like *Jaws, Close Encounters, Raiders of the Lost Ark* (1981, directed for producer friend Lucas), and *E.T.*, that tendency was of little issue, but as Spielberg tried to change direction it hobbled his work. He sanded off the more harsh and problematic edges of Toni Morrison's novel *The Color Purple* for a milquetoasty 1985 adaptation; his 1987 adaptation of J.G. Ballard's autobiographical novel, *Empire of the Sun*, inspired by Ballard's childhood experiences under Japanese occupation during WW II, was generally considered inferior to John Boorman's thematically similar *Hope and Glory* released that same year; *Always* (1989) was a woefully miscalculated remake of the bittersweet WW II fantasy *A Guy Named Joe* (1943), with Spielberg mistakenly assuming the milieu of airborne firefighters had the same gravitas as *Joe*'s self-sacrificing bomber pilots in combat against the Axis; and then there was *Hook* (1991), a misguided attempt to "adultify" *Peter Pan* with themes of menopausal reevaluation as a long absent and now grown Peter (Robin Williams) returns to Never-Never Land.

Even though he seemed to have lost his creative way, Spielberg was still capable of turning in a moneymaker. Despite predominantly negative reviews, *Hook* took in almost $120 million domestic, and was followed in 1993 by the empty-headed but technically amazing *Jurassic Park* which, with its U.S. take of over $357 million, was, for several years, the all-time box office champ.

Whatever inner governor had been holding Spielberg back creatively he finally managed to cast off—and do so with a vengeance—with 1993's *Schindler's List,* adapted by Steven Zaillian from Thomas Keneally's bestselling novel which, in turn, was inspired by the true story of a playboy German industrialist (Liam Neeson) who, during WW II, rose to the occasion and saved hundreds of Jews from extermination. *Schindler* is boldly shot in a dolorous black-and-white, and deals face-on with one of the grimmest chapters in human history. It was, in light of its somber story, surprisingly successful commercially ($96 million U.S./$312 worldwide against a $25 million budget), and gained Spielberg a level of artistic legitimacy he'd been unable to achieve with his earlier work.

Schindler's List also seemed to liberate something in Spielberg, and after the sequel *The Lost World: Jurassic Park II* (1997), he turned out a string of pictures all marked, to some extent, with a new, more mature sensibility. There was *Amistad* (1997), another true history piece, a noble—if unfocused—attempt to grapple with America's history of slavery; and then the brutally demythologizing WW II adventure, *Saving Private Ryan*, the following year. Even when he returned to the realm of science-fiction and fantasy with *Artificial Intelligence: A.I.* (2001) and *Minority Report* (2002), the moral simplicity of *Close Encounters* and *E.T.* was clearly gone.

A.I. was originally to have been a Stanley Kubrick project. Kubrick had spoken with Spielberg about the possibility of working jointly, with Kubrick as producer and Spielberg in the director's chair, but, ultimately, Kubrick felt the material leant itself better to the other director's sensibilities and turned the property wholly over to Spielberg.

A.I. is a sci-fi fairy tale, a futuristic *Pinocchio* (which the screenplay, by Spielberg from a screen story by Ian Watson adapting Brian Aldiss's short story, "Supertoys Last All Summer Long," references repeatedly), being the story of a robot boy, David (Haley Joel Osment), who longs to be a real boy so as to regain the love of the human mother (Frances O'Connor) who rejects him for her biological son. Overlong, episodic, sometimes sluggish and heavy-handed, it's an interesting debate as to whether or not Kubrick would have handled the rambling structure of the piece better than Spielberg. By the same token, it's worth arguing whether or not the more emotionally aloof Kubrick could have delivered the poignancy Spielberg brings to some of the movie's more emotionally laden scenes for, despite its flaws, the movie has moments of undeniable dramatic power.

A.I. is not a child's fairy tale, but a fairy tale for adults about a child's bruised soul. David's jealousy over his biological brother, his feelings of abandonment and loss, his horror at learning from his creator (William Hurt) that his "uniqueness" will be reproduced for mass consumption, and the longing carrying him through his long, often terrifying quest are frighteningly real, disturbing, and sometimes heartbreaking. So too is the poignancy of the movie's final scene, marked by a lyrical bittersweetness unthinkable in a Spielberg picture of twenty years earlier.

David has been recovered by alien explorers from a future ice age long after the human race has died out. Having searched his memory, they are aware of his trials and offer him the possibility of a brief bit of happiness. They can recreate his mother from a keepsake lock of her hair. However, they warn, the recreation will last for only one day, after which she will sleep and never wake. David takes the offer and the day spent alone with his mother in a replica of their home is an idyllic day of mother-and-child delights. As the day ends and she turns to bed, David turns his back on his cybernetic immortality, curling up in an unending sleep with the mother who finally loves him.

Minority Report is more of a straight-up sci-fi action thriller, and, as such, perhaps it even more clearly displays the new colors Spielberg had added to his palette, emotional colors which stand out starkly against the comparatively simple ambitions of *Report*'s futuristic fugitive story. *Minority Report* (adapted from a Philip K. Dick story by Scott Frank and John Cohen) is a less artistically grandiose but more tightly constructed thematic kin to *Blade Runner* (1982) in that it tries to retool *noir* for a sci-fi context, taking a familiar story—a cop (Tom Cruise) is framed for a murder he didn't commit—and giving it a World of Tomorrow twist (cops use psychics to apprehend criminals for crimes they have yet to commit). Spielberg and cinematographer Janusz Kaminski find a modern-day visual counterpart to the light/shadow starkness of the classic *noirs* with a color-drained look of charcoalish harshness. And, like the classic *noirs*, this visually abrasive scheme mirrors the rough-edged content; a hardboiled cop now desperately on the run, hiding out among the future's demimonde, forever haunted—and somewhat twisted—by his guilt over the long-ago loss of his son snatched away at a public pool outing during an ever-so-brief moment of distraction.

In the early twenty-first century, of the two men, Spielberg emerges as the more vital, more exploratory moviemaker. In fits and starts, he has broadened his emotional range both as a director and producer. While Spielberg's various production brands have turned out an astounding amount of disposable, forgettable kiddie fodder, their output has also expanded to include such *un*-Spielbergian works as *American Beauty* (1999), *Collateral* (2004), the matched pair of WW II stories *Flags of Our Fathers* and *Letters from Iwo Jima* (both in 2006), and the HBO WW II mini-series' *Band of Brothers* (2001) and its Pacific war counterpart, *The Pacific* (2010). He has not only maintained the creative collaborations he established in the earliest days of Amblin (Robert Zemeckis directed *Cast Away* [2000] for Dreamworks), but continues to offer opportunities for new directorial talent, giving TV director Mimi Lederer her theatrical feature break on *The Peacemaker* (1997) and *Deep Impact* (1998), and doing the same for stage director Sam Mendes with *American Beauty* and *Road to Perdition*.

At the top of his creative game, Spielberg continues his incredible output, moving from the sentimental escapism of *The Terminal* (2003) to his 9/11-referencing revamp of *War of the Worlds* (2005) to his disturbing take on the unending cycle of violence and revenge in the Middle East with *Munich* (2005), while wearing his producer's hat for the blockbuster *Transformers* franchise, an upcoming fourth *Jurassic Park*, and a planned remake of the 1951 George Pal sci-fier, *When Worlds Collide*.

Still, however accomplished Spielberg stands as a filmmaker, and however impressive his artistic growth may be, it is George Lucas's stamp which is most indelible on the industry today. *Jaws* may have given Hollywood its taste for the summer blockbuster, but *Star Wars* demonstrated the full potential of the present-day film franchise. And, it is also the Lucas aesthetic which holds sway.

As far back as his earliest days as a feature director, Lucas had come to believe the most important parts of a movie were its opening five minutes and its climactic twenty, with everything in between no more than filler. He felt simplistic characters and stories could be eclipsed by sufficient doses of fast-paced action. There is hardly a big-budget thriller today which does not seem poured out of that mold.

And so Spielberg, the one-time *wunderkind*, becomes Hollywood's Old Guard, one of the last few at the major studio level who believes in the antiquated idea that movies—even the most fantastic of adventures—should be about people.

Pyromaniacs: Hollywood's Bad Boys
(posted 5/15/11)

A man who works with his hands is a laborer;
a man who works with his hands and his brain is a craftsman;
but a man who works with his hands and his brain and his heart is an artist.

Louis Nizer

In his indispensable film study text, *Understanding Movies*, Louis Gianetti held forth on what separated craftsmanlike directors from those who rise above the norm:

> *... what differentiates a great director from one who is merely competent is not so much a matter of what happens, but <u>how</u> things happen...*

In other words, Gianetti continued, the difference was in how effectively the director used form—visual style, composition, editing, *mise en scene*, and the rest of the directorial toolbox—to "... embody (a film's) content."

But with the rise of big budget blockbusters in the '70s and '80s, there came the ascendancy of a breed of director for whom content mattered less than form. In fact, there were, actually, some for whom content seemed not to matter at all. For them, visual virtuosity was not, in Gianetti's words, a means of embodying content, but an end in itself; they were purveyors of what detractors often referred to as "pretty pictures" and "eye candy." As opposed to Gianetti's content embodiers, they represented a new directorial species presciently limned by film theoretician Siegfried Kracauer over a half-century ago:

> *The technician cares about means and functions rather than ends and modes of being... he will be inclined... to conceive of them in an abstract way...*

The movies have always had their share of visual virtuosos (think Orson Welles, or consider the shadow play of the 1940s/1950s *noirs* growing ever more baroque with each passing year), but visual style stepped to the fore during the '60s and '70s as never before. Inspired by European flamboyance and with the traditional conservative Hollywood aesthetic of form-follows-function having faded with the old studio system, there came a generation of directors who were as expressive visually as they were in the stories they told. At their best, visuals and narrative acted as a powerful team, each reinforcing the impact of the other, e.g. the bleak modern urbanscapes of *Point Blank* (1967) and the movie's theme of dehumanization; the near-documentary look of *The French Connection* (1971) and its realistic police procedural tale; the elegant pacing and deepening visual gloom of *The Godfather* movies (1972 and 1974) and their epic narrative arc of devouring moral corruption amid Mafia royalty.

But there were also directors who seemed more intent on dazzling than conveying, like Sidney J. Furie *(The Appaloosa* [1966], *The Naked Runner* [1967]), Richard C. Sarafian *(Man in the Wilderness* [1971], *Vanishing Point* [1971]), and Peter Hyams *(Busting* [1974], *Capricorn One* [1978], *The Star Chamber* [1983]). And, there were also directors—like John Milius *(Dillinger* [1973], *Red Dawn* [1984], *Farewell to the King* [1989]) and Walter Hill *(The Driver* [1978], *The Long Riders* [1980], *Extreme Prejudice* [1987])—who seemed to consciously and conspicuously strip-mine the work of directors of greater stature for the superficial stylistic tics of the originals only to regurgitate them in pretentious but dramatically inferior fare, sometimes even copying the work of their inspirations shot-for-shot, e.g. Hill's *The Long Riders* aping Sam Peckinpah's *The Wild Bunch* (1969).

*****

Perhaps no director defined the aesthetic of visual indulgence with more clarity and with less apology during those creatively explosive years of the 1960s/1970s—and up through today—than Brian DePalma. On the eve of the 2002 opening of DePalma's twisty-turny neo-*noir Femme Fatale*, critic Gavin Smith glowingly described DePalma's canon in, ironically, the same terms often used by his detractors, saying DePalma's filmmaking "... delights in taking liberties with suspension of disbelief in sequences of absurd, impossibly escalating jeopardy... logic and believability aren't important... (his movies are) adventures in cinematic form masquerading as genre exercises."

DePalma himself has been openly dismissive of the human dimension of his movies, confessing to boredom with shooting scenes stressing emotion and character, while, instead, primarily concerning himself with visual concepts that may have little to do with the dramatic content. By his own words, he is, according to a 1984 interview,

"… a visual stylist, a *visual stylist*…" (his emphasis) for whom dramatic content is, at best, a secondary concern.

DePalma's near-exclusive obsession with visual imagery explains his frequent turning to tales featuring macabre and sometimes grotesque violence *(Carrie* [1976], *The Fury* [1979], *Scarface* [1983], *Body Double* [1984]), and lurid sexuality *(Dressed to Kill* [1980], *Casualties of War* [1989], and, again, *Body Double)*. In the same 1984 interview, DePalma explained his penchants saying that, motion pictures being "… a kinetic art form…," acts of violence make a natural fit for cinema and for his desire to fully exercise the visual potential of the medium.

Unsurprisingly, then, some of DePalma's biggest disappointments have been movies demanding a strong dramatic foundation, like his Vietnam War-set *Casualties of War* (1989) and its Iraq war counterpart *Redacted* (2007), crime drama *Carlito's Way* (1993), and his attempt at a *The Conversation*-type political thriller, *Blow Out* (1981). By the same token, some of his biggest commercial successes have been movies whose near-cartoonish plots provide the perfect vehicle for his brand of visual hyperbole like his almost wholly fictional take on the bringing down of gangster kingpin Al Capone in *The Untouchables* (1987), and the first big screen interpretation of the far-fetched 1960s TV spy series, *Mission: Impossible* (1996).

*****

The success of *Star Wars* (1975) further catalyzed the popularity—among a new generation of audiences, moviemakers, and even studio executives—of the visual stylist aesthetic. *Star Wars* creator George Lucas himself often professed a dismissive attitude toward the elements of drama and character, and it was a mindset which would often become couched in the lofty terms of "pure cinema," and in being supposedly truer to film's visual nature than the more narrative-driven movies of an earlier age.

The result, in the eyes of many in the critical establishment as well as from more drama-centric moviemakers, has been thirty to forty years of thrillers and adventure films marked—according to film critic Richard Corliss—by ever more innovative "… eye-popping visuals…" buoying up "… straight-ahead, easy-sell scripts that are routine and familiar," while traditional story-telling values of "… situation, character, wit, subtlety…" have degraded. By the early 1980s, there was already a critical constituency gagging on a wave of visually indulgent, dramatically vapid big studio fare. As long ago as 1984, *Film*

Comment's David Chute was complaining, "In the post-Lucas period, 'pure cinema' is synonymous with sensationalism... I'm sick to death of all this empty style."

In a 1996 cover story, "Who Killed the Hollywood Screenplay?", *Entertainment Weekly* gave, as an illustrative example of the excesses of the visual stylists, the "ludicrous" climax of the stalker thriller *The Fan* (1996), set at a baseball game during a torrential downpour. According to *The Fan*'s screenwriter, Phoef Sutton, a number of people on the production argued with director Tony Scott over the scene, pointing out baseball games are called because of rain: "In fact, *everybody* argued with him. But I don't think Tony cared about the plausibility of it."

Almost a decade later, demonstrating the same dismay for a trend which has only grown more pronounced, writer/director Ron Shelton, responding to a young generation of moviemakers' disdain for dialogue, argued in an interview, "... the old canard that action defines character is only partly true. Hamlet wasn't doing a whole lot when he said, 'To be or not to be.'"

In Hollywood, the argument has been less an aesthetic than a commercial one. Action and visual excitement sell better than character and drama at the major release level, and, as style/action-driven movies have come to dominate box office charts, the industry has looked to areas producing the kind of eye-tickling talent the studios feel the blockbuster brand of thrillers needs such as cinematography (Jan De Bont, *Twister*, 1994), advertising (Tony Scott *[Unstoppable*, 2010] and his brother Ridley Scott *[Robin Hood*, 2010], Gore Verbinski *[Pirates of the Caribbean*, 2003), and music videos (McG, *Terminator Salvation*, 2009).

The career of Ridley Scott, one of the Grand Old Men of the school of visual stylists (his feature directorial debut was 1977's *The Duelists*), provides an apt microcosm for the trend at large, with its few nuggets of gold scattered across an ever-widening vein of pyrite. Within Scott's filmography, every *Alien* (1979), *Thelma & Louise* (1991), or *American Gangster* (2007) is offset by a surfeit of gorgeous but empty—and sometimes silly—movies like *Legend* (1986), *Black Rain* (1989), *1492: Conquest of Paradise* (1992), *G.I. Jane* (1997), and *Hannibal* (2001). Wrote *Star-Ledger* critic Stephen Whitty in his pan of "purely visual filmmaker" Scott's failed con man comedy *Matchstick Men* (2003), "For twenty-five years, Ridley Scott has been a style in search of a story… (He) has always known how to make gripping, memorable pictures. Telling tales… has been another matter."

*****

Ridley Scott's career may stand apropos as an in-miniature representation of the forty-year post-*Star Wars* trajectory of the visual stylists, but if one is looking for a more contemporary poster child for the aesthetic, an equally on-point choice would be Michael Bay. In the years since his 1995 theatrical debut with *Lethal Weapon* (1987) clone *Bad Boys*, Bay has, for many, come to stand, for good and/or for ill, as the top of the visual stylist heap.

Bay's career began in advertising and music videos, his work on an award-winning series of "Got Milk?" ads bringing him a 1994 Director's Guild nomination for Best Commercial Director. The following year, the producing team of Don Simpson and Jerry Bruckheimer, with their eyes on slick-looking, action-driven fare like *Top Gun* (1986) and *Days of Thunder* (1990) (both directed by Tony Scott), brought Bay on board to helm the light-hearted cop actioner *Bad Boys*. A mid-range hit in the U.S., *Bad Boys* ultimately pulled in a worldwide box office of $150.8 million, a tremendous return on a budget of just $23 million. Bay thereafter became a regular member of Bruckheimer's directorial stable, subsequently turning out a series of evermore extravagant and expensive blockbuster thrillers. On only his second film, *The Rock*, with its $224 million worldwide gross against a $75 million budget, Bay graduated to the A-list ranks, and remains one of present-day Hollywood's premier purveyors of the big budget actioner.

Though Bay does have his supporters among action aficionados, the general critical view of his work slants negative and often even hostile. In a review of his historical epic *Pearl Harbor* (2001), perhaps his most reviled work, *Entertainment Weekly* described Bay as a director with a "… near-fetishistic love of sleek, macho gadgetry… whose films rarely flirt with notions of brevity or subtlety…," while another critic, reviewing the same picture, ranted that Bay "… proves his generation of single-minded directors-as-demolition experts knows little about inspired filmmaking."

Bay's movies are about action, noise, pace, and the striking, often pretentious image (Nicolas Cage's Christ-like pose during the climax of the empty-headed *The Rock*; Ben Affleck striking a heroic stance on a parked fighter plane's wing, backlit by a setting sun in *Pearl*

Harbor although the Japanese attack took place in the morning). In a 2001 consideration of Bay's work, which damned the director with the faintest of praise, *Film Comment*'s Kent Jones wrote that his enjoyment of Bay's work was the "guiltiest of pleasures." And that "Bay uses (explosions) the way that Bresson uses doors—liberally."

Neither characters nor plots have to play out credibly, or even consistently in Bay's thrillers—they serve only as functions to take his movies to their next spectacular display of action and effects. In *The Rock*, for example, supposedly crack military officers make the most boneheaded of misjudgments (one blunders into an achingly obvious ambush site; another hand-picks the most unreliable of troopers for his moral crusade to force the U.S. to own up to forgotten covert operatives). In *Armageddon* (1998), NASA official Billy Bob Thornton lobbies his agency to use Bruce Willis's mining outfit rather than trained astronauts for a space mission to blow up an Earth-threatening asteroid because of their unique abilities, although the only unique ability they demonstrate on the mission is their collective talent for standing around grimly watching a power drill grind away.

Peter Bart, in his 2000 book, *The Gross: The Hits, The Flops—The Summer That Ate Hollywood*, recounts *Armageddon* screenwriter Jonathan Hensleigh's creatively frustrating experience with the director. As Bay ran Hensleigh through one rewrite after another, Hensleigh, irritated at Bay's increasing obsession with the physical side of the film, thought back to a remark *New York Times* film critic Janet Maslin had made about film directors coming up from the world of music videos: "They haven't just undermined film narrative, they've demolished it."

One of Bay's signature tics is a rocket-fired pace maintained by an editing style so frenetic one film director declared, "... it felt like (*Armageddon*) was made for people with attention deficit disorder." Bay's handling of exposition scenes is no different, using the same restless camera and exhausting cutting rhythm he uses for his often incomprehensible action sequences, almost never repeating a shot within a scene. Kent Jones describes Bay's sensibility as being one of "... downsizing narrative coherence and capitalizing on his audience's urge toward mental statelessness... Clarity? By Bay's lights an outmoded concept... ."

Bay is both frank but dismissive about the continuity problems his style often produces. "I don't get hung up on continuity too much," he told an interviewer. "When you get hung up on continuity, you can't keep the pace (up) and price down… ."

Bay's cutting can grow so chaotic it actually works against the very overwhelming impact he's trying to create. Kent Jones confesses that during the attack scene in *Pearl Harbor*, the editing grew so jumbled he could no longer keep track of which character was on which ship. One of the peak moments during the attack scene comes when a Japanese bomb pierces the magazine of the battleship *Arizona*, touching off an explosion so powerful it lifts the massive dreadnought clear out of the water. Bay cuts through the moment so quickly—it's little more than a flash cut of the ship lifting out of the harbor waters—that the horrible grandeur of the moment is lost in the rushing on to other things. Compare this to the attention the same moment gets in the more traditionally constructed big budget Pearl Harbor recreation of three decades earlier, *Tora! Tora! Tora!* (1970).

Though a particularly dreadful release like *Pearl Harbor* pushed Bay to the post of whipping boy for a generation of visually addicted, speed-freak-paced, action-immersed, dramatically underwhelming directors, there's no refuting his box office track record and Bay points to box office numbers as the strongest indication he is obviously "… tapping into something people want to see."

And moviegoers do want to see Bay's movies. Each of his first four movies released after *Bad Boys* easily crossed the $100 million blockbuster barrier, their average domestic take standing at $168 million with, frequently, even better earnings overseas. *Armageddon* alone pulled in $452.8 million worldwide while Jon Amiel's vaguely similar sci-fier *The Core*, with its Amiel-admitted anti-Bay sensibility, achieved better reviews, but did a worldwide business of only $72.7 million. Bay stumbled the first time he moved out from under the Bruckheimer label with the sci-fier *The Island* (2005) for DreamWorks. The $126 million picture did only $35.8 million domestic (although it compensated somewhat with a $124.5 overseas take), but then he roared back with another sci-fi effects fest, the $150 million *Transformers* (2007, also for DreamWorks), which turned out to be his highest grosser with a worldwide take of $706.5 million. Bay followed with the 2009 sequel *Transformers: Revenge of the Fallen* which, despite poor reviews, did over $836 million worldwide. The cumulative domestic take alone for Bay's eight theatrical features amounts to approximately $1.5 billion.

That in mind, for all the critical carping—and for whatever statement that obvious popularity makes about today's blockbuster audience - Bay is correct when he says the stories he tells and the way he tells them are something "... people want to see."

Bubbas, Chop-Sockies, Splatters and Sleaze—Oh, My!
(posted 1/23/11)

Since the earliest days of American cinema, there has been a shadowy counterpart to the commercial mainstream: exploitation movies—pictures whose appeal lies in their sensational treatment and leering promotion of often lurid and prurient material. Pre-1960s, when mainstream Hollywood worked within severe restrictions on content, exploitation movies offered audiences titillating glimpses of the deliciously taboo, usually under the guise of being some sort of instructional cautionary *against* the very subject matter being exploited, e.g. sex in "hygiene" movies like *The Road to Ruin* (1934), drugs in anti-drug movies like *Tell Your Children* (1936—rereleased in the 1960s/'70s as camp classic *Reefer Madness)*, and gambling in the anti-vice *Gambling with Souls* (1936).

By the 1950s, as the studios entered their long postwar decline, downscale producers launched a new vein of exploitation moviemaking, churning out low-budget thrillers (mostly sci-fi and horror) aimed squarely at the burgeoning youth audience. Again, the movies were cheap, the stories ritualistically formulaic, and the thrills purely visceral and often gimmicky. Writer/producer/director William Castle, for example, one of the most colorful of the 1950s low-budget showmen, tickled youth audiences with such gimmicks as "Emergo" in his feature *The House on Haunted Hill* (1959); a plastic skeleton flying across the theater on a wire over the heads of screaming teens. For his 1959 *The Tingler,* a number of auditorium seats received mild electric shocks every time the eponymous creature appeared on screen.

The heroes of these cheaply ground-out thrillers were often misunderstood youths, an archetype with automatic appeal for their intended teen audience. Young heroes saved the world from alien invaders in *Invasion of the Saucer Men* (1957), from an all-devouring pile of goo in *The Blob* (1958), from an oversized lizard in *The Giant Gila Monster* (1959). There were misunderstood teenaged aliens *(I Married a Monster from Outer Space,* 1958), misunderstood teenaged cavemen *(Teenage Caveman*, 1958), misunderstood teenaged monsters *(I Was a Teenage Werewolf,* 1957), and so on and so forth *ad nauseum.*

With the 1960s, exploitation movies moved into yet another cycle. Most of the major studios were in dire financial straits, and content restrictions, which had been gradually easing for years, almost completely collapsed. Desperate to pull viewers away from their TV sets, the sex in movies became raunchier, the violence bloodier, and once-taboo subjects were now considered legitimate subjects for exploration (and exploitation). Nowhere was the sex raunchier, the violence bloodier, or the subject matter more outré than in exploitation movies.

In the 1960s and 1970s, the exploitation arena boasted its own peculiar array of genres, a canon including "sexploitation," "blaxploitation," "splatter," and "chop-socky" movies. Whatever the genre, they were invariably cheap—often made for just a few thousand dollars—and skated along (and often teetered over) the edge of absurdity and stomach-turning grotesqueness.

*****

In some cases, exploitation genres took their cue from mainstream hits as was the case with blaxploitation movies. The success of upscale, racially charged releases like murder mystery *In the Heat of the Night* and comedy *Guess Who's Coming to Dinner?* (both 1967) alerted Hollywood to a long-underserved black audience starved for entertainment expressly designed for the black audience, preferably by black filmmakers, and which—even if in lightweight or sensational fashion—somehow reflected the black experience. The exploitability of the situation was further confirmed by the success with black audiences of the seriocomic *Watermelon Man* (1970), the uncompromising and angrily defiant *Sweet Sweetback's Baadasssss Song* (1971), and the first black-oriented thriller to come from a major Hollywood studio (MGM), *Shaft* (1971), with a script from *The French Connection* (1971) scribe Ernest Tidyman, and directed by noted black photojournalist Gordon Parks.

Quick to capitalize on this emerging opportunity, Hollywood began sausaging out a steady stream of what were soon dubbed "blaxploitation" movies. While a few of these urban thrillers—e.g. *Across 110th Street* (1972), *Cotton Comes to Harlem* (1970), *Super Fly* (1972)—tried, at least in some measure, to earnestly reflect identifiable aspects of the lives of their intended audience, as a rule, blaxploitation movies were produced on the cheap and looked it, with cartoonish storytelling interrupted at regular intervals by major doses of bloody violence.

The biggest blocs of blaxploitation films were knock-offs of mainstream horror forms tailored for black audiences—*Blacula* (1972), *Blackenstein* (1973), *Dr. Black, Mr. Hyde* (1976), The Exorcist clone *Abby* (1974)—and formulaic, shoot-'em-up crime stories like *Black Caesar* (1973), *Slaughter* (1972), *Hammer* (1972), *Black Mama White Mama* (1972), *Coffy* (1973), *Godon's War* (1973), *Cleopatra Jones* (1973), *Black Godfather* (1974), *The Mack* (1973), *Trouble Man* (1972), *Dolemite* (1975), *Foxy Brown* (1974), *Hell Up in Harlem* (1973), *Truck Turner* (1974), *Three the Hard Way* (1974), *Friday Foster* (1975).

*****

Another low-end 1970s fad kicked off by a breakout hit were rural-set thrillers spinning off from the success of *Billy Jack* (1971). Made for a meager $800,000, this independently produced back-country story of a Vietnam vet espousing peace while karate-chopping his way through bigots and rednecks went on to bring in an eye-popping $35 million, in the process inaugurating a wave of similarly simplistic actioners set in the American south and southwest.

Again, here was a genre boasting a few more-polished studio efforts like *White Lightning* (1973), *Smokey and the Bandit* (1977), and *Convoy* (1977), but more typically movies looking to exploit the so-called "bubba" market—many of which received only regional releases—were low-budget quickies flogging the same few formulas to death: either a "good ol' boy" of a hero looking to mind his own business (or one engaged in light criminality) is impressed, persuaded, or otherwise incented into combating a corrupt establishment *(White Line Fever* [1975], *Vigilante Force* [1976], *The Black Oak Conspiracy* [1977], *A Small Town in Texas* [1976], *Macon County Line* [1974], *Jackson County Jail* [1976], *Dirty Mary, Crazy Larry* [1974], *High Ballin'* [1978], *Smokey Bites the Dust* [1981], *Breaker! Breaker!* [1977], *Thunder and Lightning* [1977]*)*, or the protagonist is involved in impish but more-or-less innocent fun tweaking a repressive, sometimes corrupt law enforcement establishment *(Eat My Dust* [1976], *The Great Smokey Roadblock* [1976]*)*.

The regional grass roots appeal of these "redneck" movies was never better illustrated than with *Walking Tall* (1973). Based on the true story of Tennessee sheriff Buford Pusser, *Walking Tall* was made for a modest $500,000 with minor stars (Joe Don Baker played the lead), a long-time B-list director (Phil Karlson), and released initially with little media support.

Next to the ham-fisted moralizing and Constitutional transgressions of Baker's Sheriff Pusser, Dirty Harry Callhan's frequent legal oversteps pale by comparison: Baker waylays villains with a massive club, tortures confession out of a corrupt deputy with a beating and a threat to blow the man up, and responds to a demand to produce a search warrant with, "I keep it in my shoe!" before kicking in a door. Yet, in one southern city alone, the movie played for twenty-one straight weeks at a downtown theater before continuing for another six weeks at a second venue. Ultimately, *Walking Tall* grossed a commanding $23 million nationwide.

*****

While some exploitation genres keyed off mainstream successes, others belonged almost wholly to the exploitation circuit. There were the stomach-churning gore fests—dubbed "splatter" movies—like *Blood Feast* (1963), *The Driller Killer* (1979), and *Maniac* (1980); and "sexploitation" films like *Faster, Pussycat! Kill! Kill!* (1965), *Caged Heat* (1974), and *Ilsa: She Wolf of the SS* (1975), which combined a lurid, often fetishistic eroticism with overdone violence.

The exploitation circuit also cornered the market on martial arts films during a 1970s explosion in the genre's popularity. While there were occasional upscale American-produced forays into the martial arts scene, like *Enter the Dragon* (1973) and *Circle of Iron* (1979), the American market for "chop-socky" movies was, for the most part, strictly downscale, dominated by foreign imports from two Hong Kong-based companies: The Shaw Brothers, and Golden Harvest.

As a rule, the product from either company was indistinguishable from the other. Their films were all made cheaply, quickly, with the flimsiest of plots, horrendous dubbing, featuring sadistic violence and blood spilled by the bucketful, and were packed with the most outrageous renditions of Asian hand-to-hand combat. Just to name a few: *The Street Fighter* (1974), *Master of the Flying Guillotine* (1975), *Fist of Fear, Touch of Death* (1980), *Fists of Fury* (1980), *Chinese Connection* (1973), *Return of the Dragon* (1973), *The Chinatown Kid* (1978).

*****

Whatever the genre, the key to the exploitation market was cost. Most exploitation movies were so cheaply produced it was nearly impossible for them to lose money despite the limited distribution they usually received. Even returns any major studio would have considered microscopic were enough to keep the exploiters and their exhibitors in business.

The exhibition cornerstone for exploitation movies was the urban "grindhouse." Despite the pornographic ring of the sobriquet, "grindhouse" simply referred to a movie house which screened its attractions from the time the auditorium doors opened until they closed usually in the wee hours of the morning... providing they closed at all. Some grindhouses remained open twenty-four hours a day, 365 days a year.

Typically located in economically disadvantaged urban areas, grindhouses were often once reputable cinemas or one-time live theaters which had deteriorated along with their surrounding neighborhoods. They offered a hodge-podge of less-than-prime film entertainment at low prices. Depending on where a grindhouse was located, patrons were likely to find themselves sitting in close proximity to working prostitutes, college students taking a break from all-night cramming sessions, or junkies and the homeless looking for a cheap night's shelter.

One of the most impressive collections of grindhouses existed in New York City's Time Square area from the 1970s into the 1980s. One block of Manhattan's famed Forty-Second Street between Eighth Avenue and Broadway was lined on both sides with nearly unbroken ranks of twenty-four-hour porn shops, strip joints, "skin flick" theaters and grindhouses. This block of "The Deuce," as locals dubbed Forty-Second Street, was, during an economically troubled time for the city, considered so much the epitome of urban physical and moral decay it was often used as the background for crime thrillers and dramas set among the demimonde e.g. *Shaft* and *Midnight Cowboy* (1969).

Grindhouses benefited from the limited exposure movie releases had in those days before wide national releases became the norm. A grindhouse might not receive a print of a mainstream release for six months or better after the film had first hit theaters, and by that time the print might be pitted and scratched, perhaps even missing footage. Still, with the grindhouse likely the only convenient and affordable cinema in the neighborhood, it offered the one chance for area residents to see that movie—or *any* movie—on the big screen.

Also working for the grindhouse was the limited aftermarket exposure movies had at the time. A major feature during the period might've been in theatrical exhibition anywhere from one to three years, gone through a cooling off period thereafter, then later be sold to one of the then three broadcast networks which would air it once or twice a year for a few years. Lesser features might not make it to network TV at all. After the network TV license expired (or in lieu of it), a title would be "packaged" with other titles from its studio and put into syndication with individual local stations around the country licensing the package for from five-twenty years. Since these packages were sold on a market-by-market basis, some markets—particularly smaller ones with few local stations, none of which might have much money to spend for movie programming—might never see any number of syndicated titles.

This preserved the value of older studio product for the grindhouse and its patrons. To give an example of how this might work for an exhibitor, one Forty-Second Street house capitalized on the 1973 release of *Battle for the Planet of the Apes*—the last entry in the original film series—by bringing back the previous four films, some of which hadn't been seen in years, offering patrons the opportunity to, as the marquee read, "Spend the day on the Planet of the Apes."

In fact, it was not unusual for grindhouses to pad their bills by supporting a new release with an older (and therefore cheaper to acquire) actioner. For example, another Forty-Second Street grindhouse backed up its plays of new release *Ben*—the 1972 sequel to 1971's horror hit, *Willard*—by bringing back 1969's special effects spectacle *Krakatoa, East of Java*. So that the 131-minute *Krakatoa* wouldn't be a drag on the program when coupled with the 94-minute *Ben*, the management trimmed down the dramatic sections of *Krakatoa* shortening its running time and emphasizing the action elements for its thrill-hungry audience. That this also made the movie occasionally incomprehensible was of little consequence to the management, or, for that matter, the grindhouse customers.

Because they were usually the last stop in the life of a mainstream release—or were sometimes skipped entirely by the major distributors—urban grindhouses were consistently hungry for product. Consequently, the bread-and-butter for most houses were exploitation films. Where there was more than one grindhouse in an area, it was not unusual for different theaters to specialize, some offering only tired prints of mainstream releases, while another might exclusively present chop-socky films, another only blood-soaked splatter titles, another solely blaxploitation pictures, and yet another specialize in cannibal films and "shockumentaries" about grotesque cultural practices around the world. Exploitation titles changed weekly, with distributors "bicycling" their small number of prints from one market to the next, booking them into individual theaters.

With the 1980s, the network of circumstances supporting the grindhouse—and its rural counterpart, the drive-in—began to disintegrate. Rising real estate values induced some owners to sell out, while other theaters folded unable to meet rising rents and property taxes with their bargain basement offerings. Still others fell victim to urban renewal programs targeting blighted neighborhoods for razing and redevelopment. Such was the fate of the Manhattan groundhouses along The Deuce as the Times Square area was transformed through the late 1980s and 1990s from a nationally recognized bit of urban infamy into a glittering and family-friendly tourist Mecca.

Changes in film distribution dealt the grindhouse circuit another body blow. The limited release patterns which had maintained the theatrical value of a title months after its debut gave way to national saturation releases, while the blossoming cable and home video markets kept older titles constantly exposed and easily available to the viewing public. Individual neighborhood movie houses were replaced by suburban shopping mall multiplexes; venues where, at prices far above grindhouse rates, chop-socky flicks and other shabbily produced exploitation movies couldn't compete in head-to-head competition against major studio gloss and heavily hyped blockbusters. By the 1990s, the grindhouses were gone.

 The extreme nature of grindhouse movies in the 1960s/1970s was, in its left-handed way, a mark of the same changes in the domestic movie business which had produced the best-remembered films of the day. Old strictures were crumbling, and the same creative freedom producing an incredible body of high-quality and daring mainstream cinema was also responsible for the exploitation boom. Though most exploitation moviemakers may have been purely mercenary in their aims, some exploitation film fans saw in their work a blatant rejection of Hollywood homogeneity; they were movies whose very outrageousness and contrariness to acceptable norms was their attraction.

In contrast, in this age of the multiplex, wide releasing, and the blockbuster, outrage seems to have been outlawed, and the homogeneity against which the exploitation movie and its fans rebelled now reigns, not by banning the extremes of the grindhouse shockers, but by co-opting them.

Any episode of cable programmer AMC's *Walking Dead* series now offers as much gore and dismemberment as the old splatter flicks of the 1960s, and mainstream releases like the *Scream* movies, *Watchmen* (2009), *Hannibal* (2001), et al go much further. *The Green Hornet* (2010) features martial arts derring-do every bit as outrageous (if not more so) than the absurdities of vintage chop-sockies. The abnormal, the freakish, the taboo, as well as the absurd, the improbable, and the over-the-top, have become de rigueur.

It was perhaps this absorption into the mainstream which undercut *Grindhouse* (2007), a cinematic salute by writers/directors Quentin Tarantino and Robert Rodriguez to the seedy theaters and delightfully awful movies which had occupied so many hours of their respective youths. Tarantino and Rodriguez sought to recreate the grindhouse double bills of old, though in more polished fashion, with a tongue-in-cheek double bill of their own: faux grindhouse horror flick *Death Proof* (Tarantino's contribution), and faux grindhouse sci-fier *Planet Terror* (from Rodriguez), along with coming attractions for equally over-the-top fare produced by several guest writer/directors like Eli Roth and Rob Zombie.

But *Grindhouse* may have worked better as a demonstration of why the exploitation movie had died out rather than as a campy tribute. Despite a major promotional push by production company Dimension Films (the horror arm of The Weinstein Company), and predominantly supportive (and equally nostalgic) reviews, the movie's earnings capped out early at just $25 million—a particular disappointment in light of the picture's $53 million cost.

Perhaps today's youth-dominated audience—too young to remember the originals *Grindhouse* was referencing, too cinematically illiterate to appreciate the *homage*, and to inured to the kind of outrageousness which had once been, well, outrageous—didn't get the joke.

Right-Hand Man: Mike Elliott
(posted 9/22/10)

Throughout history, standing to the right of every great king one usually finds a great prime minister turning the king's vision from abstract ambition into fact. During critical years for Roger Corman's Concorde studio, the man at Corman's elbow was Mike Elliott.

Look up Mike Elliott on the Internet Movie Database (www.IMDb.com) and you'll see over 100 credits attributed to him as a producer… and, as extensive as it is, that list may not be complete. Elliott admits he was attached to so many movies he can't remember them all. "Occasionally people come up to me and mention a movie they say I worked on and I go, 'I did?'"

But that's a natural product of having been production chief at a company that was a veritable movie-making factory during the height of the Direct-To-Video (DTV) boom: Concorde New Horizons, which had been launched in 1983 by the legendary "King of the Bs," Roger Corman. Considering the weight of Elliott's filmography, it's a curiosity that his desire to get into the motion picture business was based simply on the idea of not wanting to wear a jacket and tie to work.

Elliott was born in Ventura, California, but grew up outside the town of Bend, Oregon, on a cattle ranch. When his thoughts focused on his future, he had something more cosmopolitan in mind than being a cowherd and wound up on the other side of the country at Cornell University majoring in Soviet Studies. "International politics, that's what I was into then."

Along about his junior or senior year, Elliott began to think about his post-graduation professional direction. "Everybody I knew (at Cornell) was either going to be a management consultant or an investment banker. My only experience with banking was with the teller at my bank, and I could never understand why anybody would hire people with no experience to be a consultant in *anything*."

Still, it seemed as if those were the areas where the jobs were, so Elliott "bought myself a crappy suit" for interviews and headed down to New York City and Manhattan's financial district. But, once on the scene, "I realized in a half-second I didn't want to be there."

Then, fatefully, Elliott remembered somebody telling him no one had to wear a suit, crappy or otherwise, in the movie business.

Elliott crossed the country again, to Los Angeles this time. Knowing nothing about the motion picture industry, he pulled out a phone book, looked up addresses of TV and movie companies and began knocking on doors. Ironically, despite the motive of wanting to work in a business not requiring a jacket and tie, Elliott decided to play things safe on his first interview and wore his crappy suit. "They laughed at me."

Eventually, he landed an internship at a TV production company, and then another and another until he was juggling five internships at once, doing Mondays at one site, Tuesdays at another, and so on, filling out the week. It would turn out to be an effective education as, after a time, Elliott could walk onto any set and say, "I get it," being able to instantly understand what was going on, who was doing what, how it was being done, and why.

He also landed a slot in CBS's "management" program. "It sounds lofty," says Elliott, "but it wasn't." He was handed a red jacket and assigned such duties as answering phones, running errands, taking out the trash... he was a network page.

His supervisor was a woman of certain years who was the head of pages. "I think she'd been a page, like, in the '20s." She would, Elliott reflects, represent the only time in his twenty-odd years in entertainment "... where someone had it in for me." Elliott had an assignment on the daytime soap opera, *Capitol*. His job was to stand at one end of the sound stage and watch a red light. If the light went on, it meant someone was trying to call in on the silent stage phone. When that happened, it was Elliott's job to pick up the phone and whisper, "We're rolling." To this day, Elliott still wonders over the fact that "I don't remember that light ever going on when we *weren't* rolling!"

Elliott had been placed in a position where he could only see the light by awkwardly craning his neck, and also which inhibited his view of the production. He found a position about thirty feet away which allowed him to watch the taping while still being able to see the warning light. His supervisor was furious: "What're you doing over *there?*"

Back in the original position, Elliott whiled away the time reading, able to still mind the telephone warning light through a small, strategically placed mirror. Upon seeing his new set-up, the supervisor did not compliment Elliott on his ingenuity or through finding a more productive use of his time standing in the wings. She kicked the mirror across the floor: *"No mirrors!"* She had, Elliott surmises, done the job a certain way herself, and that, apparently, was the way she determined it was always going to be done.

Elliott had another position on the game show *The Price Is Right*. It was his job to help the audience file in and find seats. He had a chance to see how the producers, standing near the auditorium entrance, decided on who among the audience would be chosen to go on stage. As the audience filed by, every so often Elliott would hear one of the producers say, "That's interesting." Later, he would notice everyone selected to play the game had been tagged with a "That's interesting."

During one taping, two Canadian women asked Elliott if it would be possible to meet game host Bob Barker; they had some sweatshirts they wanted to give him. Elliott explained the show policy: *if* Mr. Barker chose to come out into the audience after the taping, they could raise their hands to try to get his attention, and *if* Mr. Barker chose to do so, he'd come over and they could give him any gifts or make a request for autographs, etc.

As it happened, this was an occasion when Barker decided *not* to come out after the taping. Elliott describes what happened then as if it was a movie:

"I look over and SNAP ZOOM in on the two Canadian ladies talking to my boss. SNAP ZOOM on my boss as she looks over at me." She was, as usual, angry, stormed over to Elliott and demanded to know why he'd promised the women they could be on the show. As Elliott described his exchange with the women, his boss seemed of little mind to hear he'd said no such thing.

Beginning to sense his days in CBS's management program might be numbered, that night he leafed through one of the local papers and found a small notice that Roger Corman's Concorde New Horizons was looking for interns. Elliott called to set up an appointment to speak with Corman.

"Oh, you don't speak with Roger Corman," it was explained to him. There was another individual charged with interviewing the intern candidates. But when Elliott showed up for his interview saying he was there to see Mr. Corman, the other person wasn't there and he was ushered directly in to see Concorde's top man.

This was, as Elliott would later find, not an anomaly. "Roger was always very approachable," he says. Corman was not an isolated or aloof company chieftain. The Concorde head—at least in those early years of Elliott's tenure with the company—"read every draft of every script, saw every cut of every movie, watched every trailer, looked at all the marketing materials, went onto the sets…"

Corman looked over Elliott's resumé. "I see you went to Cornell." Elliott would come to learn Corman was a fan of Ivy Leaguers. Elliott made his pitch offering to work six months for Concorde without pay. If Corman was satisfied with his performance at the end of that period, he'd hire Elliott. With an eye always fixed on the bottom line, "That was an offer Roger couldn't refuse."

As might be expected, Elliott's first jobs were fairly menial. One of his duties was as projectionist. The company had one projector which Elliott guesses was from the 1930s or so. Only one other person in the company knew how to run it. Not only did no one else know how to work the machine, but no one else *wanted* to know because every time the projector broke down—which happened on a regular basis—a director and producer would soon be in the projection booth berating the projectionist for ruining their screening for Corman.

There was a fairly high and regular turnover at Concorde and this provided an opportunity for Elliott to expand his responsibilities. There was a runner making $190 a week who quit, and Elliott took on his job. It turned out to be grueling in unexpected ways. "I had to pick up Roger's kids at 6:30, take them to school, then make runs for the company…." All this and still handle screenings with the cantankerous vintage projector.

At that time—c. 1987—Concorde was putting out about seven-eight theatrical releases per year. Elliott found his hodge-podge of menial chores back-breaking, the pace non-stop. "It was a crazy place," he says but with a sense of warm nostalgia. "But I have to say it was fun -probably the most fun I've ever had." Undoubtedly part of the fun—and the craziness—came from Corman's willingness to take flyers on untried people.

Corman regularly acquired foreign theatricals for U.S. release under the Concorde banner, but the films needed to be tailored for the American market. Corman asked Elliott to trim the movies for length as well as insert stock footage of nudity and action. Some of the movies, in fact, were from some of Europe's more prestigious filmmakers.

"I'm just an intern!" Elliott protested, but that seemed to matter little to Corman. "It's funny," Elliott says, "but after a while I'd be cutting these movies from some pretty big names and be thinking, 'Ya know, it *could* use a little action here!'"

Elliott's first major opportunity to move up at Concorde came when the company's marketing and advertising chief quit. Elliott went to see Corman: "You know, marketing is what I'm *really* interested in."

"What do you know about marketing?" Corman asked. "Was that your major?"

"No. Soviet Studies."

Nevertheless, Corman gave Elliott the job of coming up with a marketing campaign overnight for an upcoming Concorde film then titled *Charlie Guitar*.

Elliott stayed up all night composing an "awful collage" that was supposed to represent the marketing campaign. He changed the title, and came up with the key image of a pretty young woman holding up a pair of beach balls over her breasts. The next day, Elliott trooped into Corman's office with his awful collage. Corman looked at the woman and her beach balls. "What's the line?" he asked, meaning the promotional tag line.

"'At Big Top Beach, everybody finds a treasure chest!'"

Corman turned to him and announced, "You're hired."

Elliott was now the head of marketing and advertising for Concorde New Horizons. He'd only been out of school nine months. And, he was still one of Concorde's house projectionists.

Elliott doesn't remember the title of the first movie whose campaign he handled as head of marketing—"Something-*Dead,*" is all he can recall. Corman introduced him to the director and producer as his marketing "expert." Despite his success with the *Big Top Beach* line, Elliott felt like anything *but* an expert, and, as he presented his ideas, the director and producer worriedly asked, "Are you *sure* this will work?"

Working on the marketing materials, Elliott spilled White-Out on the key art, then tried to draw through it with a marker. "This poor guy (in the picture) looked like he was wearing goggles." When Elliott turned in the materials, he got questioning looks about the goggle-eyed artwork. "It doesn't matter!" Elliott told his people, "We've got to send it in! There's no more time!" Looking back on it today, Elliott laughs. "I didn't know *what* I was doing!"

But he learned as he went and, ultimately, did some fifty to sixty marketing campaigns.

And then, in typical Concorde fashion, the company's regular turnover presented Elliott with yet another opportunity to advance in the ranks when the head of production quit. Again, Elliott went into Corman's office: "You know, production is what I'm *really* interested in."

"We need you in marketing," Corman told him.

"I'll still do marketing," Elliott said, again making Corman an unrefusable offer.

Corman said he would think about it. The next day, he walked up to Elliott, a grave look on his face. "We hired somebody from Oxford." A beat, then a smile: "Just kidding." And then Corman gave Elliott his mandate: "I want you to double production, and halve the cost."

As it happened, Elliott had come into Concorde at a time when the company was transitioning from a struggling theatrical company to one wholly dedicated to home video and television. By the time Elliott left Concorde eight years later, the company's seven-eight theatrical releases per year had expanded to an annual slate of thirty-eight video features.

The pace at Concorde—which had always been hectic—only became more so. Elliott had three line producers working for him, and the company might be shooting five films at any given time. There was always a Concorde film shooting somewhere in Los Angeles twenty-four hours each day as well as projects being prepped and others in post-production. One crew might be working on a set from 6:00 a.m. to 6:00 p.m., and no sooner had they left when a second crew would take their place. Elliott describes the process as "Churn and burn. Was that the best way to make movies? No. Was that the best way to make a *lot* of movies? Maybe."

Elliott would bounce from set to set to keep an eye on how things were going, but with so many projects in progress at any given time, "I couldn't focus on any one flick." At the same time, he was running up an enormous amount of frequent flyer mileage as he visited Concorde shoots overseas. "We had stuff shooting in Peru, Chile, The Philippines, not so much in Canada..."

There were so many movies being pounded out in those years that when asked if he remembers any of them as being particularly good—or even particularly bad—Elliott seems aware of how difficult a concept he's trying to communicate when he says, "You don't think of them that way. You don't think of 'good' or 'bad.'

"If you see one, you remember, 'Oh, yeah, I remember how we did that,' or 'I can't believe that one cost so little!' Or you don't remember some of them at *all!* Some *were* awful!"

After a bit more reflection:

"There's three things I'd say about it, that you come away with:

"One: working that fast, it's easier to live with something that sucks because you *have* to move on. You can't mope; there's no time.

"Two: the special generosity of Roger Corman. He opened his checkbook to people like me. Granted, he didn't pay much but he let you learn, you earned your stripes on his dime, he let you make mistakes.*

"Three: it teaches you to make quick decisions."

(*At the time Elliott left Concorde, he was head of production for the company overseeing thirty-eight titles a year. His annual salary was $38,000.)

And, as for a movie that, in some fleeting breathing space during production, might strike him as worse or better than usual:

"There were two kinds of pain:

"There was the pain of, 'Wow, we should never have done this one.'

"And there was the other pain of, 'This is special,' but it's going into the same grinder with everything else." There was simply no time for special attention and handling.

A two-tiered production system was created which accomplished Corman's goals of ramping up output, keeping costs low, and which also played to one of the company chief's pet pleasures: "Roger liked to discover new filmmakers."

In the 1960s/1970s, Corman's productions regularly served as a proving ground for new talents who would go on to rank among the most popular and/or acclaimed directors (as well as actors and writers) in the mainstream movie business such as Francis Coppola (whose Corman credits include *Dementia 13*, 1963), Ron Howard *(Grand Theft Auto*, 1977), Jonathan Demme *(Caged Heat*, 1974), and Martin Scorsese *(Boxcar Bertha*, 1972). By the 1980s, however, the B-movie circuit was no longer the point of entry into the movie mainstream it had been. As cable TV entrenched and expanded in the 1980s, it brought with it a field of low-budget production from which, more often, the next generation of mainstream moviemakers arose. "They came out of music videos, commercials—cheap TV."

So, Concorde began to look to its own. The company would set up an A-picture—"Maybe for around $800,000"—then piggyback a B onto the same production, sometimes for budgets as low as $150,000. The B would shoot on the same sets with the same crew as the A. The director might be one of Concorde's young Director of Photography's whom the company felt showed directorial promise. "We'd pay the (A) crew $100 or something to work (the B)." Since all involved knew each other, "The whole crew wanted to help the guy." As a grooming and discovery process, the A/B process worked quite well. "That low cost allowed us to move up some great DPs," says Elliot. "Some of the best DPs working in movies today worked for us."

Still, even $800,000 isn't a lot of money to make a movie, not even back in the 1980s, but Concorde was able to get more than twice as much for its buck as much bigger movie companies.

"What another company could do for $2 million we could do for $800,000," says Elliott. "They were paying out for finance fees, for their insurance bond, equipment rentals, sound stages. We didn't have any of that. When we made a movie, it was *our* cash. We didn't have to pay fees to a bank. We *owned* the cameras, we *owned* the editing suites." As Elliott describes it, Concorde was, in a small-scale way, a throwback to the self-contained, cost-efficient movie studios of Hollywood's mogul age.

In those first years of Concorde's morphing into more of a DTV and TV outfit, nobody at the company—or any place else for that matter—quite understood the new dynamics of the developing DTV market. For one title, Concorde tried the stunt of releasing the picture in a single theater in Orlando while Blockbuster was having its annual convention there, hoping the movie would catch the eye of the video chain.

In the late 1980s, there was still a widely held belief that a theatrical release was a must to prime a title for the home video business. At the time, Concorde's movies received limited releases (compared to films from the major studios), with fifty prints bicycled around 500 screens for a period of ten weeks "... or until we couldn't book it anymore." The company began reducing the scope of its releases, trimming them to ten prints bicycling around fifty screens for five weeks. As the margins on theatrical releases shrank, they were making less financial sense to do, but, more importantly, Concorde was seeing there was no evidence a theatrical release was helping its product in ancillary markets.

"It got to a point where we shrugged our shoulders and slowly realized theatrical was about prestige more than it was a sales factor," says Elliott. "The box and the cast became more important."

While eliminating theatrical release didn't impact Concorde's video business, something *was* lost. "You know, if you go through the company's files you find a lot of interesting stuff," says Elliott with what almost sounds like a sense of wonder. "You can find a check to Francis Coppola for $23. When you look around in there you find out that Roger's movies opened at Number One! *X: The Man with the X-Ray Eyes* (1963), the (Edgar Allan) Poe movies, *Death Race 2000* (1975). In the video world, that doesn't happen."

One of the new business wrinkles Elliott brought to Concorde was multi-picture output deals for overseas markets. Elliott—taking on a new job yet again—became the company's international sales person, negotiating sales of Concorde titles in five, ten, fifteen, even twenty-title batches to overseas buyers who would strip off Corman's brand and distribute them under their own names in their domestic markets.

During his last years at Concorde, Elliott was actually Corman's financial partner in projects. Corman himself—"Maybe it was because he was getting older, or because we were doing so many pictures, maybe both"—had become less hands-on, relying on the system in place at Concorde to keep doing what it'd been doing. According to Elliott, "He became more of an elder statesman" in the company, presiding rather than directly managing day-to-day operations. He no longer read every script. Elliott would present Corman with a piece of paper with ten sentences or so describing the movie he wanted to put in the pipeline. Corman might cross out a sentence or two, and when he was done reading he'd either make a "+" or "-" at the top of the paper, or simply X out the whole page. The "+" meant "yes," the "-" meant he didn't like it, but if Elliott wanted to make it, he could go ahead, and the cross-out was—obviously—a "no."

In 1995, Elliott decided to buy the company from Corman. He put up what money he had, put some partners together, and went looking on Wall Street to finance the purchase. Curiously, none of the banks typically involved in media and entertainment were interested. Instead, Elliott found financing among mercantile banks specializing in manufacturing which somehow seemed fitting considering Concorde's production line type of moviemaking.

On the eve of concluding the deal, Corman raised the purchase price. Elliott managed to raise the additional money, but then Corman hiked the price again, and, at that point, the deal collapsed. Elliott and his associates left the company and formed Capital Arts.

Although it had been a frustrating and aggravating process, Elliott still tips his hat to Corman. The Concorde boss wrote a "really nice release" announcing the departure of Elliott and Co., and the launching of Capital Arts, and even offered them their first film project.

Still, this was not a good time. Elliott was, for the moment, bitter, frustrated, and maybe most importantly, broke and in debt, having spent all his money (and more) trying to set up the buy. Yet, when another company which had done work with Concorde approached Elliott about helping them with a suit against Corman over what they felt were financial "irregularities," Elliott refused. "Roger is being straight with you," he told them flatly. Then the company changed course and asked if Elliott and Capital Arts would make movies for them.

Initially, Capital Arts was making the sort of low-budget films Elliott had made at Concorde, but with one exception. A certain amount of gratuitous nudity had long been a Corman staple as far back as his 1970s theatrical releases. "Back when nobody was showing boobs, that was Roger's bread and butter," explains Elliott, and it remained a prerequisite element as the company moved into home video. Elliott and his associates were of like mind; it had been an aspect of Concorde product they hadn't been particularly proud of, and decided Capitol Arts would take a different tack.

In time, the company found solid footing, the work became steadier, the projects coming the company's way more upscale, made for bigger budgets, done for bigger companies. Capital Arts moved into TV movies, family films, and direct-to-video sequels which were becoming the mainstay of low-budget studios.

"I claim I made the first DTV sequel (with *Casper: A Spirited Beginning* [1997])," laughs Elliott, meaning a home video sequel to a theatrical hit. "Stephen Einhorn'll tell you *he* did with *Poison Ivy 2* (1996), but I'm pretty sure they thought they were making a theatrical while they were doing it. I suspect Stephen thought it was a theatrical, too."

Reflecting on how the business has changed in his twenty-odd years in it, one senses a certain unease... and wistfulness in Elliott. At the same time, his own experience gives him a level of empathy—and even sympathy—with today's movie industry executives.

"In the end, a studio executive is somebody who's guessing," says Elliott. "Enough bad guesses and you lose your job." Elliott believes any good movie, in time, can be recognized. He points to *The Princess Bride* (1987) and *Office Space* (1999) as movies that did poorly in theatrical release, but whose acclaim and fan base grew over the years. But that kind of long-term appreciation doesn't solve the immediate tactical problems of putting out small, singular movies in today's blockbuster-dominated environment.

There is never enough time to give the care and attention to those projects requiring a certain amount of special care and attention. "Go to a studio marketing guy," says Elliott resignedly, "Glance at his desk. How can he concentrate on one movie? He's got ten titles sitting there. There's a movie coming out every Friday. Look at Lionsgate, they've got a horror movie coming out every week either in theaters or on video. You go into these meetings to talk about what's coming, everybody nods, says yes, and that's the last you hear about some of these titles." He sighs. "They don't say, 'Mike's little $7 million movie needs to be worked on.' It's, 'Bruckheimer's $200 million movie needs it.'"

He considers a moment, then, "Certainly, it's a sad and weird change that a movie has to play in one week (meaning score a good opening week). Is that an audience-driven thing? Executive-driven?"

As a producer and filmmaker there are always two impulses at war, he says:

"One: give them what they want, or Two: give them what they need."

It had always been Corman's mantra at Concorde that, "The only person we work for is the audience." But along with the business, the audience has changed as well. Another sigh: "I can't tell if it's my age and I fight my urge to disdain... or has there been a change. The audience has certainly become less interested in drama and more in spectacle. They're younger, less sensitive to obscene violence. Maybe that's just a natural progression of humankind... and marketing."

On Corman's Front Line: Travis Rink
(posted 9/22/10)

If Roger Corman was the commander-in-chief, and Mike Elliott his field marshal, than Travis Rink was among the front line troops who actually had to carry the fight.

Writing several scripts for Concorde in the early 1990s, Rink had a close-up look at the factory-like process that made Concorde's prodigious output possible.

Rink had made a number of short films and written small comic pieces as a teen back in Poughkeepsie, New York, and headed to Los Angeles in the late 1980s intending to go to film school with the idea of becoming a director. Rink was not in L.A. long before he became diverted. "That was Hollywood at the absolute height of the coke craziness," he says. Rink became involved in the motel business, wound up with his own place on Sunset Boulevard. He was making good money and got caught up in the coke-fueled party-and-club scene, which didn't leave him much time for film studies.

In time, he reined himself in and began to focus on why he'd come out to L.A. in the first place. An acquaintance who had done some television work made a suggestion: "You know, you've written in the past. A good way to get into Hollywood is to write a script." Rink picked up a copy of Syd Field's book *(Screenplay: The Foundations of Screenwriting)* and began taking film classes here and there, including classes at the American Film Institute.

"I started putting together some scripts. Probably the first three were complete *crap!* I don't even have copies anymore."

But, the more he wrote, the more his writing improved.

He began turning out short stories, little hard-boiled mysteries and thrillers, some horror pieces, and was able to regularly place them in men's magazines. "I found," he explains, "that men's magazines paid the best compared to magazines like *Alfred Hitchcock Presents* and *Twilight Zone*. I wrote the same kind of stories—I just tossed in two sex scenes." The men's mags were buying Rink's stories for $500 apiece, and he was managing to place one a month.

But, in time, the market changed. Whatever obligation skin publications had once felt to offer something worth reading along with their T & A was dissipating and his story sales were tapering off.

Rink knew a woman hired as an assistant to a producer who'd optioned a Western novel. "This wasn't a Louis L'Amour," Rink says dryly. "This was more of a Grade D, loosely based on historical fact, set in Denver in the mid- or late 1800s." The novel's author had insisted on writing the screenplay himself although he had no screenwriting experience. The producer had tried circulating the author's script around town without any luck. Rink's friend talked him up to the producer who finally decided to give Rink a shot at rewriting the script. "I did a complete overhaul," he says. "I turned it from a straightforward Western into something like a gangster film, kind of like (the HBO series) *Deadwood*."

When the producer began sending out Rink's version of the story, the project finally began to get some traction. "We got a lot of response," says Rink. "There were a lot of meetings." Unfortunately, the producer's option on the book was running out, and the very interest the material was getting—thanks to Rink's script—began to work against them: "Now the author thought he had this hot property because of all the response. He wanted more money to renew the option." The producer couldn't raise the money and the project died.

Still, it had been a paying project for Rink, had earned him membership in the Writer's Guild, and landed him with a good agency, Paul Kohner, Inc. Rink set about writing an original screenplay and came up with the mystery thriller *Cold Comfort*. His agency began circulating the script, the responses were good, but potential buyers choked on Rink's killing off his protagonist three-quarters of the way through the story. "They had a problem with that," he says, and the Kohner agency couldn't make a sale.

Still, the agency's efforts on *Cold Comfort* had gotten Rink's name out among a widening circle of contacts, and the quality of his writing gave those contacts reason to remember him. Rink put aside *Cold Comfort* and focused on a new piece of material inspired by a walk through a cemetery and a magazine story he'd saved about a police corruption trial in Italy. He came up with a tight little neo-*noir* he titled, *Caroline at Midnight*.

A producer took a six-month option on the material and introduced Rink to Scott McGinnis, a TV and film actor looking to move into directing. The producer tried to get the project off the ground but the option expired without *Caroline* having found a home. The producer dropped out, but Rink and McGinnis stayed in touch. In the hopes of making the screenplay a more attractive prospect to potential buyers, McGinnis showed it around his circle of acting acquaintances and was able to attach some talent to the property including one-time Brat Packer Judd Nelson, Clayton Rohner (who would play the male lead), and Mia Sara (playing the female lead).

As it happened, McGinnis had contacts over at Concorde New Horizons and sent the script over. Although Rink didn't object, privately he wasn't completely comfortable with the idea of Concorde as a home for the project. He'd heard stories about new talent being taken unfair advantage of, and of financial shenanigans.

It was early 1994 when Concorde production chief Mike Elliott saw the script. He was interested, but there was a hitch: Concorde only wanted to put up half the budget. However, if McGinnis and Rink took too long to get another party to step up with the other half, they risked losing their attached actors. "The actors were only available for a short window," explains Rink, "so it was now or never."

Rink called Lance Robbins at Saban Entertainment. The scripts for both *Cold Comfort* and *Caroline at Midnight* had been in front of Robbins and he'd liked Rink's work. Rink told him Concorde was interested but was looking for a partner. If Saban came in for half the money, Saban could have the international rights while Concorde retained domestic rights. "I'll put in up to $1 million," was Robbins response. Rink put Robbins and Elliott in touch and by the end of the day a deal was in place to shoot *Caroline* for $800,000 (Rink estimates that because Concorde owned all its own equipment instead of having to rent it as did many other production companies, the $800,000 budget was actually buying $1 million worth of production value).

Those were the days when Elliott was submitting one-pagers of prospective projects to Corman. Corman okayed the *Caroline* synopsis, but the material would require some changes.

Rink, Elliott and McGinnis met in Elliott's office one afternoon. Despite the whirlwind pace at Concorde, Rink found Elliott – as he would always find Elliott—"cool, calm, collected."

"These are the changes we need," Elliott told him.

"There were two kinds of changes," says Rink. "Most of them were for budgetary reasons, and I had to add in 'The Corman Style'... which meant one car chase."

There was one other mandate for the rewrite. Again, for cost reasons, Rink had to eliminate as many of the more-costly-to-shoot exterior settings as possible.

With that, Elliott reached into his desk and held up a check. "We want to do this movie," he told Rink and McGinnis. "I am prepared to pay—" and he gave Rink a number. "This check is for 80% of it. You'll get the rest when the rewrite is done." They sealed the deal then and there and Elliott handed over the check. "What do we need to get started?" Elliott asked.

"I can be ready to start in one hour," Rink told him, then took the check to his bank, made sure it was good, deposited it, and headed back to the office.

There'd been no bankers, no lawyers, no agents involved. The deal had been sealed with a handshake. Despite Rink's early trepidation about becoming involved with Concorde, he would find his dealings with them candid and forthright. "Mike Elliott was a straight shooter," Rink remembers, never promising what he couldn't deliver, always delivering what he'd promised, and all of Rink's dealings with Concorde followed suit. In retrospect, Rink thinks of his work with Concorde as, "Kind of an ideal. I'd been skeptical because of all the things I'd heard about how (Corman) ran his business. However, I have *never* dealt with nicer people. All I can attribute it to is they loved what they were doing."

After depositing his check, Rink returned to the Concorde offices. "It was 6:30 (in the evening)," Rink remembers. "I had a portable word processor with the script on it. They asked me what I needed. I said, 'I need Chinese food, a six-pack of beer, two packs of cigarettes.' Elliott and McGinnis went out and got the supplies. I wrote from about seven that night to five the next morning. And that was it. Except for some minor things Saban needed—maybe an hour's worth of work – not another change was made to the script."

With a finished screenplay in hand, the Concorde gears began to whir. The company's in-house casting director immediately began sending out casting bulletins. Within two-three days, the rest of the cast filled in, among them Tim Daly who was then starring in the popular TV sitcom, *Wings*. The script also provided a number of small but attractive roles that would require only a few days work. As Concorde and McGinnis continued to pass the script around town, *Caroline at Midnight* began gathering buzz as a "cool little project" and those juicy supporting parts quickly filled in with a still up-and-coming Virginia Madsen, Paul (*American Graffiti*, 1973) LeMat, Zach (*Gremlins*, 1984) Galligan, Tom (*Back to the Future*, 1985) Wilson, Xander (*A Few Good Men*, 1992) Berkeley. So many actors were calling to get on the film, says Rink, that, "It got to the point people were calling and we had nothing left to give them."

Just three weeks after Rink and Elliott had shaken hands on *Caroline* in Elliott's office, the film was in production. The company shot the movie's few exteriors first. Rink was invited to come down and see them shoot the first scene, a night scene in a parking garage between Tim Daly and Xander Berkeley. It was, as Rink remembers it, an unforgettable feeling: "As I pulled up, I saw all these trucks, these generators, all these people. I thought, 'Wow, this is because of *me!*'"

Out of a trailer popped Mike Elliott and his assistant. Elliott had his assistant take Rink up to the garage level where the crew was filming. She introduced him around and then Rink watched them shoot the same scene from various angles for about two hours. Rink remembered why he'd come to L.A. several years earlier, and had an epiphany. He looked around at the dozens of people, the equipment, the juggled logistics, the grind of filming. "I decided then and there I'd *never* want to direct in my life. It was about eleven at night: I was bored, I was cold, and I wanted to go home."

After the exterior shooting was completed, production moved to Concorde's "studio"—a converted warehouse in an industrial part of Venice. Another production had been shooting on *Caroline*'s soundstage the day before—Sunday. A crew had worked all night striking the old sets and building the sets for *Caroline*. The sets were ready by the time the *Caroline* crew began shooting on Monday morning.

For some reason, Rink would always remember the "Costume Department." "It appeared to me to consist of clothes people had left there and forgotten to take with them. There were virtually *no* costumes! All the actors wore their own clothes." Every few days over the course of the twenty-one-day shoot, Rink would stop by to see how filming was progressing, and usually ran into one of the actors heading into the studio for his or her scenes carrying a bag of their own clothes.

Although McGinnis always invited Rink to stay, the tedium of shooting was too much for him and he never hung around, but he did begin to spend more time at the studio when *Caroline* went into its fourteen-day editing stage.

Concorde's editing facility was in one of the outbuildings around the warehouse studio. The editing rooms were rooms in name only: "It basically appeared to me to be one big room divided by drapes (into individual editing suites). You could always hear dialogue and car crashes from the next bay over. Each 'room' was about the size of a bathroom. Two people could fit in one room kind of comfortably, and that was usually the director and editor. You could add a third, but then you had to drag in a chair from another room and sit behind them. One time (on *Caroline*), they squeezed *four* of us in there. We were literally knee-to-knee."

There was one "assistant editor" to serve all the various editors at work. Rink remembers her constantly running from one editor to the next grabbing new reels as the editors called for them.

There was a small screening room of maybe ten seats at the studio. Directors could view their dailies there, then, if necessary, take a short walk across the lot to the editing building to make changes (there was also a larger projection room at Concorde's offices which, according to Rink, had "... forty chairs, but only twenty seats. They were regular movie theater seats but only twenty of them had cushions").

Editing completed, a few prints were struck and it wasn't much later before Concorde was cranking out VHS copies. Rink estimates that, from the time he finished his early morning rewrite to the time the VHS was appearing in stores, was a span of "probably three months."

What made such speed possible, Rink says, was passion. "It was because Corman owned his own stuff, but he also had a lot of talented, young people there who *loved* movies; they were definitely not there for the money! Go there morning, noon, and night, and they'd be there."

Caroline at Midnight did good overseas business for Saban (which would go on to continue doing co-productions with Concorde including a series of made-for-cable movies under the umbrella title, *Roger Corman Presents)* and for Corman's company in the U.S., even nabbing a pay-TV sale. This was all no doubt why several months later—around the end of November or beginning of December of that year—Rink received a call from Mike Elliott. "We have a hole in the December schedule," Elliott told him. Lance Robbins at Saban had sent over *Cold Comfort* (which Rink had rewritten and renamed *Unfaithful*—no connection to the 2002 Diane Lane starrer). "We want to do it."

"What are we talking about money-wise?" Rink asked. Elliott offered a little more money than Rink had been paid for *Caroline*. They struck the deal right then on the phone.

The process of getting *Unfaithful* done was even faster than that of *Caroline*. Rink had one script meeting with Elliott, Robbins, and the director, Catherine Cyran. They presented Rink with their notes. *Unfaithful* required less rewriting than *Caroline*. "But in this case, once I turned in the rewrite, I was out of the loop. I didn't even know who was in it until I called up Elliott in mid-January to ask him how things were going. He said it was *done!* He said, 'If you want, come over and pick up a screening copy and copies of the posters' which were already made up."

When Rink went over to get his copy, he got a taste of Cormanesque salesmanship: according to the posters, *Unfaithful* had been rechristened, *The Heat of Passion II: Unfaithful* "—even though it had *nothing* to do with (Concorde's) *In the Heat of Passion*."

Several years later, dealing with World International Network (WIN)—a production company aspiring to be something more upscale than Concorde, and that was offering Rink a chance at his first theatrical release—Rink was almost constantly dismayed at how unfavorably his WIN experience compared to dealing with Corman's outfit. "You're sitting in a room with six people all shooting notes at you," he says unhappily. "You can be in a room with six people all working for the same company, all having six different opinions." Trying to keep the project alive, Rink kept rewriting his script to try to satisfy the development notes. But with each draft, he found his script—a twisty-turny bit of neo-*noir*—being hammered into something more formulaic, familiar, and forgettable. No matter what he did, there were always more notes as if there was a concerted effort on the part of WIN's staff to make sure anything distinctive about Rink's material was sanded off. He eventually came to despise the rewrites and finally walked away.

In Rink's opinion, what happened at WIN is representative of trends in the motion picture industry at large. At the larger movie companies, there exists, he says, a bureaucratic layer of development people "… who've never written anything in their lives…" who justify their existence by meddling with material. There are, he says, too many "… chefs trying to make the meal who you go into a meeting with, and come at you with their own set of notes and take on what the film should be."

In the majority of studio films, Rink adjudges, the results are movies with "… vast holes in the logic of the story… Holes big enough you can drive a truck through," as well as movies—with very few exceptions—which "… do nothing to challenge an audience's mind. The audience is vastly underestimated as to their intelligence."

He contrasts that with his experience with Concorde: "Elliott and them trusted what the writer was trying to do." The quick efficiency of Concorde, as well as their cost-effectiveness has often left Rink wondering just how much of the cost and energy involved in major studio productions is wasted. At Concorde, moviemaking was, "All very straightforward. It wasn't brain surgery."

But there's another difference Rink sees as well. At the major level, there are, he speculates, too many money people involved. "Even the (major) studios answer to stockholders; even *they* can't just greenlight anything they want without thinking about their bottom line." As for financing outside the studio system, that comes from "… investment groups who can range from a group of dentists to some rich businessmen who want to get into the movie business. And those people really know nothing about and don't really love film as much as Corman and people like Mike Elliott."

The Grindhouse That Wouldn't Die!
(posted 5/13/11)

By the 1980s, the glory days of the movie grindhouse were over. Rising real estate values and rents, and urban renewal ate away at the grindhouse circuit, and down the houses came, one seedy, sticky-floored theater after another.

But even though the grindhouses died out, grindhouse cinema didn't die with it. Like some sort of adaptive mutation, it found a new way to live in the reconfiguring terrain of the 1980s movie exhibition that provided every consumer with the ability to create an individually programmed grindhouse in his/her very own living room.

The first commercially successful VCR was introduced to the American buying public in 1975, the same year HBO became the first nationally available pay-TV service. By the end of the decade, a few major studios had formed "home entertainment" divisions for the purpose of producing videocassettes of their theatrical features for the home market. Within a few years, the home video business was booming, and by 1991 there was a VCR in almost three-quarters of American homes.

But even before the new ancillaries of home video and cable had matured, the expanding streams of revenue they were throwing off were reshaping the motion picture business. With their insatiable need for product, advance commitments from video distributors and cable channels (as well as foreign markets) were often key to financing major films. In fact, as budgets increased to the point where few films could reach breakeven even with a respectable domestic theatrical release, ancillary monies were often the margin between a film's financial success or failure.

These new ancillaries also provided a growth culture for a new kind of cinema underclass. These "minors" worked from a simple economic premise. They saw how the majors could lay off a goodly amount (and sometimes all) of production costs against projected and/or advanced ancillary revenues, effectively amortizing a production even before it went in front of the cameras. Successful minors correctly gauged the hunger of niche audiences with appetites for lesser product as long as it was heavily laced with the old grindhouse staples of hyper action (or sex or gore etc.), and calculated that, if the majors were able to offset the costs of a big picture with the new ancillary dollars, it could be possible to put a small picture into profit the same way simply by making it cheaply enough. Two exemplars of the minor producing ranks of the 1980s were Cannon Films and Troma Entertainment.

*****

A small-time production company acquired in 1979 by cousins Menahem Golan and Yoram Globus, under their leadership, Cannon in the 1980s became a moviemaking machine grinding out an endless succession of often cheap-looking, dramatically indistinguishable actioners and their sequels, and rolling them into theaters on a wave of hype. It was assembly line filmmaking: the company churned out nearly 125 movies in the space of ten years, forty-three in their peak year of 1986. Typical Cannon fodder: five *American Ninja* pictures; house star Chuck Norris going through his martial arts paces in three *Missing in Action* movies, two *Delta Force* entries, and *Invasion U.S.A.* (1985), all turned out between 1984-1988; taking over the *Texas Chain Saw Massacre* brand for *The Texas Chainsaw Massacre 2* (1986); and likewise adopting the *Death Wish* title for a long-running franchise with no less than four increasingly lurid sequels. There was such a regular, if limited, audience for this kind of generic action fare it was not unusual for Cannon to aggressively mine enough in advances from cable, video, and overseas markets to put a Cannon movie in the black before it ever opened.

The key, of course, was in producing movies for a price. Cannon's four *Death Wish* sequels, for example, were produced for slightly more than $5 million per, while the three Chuck Norris-starring *Missing in Action* movies were turned in for a little under $4 million per, and the budgets of the studio's five *American Ninja* movies didn't even average $1 million each—this at a time when the average cost of a movie produced by one of the majors was approaching $18 million.

*****

Troma got by on even slimmer budgets (*The Toxic Avenger* [1984], one of Troma's signature titles, was produced for less than $500,000), but took a creatively different tack from Cannon. While Cannon movies were—despite their often ludicrous plots—straight-faced thrillers, Troma dealt exclusively in a blend of the grotesque and kitschy camp.

Troma films were so knowingly ridiculous that the undernourished quality of their productions only added to their absurdist charm. Part of Troma's success was—and remains—its ability to actively cultivate a cult-like devotion to their often outré, tongue-in-cheek horror thrillers, films branded with such proudly off-the-wall titles as *The Toxic Avenger* (plus three sequels), *Fat Guy Goes Nutzoid* (1986), *Sgt. Kabukiman N.Y.P.D.* (1991), *Class of Nuke 'Em High* (1986, plus two sequels), and *Surf Nazis Must Die!* (1987).

*****

Key to the viability of companies like Cannon and Troma was that it was not necessary for their movies to succeed—or even make much money—at the box office; only that their titles appear on the theatrical circuit even if only for a brief time. Theatrical release acted as little more than a primer for the ancillary markets that were the bread and butter of the minors. Theatrical release granted a cachet to even the most junior level foray when it eventually appeared on home video, escalated the floor on pay-TV fees (premium services routinely paid more for a theatrical release than for comparable direct-to-video fare), and established a valuable brand name-recognition factor with consumers, prepping them for that time when the picture moved—quickly—to home video.

From major movies partly underwritten by ancillary advances to smaller theatricals completely subsidized by ancillaries, making product directly for ancillaries—specifically, home video—was a natural evolutionary/entrepreneurial jump. The driving force behind direct-to-video production was the bottomless hunger for product in the home video market.

Over the space of about a decade—from the mid-1970s to the mid-1980s—the cost of a home video player went from about $1000 to just a few hundred dollars. The explosive popularity of home video created a gold rush-like environment. Stand-alone video stores and chain franchises appeared in every neighborhood. Any number of non-video establishments tried to cash in on the boom: convenience stores, magazine shops, motels/hotels, even neighborhood gas stations began offering a selection of videos for rental as a sideline.

This tremendous growth in home video retailing meant there were – literally—hundreds of miles of shelf space requiring stocking. In what was becoming a tremendously crowded, fiercely competitive environment where it often seemed some kind of video rental was available in some kind of business on every street corner, it was a valuable marketing hook for a video store to be able to brag about the hundreds – even thousands—of titles available on its shelves.

Home video in the 1980s was, after all, a rental-driven business. With tapes of major titles retailing at first issue in the neighborhood of $100, tape purchases were rarely an attractive option for VCR owners (prices on home video titles did drop after their debuts to more affordable sell-through levels, but sell-through always remained secondary to rentals in the home video market). Even when video entertainment was at its most popular, VCR owners only averaged a half-dozen tape purchases annually. Most tape sales went to video stores who offered them as rentals, but even video stores only purchased limited copies of new releases.

A store needed a title to do so many "turns" (individual rentals) for it to pay for itself. The more copies of a title a video store stocked, the more turns needed for the store to get its money back. Stores aimed to stock enough copies to provide a certain level of convenience for customers, but not so many as to push breakeven to chancey levels. When consumers had to deal with a store's limited "depth of copy," it behooved the store to be able to turn a customer loose among long ranks of stocked titles to look for a second choice.

The major movie companies saw an opportunity here to milk revenue out of their thousands of older library titles as well as newer movies that had, for one reason or another, been denied a theatrical release. Video store shelves began to fill with old and unreleased theatricals as well as vintage TV shows.

While the majors were plundering their libraries for home video material, developing outside the circle of mainstream movie studios was another tier of movie companies with the goal of exploiting the home video market not as an ancillary, but as the basis of their businesses.

Direct-to-video (DTV) producers like Full Moon Entertainment, Seduction Cinema, PM Entertainment, Spectacor, Empire Pictures, and Tempe Entertainment—just to name a few—were very much informed by the exploitation movie experience of the 1960s/1970s. They knew there were niche audiences attracted to certain genres (horror, action thrillers, martial arts, softcore sex, etc.) on a more-or-less generic basis. For the fan of splatter horror films, for example, it didn't matter if there was a familiar star headlining the film, or what the quality of the production values were, or even if there was a modicum of cleverness to the story as long as the movie ran briskly and was regularly interrupted by scenes of gore and bizarre death. Likewise, a fan of actioners didn't care if a police thriller was all that realistic or even remotely credible as long as the action was loud and plentiful.

Camilla Carpenter, a one-time film acquisition executive for pay-TV service Cinemax, illustrated the almost primal appeal such generic grindhouse-caliber fare could have while discussing the consistent popularity of a series of DTV actioners the service had picked up in the early 1990s featuring martial artist Cynthia Rothrock: "They love 'em. I don't know what it is, but you'd be surprised how many guys enjoy watching an attractive girl kick the hell out of people."

DTV titles were made for budgets ranging from just a few million to under a hundred thousand, sometimes boasting a minor or fading star, usually adhering religiously to genre conventions, had a running time of less than ninety minutes, received comparatively little promotion, and often served little more purpose than to offer the undiscriminating video store browser a second (or third) rental choice on the tacit promise of the prerequisite amount of mayhem and/or titillation in a favored genre.

As disposable as most DTV movies were, some companies—in Troma fashion—were able to cultivate followings if not for their brands than at least for some of their franchises. Full Moon Entertainment, for one, which specializes in a blend of horror/sci-fi/fantasy, managed to turn its 1985 *Trancers*—a sci-fier about a futuristic bounty hunter –into a franchise with no less than three sequels, while the company's 1989 *Puppet Master*—about a collection of sentient dolls carrying out the evil bidding of the title character—was also followed by three more installments.

*****

By the mid-1990s the boom in home video had crested. VCR ownership was plateauing, and there was a glut in the kind of B- and C-caliber titles that made up most DTV product. Said one DTV director at the time, "There's just too much stuff out there. The buyers can pick and choose and it's hard to get a good price for a picture now."

Consequently, the end of the decade saw an enormous shakeout among the ranks of low-budget DTV producers. Companies like Troma and Full Moon, which had managed to build a brand name-loyal fan base, were able to survive, but most either folded or found themselves struggling in an overstuffed and contracting market.

As the century turned, DTV producers also found themselves challenged by shifting in the financial base of the business due to the introduction of yet another new home entertainment technology: DVD.

As lucrative as the home video business had been for Hollywood, there had always been a level of dissatisfaction with the way home video had played out. Movie studios had made their money primarily on the sale of product to video rental outlets, but hadn't shared in the enormous revenues generated by rentals. The movie industry looked to avoid repeating that strategic error with the DVD business.

From the outset, Hollywood thought of DVD distribution as a sell-through business, setting prices on DVDs low enough at first issue to be attractive to the average consumer. As a consequence, DVD played out in a reverse of home video, with revenue from consumer DVD purchases far outstripping rental revenue. By the mid-2000s, the average DVD owner was buying 17 titles per year; a nearly three-fold improvement over the VHS years.

As the home market shifted from rental- to purchase-driven, the majors' view of direct-to-video/DVD production also changed.

During the early, tentative years of the home video business, a number of movie companies had ceded the task of distribution to independent video distributors (e.g. Vestron, Thorn/EMI and so on) and co-ventures (CBS/Fox, for example). But, as the potential of home video became more manifestly clear, the majors moved to fully control their product from production all the way through ancillary distribution. Eventually, every major studio came to establish its own video arm, leaving indie distribs to either fold, or fill their catalogs with DTV product and titles from production companies too small to have their own home video arms.

The attitude of the majors similarly evolved with respect to direct-to production. Much as they had bulled aside the independents and taken control of distribution during the home video era, they now looked to muscle aside the smaller companies that comprised most of the DTV ranks. In the purchase-driven DVD era, the majors' preferred strategy was to build their DTDVD product on established brand names, turning out DVD sequels to theatrical hits and launching them into the marketplace with promotional campaigns comparable to those supporting the DVD debuts of their theatricals. As of this writing, most—if not all—of the major motion picture companies have established divisions for the express purpose of exploiting popular theatrical titles with spinoffs for the DTDVD market.

Warner Bros., for example, created Warner Premiere in 2006 with the goal of turning out DTDVD features in the $5 million budget range, preferably theatrical spin-offs, its inaugural effort being *The Dukes of Hazzard: The Beginning* (2007), a DTDVD sequel to its $80.3 million grossing 2005 theatrical, *The Dukes of Hazzard;* Universal has turned out three DTDVD sequels to its 2000 teen comedy *Bring It On*, two direct-to sequels to its *American Pie* series of theatricals, and continues to extend its *The Land Before Time* "kid vid" franchise through a dozen direct-to follow-ups to the 1988 animated feature, the most recent of which was produced in 2007.

Surviving DTV companies (now DTDVD companies) not only have to contend with being in head-to-head competition against more upscale, heavily promoted direct-to product from the majors, but they also have to deal with a reconfiguration of the retail terrain. The video store had been the cornerstone of the home video rental business, but with the stress on sell-through, any number of retail outlets—from chain stores like Wal-Mart to supermarkets—have come into play presenting a problem for the low-budget DTDVD producer.

The DTV business had been predicated on the idea that for the two-three dollar cost of a rental, video store browsers wouldn't mind settling, as a second choice, on the kind of generic product most DTV producers turned out. However, *selling* that same product for $15-25 turns out to be a significantly different proposition.

Trying to get consumers to make the greater investment in a permanent acquisition of DTV generics is hard enough. Making it harder is that stores like Wal-Mart, Target, etc. tend to favor mainstream, easily recognizable titles they feel they can sell in bulk. And, in maintaining a family-friendly retail environment, many such chains have policies against stocking certain kinds of extreme material—the kind of graphic/bizarre sex and/or violence offering that had been the mainstay of many a low-budget grindhouse-type film producer.

As if exploitation producers didn't have enough to contend with on the business front, their business was also being eroded on the creative side as well. Bluntly: the audience didn't need them anymore.

Exploitation cinema had always been about offering moviegoers the taboo, the forbidden, the mainstream no-nos. But sensibilities have changed since the grindhouse Golden Years of the 1960s-1970s, and what once had been confined to the grindhouse and midnight show has long since found its way into the mainstream.

The old splatter films have nothing on movies like *Saw* (2004) and its sequels, *Hostel* (2005) and its sequel, *Cabin Fever* (2002), *House of 1000 Corpses* (2003) *The Devil's Rejects* (2005) et al, all screening at the nearest multiplex just down the hall from *Yogi Bear* (2010) and *The King's Speech* (2010). If you were into the grindhouse S & M kink of *Ilsa: She Wolf of the SS* (1975), you can find much higher quality stuff on Cinemax or Showtime after midnight without the indignity of having to sneak into a theater, and/or find infinitely more of infinitely varied hardcore kink at free online porn sites.

Still, for all the alternatives and challenges, the exploitation movie lives... if barely. There is still a DVD rental business, though it is vastly diminished from the home video peak years. Veteran low-budgeters like Roger Corman and companies like Troma and Full Moon have their fan bases, and other DVD distributors have found a business in repackaging vintage exploitation films from the grindhouse heyday for exploitation aficionados... and there are more than a few. So, the low-budget exploitation movie may not be extinct... but as a distinct species, it certainly appears endangered.

The question, then, is there anything to mourn in its threatened demise?

After all, for most casual moviegoers, the exploitation movie—from its grindhouse Golden Age through its home video profligacy—was something invisible, or, at best, little noted; the exploitation movie's appeal was always a narrow one. Other than possibly expanding the boundaries of what was tolerable in mainstream movies in terms of gore and perverse violence—a debatable accomplishment—exploitation movies have had little impact on the direction of the business or creative evolution of Hollywood movie-making. Does the exploitation movie signify anything other than opportunism built on appealing to the basest, most voyeuristic instincts in its audience?

There may be little to mourn, but possibly something to miss. Here and there among the splatter and flying kicks and jiggling bosoms of the exploitation era, there was—at least on occasion, to some eyes anyway—something truly creative and inspired happening out there beyond the fringe of mainstream commercial moviemaking. Although thrillers like *Night of the Living Dead* (1968), *The Texas Chain Saw Massacre* (1974), *The Last House on the Left* (1972), and the other well-remembered Grand Guignols from the period were typically dismissed at the time as just another strain of splatter movie, the years have seen both their cult fan bases and critical cachet rise. There was, so goes a revised view, a sense of style and craft at work in some of these horrific rule-breaking shockers, and in their extreme carnage some saw a funhouse mirror reflection of the violence, moral chaos, and social upheaval of one of the most tumultuous periods in American history.

In comparison, the graphic horrors of today—including remakes of those 1960s/1970s touchstones—are often about little more than delivering jolts to young ticket buyers. One of the patron saints of graphic horror—*Night of the Living Dead*'s writer/director George Romero—has rued the so-called torture porn horror movies (movies like *Saw*, *Hotel*, et al) as "... cruelty for the sake of cruelty... Everybody wants this sort of, bim-bam-boom shock effect."

In the passing of the grindhouse and its distinctive fare, there is also a nostalgia factor. There are those who look back at the threadbare productions, the audacious stories, transparent shock effects, and bad acting and see a kind of campy charm.

And who doesn't miss charm?

Guerilla Filmmaking
(posted 4/10/11)

Blockbuster—the one-time giant in the home video rental business that went bankrupt last September—was bought at auction this past week by Dish Network for $320 million. According to Dish, it intends to combine its wireless technology with Blockbuster's brand name recognition, studio relationships and digital rights to reestablish Blockbuster as a player in the direct-to-home market against Netflix and newer contenders like Amazon and a Warner Bros. online rental service to be offered on Facebook.

However this plays out long-term, the auction buy is the last page in a final chapter begun back in September when Blockbuster busted. To trot out the old cliché, it's the—everybody now—end of an era.

The business Blockbuster used to be in seemed revolutionary in its day, though it seems almost quaint now; come Friday, some delegate from the family would trot to the neighborhood video store hoping to get there early enough to get dibs on the weekend's new major releases, and, failing that, roam the aisles looking for a couple of flicks for the weekend. Movies in the comfort of your own home; amazing! And, unlike pay-TV, you only had to pay for what you wanted to watch, and watched on your schedule, not HBO's or Showtime's. The home TV set had truly become the home movie theater.

But in an era of digital delivery, the idea of brick-and-mortar stores quickly became an antiquated one; a sea change Blockbuster grasped too late. But there could also be some collateral damage as well as there's a good possibility that, with the passing of the video store, an entire tier of moviemaking may pass with it.

Direct-to-Video—and later, Direct-to-DVD—was built around the needs, limitations, and dynamic of brick-and-mortar retailing. Stores couldn't stock an infinite number of copies of the big movies people most wanted to see. The stores needed supplementary titles to fill their yards of shelf space so no one went home frustrated and empty-handed and thinking maybe pay-TV wasn't such a bad deal after all. Consumers, having failed to get their first—or even second choice—could roam those aisles and maybe something—an eye-catchingly lurid box cover, a vaguely familiar actor's name, *something*—would hook their attention. For the less-than-discriminating viewer willing to settle for generic thrills and jollies, DTV/DVD fare was sometimes enough.

But in the digital world, there is no depth-of-copy problem, and flat monthly subscription rates—such as Netflix offers—means a digital subscriber can watch any movie he/she wants as often as he/she wants whenever he/she wants. Who needs generic when the top-of-the-line is always available?

The direct-to business was already dying before Blockbuster went under; had, in fact, been dying for years. The Blockbuster auction may only be the death rattle. But in its glory days—the 1980s into the early 1990s—DTV offered people in that business a hell of a ride.

As one might reasonably suspect, DTV attracted its share of hucksters, quick-buck artists, schlock-mongers, exploiters and sensationalists. Still, such types did not monopolize this lowest tier of commercial filmmaking, nor, some DTV veterans might argue, did they even comprise the majority of working low-budget moviemakers. There were as many different kinds of people making DTV features as there were making mainstream theatrical releases, and for the same variety of reasons: from the coldly mercenary to the professionally and/or creatively ambitious to the gracefully resigned and pragmatic.

*****

It had never been Abraham Gordon's intention to be *any* sort of a film producer. Back in his native Wisconsin, he had majored in Theatre and Communication Arts at the University of Wisconsin-Madison, becoming something of a "hotshot actor" on the local theater scene although he admits it was a case of being "... a big fish in a little pond." It was, however, accomplishment enough to make him feel ready to graduate to a higher echelon of the business. He moved to Los Angeles in the late 1970s, his eyes on the movies and TV, his intent to "... become a hotshot actor *there*."

At first, it seemed his career was off to a fast start. He wasn't in L.A. long before he landed a part in a *Star Wars* TV special. "I had to wear an alien monster costume. I couldn't see a thing out of it. I worked for 24 hours *straight!* But I made an ungodly $1600 for a single day's work and got my SAG card." Sadly, this would turn out to be the high water mark of Gordon's Hollywood acting career.

He was unable to find work after the *Star Wars* TV gig. In the early 1980s, he took a job working in the mailroom on the lot at 20th

Century Fox, a bonus of which being he was now in a position to maneuver himself into more bit-part work. He would call in sick for his mailroom job, then slink around the lot hiding from his supervisors while waiting for his shooting call.

Gordon teamed up with some other frustrated actors on the lot and formed The 20th Century Fox Repertory Theater. They found a space on the lot large enough for a forty- to fifty-seat theater and used sections of sets the studio was throwing away. "We did good work," Gordon says. "A lot of people came to see us."

Unfortunately, someone at the Fox payroll office had noticed Gordon's name appearing on twin sets of paychecks: one for his job in the mailroom, and another as an actor in films shooting on the lot. "'You can't do both,' they told me and I got fired from the mailroom. That was the beginning of the end of my acting career."

There were still occasional performing jobs. The parts may have been small, but his exposure to the practicalities of low-budget commercial filmmaking would later prove invaluable. One of his more memorable adventures—and lessons—was on the set of a Roger Corman-produced monster movie.

"I played a cop who gets eaten by a giant reptile in *Carnosaur 2* (1995)," Gordon recounts. "I learned how Corman was able to make these movies for just a couple of hundred thousand bucks. I showed up and the wardrobe guy handed me a police uniform that was *huge!* I could've put *three* of me in those pants! I told the guy, 'These are too big!' They just tightened the belt. It didn't matter. I wasn't going to be on-screen long before I got eaten."

Gordon visited the set of another Corman production at the invitation of a friend who was the director of photography. "It was some ridiculous sci-fi picture," he remembers. "The set was just egg cartons stapled to a wall and painted. I swear: egg cartons! But that's how Corman made those things for $300,000."

But, there were no significant jobs, no professional breakthroughs. "It was getting to the point where I thought I should do something with my life besides become a cab driver or a bartender," which, Gordon estimated, was where his faltering acting career was likely to leave him. Luckily, one of his friends in 20th Century Fox Rep had taught him accounting as a professional fallback, then helped Gordon get a job doing accounting for a small production company called Spectacor, which was turning out DTV and made-for-cable features.

Working on Spectacor's financial books Gordon noticed, "They had all these non-union scripts lying around and no one was reading them. I started reading some of the ones they were producing. They were *awful!* I went to them saying, 'These are *horrible!*'" Eventually, Gordon wrangled himself the job as Spectacor's head of story development.

Actually, Gordon was Spectacor's *entire* development staff. The company had a handsome suite of offices overlooking Sunset Boulevard, but most of the offices were empty since the company's entire personnel roster consisted of just four people: "There was the head of the company, a marketing guy, me, and a young guy who was kind of the assistant for all of us."

Like most low-budget production outfits, Spectacor worked along a strict financial formula. The company was, in effect, the production arm of distributor Promark Entertainment. Promark would routinely put up half the cost of each Spectacor film while it fell to Spectacor to find the rest, often through pre-sales. Budgets typically fell between $2 and $2-1/2 million. "They freaked out if the budget went to three."

Gordon sighs. "In my experience," he says, "you take work to pay the rent." At Spectacor, he explains, if the financial paradigm were adhered to, and based on the talent, the nature of the material, and the other creative elements, any given Spectacor title's performance would range from breakeven to $300-400,000 profit, and the company could "pay the rent" with four-five releases per year.

Spectacor's distribution was such that a film's international sales were fairly predictable and normally covered a feature's cost. "The profit," Gordon says, "was in domestic. If we got nothing domestically, we broke even. *Any* sale and we were in the black. What you really hoped for was a sale to HBO. That was the best thing." In fact, one of Spectacor's few sales to the pay-TV giant—the 1991 sci-fier *Wedlock* (aka *Deadlock)*—was, for many years, HBO's highest-rated "original" movie. (Occasionally, HBO has acquired completed films—sometimes intended theatricals that have failed to find a distributor, projects produced for overseas TV, or high end DTV features—which the service feels make a good fit for its programming, and presented them as an "HBO original film.")

Gordon's accounting experience turned out to be a boon in developing material to fit Spectacor's tight budgets. "I could figure costs. Going through a script I could tell, 'We don't need this, we don't need that.' And I could get a property to a number of people who could produce it."

Gordon didn't look at material from WGA writers—"We couldn't afford it"—but would look at almost anything else. Screenplays came to him from "... all over the place. I looked at everything." Anybody Gordon met—at a party, at a lunch, a friend of a friend—who pitched him a piece of material was sure to get their script read. Since a small company like Spectacor didn't have much money to spare for development, "I rarely optioned anything unless I was confident it would go." Spectacor paid between $25-40,000 for a script, but never more.

Scripts often came with a director already attached. While the low budget tier had its share of hacks, Gordon just as often found himself working with quality directors like the late George Hickenlooper *(Hearts of Darkness: A Filmmaker's Apocalypse,* 1991; *Casino Jack,* 2010), and Rick King *(Hard Choices,* 1985) whose work had twice been to Sundance. That such directors were available for low budget work illustrates Gordon's point that, "It's hard to work your way up."

Most of Spectacor's films, like most other DTV product, were actioners because they were deemed the most sellable, but Gordon wasn't particularly fond of action-driven DTV thrillers. "I always thought on our budgets the action looked kind of cheesy. The action stuff always looked so lame I could never see why (Spectacor) bought (those scripts)." Gordon's penchant was for more suspense- and character-driven pieces, which he felt would come off better on Spectacor's $2 million budgets than action-carried pictures. Whatever the script, Gordon's job—as he saw it—was to work with the screenwriter to make the "... script so good that even if they screwed it up (in production) it wouldn't suck."

Whatever his personal preferences, Gordon still had to operate within Spectacor's rigid financial paradigm. Whenever he considered a piece, he had to consider opinions other than his own. "You gotta make the distributors happy," he says resignedly. "They're reading it, too."

On one project—the kind of character-driven thriller Gordon liked—after working with the screenwriter on several rewrites, he sheepishly had to ask the writer if it were possible to incorporate a sex scene between the male and female leads.

The writer balked: "The guy's supposed to be happily married. If he sleeps with the girl, he's not so much of a good guy."

"Well, is there anybody else she can sleep with?" Gordon asked. He already knew the answer and wasn't surprised when the writer said no. "Can you get her naked coming out of the shower or something? Anything like that?"

When the writer asked why Gordon was lobbying for such an obviously gratuitous—and fleeting—bit of nudity, Gordon explained, "The marketing guy says if you get the girl naked it'll add fifteen percent to the overseas sales."

"It got so when I read a script I just thought that way," he says. "I'd think, 'Hey if we get an *Asian* girl naked, we get a great pre-sale in Japan or another Asian market. If I can find a *Canadian* woman, we can film in Canada and qualify for rebates. It was exciting for me to see how good I could make a picture with these requirements. That was the fun of it."

Gordon assuaged the squawking writer with another fact of the business: "Don't worry, if we get a big enough name, she won't do it anyway and it'll come out," which was exactly what happened.

In fact, an actress didn't always have to have the power of a big name to affect the same outcome. Gordon says actresses wanting the job would often agree to a film, then object to a nude or sex scene "... at the last minute" when it was too late to replace them.

At the time, the American motion picture industry had an annual output of about 400-500 titles covering everything from major mainstream releases to limited art house releases and imports. Five hundred titles may sound like a lot but measured against the thousands of actors, writers, directors on the lookout for work at any given time, 500 turns out not to be a very large number at all. For someone in Gordon's position, this meant a large pool of talent available for low-budget work from directors like Hickenlooper and King to actors of all stripes. "We usually caught actors on the downside of their careers," Gordon says. While they might no longer have been bankable names for mainstream releases, their names were still familiar enough to be an asset on the box of a DTV feature; enough to catch the eye of a video store customer wandering the aisles looking for an impulse rental. However, some actors—downward trending career or no—thought going straight to video was beneath them. "To get some of them you had to promise a theatrical release. If you couldn't guarantee theatrical, the agent wouldn't let the actor do the picture."

No DTV financial paradigm could survive the changing nature of the DTV market. By the 1990s, the DTV business was already on a downhill trend. The cynical calculation that drove so much of the DTV market—providing generic action fare featuring a few faded but familiar names on the case—was failing. "There were too many titles and they sucked," is Gordon's analysis. "Nobody wanted to rent them." Most of the DTV producers Gordon remembers from his days with Spectacor are gone, having either folded or been absorbed by larger film producers. "The studios got smart," Gordon says. "They bought up all these little companies and stocked (video) stores with *their* library titles."

Gordon left a faltering Spectacor in the late 1990s taking a job with a company handling payroll operations for feature productions (that life-saving accounting experience coming to play again). Occasionally, some of the talent contacts he made from his Spectacor days ask him to show a script around, and Gordon was instrumental in helping screenwriter Cliff Hollingsworth find a home for his screenplay, *Cinderella Man* (2005).

There are other echoes of the old days. One day on his accounting job, an IT technician working in the office came up to Gordon wondering if he'd ever acted. It turned out the tech—obviously an insomniac of sorts—had seen Gordon get devoured the previous night on a 4 a.m. airing of *Carnosaur 2*.

*****

Unlike Abraham Gordon, director Rick King knew what he wanted to do early in life. He'd had a passion for movies in high school, and after leaving his home in Virginia to begin college studies at Stanford, he transferred back east to MIT "… where I knew I could get hold of cameras."

King learned filmmaking at MIT under the guidance of Richard Leacock of *Monterey Pop* (1966) fame. "A friend put us in touch," he says. "Ricky Leacock was one of the great documentary filmmakers of all time. Just a brilliant guy."

The program at MIT wasn't the kind of film study dreadnaught as those at USC or NYU. The program, says King, "was tucked away in MIT's Architecture Department," and there was no graduate program. But, the program had equipment and Leacock put his students immediately to work.

The act of *doing*, King found, was the best form of filmmaking education. "You learn as you go along." He recounts, as an example, a story told by Peter Bogdanovich about his filming of *The Last Picture Show* (1971) at a screening of the film at the DGA the night previous to this interview. Bogdanovich was filming a fight between Jeff Bridges and Timothy Bottoms where the camera followed them around a parked car as they tussled. When the shot was finished, Bogdanovich was satisfied and called, "Cut."

Cinematographer Bruce Surtees then asked him, "Don't you want a master?"

To which a puzzled Bogdanovich asked, "What's that?"

King spent a year in the program and then "just hung around for another year helping out" so he could continue to have access to filmmaking equipment. Over the course of his time at MIT, King made about a dozen short documentaries. "I did them about everything. There was one about this little diner in town, there was another one where me and this other guy were going to go down to Louisiana to film the guys on the oil rigs in the Gulf (of Mexico). I did one about Chinese poetry that was structured kind of like a Chinese poem. Any excuse to make a film and I made one."

Asked why he never made a fiction short, King says, "It never occurred to me to make a short fiction film. I always thought if you wanted to make fiction, you made a feature." The documentary-driven MIT program was, nonetheless, an excellent exercise in learning the craft of filmmaking, particularly in trying to get the work done on little money with minimum resources.

After his second year at MIT, King returned to Stanford, graduated, and took a job in an automobile factory. He used $30,000 of his factory earnings to self-finance his first feature, *Off the Wall* (1977), an adroit use of what King had learned at MIT incorporated into a fiction vehicle drawing on his most recent life experience. Written by King and Marly Swick, *Off the Wall* concerns an automobile factory worker (Harvey Waldman) who is the subject of a documentary film. About halfway through the movie, faced with the nothingness of his life, Waldman commits a bank robbery filmed by the documentary crew, then takes the camera and uses it to record a diary of sorts. *Off the Wall* earned King his first trip to Sundance.

The film was critically respected but didn't provide a major commercial breakthrough. King spent the next few years making money editing, writing, shooting political commercials and whatever money-earning jobs he could find in the film business while all the time trying to develop new material.

He moved to New York and partnered with Robert Mickelson who acted as his producer. Mickelson would leave King to develop material while he tried to put together the money and logistics. "Robert sheltered me from a lot of headaches," King says. "He insulated me from the money problems, but we made the big decisions together.

"The big thing for us was to keep creative control. If someone offered to put up some money in return for having a voice in making the movie, Robert's response was to put up money of his own so we could keep that control." One idea Mickelson drove King to finish developing became King's second directorial feature, *Hard Choices* (1985).

Hard Choices was produced for $450,000. "Robert raised money on pay phones," King chuckles admiringly. The process of actually shooting the film was no less a matter of "winging it."

"We had a scene at an ice cream stand, a Dairy Queen. The location person walked into this place in the Catskills. 'Hey, how would you feel about having your establishment in a movie?'

"The guy thinks about it, he says, 'Well, it's kind of a slow season, ok. When would this be?'

"'How'd you like having it in a movie in fifteen minutes?' And he looks out his window and sees the crew waiting to swoop in."

While that kind of guerilla filmmaking made for a certain amount of stress, King also says, "It was the purist experience I ever had. Everybody had their reason to be there, they all generally believed in the project. Everybody was enthusiastic." On a budget of $450,000 he says, "Nobody's doing it for the money."

Hard Choices provided King with his second trip to Sundance and to another festival—now long gone, he doesn't recall the name—in Los Angeles. "We got two, three nights at the Beverly Wilshire but had no money—we'd spent it all on the movie!" King and Mickelson whiled away their time driving around L.A. in their rented car having little money to do much else. At one point, they blew a tire, then drove around on the spare "donut" until that gave out. "We'd call in and people are asking, 'Where the hell are you?' Oh, we're just driving around. Got a flat.'"

The reception for *Hard Choices* at the festival was positive enough to bring King phone calls from agents. "I was so naïve at that time I didn't know what an agent was!

"'Hi, I'm from ICM.'

"'Yeah? What's ICM?'"

King and Mickelson settled in L.A. Despite the positive reviews for *Hard Choices*, even though the film was picked up for distribution "... it got lost for one-two years." In the meantime, King was in Hollywood trying to get projects off the ground, doing low-level development deals. While King did get some work, the strategic commercial breakthrough any director new to the industry hopes for didn't happen.

There was the cop-and-robber thriller *Point Break* (1991) for Fox, for example. "The movie was my idea," says King. "I sold it to the producer of *Killing Time* (a 1987 noir King had directed) and was slated to direct. (W.) Peter Iliff is my friend and I wanted him to write the film. I wrote parts of it uncredited and was a co-producer as well as having a story credit," but ultimately the project—starring Patrick Swayze and Keanu Reeves—went to director Kathryn Bigelow.

And there was *Traveller*, a Nicholl Fellowship-winning screenplay by Jim McGlynn inspired by the insular Irish-American clans who make their money from housing repair scams.

At the time, King was in the process of switching agents. One prospective rep he was talking to showed him the screenplay for *Traveller* after King asked for a sample of the kind of material he handled. King was so struck by McGlynn's screenplay he took out an option, then he and Mickelson worked closely with the writer to further develop the material with the plan being Mickelson would produce and King direct. But they couldn't find a home for the project and after a few years their option expired. A management company handling Bill Paxton picked up the rights as a project for Paxton to star in and also produce. "They had the money to get the film made," King explains simply. The script was revised and finally made it to the screen in 1997 starring Paxton and Mark Wahlberg, and directed by Jack N. Green. While King's early role developing the material warranted an executive producer credit, *Traveller* was still a disappointment and in more ways than one. Despite generally good reviews, King maintains, "We had a better script, frankly."

It was coming time for King to rethink his priorities and his strategies. "When you get to the point of having a family, a mortgage, that becomes a major consideration," he says. He pauses reflectively, considers a career path that began with art house features like *Off the Wall* and *Hard Choices*. "Looking back on it—and I'm not sure that's always a good thing to do—but in retrospect it might be better to do those kinds of films where you make money first, and then every so often do an indie." Besides, that kind of guerilla filmmaking was exhausting. "Now," says King, "because of HD video, people are just churning 'em out, but, back then, it was an event just to get (the movie) done." For King, the direction was now to "… move into taking whatever work I could, but sure I could invest it with something."

He directed a number of direct-to-video features thereafter with budgets typically ranging from $1.5-2 million. According to King, most of the DTV companies were primarily concerned with getting films turned in on time and on budget. DTV producers worked on small margins and needed their films turned around quickly. The profits may have normally been thin, but occasionally one of these low budget efforts could produce substantial money.

King directed *Prayer of the Rollerboys* (1991) (from a screenplay by Peter Iliff) working with Robert Mickelson. "We teamed up, we made the movie for $1.5 million, half from overseas. It came along at the right time." The movie, starring Corey Haim, was set in a dystopic near-future and concerned a fight between warring gangs. King estimates *Prayer* sold 30-40,000 units on video at maybe $30 per unit meaning the domestic take for the film from video sales alone was close to $1 million.

The budgets might have been tight, but King generally found DTV companies quite liberal in granting him creative control. As long as he managed to touch the necessary bases—including the action and sex in the script that made the property saleable (which, King points out, is no different than the agenda for most mainstream theatrical fare)—King found most DTV production companies tended to leave him alone on a shoot.

Take *Road Ends* (1997), for example. King brought the project to DTV company PM Entertainment. At the time, PM was normally producing films—thrillers featuring heavy doses of action and nudity—for under $1 million. *Road Ends* was announced as part of a PM move to upgrade the company's output and visibility. The company substantially upped its usual outlay for *Road Ends* to $1.6 million. Aside from relocating the screenplay's setting from the Florida Keys to California where PM was based (for budget reasons), and mandating King use the PM house production staff (also for cost reasons), King was otherwise left to make the movie as he chose.

"I loved making those films," says King. "There was always a positive attitude on the set. You can always take these B kinds of movies and invest them with something."

Still, the tight budgets came with problems. "Compromises always had to do with money. You might want a better restaurant for a scene, a better location, more stuns, but you had to settle."

Again, *Road Ends* is an example. King and co-producer (and *Road Ends* star) Chris Sarandon got a greenlight from PM on the basis of Dennis Hopper's agreeing to take a principle role in the film. However, to get Hopper, King had to agree the film would be shooting in a matter of weeks to take advantage of a hole in Hopper's schedule. At the time, King was still refurbishing the screenplay and Sarandon was shooting another project. King began filming while Sarandon was still on the other set, tweaking the script to suit locations, shooting most of Hopper's scenes so he could be released on schedule. Just as Hopper's time on the film was coming to an end, Sarandon completed his work on his other project and stepped into *Road Ends*. Even with all the schedule juggling, King completed the film within its approximate two-week schedule on time and on budget.

Road Ends also re-illustrates how much talent was available for low budget shooting. Despite only having $1.6 million, besides Sarandon and Hopper, the film's cast also boasted Mariel Hemingway, Peter Coyote, acclaimed stage actress Joanna Gleason, Geoffrey Thorne (who was coming off a stint on the successful CBS series *In the Heat of the Night*) and veteran character actor Bert Remsen.

But by the time of *Road Ends*, the DTV market had already peaked and was in decline. "PM would've been really smart four years earlier," says King. He remembers going over to the PM offices. "The place was *busy!* There were people running everywhere, all these people carrying cans of film... They were for real, this wasn't some fly-by-night outfit." Today, there's no listing for them in any of the usual producers' registries. "Their business model dissolved," says King. Like a lot of other DTV producers, "they made a lot of terrible movies. The business dried up."

The major studios, King surmises, saw a huge business in DTV. Movies that were not going into wide release were going into the video market with a studio-sized push behind them. Even if it was a small film coming from a studio's art house "classics" division, it was being hyped to a degree DTV producers couldn't match. "You've got some direct-to-video feature with Jeff Fahey going up against a studio film that didn't do well but it has Jeff Bridges and it cost $5-12 million, they couldn't compete against that."

Road Ends would be Rick King's last fiction feature. He went to where the work was, and found it back in documentaries. He made his own theatrical documentary *Voices in Wartime* in 2005, and since then has been steadily turning docs out ever since for cable channels like Turner and The History Channel. "I enjoy the documentaries a lot," says King, "they take me all over the world, but, at the same time, fiction is my first love."

*****

PM Entertainment's million-dollar budgets were epic in size compared to the money George Barnes and his Take 2 Productions frequently had to work with when Barnes began making features in Florida during the late 1980s.

Raised in River Edge, New Jersey, Barnes grew up helping his father build houses. During one bitter, New Jersey winter day, Barnes was helping his father pour the concrete footings of three houses in a cold, freezing rain. The concrete truck was stuck, and Barnes and his father had to lug concrete from the truck to the site by hand in buckets. Barnes looked up, saw his father had an ice beard three inches long hanging from his chin, and came to the realization, "This ain't for me."

At seventeen, he headed for Florida to build houses, but building in Florida and building in New Jersey were day-and-night contrasts. Back in New Jersey, it typically took Barnes three-four months to complete a house. In Florida, because of the tangle of regulations and building codes, the first house took two years. The frustrations were too much for Barnes, and after that project he decided, "I quit, I'm doing something else."

He spent a year looking at different industries, and began to focus on entertainment. In the late 1980s, America was experiencing a boom in TV and film production. These were the peak years of the home video business, music video-fueled MTV was coming into its own, cable TV was expanding, and Florida was an attractive filming site. The state offered a host of exotic locales, labor and material costs were cheaper than in major urban locations like Los Angeles and New York, Florida was a right-to-work state, which allowed shoots to use less-expensive non-union talent and craftsmen, and the state was generally film-friendly in terms of police cooperation, permits, etc.

But, at the time, Barnes didn't know anybody in the film business to provide him with an entree. His karate instructor's wife owned a talent agency and suggested Barnes "... try modeling and acting. I'll send you on some auditions."

Barnes felt that would at least get him on film sets. Once there, he began hanging out with the crew rather than the cast. "The *business* interested me," says Barnes. "And at the time, I didn't think of day-player actors and local models as being in the business."

Barnes appeared in advertising spots for Schick, Otto Sportswear, Riddell Sportswear, Ryder trucks, Gillette, and Champion Sportswear. He finally made the move over to production on the Robert Redford starrer, *Havana* (1990).

The casting director asked Barnes if he'd be willing to help with the production: "You know, check people in and this and that. I was like a second second AD." After *Havana*, the same person called Barnes in for other jobs as production assistant and grip. Barnes eventually landed an internship with Polydor Records UK, which took him through the production on 10-15 music videos. Eventually, Barnes started receiving calls to manage the company's US/Florida location productions.

He worked out of Greenwich Studios, a major production facility in North Miami, working directly for the studio on films like the Jim Carrey vehicle *Ace Ventura: Pet Detective* (1994), *Rough Stuff* aka *Mr. Nanny* (1993) with wrestler-turned-actor Hulk Hogan, and *Deadly Rivals* (1993) with Richard Roundtree and Margaux Hemingway. Barnes's responsibilities at Greenwich continued to expand and he began traveling overseas to negotiate distribution agreements on some of the films Greenwich was turning out. His first job acting as a full-fledged producer was on the low-budget thriller, *South Beach* (1992).

A $1.3 million production shot in eighteen days, *South Beach* starred a veritable gallery of B-list familiar faces: Peter Fonda, Gary Busey, Robert Forster, Stella Stevens, Henry Silva, Isabel Sanford from the 1970s/80s TV series *The Jeffersons*, ex-model Vanity, and Fred "The Hammer" Williamson, an ex-football player who'd starred in a number of 1970s blaxploitation films and who was acting as *South Beach's* director and one of its producers.

South Beach turned out to be an instructional lesson for Barnes in how to shoot low-budget films. The secrets, he says, are, "A lot of cash, immediate decisions." Barnes talks of being out on the shoot, going up to Williamson and explaining the need for some materials, Williamson pulling a wad of cash out of his pocket, handing Barnes a few bills and pointing him to a hardware store across the street warning him, "Don't forget to bring me back a receipt!"

The ready access to cash had a practical aspect. "You can't beg someone to do something for you and then tell them you're going to have a check for him in thirty days," explains Barnes. "You go into a restaurant, you tell the guy, 'I'll give you $500 if you let us shoot here tonight,' the guy says, 'Absolutely!'"

Barnes wound up managing Greenwich for a few months but eventually he left. "They wanted me to be a property manager," Barnes says, and that was "Totally not for me. I'm not an office guy. I don't like the studio management end. I like managing shoots, crews, locations, I like the creative end."

He set up his own production company—Take 2 Productions— and took on a business partner. The arrangement was Barnes would handle the creative and production side, while the partner was tasked with the business side, primarily raising financing. Barnes made small commercials and music videos while he set about trying to get Take 2 into DTV features. He ran an ad in *The Hollywood Reporter* calling for material. "I was getting a million scripts. They all sucked. Everything was crappy reads."

He finally came across *Dinosaur Babes* (1996), a quirky script by Brett Piper about loincloth-clad amazons, cavemen, an ancient crashed UFO, and, of course, dinosaurs. The script promised a campy, kitschy kind of fun bolstered by impressive special effects. Piper had already completed a half-hour short: "The Return of Captain Sinbad."

"Sinbad" had been shot in stop-motion, and executed so deftly that Barnes and his partner were sure *Babes*—if pulled off with the same technical expertise—would do well.

Barnes went up to Maine to meet with Piper whom he found living in his grandmother's unfinished, dirt floor basement. The basement, Barnes remembers, was cluttered with Piper's effects paraphernalia: the table top set on which he'd shot "Sinbad," fully articulated dinosaur heads as big as an office desk, and so on. Barnes and his partner were so impressed at Piper's evident technical skill that until production began on *Babes* they would often wonder why Piper was not working at a higher level in the business.

Barnes soon found out the reason: "He's extremely talented but he's insane."

Take 2 acquired "The Return of Captain Sinbad," and then Barnes and his partner put up $300,000 to make *Dinosaur Babes*, with Piper as writer/director, and Barnes taking on the jobs of producer, director of photography, editor, and post-production supervisor. Piper may have been an effects wizard, but was less adept at dealing with cast and crew. His behavior on the set was so erratic that, at one point, Barnes had to take the helm because Piper refused to come to the set. "Here was a guy who told me he was gonna do the entire movie for $35,000," says Barnes. "$250,000 later, I have some problems."

The end product was not the fun tongue-in-cheek caveman flick Barnes had envisioned. The effects sequences were truly impressive – Piper was, indeed, a *maestro* of such old-school effects techniques as stop-motion animation, forced perspective, glass mattes, and miniatures—and gave the film the impression of having been made on a larger budget, but the film was still a disappointment creatively. However, Barnes did secure a sale with Blockbuster and while *Babes* was "obviously no big hit," it did manage to make its money back.

The fate of *Dinosaur Babes* may have been frustrating, but Barnes was soon dealing with a much bigger setback. The plan he and his partner had worked out was to pitch a slate of projects—led off by *Babes*—to a pool of investors. The thinking was: once Take 2 was regularly turning out low-budget features, Barnes was confident—based on his previous distribution experience—he could negotiate enough sales to insure a more-or-less steady revenue stream and Take 2 would become a self-fueling outfit. The trick was to get the initial investment to prime the company's financial pump—and that had been his partner's task. The partner didn't come through and quit.

For a moment, it seemed to Barnes that Take 2 had hardly taken its first breath before it was dying on its feet. But Barnes is nothing if not resilient, and certainly resiliency was an asset in the volatile low-budget market. He gave himself an hour on the beach one afternoon to mope, than decided he was going to stay in Miami. "This is where it's going on," he told himself and settled on a strategy of doing commercial work while trying to see what feature projects he could find. The next day he was in a working relationship with a new low-budget company called Pan Am Pictures run by a refugee from the collapse of Cannon Pictures.

Pan Am soon had a workable financial model making movies for $250-300,000, with Barnes negotiating distribution deals that would bring in anywhere from $3-7 million. The investors were, "Private guys, doctors, friends, lawyers. Once they saw the model work, it was easy to get money."

Because budgets were so tight, Barnes couldn't always spend time or money on the niceties.

On Pan Am's thin budgets, the keys were to move quickly, shooting without permits, and developing a crew running smoothly "... like a SWAT team..." with everybody always knowing beforehand exactly what needed to be done. Notes Barnes, "Every position is really important. You have a three-hour delay because a PA forgot a screw that held a camera plate on. That's the kind of shit that just kills you; you can never make up that time."

The financial model was workable—as long as Pan Am paid back its investors. The problem was, says Barnes, that the man running Pan Am "was crazy. He'd take the money, go out and buy a Jaguar or something, and wreck it." The money was frittered away on everything but recoupment and, eventually, Pan Am collapsed. The Pan Am man disappeared owing Barnes money ("People *always* owe me money," Barnes sighs resignedly). As for Mr. Pan Am, he was spotted resurfacing several years later in Los Angeles trying unsuccessfully to put together a package of softcore porn films.

Yet, again, Barnes found himself having to regroup and commit to a new tack. What always helped Barnes survive his feature setbacks was that Take 2 was amply succeeding in other avenues. He became involved with German-based commercial-maker Filmhouse, working as a DP and producer. "They were doing a commercial a day," says Barnes, "and had a $1 million minimum (budget for their commercials)." He also spent a year in Chile designing a media campaign for a presidential candidate working with a production staff of 1400 and a budget of $45 million.

He returned to Florida, sank a half-million dollars into building a studio in South Beach, and was almost immediately confronted with disaster. He'd taken an eight-year lease, but just three months after he'd moved in the landlord filed for bankruptcy in Texas. Barnes spent a year and a half fighting in Federal court in Texas trying to keep his lease, but the bankruptcy court judge ruled Barnes's lease was "not in the interest of the creditors" and gave him fourteen days to vacate.

Barnes bounced back still again, slapping a studio together quickly in offices provided by the Adkins & Associates agency for whom he wound up doing a good deal of commercial work over the next year-year and a half, after which Barnes bought his own building.

He continued to keep an eye out for feature work. He was brought a project called *All Men Are Beasts* (2001), but the project went bad after shooting. "It was a post-production debacle," sighs Barnes. "A lot of indie films come apart in post because everyone underestimates what's involved." It was a "very cute movie," says Barnes, which, following its post-production problems, then fell victim to producer Elvis Cruz's unrealistic expectations. "I said, 'Let's go around to the markets," explains Barnes, "'You won't get rich, you spent $1 million, you'll get two-three million back,' but he wouldn't do it." Cruz set his sights on a much bigger payday and, as a result, the film was never released.

Barnes also worked on the 2003 indie film, *Valley of Tears*, but it was another film that ran into trouble in post-production, a process that eventually ran to three-four months. "That's a myth that you can fix a picture in post," declares Barnes. "You can fuck it up in post, but you can't *fix* it. It's got to be shot right."

That would be Barnes's last feature work to date but Barnes is not short of work. Take 2 Productions now has offices in Florida, New Jersey, and Europe, and Barnes works regularly on commercials, corporate videos, music videos, and political media. His advertising spots are often done on a scale that not only dwarfs any of Take 2's features, but rivals most major film productions in both complexity and comparative cost. For example: an Audi spot he shot in Manhattan that involved closing Park Avenue from the Helmsley Building up to Grand Central Station. "The mayor drove one of the cars!" chuckles Barnes. "What a great guy! And the film office in New York delivers the best service I've ever experienced."

He has not given up on features, however. "I would love to do great movies. I do not miss bullshit. I don't miss the sacrifices you have to make because of the (small) budgets that you don't have in commercials."

In 2007, working with his one-time neighbors at Adkins & Associates, Barnes put together a proposal for a slate of $2-3 million DTDVD features that he took to The Weinstein Company. Discussions went on for several weeks and looked promising but then, without explanation, the Weinstein contact evaporated. Barnes took the same proposal to Warner Premiere, but, as impressed as they were, Warner wasn't interested in originals, their mandate being to exploit Warner Bros. theatrical brand names for the DTDVD market.

It was a mark of how much the business had changed since Barnes had first gone to Florida twenty years before; DTV indies being crowded out by studio-produced DTDVD features. Even filming in Florida became a more grueling experience than it had been during the wide-open gold rush days of the late 1980s-early 1990s.

Back in the days when he'd worked on *South Beach*, Barnes remembers how film-friendly Florida was. "The Colony and The Breakwater and those Ocean Drive restaurants paid *us* to shoot there! We got $10,000 from The Boulevard, $20,000 from the Colony. It brought them awareness. The police support was fantastic. The parking was great. All of the streets from Washington to Ocean, from Fifth to Eleventh were production vehicles only. That eroded. The locations got expensive, the permitting is disastrous. One time I got thrown out and closed down for *having* permits. I don't want to bad-name a town, but it's not really film friendly anymore, and it's more expensive (to shoot in Miami) than in New York now."

But Barnes, with the bounce-back ability of a Super Ball, is not done with features. Still, "The hardest thing? Finding a project worth shooting. That, and finding people that can do it. It's not easy, it's not something anybody can do."

Neo-Noiriste: John Dahl
(posted 11/10/10)

By the time John Dahl had directed his third feature—1994's *The Last Seduction*—critics had anointed him as a contemporary torch bearer—perhaps the lone, consistent one—of the *film noir* ethos. Even today, with his filmography having grown to include the less *noir*-ish thrillers *Unforgettable* (1996) and *Joy Ride* (2001), a tale of card sharks prowling New York's underground big-money poker circuit in *Rounders* (1998), and a true story of WW II adventure and valor in *The Great Raid* (2005), Dahl's name is still most closely associated with modern day *noir* thanks to the three indelible thrillers that launched his career: *Kill Me Again* (1989), which he co-wrote with David W. Warfield, *Red Rock West* (1992), on which he collaborated with his brother Rick Dahl, and *The Last Seduction*, written by Steve Barancik.

Dahl's working in movies represents a formidable leap from a less than cosmopolitan upbringing in Billings, Montana. Although he turned out some short films in high school, Dahl was not an avid young cinephile in the Scorsese/Spielberg/Coppola/Lucas mold. His interests lay primarily in art and music. Movies, he says on reflection, were something "... very, very far away" from Montana, never an option to consider for one's future.

Music and art helped carry him through high school, after which he attended the University of Montana where he entertained notions of becoming a commercial artist while indulging his musical interests playing in bands. By age twenty-one, he sensed neither his penchants for art nor for music were going to put much food on the table, so his interest subsequently turned to film—which some might hardly consider a less quixotic pursuit.

But, again, Dahl was no aspiring cineaste. His graphic arts sensibility was attracted to the visual qualities of animation, and it was only after he began attending film school at Montana State in Bozeman to study animation that he became interested in feature filmmaking.

Interest grew to passion, and when his class of nine graduated from Montana State, Dahl boldly announced to his professor that he "... was going to L.A. to make movies."

His professor laughed.

It was no direct route to Los Angeles. In fact, there was a moment when it was an open question as to whether or not Dahl would continue to pursue film at all. A friend of his in Washington, D.C. helped him secure work as an assistant director, and "... after about a year of that I knew that wasn't what I wanted to do." He spent time in an art department after that, then applied to both the American Film Institute and law school. In *Rounders* fashion, Dahl's future hung on the turn of a card (actually, his applications). "If the AFI *hadn't* taken me, and law school *had* accepted me, I'd probably be a lawyer somewhere in Montana today," says Dahl.

Unlike the "film brats" who had come out of NYU and USC in the 1960s and 1970s, Dahl didn't go into the AFI drawing on a long-held interest in and an encyclopedic knowledge of films. Many of the classic titles the AFI screened hit him fresh. On the occasion when director Billy Wilder's malevolent classics *Double Indemnity* (1944) and *Sunset Boulevard* (1950) were screened back-to-back, something in the unique stylishness of *film noir* appealed to the visual artist in Dahl. Living in the same neighborhood where many scenes from both movies had been shot—"I'd be walking and realize, 'Hey, this is the street where Fred MacMurray was walking in *Double Indemnity!*'"—only made what he'd seen in the movies more vivid and concrete for him. That in mind, when he began musing on what kind of movie he wanted to make, it's no surprise his thinking drifted toward something *noir*-ish.

He remembered a bus trip he'd taken from Montana to San Francisco to visit a friend several years before. The bus had stopped for a few hours in Reno. Says Dahl: "Reno struck me as the most decadent, weirdest place I'd ever seen in my life at the time—" he had been nineteen "—I couldn't believe a place like that could really exist. Years later, when I was heading to L.A. from Montana, I passed through Vegas and that stopover in Reno came back to me. Remember, this was years ago when Vegas was Vegas. Now, Vegas is a theme park."

The refreshed memory of that stretch-your-legs-and-bathroom-break in Reno years before produced *Kill Me Again,* and then came *Red Rock West,* which Dahl describes as "... kind of an extension of *Kill Me Again.* All the things I didn't get to do in *Kill Me* I put into *Red Rock West.*"

Despite receiving critical acclaim on the film festival circuit, *Red Rock West* was years getting into theaters. When Roger Ebert reviewed the movie after its 1994 theatrical release, he remembered being blown away by the movie years earlier at the Toronto Film Festival. He speculated—correctly, according to Dahl—the hold-up was a product of the movie's hard-to-categorize but quintessentially *noir*-ish story about a drifter (Nicholas Cage) mistaken for a hit man by a local sheriff who wants Cage to kill his wife.

Ten or fifteen years earlier, when the financially desperate studios were almost reckless in their creative daring, Dahl might've had an easier time carving out a commercial niche for himself. By the 1990s, however, the industry had not only grown more creatively conservative, but much of the decision-making had come to be dominated by marketing departments. "Marketing departments have a big voice," he says.

Dahl remembers the gent handling marketing for *Red Rock West* telling him, "Well, it's kind of an action movie, Nicholas Cage has a little bit of a reputation for action stories. You've got some action, but not enough. You've got some comedy. Hmm. You need to make it more of an action story, or more of a comedy." It never seemed to occur to them, says Dahl, "to sell it for what it was. They didn't know what to do with it, they couldn't figure it out."

Still, *Red Rock West* earned Dahl the widespread attention and respect of reviewers, and then *The Last Seduction* came along and cemented his reputation as a *noiriste*.

Part of the strength of Dahl's work may have come from his *not* having been a lifelong film aficionado. So many of the neo-*noirs* that have crossed movie screens over the last twenty-five to thirty years—even memorable entries like Lawrence Kasdan's *Body Heat* (1981) and Bob Rafelson's remade *The Postman Always Rings Twice* (1981)—play like, at best, artful pastiches of the *noir* classics of the 1940s and 1950s, echoing the oldies rather than establishing their own distinctive voices. Dahl, on the other hand, was coming to the genre from another place, and didn't so much feel a need to honor the old tropes as build on them, giving his *noirs* their own, completely contemporary feel. In fact, Dahl didn't even consider *The Last Seduction*—easily his most recognized work up to that time—a *noir*.

"When I read the script (for *The Last Seduction*), I thought it was a black comedy," says Dahl. "It didn't even occur to me that Linda Fiorentino's character was a *femme fatale* until after the movie was released and reviewers labeled her one."

If Dahl had first been attracted to *noirs* by the visual stylishness of the vintage genre classics, what he later found so enticing as a storyteller was the form's trademark moral ambiguity/ambivalence.

Right and wrong were rarely clear, even less rarely constant. "We shouldn't like (Fiorentino's character)," Dahl says, speaking about *The Last Seduction*, "but once her husband slaps her, our sympathy tilts toward her. We keep thinking after that she must redeem herself at some point, but, in the end, a good guy goes to jail and she gets away with (betrayal and murder)."

That kind of moral complexity, says Dahl, is hard to find today in a movie mainstream dominated by big budget action-driven movies targeting a young audience. "Consumers of movies tend to be teenagers and young adults, and their tastes are driving the movies," he says, and, as a consequence, "Movies have become more of a thrill ride and a spectacle. It's hard to imagine *Snakes on a Plane* (2006) being made in the 1960s as anything but a low-budget drive-in movie, but it's the perfect example of what I'm talking about when I say movies today are more about marketing."

Still, Dahl concedes the major movie companies are in a tough situation. "There really isn't a *film* company anymore," he says, and points back to the 1960s and 1970s when the major studios began evolving into massive entertainment conglomerates. "They own music companies, a film studio, theme parks, TV networks, some own magazines and newspapers." This kind of growth and amalgamation was necessary, says Dahl, for the studios to survive and shield their risks. These growing entertainment complexes became focused on teens and young adults—a relatively easy market to sell to, he posits—with a fair amount of expendable income. "They can buy records and lunch boxes and movie tickets."

Dahl sighs. "Who was it? William Goldman who said that in this business nobody knows anything? Now they *know* nobody knows anything. Today, people throw their hands in the air; 'I don't know what works! I'm tired of having the marketing guy yell at me on Monday morning! Let *him* run the studio!'"

The end result is a multi-billion dollar a year industry focused on entertainment, managed by a handful of "gatekeepers"—creative executives but particularly marketing chiefs—deciding what's going to go out into the mass entertainment arena. "There's what, eleven major movie companies?" Dahl muses. "That means eleven people decide what movies are going to get made, there are eleven 'filters' on what's going to go out there." And, because studio movies have become so costly to make, and because the various arms of these multi-faceted entertainment companies look to feed off a box office success, the risks to studios are greater than ever. "The necessities of the business have made (movie companies) risk-averse," judges Dahl. "By their very *nature*, they are risk averse."

It explains movie companies' reliance—over-reliance, Dahl judges—on the test marketing process. "Their investment is so great you can understand it," he says, "but it means anything that remotely makes people uncomfortable is taken out. You know, some things are *supposed* to make you uncomfortable."

And, in today's cluttered entertainment environment, studios need films with the kind of marketing hooks that can cut through the clutter. "There's a lot more demand for people's attention," says Dahl. "There's a couple of hundred channels of television you can watch, pay-per-view, you can buy a surround sound system for your house, DVDs are great little products with extra bonuses and you can watch DVD films in widescreen, people are plopping down $2-3,000 for big screen TVs."

The choices are endless, says Dahl, which pushes studios to gravitate toward movies whose chief quality is their ability to get attention, like big-budget special effects fests or movies with poke-in-the-eye hooks like *Snakes on a Plane*.

Dahl hopes the big studio strategy will actually cultivate fertile ground for an alternative: "I think there'll be a brand new explosion of independent films in the next few years. People have been fed a diet of one, big, bloated film after another. I don't know that anyone feels any great joy when they leave these films. When I saw *Capote* (2005), I thought that was as good a movie as I'd seen in a long time. Well-written, well-shot, well-acted, well-directed, extremely well-edited, it was a brilliant little film."

But this kind of filmmaking has to happen outside the major studios. "The studios don't know how to make (these kinds of movies)," says Dahl. "They couldn't afford to make them if they wanted to. Between the insurance, what the unions have done to them in terms of cost, they can't do it."

In one of the few instances Dahl's usual Montana reserve falters, he issues a call-to-arms to filmmakers themselves. "It's up to filmmakers to take risks!" he charges, "Sell their stupid big-ass car and make their own movie! Get your friends, get people you know!" He ponders a cinema counterpart to community theater, something outside the chokehold the major studios have on commercial filmmaking. "It's kind of a great time making your own movie like that. It's interesting for (filmmakers) to spend their own damn money, it's a lot more liberating and creative. There's an incredible sense of liberation in not having to consider what a studio exec, what those eleven people sitting at the gateway want to see!"

New technologies and venues make it possible, says Dahl. "You can edit a movie on a laptop and buy a high quality HD camera for $3,000. Somebody has to crack the distribution nut, though. The studios have this huge distribution machine. Think of what it takes to manufacture 3,000 prints of a movie, ship them out to thousands of theaters so they're there when they're supposed to be, all opening on the same day. And this massive studio distribution machine is governed by a small number of filters, the people who decide what movies are going to be made.

"The Internet, on the other hand," he proposes, "is very democratic. You want something to bring joy to your heart? MySpace is getting more hits than Google." On-line venues can provide an alternative to theatrical distribution, says Dahl. "The public is going to find a way to find something interesting."

The trick—and Dahl's largest, nagging doubt about the future—is in the "something interesting" part.

Dahl frequently speaks to film students. He's impressed with their technical expertise—"Their movies look good, they look like movies"—but, in terms of content, he finds what he sees "a little depressing. I see them imitating."

He senses little of the artistic aspiration that seemed to mark earlier generations of aspiring filmmakers; the kind of creative ambition that produced a personal and/or personalized kind of commercial filmmaking evidenced among so many of the most memorable movies of the 1960s/1970s. Rather, says Dahl, so many of the young filmmakers he meets seem to be striving "... to reach that point where somebody gives them $80 million to direct the next superhero epic. That's the goal it seems."

And that lack of hunger to creatively say something distinctive is something he feels isn't just confined to fledgling filmmakers. He sees it throughout the commercial entertainment spectrum; a new across-the-board creative ethic. "When I was growing up, playing music was an important thing, and there was an artistic *thing* people were striving for in the 1960s and 1970s. Now, you have *American Idol*. In the 1960s, 1970s, the big thing was, 'I won't sell out!' It's hard to see any of these *American Idol* kids having that argument. These young singers, young actors, musicians... it doesn't feel like there's an artistic integrity they're striving for. How else do you explain the phenomenon of Paris Hilton?"

He sees a similar trend in theater. He remembers taking his son to a production of the Disney stage show, *The Lion King*. "It was fun, it was spectacular, but I kept thinking, 'This is from a *movie!*' and I thought that was a little sad. It's not exactly Ibsen, is it? It's a far cry from *A Doll's House* or *The Glass Menagerie*. American theater history was pretty vibrant up to a certain point. Theater in the 1940s and 1950s was an elegant art form. Broadway today is recycling movies as plays. Broadway today is a joke."

Not only has the ambition among aspirants changed, but so too, thinks Dahl, has the creative sensibility. He remembers one young filmmaker who "... had decided the audience only had a long enough attention span to see an image for four seconds, then it had to change. I asked him, 'How'd you come up with that?' He said, 'Watch a classic movie like *The Rock* (1996). (Director) Michael Bay figured out you had to cut all the time.' I asked him, 'What year were you born?' 'Nineteen eighty-two'—about when MTV was launched." Dahl chuckles ruefully: "A 'classic' movie like *The Rock*."

Dahl remembers a four-hour compilation reel of movie car chases he put together as research for one of his projects. When he screened the reel, "You'd be surprised how many people came by and wanted to see that. I had to make copies for people!" According to Dahl, by wide consensus the car chase people thought was the best was the one from the 1968 cop thriller *Bullitt*. "Which is funny because, by today's standards, it's incredibly long, it doesn't have a lot of cuts, there's not a lot of damage. *The French Connection* (1971) came in a close Number Two. But the chase from that 'classic' *The Rock?* It made little or no impact. It seemed forced."

In Dahl's opinion, what those chases from earlier movies have going for them is not just the skillful ways they are assembled, but their sense of possibility; that they *could* happen. Whereas the chase from *The Rock*—as with many action sequences in today's thrillers— is so over-the-top, that sense of *impossibility* actually undercuts its effectiveness. "People didn't care."

He sighs. "These young people have never seen *Double Indemnity* or *Treasure of the Sierra Madre* (1948). They probably think they're just dusty old pictures."

Asked what movies he remembers and treasures, he replies, "*A Clockwork Orange* (1971) was the first time I really watched a move and said, 'Somebody had to *make* this thing! It didn't just show up in Billings, Montana.' Billy Wilder's films, Hitchcock... I thought they were great. Still do. *In Cold Blood* (1967) is a terrific film, *The Godfather* (1972) of course, *The Conversation* (1974)...

"I don't know that people are really interested in taking up the big issues of today." But, Dahl says, that's not something he particularly yearns for. While that's all well and good, he looks for the artistic drive to create something still more substantive than topical relevance. "It's pretty easy to beat up on George Bush. Do something different.

"I want a movie to be a timeless piece of material that can be watched now, ten years from now, and still have some resonance; to be lost in time. I never tried to make a movie that was hip and of the moment."

Asked to ruminate on the changes in audience tastes and the derivative tendencies of young filmmakers, Dahl is asked if he ever considers the possibility he might be making movies for an audience that no longer exists.

"I'm amazed anybody's *ever* seen the movies I've made!" he says, sounding earnestly surprised. "My world revolves around trying to find a movie, make a movie, then go on to the next one."

Scorsese & Tarantino: Whose Streets Are Meaner?
(posted 12/17/12)

I've got Martin Scorsese and Quentin Tarantino on my mind these days. It's a product of the end-of-year hurrahs for Scorsese's *Hugo*. The film goes into the Academy Award ceremonies with 11 Oscar nominations—the most of any film this year—including a Best Director nod for Scorsese. Win or lose, Marty's on a roll having already taken a Golden Globe for his work on the film, and selection as Best Director by the National Board of Review (the Board also named *Hugo* Best Picture). And that doesn't include the film's placing on any number of critic's Year's Best lists.

What does all this have to do with Tarantino? It brings to mind a statement the younger filmmaker had made about Scorsese some years ago.

They've always been linked, these two. Tarantino had been anointed by more than a few as "the next Scorsese" with his 1992 directorial debut, *Reservoir Dogs*. *Dogs*'s mix of unrepentant low-lifers and profanity-as-gutter-poetry dialogue harkened some reviewers back to Scorsese's own breakout nearly twenty years before: *Mean Streets* (1973). Tarantino himself has often cited Scorsese as one of the filmmakers whose work has had a "huge" influence on his own filmmaking (along with Howard Hawks, Brian DePalma, and Sergio Leone).

I've tried to run the quote down to make sure I have it exact (I'd hate to stir up a fuss with a bit of misremembering), but haven't been able to trace it. It would've been after the releases of Tarantino's *Kill Bill*s (*Vol. 1*–2003; *Vol. 2*–2004) and Scorsese's Howard Hughes biopic, *The Aviator* (2004). Tarantino said something to the effect that he didn't want to wind up in his later years like Scorsese making movies about Howard Hughes.

I don't know if Tarantino was suggesting Scorsese had passed his peak, or that he'd reached a point in his career where he had to make movies—as Tarantino once said of a certain tier of directors—"… to pay for (his) pool." Or, perhaps the notoriously motor-mouthed filmmaker was just on a jag and his tongue got a little in front of his head. Whatever: dig, observation, or slip of the tongue, I remember thinking it wasn't particularly flattering. Or fair.

Since then, Scorsese's filmography has been extended by the Oscar-winning *The Departed* (2006—which also copped him the

Best Director trophy); the Rolling Stones rockumentary *Shine the Light* (2008); his biggest hit in thriller *Shutter Island* (2010); the docs *A Letter to Elia* (about director Elia Kazan), and *Public Speaking* (about writer Fran Lebowitz) (both 2010); the pilot for the HBO series *Boardwalk Empire* (2010—for which he won an Emmy); the HBO doc *George Harrison: Living in the Material World* (2011—named among the Top Five Documentaries of the year by the National Board of Review); and, of course, *Hugo*. That's almost as much directorial work as Tarantino has turned in since and including *Reservoir Dogs* nineteen years ago.

But as much as Tarantino might have been influenced by Scorsese, and for all the comparisons made – at least early in Tarantino's career— between them, it is, at best, a tenuous, wholly superficial connection. Lean back and squint, and maybe they look related. Close up; not so much.

*****

Scorsese had been a frail and sickly child, unable to run the vibrant streets of his Little Italy neighborhood like the other kids. Instead, there were hours spent in front of the TV with the then movie-heavy New York channels. His father, a film buff, tried to compensate for young Scorsese's home-bound days by taking him to the local movies houses, sometimes twice a week or more. Between what he caught on TV and what his father exposed him to at Manhattan cinemas, Scorsese was introduced to a wildly eclectic range of films and filmmakers at an early age, from Ford and Fuller to Powell and DeSica; Hollywood schlock like *Land of the Pharaohs* (1955), to the dark poetry and startling color palette of *The Red Shoes* (1948).

He may have been too often stuck in his family's lower East Side apartment, but he was not oblivious to the world around him. He soaked up the drama, the humor, the color of the New York streets, of the urban Italian-American experience, came to understand the double-edged sword of family/tribal loyalties—how they brought belonging but also how they stifled and strangled, and how they could cultivate a culture of compelled, sacrificial self-destruction. After years percolating and ripening, that sensibility would become one of the most vivid and integral textual colors, almost a character in itself, in movies like *Mean Streets, Raging Bull* (1980), *Goodfellas* (1990), and others. It morphed and mutated, transposing itself to the Boston crime scene for *The Departed,* and to a New York long gone and nearly forgotten in *The Age of Innocence* (1993) and *Gangs of New York* (2002).

He acquired more than a passion for movies from his upbringing. His was also a spiritual family, devoutly Catholic, and that sensibility imprinted on Scorsese's creative self just as deeply as his feel for The City and his sense of his Italian blood. It was a feeling held deeply enough that Scorsese considered the priesthood as a vocation, even attended seminary school for a year. He never gave up his spiritual quest, continuing his investigation of conscience and soul, of spiritual uplift and human foible in his films, sometimes overtly (*The Last Temptation of Christ* [1988]; *Kundun* [1997]), sometimes obliquely (*Mean Streets's* Charlie [Harvey Keitel] oblivious to the paradox of trying to stake out his nobility amidst the ignobility of his street hood existence). "My whole life," Scorsese has said, "has been movies and religion. That's it. Nothing else."

He gave up pursuing one passion—religion—for another, dropping out of his studies for the priesthood to study film at New York University.

In the early 1960s, the two great centers of film study were NYU and the University of Southern California, but their philosophies were markedly different. Admittedly speaking purely in broad strokes, USC looked at film as a trade (unsurprisingly as the USC film program had been co-founded by the Academy of Motion Picture Arts & Sciences), concentrating on practical skills and the business of making movies. NYU looked at film as an *art;* film not just as a form of entertainment, but as a means of personal expression. NYU was the perfect greenhouse for the soulful Scorsese.

At NYU, Scorsese's already broad film sense was widened still further. The French New Wave, the *cinema verite* documentary movement—all made their mark on the avid young film student. Look at *Mean Streets* with Scorsese's bio in mind, and it's impossible *not* to see the interplay of Italian neo-realism, French New Wave, and *cinema verite* combining with Scorsese's view-from-the-stoop of life on the New York streets, and his own search for a spiritual centeredness in a non-spiritual world.

His appetite for all things cinematic was—and remains—voracious. Ben Kingsley, who plays film pioneer Georges Méliès in *Hugo*, recently told *USA Today*, "We overuse the term until it's meaningless, but Marty truly is passionate, especially about the legacy of movies… I'm not sure there's a movie Martin hasn't seen." Late last year, Sound on Sight posted a video interview with Scorsese where he commented on the passing of British director Ken Russell. Watch how easily Scorsese references Russell's obscure early work, the black-and-white shorts done for the BBC profiling figures from the arts like Isadora Duncan, Rosetti, Sibelius, Coleridge. What strikes me watching that clip isn't just how Scorsese's knowledge of cinema seems bottomless, but how he also seems well-acquainted with the *subjects* of Russell's BBC works. It's not hard to imagine the self-admitted obsessive watching Russell's film on Sibelius, say, then, ignited by what he saw, going on to read up on the Finnish composer, listening to recordings of his work, and on and on and on.

At a purely intellectual level, Scorsese's closest filmmaking relative would be, to my mind, Woody Allen. Though stylistic and thematic opposites, both inform their films not just with their passion for classic and art house cinema, but in drawing from centuries of western art, culture, and thought. Allen digs into it all—philosophy, spirituality, psychology, the whole shmear of western intellectualism—and boils it down to an on-the-nose joke (in *Hannah and Her Sisters* [1986], Allen's character grapples with the idea of persistent evil in the world, asking his father how God could permit the existence of Nazis; "How the hell do I know why there were Nazis?" his father replies, "I don't even know how the can opener works!"). Scorsese dips into the same, big pool, only instead of a joke, brings it to a tragic—and often violent—demonstration of human frailty and fallibility. (*Mean Streets's* Charlie doomed by his self-appointment as savior to Robert DeNiro's reckless, impulsive Johnny Boy.)

If he somewhat resembles Woody Allen intellectually, the course of his career mirrors, to some degree, that of his good friend Steven Spielberg. Thematically, they're night and day. Even Spielberg at his darkest believes in an ultimate demonstration of good, whereas Scorsese's work usually works from the idea that we're born into shit, then things go downhill from there. They're polar opposites stylistically as well. Spielberg is a classicist and will take a graceful dolly shot over a smash cut any day. It's hard to imagine Spielberg putting together a sequence as fragmented and fevered as Ray Liotta's coke-fueled, rock-scored down-spiral into *Goodfellas's* climactic dope bust.

But they are both cinematic adventurers. It came late to Spielberg. Liberated from an over-reliance on audience-friendly fantasy and romanticism by the grim material of Holocaust drama *Schindler's List* (1993), Spielberg has since felt free to follow his interests, light and dark, through an impressive, increasingly eclectic body of work ranging from the Capra-esque *The Terminal* (2004) to the controversial political thriller *Munich* (2005); from the breezy chase flick *Catch Me If You Can* (2002), to his disturbingly brutal re-envisioning of World War II in *Saving Private Ryan* (1998).

The difference is Scorsese has *always* been such an explorer, adamantine in chasing off after whatever engaged him oblivious to its commercial appeal. Look at just his early years: he pinballed from the *Mean Streets* of New York to the sun-baked southwest in one of the best women's movies of the 1970s, *Alice Doesn't Live Here Anymore* (1974), then back to New York for the near-surreal *Taxi Driver* (1976), then a jump back in time for the period musical *(New York, New York* [1977]), and then off to San Francisco's Winterland Ballroom to film the final performance of The Band for the rockumentary *The Last Waltz* (1978).

He didn't hit the mark every time: *New York, New York*'s pair of unlikable lead characters (played by Robert DeNiro and Liza Minnelli) left audiences cold; some felt his Ophuls-influenced *The Age of Innocence* could have used a little less Ophuls and a little more Scorsese heat; by his own admission he was trying to make too big a movie for too little money in *The Last Temptation of Christ*; his remake of *Cape Fear* (1991)—one of his few admitted mercenary forays into the commercial mainstream—doesn't have the same low-key queasiness of the 1962 original; *The Gangs of New York* has a second-act sag; Leonardo DiCaprio comes close but doesn't quite cut it as Howard Hughes in *The Aviator*...

But the point isn't that he's made a number of flawed films. The point is that despite Scorsese's close identification with violent crime stories, almost three-quarters of his nearly thirty theatrical features are about something *else*: romance, music, history, the quest for spiritual inner peace. *Hugo*, as his latest example, is his passionate tribute to the medium that has meant so much to him.

As the range of his interests has widened, his technical ability has also grown, sometimes in quantum leaps. Look at the rough-edged, near-documentary feel of *Mean Streets*, then look at *Raging Bull* seven years later, exchanging *Streets*'s lurid neon colors for *Bull*'s harsh black-and-white, the gritty hand-held camerawork of the former for balletic swoops and swirls inside the boxing ring. Then jump ahead again for the Ophuls-like classicism of *The Age of Innocence,* and then again to see him take command of CGI for *Gangs of New York* and *The Aviator,* growing so deft in its application he knew how to use it to sweeten even a naturalistic, contemporary work like *The Departed,* adding a computer-generated rat scurrying along assassinated Matt Damon's apartment balcony as a punctuation mark to a film about betrayal layered on betrayal layered on betrayal.

Nearly every review of *Hugo* calls it an uncharacteristic work for Scorsese; that the last thing anyone expected from Martin *Mean Streets/Taxi Driver/Raging Bull/Goodfellas/Casino/ The Departed* Scorsese is a gentle, lovely, period piece dedicated to childhood wonder and curiosity. But looking at his body of work, in its supposed uncharacteristic-ness *Hugo* is actually quite in character for the filmmaker; it's right in line with his willingness to follow his own sense of wonder and curiosity, to tell a story he hasn't told before in a way he hasn't told one before. His use of 3-D for the film—a first for Scorsese—is considered the best application of the process since James Cameron's *Avatar* (2009), even by Cameron himself who has called it "absolutely the best 3-D photography that I've seen." This, too, is quite in keeping with Scorsese's ongoing evolution; Scorsese remaining the committed, voracious student he was in his NYU days. "The fun part," Scorsese told *USA Today* recently, "is trying new things. It's still magic. Someday, movies will just be holograms. I'd like to make one of those, too."

Hugo also shows—despite what Tarantino *might* have meant those years ago—that Marty's still got it.

*****

From the ground up, Tarantino is a different animal. But then, he's traveled a wholly different route to the director's chair than Scorsese.

Scorsese was born to a tight-knit family in what is certainly one of the most colorful—to say the least—cities in the world as well as being, inarguably, a cultural and media Mecca. Tarantino, in contrast, was born in Knoxville, Tennessee. He never knew his father, and his teen-aged mother relocated them to a drab, downscale Los Angeles neighborhood when he was two. He was lousy at school, felt very much the loner, the outsider, finally dropping out before finishing high school. He found company with comic books and TV, famously taking a job as a clerk at Video Archives, a video store in Manhattan Beach.

Video Archives was Tarantino's NYU. He became a connoisseur of cinematic junk food, fed on a steady diet of Hollywood classics mixed with grindhouse cinema. The way the USC tradesmen could talk about Hitchcock and the NYU cineastes about Trauffaut, Tarantino could talk about splatter-master Herschel Gordon Lewis, and the subtle differences between the low-budget chop-socky flicks turned out by the Shaw Brothers and Golden Harvest. "When people ask me if I went to film school," Tarantino once said, "I tell them, 'no, I went to films.'"

He had a passion for cinema and an almost frightening gut-level understanding of how movies worked. And, as Peter Biskind put it in a 2003 *Vanity Fair* profile of Tarantino, "(he) could write like an angel, Richard Price on acid, providing a heady mix of B-movie attitude and *nouvelle vogue* cool..."

During his video store days he hammered out the screenplays for *True Romance* (1993) and *Natural Born Killers* (1994). In 1990, he landed a job at Cinetel, a production company, and when he couldn't get *Romance* financed to make himself, his Cinetel contacts got the screenplay into the hands of director Tony Scott who picked up the rights.

Scorsese's first film had been the self-financed, little-seen indie, *Who's That Knocking On My Door?* (1967), and his second feature was a hunk of drive-in fodder for low-budget king Roger Corman called *Boxcar Bertha* (1972). Scorsese's career didn't break big until *Mean Streets* the following year. But high school drop-out Tarantino had hit the big time while still in his 20s with that first sale to a major director.

Two years later, he made his directorial debut with *Reservoir Dogs*. Scott's rendering of *True Romance* followed the year after that, and provocateur Oliver Stone added to Tarantino's cachet with one of the most controversial releases of 1994, *Natural Born Killers*. That same year, Tarantino entrenched himself indelibly as one of the *enfants terrible* of the '90s indie scene with his second directorial effort, *Pulp Fiction*. The film copped seven Oscar nominations and a win for Tarantino and cowriter Roger Avary for Best Original Screenplay.

Like *Mean Streets*, for all the buzz *Reservoir Dogs* had generated, it hadn't been a particularly big hit, or much of a hit at all, pulling in less than $3 million. But *Pulp Fiction* was a monster, grossing $108 million domestic, and nearly doubling that worldwide, against a budget of just $8 million. For years, *Dogs*, the first indie to cross the $100 million box office barrier, would hold the record as highest-earning indie release.

In contrast, it took Scorsese three decades to hit the magic $100 million number. Prior, he'd done no better than moderate hits, and had actually produced a fair number of duds like *New York, New York* ($16.4 million against a budget of $14 million), and *King of Comedy* ($2.5 million/$20 million). Even some of his most memorable works were no better than mid-rangers. *Goodfellas*, for example, had done a respectable but hardly towering $47 million; *Taxi Driver* did $28 million (roughly equivalent for its time); and *Raging Bull* had been considered something of a stiff earning $23 million against an $18 million budget. In fact, until the early 2000s, Scorsese's biggest hits hadn't been his more personal films, but his gun-for-hire gigs: *The Color of Money* (1986) at $52 million; the remake of *Cape Fear* at $79 million. It wasn't until *The Aviator* that Scorsese finally turned in a big earner ($102 million).

Early success turned out to be a double-edged sword for Tarantino. He followed *Pulp* with his first non-original project, *Jackie Brown* (1997), an adaptation of Elmore Leonard's novel *Rum Punch*. While *Brown* was Tarantino's homage to grindhouse era blaxploitation flicks, it also turned out to be his most—for lack of a better word—*human* effort. To its credit, it lacks the video store sensibility underpinning all of his other work, and has, reflectively, been considered one of his most overlooked and underappreciated efforts.

It was also quite unfairly rated a flop. *Brown* earned $40 million against a budget of $12 million, which is an ROI any producer would be happy with. But judged against the high orbit performance of *Pulp Fiction*, it looked like a loser... maybe even in Tarantino's eyes. Biskind quotes a Tarantino associate as saying, "I think he (Tarantino) thinks he fucked up."

It's easy to look at Tarantino in the years after *Jackie Brown* and judge him to be a guy who couldn't come up with the answer to, 'What do I do now?' He wrote, working on the scripts for *Inglourious Basterds* and the *Kill Bill*s; he palled around with friend and fellow filmmaker Robert Rodriguez in Rodriguez' home ground of Austin, hanging out with film geeks and running mini-film festivals of obscure video-store-back-shelf directors; and, he pursued acting, another of the passions of his youth, although judging by the pasting he took from critics as the villain in a Broadway revival of *Wait Until Dark*, it was hardly one of his strong suits. He seemed to be doing everything *but* make another film.

The perceived failure of *Jackie Brown* may have left him gun-shy. Biskind quotes a Tarantino friend as saying, "He doesn't trust himself as an artist to be able to make something that is not popular." And, from Uma Thurman: "(Quentin) was waiting for something to be extraordinary, something he could top himself with, to pull him out of his house." It would be six years before another Quentin Tarantino movie hit theaters.

This is not to say that Scorsese, in contrast, was one to respond to disappointments with Tibetan monk-like philosophical equanimity. Hardly. Biskind, in his book *Easy Riders, Raging Bulls: How the Sex-Drugs-and-Rock 'n' Roll Generation Saved Hollywood*, reports Scorsese reacting to box office duds like *New York, New York* and *Raging Bull* with self-medication, therapy, failed relationships, violent outbursts. Yet the ever-obsessive Scorsese, even while still choking on the commercial failure of one film, seemed to already be chasing his next one, typically a project just as risky and daring as the one that had just withered and died at the box office. Within the six years after his first and biggest failure—*New York, New York*—Scorsese turned out the rock documentary *The Last Waltz* the following year in 1978, *Raging Bull* in 1980, and *The King of Comedy* in 1983. Though highly respected now, at the time they were, in fact, a string of box office duds that extended into 1985 with *After Hours*. It was a losing streak Scorsese didn't break until 1986's *The Color of Money*.

When Tarantino did come back with the *Kill Bills*, it was with an even stronger commitment to the hyperbolic grindhouse/graphic novel sensibility that had flavored *Reservoir Dogs* and *Pulp Fiction*. It was not just a matter of the filmmaker turning for his comfort zone, but an acknowledgment that this was where his fan base lived. Biskind quotes another Tarantino friend: "Quentin has always felt that his core audience is adolescents, geeky boys."

Tarantino held fast to that sensibility thereafter through *Grindhouse*, the 2007 homage to the films of his video store clerk days done in collaboration with Robert Rodriguez; and *Inglourious Basterds*, his biggest commercial hit ($120.5 million), and a critical triumph. *Inglourious* received eight Academy Award nominations including Best Picture and, for Tarantino himself, Best Screenplay; his first Oscar nods since *Pulp Fiction*. After the so-so returns of *Kill Bill* (*Parts 1 & 2* grossed a combined $136 million against a combined $60 million budget) and a flop with *Grindhouse* ($25 million against $67 million), *Basterds* seemed a confident reclaiming of his King of the Indies status.

For the foreseeable future, Tarantino's game plan seems to be more of the same. Later this year will come *Django Unchained,* a story about an escaped slave, which will be the filmmaker's homage to his beloved spaghetti Westerns, and then, tentatively scheduled for 2014, comes *Kill Bill: Vol. 3*.

It is that sensibility—more than temperament, more than style, more than career course—which is the defining difference between the two filmmakers.

Back in the mid-1990s, filmmaker/author John Sayles was interviewed by *Entertainment Weekly* for one of those what's-wrong-with-the-movies stories they do periodically (again, I hope I'm not misremembering something from an article I can't run down). Sayles was comparing the filmmakers who'd come up in the 1960s/1970s with the following generation, using Scorsese as an example of the former. Though he didn't mention Tarantino by name, I couldn't help, based on the thrust of his comment, but think at the time Tarantino was at least one of the filmmakers Sayles had in mind.

Sayles said something to the effect that the difference between the generations was Scorsese made movies inspired by what he saw on the New York streets from his apartment window, while the new, young breed of filmmakers made movies inspired by Martin Scorsese movies.

Tarantino talks of "the movie-movie universe, where movie conventions are embraced, and almost fetishized (e.g. *Kill Bill)*, as opposed to the other universe where *Pulp Fiction* and *Reservoir Dogs* take place, in which reality and movie conventions collide," but, with the exception of *Jackie Brown*, there's actually very little reality in *any* of his movies. The only difference between *Pulp Fiction* and *Reservoir Dogs*, and the likes of *Kill Bill* and *Inglourious Basterds*, is one of degree not nature.

The hoods and tough-as-nails situations and brutal/comedic dialogue of *Reservoir Dogs* and *Pulp Fiction* offer a patina of at-first-glance *Mean Streets* realism, but that's all it is: a veneer. They don't have so much in common with *Mean Streets* as they do with *Sin City*, the 2005 neo-*noir* Frank Miller adapted from his own graphic novel and that was co-directed by Robert Rodriguez, Miller, and Tarantino (billed as "special guest director").

Like its source material, *Sin City* mimics, in high style, the visual tropes of *noir*, but in its hyperbolic characters and story-telling, it misses the heart of what post-war *noir* was all about. *True noir* was not the freak show *Sin City* is, but was often about how one misstep, one bad break, one lapse in judgment could take Joe (or Joan) Anybody down a domino fall of faulty remedies and cover-ups that only made bad situations tragically, lethally worse. Fed on post-war disillusionment, *noir* was all about there-but-for-the-grace-of-God-go-you. *Sin City*, on the other hand, is a universe that can only exist on Miller's pages and their screen offspring.

Tarantino's crime films are the same. They ape the tough, streety tropes of Scorsese, but, at heart, they're confections, comic books for young adult males inspired by a thousand nights of grindhouse grotesques and cheap drive-in thrills, Mix Mastered into Tarantino's own, unique funny/scary/suspenseful/gag-inducing puree. The situations and characters may be more familiar than the sword-wielding assassins of *Kill Bill*, but like the denizens of *Kill Bill*, they cease to exist once the projector closes down.

What makes them work is Tarantino's utter conviction in their reality, however unreal they may be. Tarantino is like a kid playing Let's Pretend; in that moment of pretending, the most outlandish scenarios—fighting off monsters, taking Pork Chop Hill—are, for that kid, *real*. It's Tarantino's sincerity in his craziness that makes the crazy play, backed by an awesome ability with actors (he's probably resuscitated more veteran actors' careers than rehab), a gift for clever plotting, and the ability to make his "fuck"-filled dialogue play on the ears like great rock 'n' roll.

I'm not arguing who's the better filmmaker. These are both tremendously talented guys, but despite the linkage film writers built between them at the beginning of Tarantino's career, they are talented in distinct, separate ways. Scorsese is the baker telling you the difference between French and Italian pastry, while Tarantino is explaining why Hostess cupcakes are better than Tastycake's. It's not a question of "better"; it's a question of taste.

What's undeniable, in Scorsese's case—and he has the benefit of a forty-odd year career to make the point for him—is that he has created a lasting body of respected work, and that he remains a vital, exploratory filmmaker at an age when most directorial careers are slowing down if they haven't died completely. Hell, considering the changes in the American movie industry over the course of his career combined with his own rises and falls, Scorsese should get a special Oscar just for surviving this long.

Tarantino's place in the American film canon is still an open question. He may very well wind up like one of his idols—Howard Hawks—in that he finds a comfortable, clearly defined niche, settles in there and mines it comfortably for the course of his career. Which, as Hawks showed, is not necessarily a bad thing. Cautionary note: by the time Hawks remade *Rio Bravo* (1959) for the second time as *Rio Lobo* (1970), he was also showing how getting *too* comfortable in a niche could led to a staleness, to a dulling feeling of this-feels-*awfully*-familiar. We'll have to wait and see.

In the meantime, there's always been room for both breeds of filmmaker in the American mainstream: the artist who sometimes manages to also entertain, and the entertainer who sometimes manages to create art.

Cinderella Man's Cinderella Man: Cliff Hollingsworth
(posted 10/30/10)

Watching *Secretariat* fighting for box office air against much more muscular earners like comic actioner *Red* ($43.5 million after two weeks), the David Fincher/Aaron Sorkin rendering of the birth of Facebook in *The Social Network* ($72 million in four weeks), Ben Affleck's gutsy crime thriller *The Town* ($84.7million in six weeks), and box office steamrollers *Jackass 3-D* ($86.9 million in two weeks) and *Paranormal Activity 2* ($40.7 million in its first week), reminds one just how hard it is for sports-themed movies to hit the box office sweet spot Gary Ross nailed so squarely with *Seabiscuit* back in 2003 ($120 million domestic gross; seven Oscar noms). As it is, *Secretariat*—with $37.4 million at the box office at the three-week mark, a second week drop in earnings of about a third followed by a third week drop of forty-four percent and saddled with middling reviews—will have to struggle just to make breakeven (probably somewhere in the $80 million range).

Studios have been looking for that next inspiring triumph-of-the-underdog sports flick since *Seabiscuit* with mixed results. They've looked to football *(Friday Night Lights* [2004], remake *The Longest Yard* [2005], *Invincible* and *We Are Marshall* [both 2006], *The Blind Side* [2009]), boxing *(Million Dollar Baby* [2004], *Rocky* reboot *Rocky Balboa* [2006]), and, naturally enough, horse racing *(Hidalgo* [2004], *Dreamer: Inspired by a True Story* [2005]).

It's about a fifty-fifty split between underperformers and titles that hit the mark, with quality and acclaim no guarantee of commercial success. Sports movies with a higher profile and greater critical cachet than *Secretariat* have had just as hard a slog at the box office. Case in point, and easily one of the best sports films of the last decade, was 2005's critically lauded, Oscar-nominated *Cinderella Man*, written by Cliff Hollingsworth. The story behind Hollingsworth and *Cinderella Man* is every bit as much an against-the-odds, come-from-behind tale as the one on the screen.

Raised in Barnwell, South Carolina, Hollingsworth went to the University of South Carolina in the 1970s with no particular interest in film or even in writing. He majored in broadcast journalism and went on to a master's degree in teaching. It was during his years in grad school he began to consider writing a screenplay.

"My first try was so long it was absurd," says Hollingsworth. He wrote the screenplay out by hand, but as soon as he began reading it over "realized it wouldn't work." And there was that issue of the length: "It would've been a five-hour movie!"

Still, he continued to write, and, in 1982, headed to Los Angeles with a handful of what he hoped were marketable screenplays. However, as a novice screenwriter with no representation or connections to the industry, he had no access at any level of the business. He supported himself with work as a security guard while also taking a writing class at Sherwood Oaks Film College. It was the support of his instructor, Barry Snider, which helped keep his spirits up. "He told me I had talent and to stick with it." Hollingsworth put enough stock in Snider's opinion for it to keep him motivated.

Two years later, Hollingsworth still hadn't placed any work, and now his mother was in failing health. He didn't think it was fair for him to be chasing a dream in Los Angeles while his brother, Mike, was home shouldering the full responsibility for taking care of their mother. The brothers struck a deal: Hollingsworth would spend six months in L.A., then come back to take care of their mother for six months, then go back to L.A., and so on.

"That put a big crimp on things," acknowledges Hollingsworth. The bouncing back and forth between coasts was wearing. Each time he returned to L.A. he had to get a new apartment, new phone number, new job, etc. He lived this way from 1984-1997, all the time trying to break into the movie business during his six month sprints on The Coast. During his L.A. periods, he worked as a security guard at a number of places including Universal (ironic since this would ultimately become the home for *Cinderella Man*). In 1986, he began substitute teaching, which didn't pay all that much better than security work. "I lived in some real dumps," says Hollingsworth. "I'd buy a mattress from the Salvation Army, I'd have it on the floor. That and a table would be my only furniture." In 1997, with his mother's condition worsening, he returned to South Carolina permanently, taking care of her until she passed away.

Sometime around 1994-1995, Hollingsworth wrote *Cinderella Man*; the Depression Era true story of the comeback of one-time light heavyweight boxer James J. Braddock. Hollingsworth tracked down Braddock's two sons and spent hours with them listening to stories about their father. "They were invaluable," says Hollingsworth, providing him with the kind of information "... you couldn't get from books."

The appeal to Hollingsworth—to any writer, in fact—was obvious: champion boxer loses almost everything during The Depression, his situation becomes so desperate he nearly loses his family, then he mounts a bruising comeback.

Says Hollingsworth: "It was a fantastic story. If I'd written it as fiction, nobody'd believe it." The story had everything, thought Hollingsworth: a strong, human element, triumph over adversity, a rags-to-riches arc, an always-darkest-before-the-dawn suspense line, and improbable but true turn-arounds.

For instance, taking on small-time fights to make a few dollars, Braddock breaks his right hand. He takes a job moving cargo on the docks only able to use his left hand. When he returns to the fight game, the constant working of his left has turned him from a one-handed fighter into a two-handed puncher; what had been the worst possible turn of events actually helps turn his career around.

"There's usually enough drama as it is in fighting for a heavyweight title," says Hollingsworth, but ratcheting the suspense elements up still more were the real-life circumstances surrounding Braddock's climactic match with reigning champ Max Baer.

Baer had been considered responsible for the death of two of his opponents (one died in the ring against Baer, while another died in a bout against another fighter though it was speculated his death might actually have been a delayed result from the beating he'd taken in an earlier fight against Baer). There was a feeling the older Braddock might be risking more than just a lost fight climbing into the ring against Baer.

The first year Hollingsworth had come to Los Angeles, a waitress at a night club he'd met had introduced him to her husband, Abraham Gordon, who, at the time, was heading story development for a small direct-to-video company, Spectacor. Gordon encouraged Hollingsworth to go forward on the Braddock story, and tried to help him get an agent. Gordon called several reps, but none would read the material. Based on the pitch, they unanimously felt *Cinderella Man* might be a great story, but it was "just" a sports story. "It didn't help that I was a new writer," adds Hollingsworth, or that the story was a probably costly period piece (*Cinderella Man's* production budget: $88 million). Only Abraham Gordon believed in the piece, seeing it as less of a sports story, and more of a triumph of the human spirit.

A Hollingsworth friend, Ed McCormick, had recently launched a talent agency to represent musicians back in Denmark, South Carolina, working out of an office in the back of his used furniture store. McCormick also saw the potential in Hollingsworth's script, and, for Hollingsworth's sake, became a signatory with the WGA so Hollingsworth could now have representation. McCormick and Mike Hollingsworth began making calls pitching *Cinderella Man*. In the summer of 1996, Mike Hollingsworth managed to get a pitch in with someone at the production company of *Laverne & Shirley* star cum director Penny Marshall. Though Marshall's box office track record was mixed, two of her five previous films had been huge hits: *Big* (1988), and *A League of Their Own* (1992). That same summer, he also got a pitch in at Turner Communications. Both companies read the screenplay, and both wanted it.

Mike Hollingsworth's contact at Marshall's company passed it on to the director with a "recommended." Marshall gave it a read and decided she wanted the property. Thereafter, things happened quickly.

Marshall then had offices on the Universal lot; the same lot where Hollingsworth had been working night shifts as a security guard just a few years earlier. Universal decided they wanted the project as well. Turner, still wanting the property, called Marshall and told her, "If Universal doesn't make it, bring it to us."

By then, Hollingsworth was back in Carolina tending to his ailing mother. Irby Walker, a long-time friend and a Conway, South Carolina attorney, teamed up with Gordon to negotiate the deal with Universal. According to Hollingsworth, "Both Irby and Abraham did a terrific job. Irby did most of the negotiating with Abraham advising him, and making a few calls, too. They got an excellent deal for me, and a tremendous deal for the Braddock family. It had to be especially gratifying for Abraham to be part of the negotiations. After hearing from agent after agent that he was wrong, and that it wouldn't make a good movie, here he was helping negotiate the contract for the script that every agent he'd pitched it to had snubbed." Before the deal was finalized, Universal flew Hollingsworth to New York to meet with Marshall to discuss script changes.

After Hollingsworth delivered his rewrite, another writer was brought in, and then the project seemed to momentarily stall. "For a while, I thought I was getting it back," says Hollingsworth. Other parties were already interested, including Harvey Weinstein who was still at Miramax at the time. But then Universal exercised their option and purchased the screenplay outright.

For a while, the project followed a maybe-yes/maybe-no course. At one point, Marshall was out and Billy Bob Thornton was attached as director with the possibility of Brad Pitt starring, but a threatened strike caused everyone to hesitate, and, during the interval, the Thornton/Pitt team came apart. Then, Lasse Hallstrom, coming off the Oscar-winning hit *The Cider House Rules* (1999), was supposed to direct, but that arrangement unraveled too.

The project finally began to gel when Russell Crowe expressed an interest in playing Braddock. At the time, Crowe was on a streak, coming off of two massive hits—*Gladiator* (2000) and *A Beautiful Mind* (2001)—and a highly praised performance in the Napoleonic War adventure, *Master and Commander: The Far Side of the World* (2003). Crowe sent the screenplay to producer/director Ron Howard with whom he'd had a productive relationship on the Oscar-winning *Beautiful Mind*, which had earned Crowe a nod for Best Actor as well as a U.S. box office of $170.7 million—a remarkable take in an era when dramas rarely earn blockbuster revenues. Once Howard signed on, the project was underway.

Universal released *Cinderella Man* in early June 2005. Conventional Hollywood wisdom was against a summer opening for such an adult-skewing story, since the season's box office was primarily driven by young ticket-buyers usually attracted to stories of the fantastic boasting large-scale action and spectacular special effects. That May had already seen the release of the remake *The Longest Yard* and the concluding chapter in the *Star Wars* saga, *Episode III—Revenge of the Sith*. The weeks after *Cinderella Man's* release would see Steven Spielberg's remake of *War of the Worlds*, Warners' franchise relaunch *Batman Begins*, TV spinoff *Bewitched*, another remake in the horror flick *George A. Romero's Dawn of the Dead*, and action comedy *Mr. and Mrs. Smith*—all in June; and then in July would come Tim Burton's extravagant fantasy remake *Charlie and the Chocolate Factory*, franchise launch *Fantastic Four*, action thriller *Stealth*, big budget sci-fier *The Island*, and two more horror entries,

The Devil's Rejects and *Dark Water*; and finally, summer would wind down in August with suspense thriller *Red Eye*, special effects fest *The Brothers Grimm*, and another TV spinoff, *The Dukes of Hazzard*.

Universal was undoubtedly hoping for a repeat of its 2003 summer coup with another suspenseful sports tale, *Seabiscuit*. Released a month later in the summer than *Cinderella Man*, and up against equally stiff youth-skewing competition (including Pixar's animated *Finding Nemo, Pirates of the Caribbean: The Curse of the Black Pearl, The Hulk, S.W.A.T.,* and sequels *2 Fast 2 Furious, The Matrix Reloaded, Bad Boys II,* and *X2: X-Men United*), *Seabiscuit* went on to an impressive $120.1 million domestic.

Universal had other reasons to be optimistic as well. Howard's previous ten films had had an average U.S. gross of over $101 million per title, and Crowe's previous five pictures had averaged just about the same as well as bringing the actor a Best Actor Oscar and two nominations.

At first, it seemed Universal's instincts had been on-target. *Cinderella Man* opened to nearly unanimously positive reviews (a canvass of 198 reviews by Rotten Tomatoes shows 80% positive). Roger Ebert called the movie, "terrific," *Variety* labeled it, "exquisite," and Peter Travers at *Rolling Stone* declared it "(Ron) Howard's best movie." Many reviewers considered *Cinderella Man* an early Oscar contender. Still, the movie opened somewhat weaker than *Seabiscuit* despite a heftier rollout ($18.3 million from 2,812 screens v. $20.9 million on 1,987 screens).

The movie never seemed to gain traction with the audience, and by the time it concluded its run in November, domestic grosses had capped out at $61.6 million; respectable in terms of admissions, but disappointing in light of the movie's $88 million cost. Even foreign returns—$46.9 million—weren't enough to bring *Cinderella Man* close to breakeven (typically, at *least* twice the production cost).

It should be pointed out, however, that *Cinderella Man*'s box office numbers may have been less a product of Universal's flouting the conventional wisdom of summer releases than a symptom of larger problems in the industry at the time. Both attendance and box office for 2005 had been running behind 2004 since the beginning of January, and would remain so for most of the year. Year's end would see 2005 turn out to be the latest chapter in an ever-lengthening losing streak for Hollywood, attendance having dropped each year since 2002.

That aside, there was little difference between *Cinderella Man*'s earnings and those of other equally acclaimed releases that year. The average box office for the five films nominated for the 2005 Best Picture Oscar *(Brokeback Mountain, Capote, Crash, Good Night, and Good Luck, Munich)* was just under $50 million, with *Brokeback Mountain* at the high end with $83 million, and *Capote* at the low end with $28.8 million. Only two non-action-driven, non-fantasy films made it into the year's Top twenty earners: biopic *Walk the Line* (at #16), and claustrophobic suspenser *Flightplan* (#20), with most of the top earners being typically lightweight summer fare: *Star Wars: Episode III, The Chronicles of Narnia: The Lion, the Witch and the Wardrobe, War of the Worlds,* the remake of *King Kong,* franchise launch *Fantastic Four,* and the like.

There were more disappointments for the film when the 2005 Academy Award nominations came in. The oft-predicted nods for Best Picture, Best Director, Best Original Screenplay and Best Actor never materialized (*Cinderella Man* did receive noms for editing, make-up, and for Paul Giamatti's supporting role as Jim Braddock's manager, but scored no wins). A late-year surge in quality films—including, along with the Best Picture nominees, the likes of *Syriana, The Constant Gardner,* and *A History of Violence*—appeared to have edged the front-runner out.

But, the less-than-optimal box office and the lack of awards don't take away from the quality of what remains an immensely respected, entertaining, and oft-touching movie, and certainly one of the all-time great sports flicks. And, when hundreds of screenwriters try and fail to make any inroads into a hard-to-crack and fiercely competitive business, that one novice screenwriter toughed out the rejections year after year to win himself an impressive debut with a major, much-lauded film like *Cinderella Man,* is more of a fairy tale ending than most ever get

The "Gray Ones" Fade To Black
(posted 6/3/11)

"How come you only show us clips from movies none of us ever heard of?"

She was thirty, a single mom who'd admirably gone back to school for a business degree to better things for her and her family. She'd taken my film appreciation class as an elective, a break from the grind of her business classes, expecting it would be, to use her word, "fun."

But, due to the aforementioned "movies none of us ever heard of," she was not having the anticipated fun.

I explained, "Because most movies were made before you were born."

Simple and obvious, it still didn't satisfy her, and the unasked next question in her eyes I guessed to be, "But why do *we* have to see them?"

Most of my class—not all, but most—I knew felt similarly. They didn't say it but I could tell: rolled eyes, glazed eyes, eyes glued to smart phones they mistakenly thought I couldn't see hidden in their laps under their desks instead of on the projection screen. The occasional snoozer, head down on his/her desk.

Mind you, we're not talking about obscure, challenging, subtitled art house imports. The class was a chronological study and by the time my business major had been frustrated enough to say something, "the movies none of us ever heard of" included, among others, *Dead End* (1937), *His Girl Friday* (1940), *The Maltese Falcon* (1941), *Casablanca* (1942), *This Gun for Hire* (1942), *Double Indemnity* (1944), *On the Waterfront* (1954), *Ben-Hur* (1959), *Spartacus* (1960), *Dr. Strangelove: Or How I Learned to Stop Worrying and Love the Bomb* (1964), *Fail-Safe* (1964), *In the Heat of the Night* (1967), *2001: A Space Odyssey* (1968), *The Wild Bunch* (1969), *Patton* (1970), *Network* (1972), *Chinatown* (1974), *Apocalypse Now* (1979).

Not to mention they didn't know who Bogart was, or Stanwyck, Lancaster, Grant, Fonda, Bergman... Some didn't know there'd been a *The War of the Worlds* (1953) before Spielberg's (let alone that there'd been a—"Really?"—*book!*) or that there'd been a *Planet of the Apes* (1968) before Tim Burton's monkey fest. And those few who did know, hadn't seen the originals. With the exception of *Jaws* (1975), *Star Wars* (1977), and (for just a few) *The Godfather* (1972), it seemed most of them didn't know *any* movie before *Independence Day* (1996) and *Titanic* (1997).

As frustrating as it had been, something about my business major's question wouldn't let me go. It buzzed around and around in my head for days afterward. I wasn't sure why,

Then it jelled for me: why *didn't* they know? The Internet, Netflix, DVDs, dozens of cable channels... my students had incredible access to a virtually limitless library of movies, yet almost every day I went into class it was like I was speaking in tongues to them.

And then a flip side of her question presented itself, also nagging at me: how come back when I was a kid with just six TV channels, *I* knew about all those classic (and even more not-so-classic) flicks?

After mulling it over for a couple of days, I had my epiphany: an outrageous paradox. For all their access, my students saw astoundingly little; and as limited as my access had been, I'd seen so, so much more.

****

Up until about 1970, movie releases were managed as if pictures were valuable objects to be carefully nursed through the distribution system. It wasn't because Old Hollywood had any great respect or high regard for their product; they had no illusions that they were handling some kind of—God forbid—*art*. This was a matter of simple, economic practicality; they adhered to a methodology designed to wring every last possible dollar out of each title.

Wide releases were reserved for anticipated disasters: you pushed a flick onto as many screens as possible hoping to haul in some quick box office cash before the bad word of mouth got out. But what you *normally* did was this:

A movie was initially released *only* in the better theaters *only* in the major markets. When its drawing power began to fade at that level, only then was it cycled through smaller markets, more downscale theaters, and then dropping down another tier to second- and then third-run houses, finally bottoming out at drive-ins and grindhouses. It was a process with the goal of squeezing out every possible buck at a given level of exhibition before moving on to the next one.

Movies considered special, top-of-the-line, one-of-a-kind releases were kept on an even shorter leash. We're talking the kind of big budget spectaculars we'd probably refer to today as "event" pictures; movies like *Gone With the Wind* (1939) , *The Ten Commandments*

(1956), *Ben-Hur, Lawrence of Arabia* (1962), and so on. These kinds of cinematic dreadnaughts would premiere in, literally, just a handful of cities and only in the most upscale venues, like Grauman's Chinese Theater in Los Angeles, or New York's Radio City.

I'm not throwing the word "event" around loosely: that's exactly what exhibitions at these showcases truly were. There'd be souvenirs and programs on sale in the palatial lobbies, movies would open with a musical overture as if they were Broadway plays, there'd be an intermission. Only after business had peaked at these kinds of imperial displays did a trimmed-back version of the movie trickle out into the usual distribution network.

Whether the movie was a megamillion-dollar epic or a routine studio release, this limited distribution pattern could preserve the entertainment value of a title for months, with those movies generating positive word of mouth teasing out a tantalizing expectancy in markets further down the ladder. I can still remember, as a kid in Jersey, hearing about movies opening in New York, and envying the few kids whose families had the money to "jump across the river" to see a movie in The City while the rest of us wondered how long it would take to come to our side of the Hudson, and then to our neighborhood.

With this kind of release pattern, it wasn't unusual for a successful movie to be in exhibition for as long as a year. For the biggies—the *Ben-Hur*s and such—it might take a *couple* of years before the last tired, pitted print rattled for the last time through a projector at some drive-in out in the boonies.

Still, for as long as a movie might be on the exhibition circuit, it was only being seen by a limited number of people at any given time. In this way, all movies, no matter how pedestrian, were evanescent experiences. A movie came to the neighborhood theater, and, once it left, it was gone forever, like—to steal a line from *Blade Runner* (1982)—"tears in rain."

Well, most of the time.

Some of those prestigious Radio City-caliber releases were able, under this restrained distribution pattern, to retain a lasting appeal, a cultural echo, a sense that they were *too* special to only pass through this life once. When you saw *Gone with the Wind* or *The Longest Day* (1962), you knew there was never going to be another movie like that. Ever.

And the studios recognized that impact. These super-memorable flicks belonged to their own special class, were treated like rare treasures occasionally brought out of their sacred vault for rare occasions—a rerelease—possibly to be seen for the last time by an older generation who fondly remembered them, and a newer generation that had only ever heard about them.

While rereleases were a regular feature of the old distribution model, they were rare enough for individual rerelease titles to be considered as much of an event as a movie's first time on screens. It was a form of cultural resurrection. That's how I got to see, on the big screen, movies like *Ben-Hur*, *Lawrence of Arabia*, even the everybody-in-comedy-worth-a-damn *It's a Mad, Mad, Mad, Mad World* (with the rerelease promo line recognizing just how dysfunctional the 1970s were: "If there was ever a time for *It's a Mad, Mad, Mad, Mad World*, it's now!").

Considering its age, I would guess *Gone with the Wind* would probably be the rerelease champ, showing up on the big screen every so many years decade after decade (Wikipedia lists eight theatrical rereleases). But the man who had rereleasing down to a science was Walt Disney.

Disney rereleased his animation classics—pictures like *Bambi* (1942), *Snow White and the Seven Dwarfs* (1937), *Fantasia* (1940), et al—about every seven years. The calculation was that was how long it would take one generation of viewers to age out of a given movie's appeal, and a new generation to age in. Disney—always a far-sighted guy—also anticipated that at a certain point, parents who had seen these animated jewels as kids would enjoy reliving the experience with their *own* kids.

Rereleasing made sense in a cinema world where there was no aftermarket. A movie made its money in theaters and that was that.

Until television.

Initially, many of the major studios wanted nothing to do with TV. As TV ownership increased, movie attendance decreased, and Hollywood considered the little flickering box a thief in the night running off with the movie industry's audience, a pillager, a rapist, a Pied Piper seducing ever more viewers each year with its bluish glow. Television was the great evil, The Dark Lord, so much so that some studios even had embargos on their contract players making TV appearances, or even against having a TV appear in a movie as, say, part of a living room set's decor. To actually provide TV with movie programming was tantamount to aiding and abetting a Class A felony.

But in Hollywood, even then it was already a long-established tradition that the dollar spoke louder than ideals, and the big icebreaker came in 1955 when RKO sold the TV rights to 740 of the studio's features. It was kind of like, "How dare you, you miserable little box, showing up on my doorstop with your hand out, wanting my prized—. Wait, how much did you say?" The other studios—most of whom, like RKO, were financially struggling at the time—looked at the millions RKO had reaped, figured most of their oldies weren't doing them any good sitting on the shelves gathering dust, and thereafter followed suit in a torrent of similar and even bigger TV deals.

The studios bundled their old movies in packages, and syndicators sold these packages to local stations around the country. The licensing terms might run as long as twenty years, but that was fine; in those days, there was no advantage to a quick turnover. Buying these big blocks of movies, and holding on to them for such long periods gave TV stations the ability to not only build up substantial film libraries, but to develop their own market-specific programming traditions.

Where I lived in northeastern New Jersey, we were part of the New York metropolitan viewing area, then and now the biggest, most densely populated TV market in the country, big enough to support seven channels: the flagship stations for the three broadcast networks (WCBS Channel 2, WNBC Channel 4, WABC Channel 7), three independent stations (WPIX Channel 5, which would later become part of Fox; WOR Channel 9, which would later become part of UPN, and then MyTV after UPN folded; WPIX Channel 11, which, would later be part of The WB, which evolved into The CW; and one "educational station," WNET Channel 13 (later part of PBS). Every Sunday morning, Channel 11 had a Bowery Boys flick. Every Christmas, Channel 9 would air the 1934 version of *Babes in Toyland* with Laurel & Hardy. On Thanksgivings, Channel 9 would run, back-to-back, *King Kong* (1933), *Son of Kong* (1933), and *Mighty Joe Young* (1949). What giant gorillas had to do with Thanksgiving, I'll be damned if I know, but there reached a point where it didn't seem like Thanksgiving without the big apes on a tear. Saturday night was for the kids with Channel 5's *Creature Feature* at eight-thirty, and then at eleven came Channel's 9's *Chiller Theater*. Those Saturday night slots were where I was introduced to the Frankenstein monster and vampires, werewolves, and alien invaders (I've hardly met a male of my generation who doesn't remember the original *Invaders from Mars* [1953]—an indelible concoction of silliness, low-budget embarrassment, visceral childhood paranoias, and brilliant visuals).

Stephen Whitty, reviewer for New Jersey's *The Star-Ledger*, one of the largest newspapers in the New York metro area, remembers the varied "flavors" of the different NY stations: "In the NY area... you had Channel 2 running MGM pictures, Channel 5 had Warners and old Universal titles, Channel 9 had RKO and a lot of British imports, Channel 13 ran foreign imports and silents, and Channels 4, 7, and 11 divvied up the rest."

Another childhood memory: Channel 9's *Million Dollar Movie* (keeping in mind that, in those days, you could make a pretty good movie for a million bucks). *MDM* had a unique scheduling strategy: they'd run the same movie every weeknight at eight, then run it several times each day on Saturday and Sunday. For a kid, that kind of encoring was like a form of hypnotic brainwashing. There were images I still haven't forgotten after sitting through them as a thrill-hungry ten-year-old, watching them a half-dozen times in a week: a tentacled monster barging through an inn's front doors in *The Crawling Eye* (1951), Jack Palance's arm crushed by a German tank in *Attack!* (1956), Leslie Nielsen and Anne Francis watching in terror as Walter Pigeon's "Monster from the Id" burns its way through steel doors to get at them in *Forbidden Planet* (1956), John Wayne trying to single-handedly save a railroad bridge from being washed away by a flood in *Tycoon* (1947), having a crush on one of the eponymous women of Atlantis in *Hercules and the Women of Atlantis* (1961—Channel 9 had *all* those cheesy—pardon me—mozzarella-y Italian-made Hercules movies).

As much money as Hollywood could make selling its oldies, the movie industry still hadn't "gone all the way"... but the potential revenue for selling newer flicks to the major networks was too tempting to ignore for long. In 1961, NBC debuted *NBC Saturday Night at the Movies*, a weekly movie slot featuring comparatively recent films, which soon became one of the network's highest-rated spots on its schedule.

The studios were still careful about how much exposure their product received. There was an embargo period on new movies; they couldn't be sold to TV for at least several years after their theatrical runs. And some movies—*Gone with the Wind*, *The Wizard of Oz*—were held back from TV for decades.

The prices the studios exacted for their biggest features steadily rose. By the late '60s, the nets were paying an average price of $800,000 per title, a four-fold jump from what NBC had been paying at the beginning of the decade, while particularly upscale flicks went for much more: *The Bridge on the River Kwai* (1957) went for $2 million; *Cleopatra* (1963) for $5 million.

As far as the networks were concerned, the movies were worth the money. Movies quickly proved themselves to be tremendous draws. From the mid-1960s until the late 1990s, one of the several prime time movie slots on one or another of the networks finished among the highest-rated programs for the season, often among the season's top twenty-five. Network movie telecasting reached a peak in 1968 when there was a network movie on *every night of the week:* ABC had Monday and Wednesday, CBS took Thursday and Friday, and NBC copped the rest.

One memory I have shows you how big a deal movies were for the networks and for their audience. As a kid I remember that during the tail end of the summer, NBC would air a ten-minute (I think) spot at the end of one of its movie nights promoting the top end titles they'd be premiering throughout the upcoming season. Most of the movies they were running—even the best ones—hadn't gotten that kind of advance promotion when they were in theaters!

Between what the network affiliates were airing between network programming blocks, and what the indies were scheduling throughout the day, and what the nets were airing in prime time, there was almost always a movie on *somewhere* at most times of the day.

Stephen Whitty remembers: "When you got home from school, there were old movies on Channels 4, 7, 9, and 11 to choose from; weekends, Channels 5, 9 and 11 all ran horror movies on Saturdays, while *The Late Show* on Channel 2 ran classics."

Emmy-winning producer/writer/director Bill Persky *(The Dick Van Dyke Show, That Girl)* remembers the same cinematic horn of plenty: "In the '50s through '80s, movies were the equivalent of TiVo—when there was nothing to watch, there was *always* a movie... Many a bleary-eyed morning was the result of *The Late Show* and *The Late Late Show*. Since you couldn't record them for later, you had to put in real time to watch, and many was the night I was awakened at one a.m. by a call from a friend: '*The Treasure of the Sierra Madre* is on!'"

Granted, not every market was as cinematically plush as New York. I went to college in Columbia, South Carolina, a rather feeble market by New York standards. Columbia only had three network affiliates and the only movies they carried were those on the network schedule. Out in more rural parts of the country, there were areas that didn't even have all three networks!

Still, in a number of cities, a generation of young people was growing up exposed to much of what had passed for movie entertainment since the beginning of the sound era. The local stations gave us the oldies, the nets the newer flicks we might've missed in theaters (or wanted to see again). We might not have known John Ford from Henry Ford, but we saw *She Wore a Yellow Ribbon* and *They Were Expendable* (1945).

As Peter Biskind tells it in his 1998 account of Hollywood's creative explosion in the 1960s/70s, *Easy Riders, Raging Bulls: How the Sex-Drugs-and-Rock 'N' Roll Generation Saved Hollywood*, as much as TV, movies became a cultural glue holding us Baby Boomers together. We were all seeing the same movies, seeing them over and over when they were rerun on TV like some shared group ritual, entertaining each other playing out their scenes, swaggering like John Wayne, twitching lips like Humphrey Bogart, doing lock-jawed imitations of Burt Lancaster ("I'm a pig!"—*Vera Cruz*, 1954) and Kirk Douglas ("Odin!"—*The Vikings*, 1958). I can still remember when Channel 5 got the rights to *West Side Story* (1961) when I was in high school. The next day, you couldn't pass down a hall between classes without hearing the *snap snap snap* of any number of students snapping their fingers *à la* the Jets and Sharks.

Those years parked in front of the TV as kids laid the bedrock for what would become the country's first—and perhaps last—cinematically literate generation. As we grew older and went off to college, some of us actually studied movies, some studied how to *make* movies. From our ranks came a truly memorable class of filmmakers who quantum-jumped from replaying favorite scenes in the schoolyard to a stratospheric level of cinematic artistry: Scorsese, Coppola, DePalma, Lucas, Spielberg, Friedkin, Schrader and others.

The great generational irony of that time was that while the youth of the day seemed to be violently at odds with The Older Generation about damned near everything else—politics, race, the war in Vietnam, economic disparity, social conventions, music, fashion, Women's Lib, Gay Lib, sex—movies remained a point of connection, a bridge across the generational divide.

While the Boomers made the landmark convention-busting movies of the 1960s/1970s possible, they also had an affection for the classics. Long-haired peace/love/dove types still enjoyed watching John Wayne beat hell out of somebody; a generation that had never known James Dean still identified with his smoldering rebellion; Bogart had died in 1957, but you could still find his face on dorm walls in 1977, usually a still from *Casablanca* (1942), because after Vietnam and the urban riots and Kent State and Watergate, it was hard *not* to identify with tavern-owner Rick's disillusionment and cynicism; and out of that same fed-uppedness with the rather sorry shape of the world at the time, we equally identified with—and adored—the nose-thumbing, nose-tweaking, kiss-my-ass anarchy of the Marx Brothers.

I might spend one night telling my mother how *her* generation had thoroughly screwed up the world for *my* generation, but then the next night—

"Hey, I just saw *On the Waterfront* (1954) for the first time."

"Good, huh?"

And off we'd go, me babbling about how blown away I was by Brando's performance, her still blown away by how good a young, in-his-prime Brando had looked in a T-shirt.

It was the rare cultural torch that we Boomers took up from our elders. We may not have thought much of oldsters and their skinny lapels and corny music and their Richard Nixon, but *their* movies were just as much *our* movies. It was a natural feeling; after all, we'd been raised on them.

So… what changed? How did we get from there to, "How come you only show us clips of movies none of us ever heard of?"

Actually, quite a few things changed.

Distribution patterns for one. Back in The Day, wide releasing was for movies expected to bomb. Today, it's the standard. This summer saw *Bridesmaids* open on over 2,900 screens; *Scream 4* on over

3,300; *Fast Five* on 3,644; *Thor* topped 3,900; and *Pirates of the Caribbean: On Stranger Tides* debuted on 4,155 screens. On opening weekends, there's hardly a multiplex in the country that isn't running that weekend's major release often on more than one screen.

And these mass openings roll out on a tidal wave of advance, shrill, multimedia hype—promos, gossip items, behind-the-scenes pieces—searing those titles deep into the consciousness of even the most determinedly disinterested. That sense of mystery and expectancy that used to go with waiting for buzz-worthy titles to finally come to the neighborhood bijou is gone. J.J. Abrams recently told *Entertainment Weekly* how hard it was to maintain that brand of longed-for mystery around this summer's *Super 8*, the 1970s-set sci-fier he directed for producer Steven Spielberg: "There are a lot of advantages to living in the age of instant information. The downside is that we know about things more than we want to. By the time the movie comes out, not only do we know everything about its production, you've seen a trailer that's told you almost everything."

Even after TV came along, the exposure of any given title remained somewhat limited. The life cycle of a typical movie in the 1960s ran something like this: maybe a year in theatrical release, then a cooling off period of a couple of years before being licensed to one of the broadcast networks where it would air maybe twice a year over a period of three to five years, then another cooling off period before it would be bundled with other titles for syndication. TV appearances were rare enough that even some movies that had been shown on TV still retained enough drawing power to make a rerelease viable ("See *Lawrence of Arabia/The Wild Bunch/Spartacus/Gone With the Wind* et al on the big screen again as it was meant to be seen!").

Today, the theatrical window is typically only four months, and with the saturation bombing pattern of today's wide releases, most titles have exhausted their theatrical viability long before that. Pay-per-view release comes in month five, DVD release the following month, and 10 months after a movie opens in theaters it's on a pay-TV channel like Home Box Office or Showtime. In the early days of pay-TV, a movie might run four-six times a month, appearing in only three months of its one-year license period, but now it might air two-three times that many times in a single month every couple of months, and with pay-TV services now "multiplexed"—each service offering multiple channels—it may seem like a movie is *never* off the air as it rotates through a service's various channels. That kind of overexposure can't help but kill the specialness that went with rarity.

Usually after pay-TV, a movie is sold to a basic cable network like TBS or A&E for a short term (twelve to eighteen months), then is bundled with library product and sold back to pay-TV, then back to basic cable and so on *ad nauseum,* generating fresh revenue with each turnover. It's not unusual to see highly "playable" movies—the type of flick that draws an audience no matter how many times it's aired—finish their license period on one channel one week, and show up on another the very next week (in fact, at this writing, I'd just seen *Kelly's Heroes* [1970] on TCM over the Memorial Day weekend, then saw a promo for the movie's debut on The Military Channel's *Officer and a Movie* slot the very next weekend).

Whereas forty years ago or so you couldn't wait for a favored movie to show up for one of its two or three plays on a broadcast channel that year, today it seems you can't get away from a movie. Any movie.

Well, not *any* movie. If it sometimes seems cable stations continually draw from the same limited pool, you're right. Says Stephen Whitty: "TV has given up on classic movies. Yes, TCM runs them around the clock, but it's the only station (we won't count AMC, which mostly gave up...). And if you don't like TCM's theme of the day—Alice Faye, say, or Westerns—well, you're out of luck. Every other station runs films from the last five years or so, which is fine, but hardly representative of the art."

Why?

Because of "clutter."

What's clutter?

Clutter is the average cable system offering a bit over 100 channels of programming (mind you, this is an *average,* meaning there are systems with much more), so many that subscribers can't always distinguish them from each other let alone even remember all the channels they have at their disposal.

To cut through the clutter and capture eyeballs, cable channels have moved, over the last thirty years, from the kind of generic programming that marked the early years of the business (old movies and TV shows) to more channel-defining original programming. Those channels that still have a strategic use for movies tend to air—and re-air and re-re-air—those titles they know are instantly recognizable to the mass audience. And what that *doesn't* include are the old classics, the black-and-whites—what my kids, when they were younger, called "the gray ones."

Josh Sapan, president and CEO of AMC Networks that owns cable channel AMC, puts it this way: "In the '70s, each of the broadcast networks had 15-20 million people watching each show or movie in prime time. If a network—or even PBS—aired a classic film, it was inevitably seen by millions." But with the splintering of the mass audience into smaller niches by the proliferation of cable channels, "Audiences, with rare exceptions, are smaller today. The choice and diversity on TV and the Internet has made some wonderful films victims of their obscurity." This was, Sapan admits, part of the reason AMC in the early 2000s reformatted itself from a classics station—almost a twin of Turner Classics—to one focusing on original programming *(Mad Men, Breaking Bad)* and—according to the channel's promo spots—"The New Classics"—the more familiar films from the 1960s, '70s and up.

Stephen Whitty says the expansion of the cable spectrum has been a case of "... be careful what you wish for... when I was a kid, I imagined a science-fiction world where I would just push a button and be able to see any movie I ever wanted on my TV. And that's the world we're supposedly living in now. Except take a look at what TV is *really* offering: six different channels showing *Land of the Lost* (2009) with Will Ferrell, another half-dozen running *The Bounty Hunter* (2010) with Jennifer Aniston. It's like TV has become the Multiplex from Hell, only on a six-month tape delay."

There have already been any number of cultural studies suggesting a strong disconnect between Gen X/Yers and their predecessors; a disinterest in any number of topics, both of large import and small, predating their own generational awareness. But perhaps there is no disconnect as complete between this generation and those before it as the dropping of this particular pop culture torch. Or perhaps "dropping" is the wrong word; a *disinterest* in picking it up might be more accurate.

A writer who'd worked for *Saturday Night Live* in the mid-'90s tells me that even then writers were being instructed not to reference anything more than three years prior because "a lot of viewers won't get it." Compare that to *SNL*s from the show's debut years in the '70s when the show riffed on *decades* of old TV shows and movies, its writers knowing that they and we all shared the same pop culture touchstones.

My old film teacher, Dr. Benjamin "Bernie" Dunlap, now president of South Carolina's Wofford College, describes it as "... a new sort of simultaneity... wanting everything to be happening now, at this instant, with consequences still to be determined. In a curious and debased fashion, it resembles a Zen-like insistence on the here and now."

Curiously, disturbingly, that disconnect is just as strong among many young people—like my students—who study film. Says Bernie Dunlap, "Film students often need to be taught to excavate (a film), but unsophisticated viewers grow impatient with what they view as antiquated technique ("What—no color?"), and, of course, they tend to limit their experience of a film to the crudest level of storytelling."

I once interviewed director John Dahl *(The Last Seduction,* 1994) who frequently speaks to filmmaking students. The new Gen X/Y aspiring filmmaker doesn't share Dahl's generation's respect for the oldies, doesn't see their connection to the cinematic evolutionary chain. Ford, Hitchcock, Wilder—irrelevant. *Citizen Kane:* boring. "These young people," Dahl told me, "have never seen *Double Indemnity* or *Treasure of the Sierra Madre*. They probably think they're just dusty old pictures."

The question I usually come to when I write these musing pieces is, 'Does it matter?' Who cares? So what? This new simultaneity, this disconnection with the vast treasure trove of our cinematic heritage—does it really cost us anything?

Bernie Dunlap—the man who kindled a passion for movies in me, and taught me how to truly, deeply understand, appreciate, and enjoy their magic—says it *does* matter.

The new, grounded-only-in-the-present sensibility "... ignores what has always been for me the magical ability of film to capture and reenact a present instant from the past. What's so astonishing about Lumière recording of a baby's breakfast, or visitors to the Paris Exposition—or, for that matter, the ambient reality of *Casablanca* or any film from the past—is that it enables us to study and re-experience that 'now' over and over.

"This is, of course, what (film theorist) Siegfried Kracauer meant when he spoke of the 'redemption of physical reality.' It's also at the heart of Werner Herzog's new documentary, *The Cave of Forgotten Dreams* (2011), in which he attempts to retrieve the 'now' of prehistoric cave painters flickering into life—the analogy often used to explain the psychological power of film."

In the same way that cutting ourselves off from *any* older aspect of our culture diminishes us by dimming our awareness of who we *were* and how that made us who we *are*, there *is* something lost when we turn away from the gray ones.

"(The) greatest choices were made by accident," says Stephen Whitty. "The first time I saw *Laura* (1944) and *It's a Wonderful Life* (1946) and *Kind Hearts and Coronets* (1949), I'd been simply flipping the channels and was caught by an image... there are no longer any happy accidents. Just as newspapers offer surprises to their readers—you turn the page to jump with something and there's an article on something you hadn't even thought of that catches your interest—so did (pre-cable broadcast) TV. Now, though, niche cable and Netflix offer the same sweet trap as the Internet—you can always get what you're looking for, if you *know* what you're looking for.

"So people go online and read opinions they already agree with. People go on Netflix and stream movies they've already heard of. Nobody grows an inch. And our national mythology—which is The Duke and Sam Spade and *Some Like It Hot* (1959) and *Psycho* (1960)—slowly disappears."

The Life And Death Of The "Passion Pits"
(posted 6/7/12)

This past Wednesday, June 6, was the seventy-ninth birthday of the drive-in movie theater.

The story goes that Richard Hollingshead was bothered by the fact that his mother could never find a comfortable seat in a movie theater and somehow got it into his head she'd be much more comfortable watching from her car. Well, that's the story, anyway. Whatever the real inspiration, Mr. Hollingshead patented his design for an outdoor movie theater and opened his first outdoor screen in Camden, New Jersey on June 6, 1933.

On the back of the stonework frame for the screen, gigantic, black letters screamed at passersby: SIT IN YOUR CAR; SEE AND HEAR MOVIES. If those big, black letters caught both your eye and your curiosity, it was going to cost you twenty-five cents for your car and twenty-five cents each for whoever you brought along (or, if you packed up the whole tribe in Dad's Plymouth, you could all get in at a family rate of a buck). For your money, you had to hear the sound over a kind of PA system (in-car speakers would come later), there was no snack bar (yet), and Hollingshead launched the enterprise with *Wives Beware* (1932), a Brit-made comedy that had died in theaters in a single week and was picked on the premise such a turkey wouldn't conflict with any major releases at the time.

Certainly the timing was right. America had had a love affair with the automobile from the moment Charles and Frank Duryea put the first gasoline-powered four-wheeler on the road in 1893. By the 1930s, despite The Great Depression, cars were becoming less functional and more works of beauty, engines were becoming more powerful, and the idea of the weekend drive more popular. With money tight and the times less than rosy, Americans were looking for some cheap pleasures (even accounting for inflation, that dollar for a carful of kin was a bargain—the last time I took my family to the movies it cost over $40). With the drive-in, Hollingshead rolled a family night out at the movies in with a drive in the country and a picnic.

The concept didn't initially click nationally. By the time of WW II, there were still less than 100 drive-ins operating in the U.S. The boom years came after the war.

The postwar years provided a perfect growth culture. It was a time of unprecedented prosperity, people had more leisure time and money to enjoy it than ever before, the inauguration of the interstate highway system sent America's love of the open road into overdrive, cars were big and comfy (I once had the opportunity to sit in a 1950 Chevy sedan; I had enough headroom to wear a Stetson and the front seat was as big as a sofa), and gas was eighteen cents a gallon.

The drive-in became as much an icon of 1950s fun as carhop burger joints and sock hops. By the end of the 1950s, there were over 5,000 drive-ins, and they were particularly popular in rural areas. They came as small as those serving just a few dozen cars, to drive-ins that could hold as many as 3,000 cars!

Heading out to the drive-in was primarily—though not solely—a family thing, and the drive-ins strove to accommodate them. Some would open as early as three hours before showtime and offer attractions for the kiddies like pony rides, playgrounds, miniature golf. Some offered dinners brought out to your car by carhops.

By the 1960s, all those kiddies who'd ridden the ponies and played putt-putt in the '50s now had their own cars, and what they found in the drive-ins was something they couldn't find anywhere else: privacy. Drive-ins became the go-to option for teens looking for a place to canoodle undisturbed by buzz-killing adults. Drive-ins consequently earned themselves a not particularly appetizing sobriquet: "passion pits."

That was the beginning of a long, slow decline for the drive-in. As more teens showed up at the drive-ins, fewer families came, and screens started to come down.

It had never been a big-dollar business. After all, a drive-in was only open a few hours a day, and only during warm weather. As the business started to fade, drive-in owners looked for ways to generate more revenue during off hours: flea markets, swap meets, car shows, etc.

By the 1980s, new entertainment technologies were beating the hell out of the drive-in business. That was the decade cable TV took off, and then came the VCR. No one had to trek out to the drive-in to see third-rate, third-run movies; you could catch them a dozen times a month on HBO, or rent them off the back racks at Blockbuster.

The biggest stake through the heart, however, was the real estate market. Drive-ins had sat off from the cities, out where the dark was really dark and the only overhead lights were the stars. But from the postwar years on, growing out from the cities in ever-expanding rings, were the suburbs, and then the malls and business parks. What had once been "the woods" for those communities on the urban periphery had now become prime real estate… and that included drive-in acreage. By 1990, there were less than 1,000 drive-in screens left in the U.S.

There are still a few hundred of them around the country, particularly in the southwest with its favorable climate. But they're more a novelty, more a nostalgia trip than a bonafide part of the distribution circuit. It's not a business anymore; just an echo.

And one I find personally resonant.

*****

I was lucky. I caught the tail end of it.

I remember the long line of waiting cars, backed up down the gravel drive from the box office to the highway and then down the shoulder, waiting for opening time…

I can remember late night drives back from The Shore, and then, jutting up out of the darkness off to the side of the highway, a drive-in screen, a quick, teasing glimpse of a movie floating in the night…

I remember a playground in the space under the screen; a snack bar with incredibly awful hot sandwiches wrapped in foil bags and thinking how cool they looked, like some kind of astronaut food; and climbing up on the rear dash of my dad's Chevy Biscayne to fall asleep under the bubble-like rear windshield when it got late…

What's funny is I remember so much about the drive-ins from when I was a kid except the movies. The movie wasn't important. The *going* was.

*****

There were still a few drive-ins operating when the oldest of my friends started getting their driver's licenses. It was, I grant, perhaps a less innocent kind of fun… but fun nonetheless.

My friend Randy would get hold of his father's wide-ass Chevy and we'd pack six of us in there. Well, actually, just five inside. Mark never seemed to have the price of a ticket despite the fact his family had more money than some small countries. We'd have to sneak Mark onto the lot in the trunk. Having to do that for a guy whose family could've bought a good-sized Caribbean island created a bit of a resentment, which resulted in Randy purposely driving through the deepest potholes he could find, doing a tap dance on the brakes so we could listen to Mark rattle around in the trunk, and then going through an elaborate dialogue about how he'd lost the trunk key.

"I know what you guys are trying to pull!" came a muffled but still clearly irate voice from the trunk.

"Bill, do you have the key? I can't seem to find it!"

"Gee, Randy, I thought *you* had it!"

THUMP THUMP. "That's not funny! Knock it off and get me out of here!"

"How about you, Ron? Didn't Randy give the key to you?"

"That's funny, Bill, I thought he gave it to you!"

"Nope, that's what Randy thought, but I—"

"GUYS!" THUMP THUMP.

Other times, we drove out in my friend Gene's van. We'd park the van sideways and take up two spaces, open up the double side doors, set up a few lawn chairs, crack open a mini-keg, and have a night of it.

The movies were forgettable. *The Happy Hooker Goes to Washington* (1977). Some piece of crap about women of Atlantis shot in the Philippines. Movies that had been in theaters back in the 1960s.

But just as it had been when I was a kid, the movies themselves didn't matter. We didn't go to the drive-ins to go to the movies. We went to the drive-ins to go to the drive-ins.

The last time I went to a drive-in was in the early 1970s. It was on the Hackensack River in the Jersey Meadowlands. When we got bored with the movie, we'd walk over to the river and watch pleasure boats go by. Or my friend Ron would go up to the projection hut, hop up on a planter built in front to keep people clear of the projector beams, and moon the projectionist through one of the empty portals.

There's an office building there now, and on the other side of Route 3 from where the drive-in had been is the Meadowlands Sports Complex where the Giants play.

It's a piece of highway I travel on a fairly regular basis. I've never passed that damned office building without thinking back not just to the screen it replaced, but to all of them, all those little islands of Panavision dreams floating out there in the night. They all come back to me: six teens sharing the same monster bucket of popcorn; a shriveled snack bar hot dog in its aluminum sack; a yacht slipping by down the river alongside the lot with its decks glowing with a golden light and its passengers watching our movie; looking up through the rear glass of my dad's Chevy at a sky filled with stars brilliant in an ebon sky untainted by city lights.

What Makes A Classic Movie Classic?
(posted 3/27/12)

If I may, I'd like to quote from *Entertainment Weekly*'s review of the just released seventieth anniversary Blu-ray release of *Casablanca* (1942). According to Chris Nashawaty's piece, when the script arrived at Warner Bros. in December of 1941 "… there wasn't an ending yet… the movie was just one of fifty in Warner's crowded pipeline at the time… The reliably bland Ronald Reagan was considered for the lead, then George Raft, with 'Oomph Girl' Ann Sheridan floated as love interest. In other words, this forgettable little project carried all the telltale signs of becoming just another disposable feature that would run for a few weeks and then be swept away like the stray popcorn kernels and Lucky Strike butts littering theater floors."

As we all know, that's not exactly how it played out.

My point being that classic movies don't always come about because someone sits down and says, "We're making this one for the ages!" As often as not, cinematic greatness is a happy accident.

But what is it—what are the elements, the components—that turn a movie from a fun day at the matinee into an evergreen still being saluted, still moving audiences decades later? What makes a classic, classic?

In the last few years, I've been lucky enough to teach some college basic film appreciation courses, and it's become clear to me that cinematic classicism isn't always apparent to the untrained eye. I cannot tell you how many young people look at *Citizen Kane* (1941) and have declared it "Boooorrrrriiiiinnnnnng!" Does that mean that, as the years go by, *Kane* is losing its fizz? Or is movie-making greatness (or at least elements of it) sometimes an acquired taste? In the same way that the palate has to be "taught" what to look for in a fine wine ("This is supposed to be good wine? It tastes like furniture varnish!"), do we have to train the eye, the ear, the sensibility to appreciate true greatness?

Do we even understand what greatness is in a movie?

I recall a story I read some years ago in screenwriting e-zine *Hollywoodlitsales News* in which author Eva Peel claimed "plots have improved" because contemporary movies "… have taken to cramming 20-30% more plot beats into two hours… than your average action movie or thriller made before 1990." That is to say that *Enemy of the*

State (1998) is a "better" movie than Francis Ford Coppola's essay on paranoia, *The Conversation* (1974), and the glitzy but empty 1999 remake of *The Thomas Crown Affair* is "better" than the 1968 character-driven original. In other words, thrillers are "better" (sorry about the quotes, but that "better" tastes bitter to me) because they're faster and have more action in them. So, *Speed* (1994) is a better movie than, oh, say *Out of the Past* (1947), *The Third Man* (1949), *Rear Window* (1954), *The French Connection* (1971).

And for some slices of audience—the *Citizen-Kane*-is-boring crew—I think that's true.

So, then, does a movie lose its greatness because it no longer meets the demands of a new audience sensibility? Is *Citizen Kane* less the classic it's always acknowledged to be because more and more people find it a bit of a slog? Is *Casablanca* no longer one of the all-time great Hollywood movie romances because most of us no longer appreciate its wartime context and sense of self-sacrifice? Or because '40s-style screen acting might seem a bit arch by today's standards? Or because—this is for you, Eva—it has so few plot beats?

That also brings up the question of, Have we gotten a little intellectually lazy? Back in January, Sound on Sight's Edgar Chaput wrote a post on the 1954 *Godzilla* and how the movie still worked for him. Edgar, bless him, was able to extend his mind's eye to see the movie the way it must have hit an audience in 1954. But if a contemporary audience can't get past the guy-in-a-rubber-suit creature and Lego cities the Big Guy stomps and sets afire, does that make the movie bad? Does that make Edgar crazy? The 1998 remake had countless more beats and infinitely better special effects, yet even the most indiscriminate viewers agreed the movie totally, completely, and comprehensively sucked.

What is it we respond to that makes us consider a movie great? Is it purely its ability to entertain year after year? It's thirty-seven years later, and damned if *Jaws* still doesn't perform its gut-wrenching suspense magic, and, even older, *The Godfather* (1972) is still one of the most quoted movies in pop culture ("I'm gonna make him an offer he can't refuse"; "Take the cannoli; leave the gun"; "It's just business" et al).

But some movies considered "great" or "classic" are not particularly viscerally entertaining (a fancy way of saying they're not "fun"). *2001: A Space Odyssey* (1968) was *never* an easy watch, and *The*

Godfather, Part II (1974), is longer, slower, and has a considerably lower body count than its predecessor. Yet many a cineaste would argue *Part II* is the better film of the two (although by Eva Peel's gauge, not so much).

Is greatness as simple as, "I enjoyed it," or can there be something less obvious at work? Has our movie-watching sensibility been so degraded by the monumental tonnage of crap that flows into the marketplace that we may no longer have the eyes to recognize vintage good work when we see it? Can something be good even if we don't like it?

Mull that over while I load up my *Casablanca* DVD. Until you come up with an answer, here's looking at you, kid.

Comic-Con Prompts Thoughts on the Prospect of a Great Superhero Film
(posted 8/2/12)

In a July 28 post, my Sound on Sight colleague Deepayan Sengupta pondered the admittedly arguable premise that, for all their entertainment and box office value, the superhero movie has yet to provide a true cinematic classic. Back in March, I came at a vaguely similar idea but from a different angle. I suspected—as does Sengupta—that the problem could be that there might be some inherent barriers as to how far dramatic substance in the genre could be pushed: "... the form has limits, I think, more so than its printed source... and so does its core audience."

As it happens, the July 27 issue of *Entertainment Weekly* offers their annual coverage of the San Diego Comic-Con, which took place July 12-15. I think, in that coverage, possibly Sengupta and myself have our answer.

I'm sure most of the people who write or visit this site are better acquainted with Comic-Con than I am, but for you rare few who may be in the dark, let me borrow from reporter Adam B. Vary's piece: "... (what) began in 1970 as a weekend-long hangout for a few hundred comic-book aficionados... has evolved into the single most important showcase for Hollywood's biggest—and most expensive—projects." According to Vary, over 125,000 fans packed the San Diego Convention Center for the granddaddy of comic book conventions.

Whatever individual Comic-Con fans are fans of—comic books, genre movies, TV shows, etc.—they're unmatched in their rabid devotion. They come in costume, they remember franchise trivia even creators have forgotten. Their bond with their idol of choice can be frightening in its intensity. And what they feel—about preview footage from an about-to-be released blockbuster, about a treasured TV classic, about a casting announcement for a new superhero franchise—they blog, tweet, text, Facebook, Skype, email about enthusiastically (good or bad) and relentlessly. Think of it: 125,000 Comic-Conians going back to their hotel rooms, campers, sidewalk tents each night to connect with their like-minded brothers and sisters all across the country (nay, the *world!*) through every social media pipeline there is to say, "See it as soon as it comes out! It's *gold!*" Or, "Save your money; this one sucks the left hind one."

As a result, by wide admission, Comic-Con has become so important to the Hollywood hype process that the comic book element of the convention—its initial reason for coming into being—has long since been eclipsed by movie and TV displays. The value of generating good buzz at Comic-Con is so recognized, that even projects that wouldn't superficially seem a good fit alongside more expected fare—like panels for *Twilight Saga: Breaking Dawn—Part 2* and the TV sci-fi series *Fringe*—now share the convention floor, e.g. AMC's drug-fueled drama *Breaking Bad*, the Will Ferrell/Zach Galifianakis big screen political comedy *The Campaign*, and Quentin Tarantino's vengeance Western, *Django Unchained*. Comic-Con is Hollywood's version of Oprah's Book Club; one good word and you're a hit. That good word is worth crashing the door.

Actor Nathan Fillion—a Comic-Con idol for his role in the short-lived sci-fi series *Firefly*—kept a diary of his experiences at this year's gathering. One of his entries gives some idea of the kind of fan heat Comic-Con can produce.

Mind you, *Firefly* had fared so poorly in the ratings during its original run, it had been canceled by the Fox network after only eleven episodes. Yet, here was the series being saluted at this year's Comic-Con with a ten-year anniversary panel. Fillion had seen a line outside the convention center: "… it winds back, forth, and back again and then winds under tents. I see the die-hards in their sleeping bags… I wonder what event they wait for, what piece of fandom do they anticipate?" It turns out they were at the convention for the *Firefly* panel. Wrote an emotional Fillion: "It's hard to describe the feeling of vindication when your canceled TV show oversells the panel ten years later, and by 20,000."

It's that kind of fan excitement that provides Comic-Con with its greatest strength, and that makes it invaluable to big-budget Hollywood… and that also provides the greatest danger to filmmakers tempted to follow Sengupta's advice of trying for moviemaking classic status by breaking a few genre rules.

What the Comic-Con crowd feel, they feel with a passion and an awesome sense of collective identity; what Fillion describes as "… an energy of kinship…" Like or dislike, it'll be a tidal wave of judgment sweeping out across the Internet.

Again, from Vary's story: "There was no better proof of the power of Comic-Con than the moment during the *Man of Steel* (the

Superman franchise reboot) panel when a grown man stepped to the mic to ask a question of director Zack Snyder and star Henry Cavill with tears streaming down his face." The question? A rather routine one inquiring as to who the villain in the new movie might be. And for that: tears.

But an even better example of that same power—and how afraid filmmakers and studios and networks are of it—was a screening Peter Jackson held of twelve minutes from *The Hobbit: An Unexpected Journey.* Jackson screened the footage in conventional format; not in the new forty-eight frames-per-second digital format he's been using to shoot the film. According to Jackson, he didn't go with 48 fps because the convention center "... (isn't) a real cinema." But Jackson had screened footage from the movie at CinemaCon for movie business types in April in 48 fps, and the response had ranged from underwhelming to negative. I doubt the CinemaCon screening was any more a "real cinema" than Comic-Con, and it's my suspicion that Jackson, after what happened at CinemaCon, felt that a similar response in San Diego would be lethal for a two-film project with a reported combined budget of around $500 million.

Here's the statistical issue. One hundred and twenty-five thousand people is a lot of people at a convention; no doubt about it. And when they start social media-ing their observations, those 125,000 create a ripple effect that can easily translate into millions.

Yet, *Firefly* died in eleven episodes, and the 2005 big screen version—*Serenity*—which was supposed to capitalize on this fervent fan following, did only a meager $40 million worldwide. Or consider *Fringe,* which has struggled in the ratings throughout its run even though it's been another regular Comic-Con fave.

Comic-Con is like the presidential primaries. To gain the nomination, the candidate has to appeal to the party hardcore, the ideologues. The rub is they don't represent the less ideological, more centrist, more varied general electorate. In other words, everything you say, do, and promise to win the nomination can make you look like either a Commie or a neo-Fascist in the general election.

Comic-Con represents the party faithful, the true believers. They are not the general movie audience. Most moviegoers don't care whether or not Sam Raimi's *Spider-Man* (2002) or Marc Webb's *The Amazing Spider-Man* (2012) is closer to the classic comic book origin story. Most of them haven't ever *read* a Spider-Man comic book. Past

Peter Parker getting turned into a superhero by a bite from a funky spider, the Spider-Man canon is a big blank for them. The movie is either going to work for them as a movie, or it won't.

What I'm saying is Comic-Con puts moviemakers and TV producers in a damned-if-you-do-damned-if-you-don't bind. Winning over the Comic-Con crowd won't win you the box office general election, but turning them off could very well lose it for you.

And how that plays out creatively is in an artistic conservatism. *The Amazing Spider-Man* is grand entertainment, and there are scenes between Andrew Garfield and Emma Stone that are startlingly charming. But there's still gobs of action, and unless you've been hit in the head with a twenty pound sledgehammer, you know how this is going to come out: Spider-Man wins, The Lizard loses, Peter Parker and Gwen Stacy connect. Hell, you knew that when you bought the ticket.

Most superhero movies aren't about challenging our expectations, but in living up to them, affirming them, fulfilling them. Like most genres, the superhero movie has its rituals, and violating those rituals brings risks, and with the hefty price tags that go with the typical superhero flick, "risk" is not a word a studio writing nine-figure checks wants to hear.

That's the choke collar on the superhero movie. They are too big to fail, cost-wise, and a studio might let a filmmaker like Christopher Nolan push at the limits, maybe even put a toe over them, but that $250 million *The Dark Knight Rises* is still going to have a clearly evil super-villain, tons of incredible action, and more or less touch most of the superhero bases (if with unmatchable deftness).

There was a time when rule-breaking risks—and I mean clean, through-the-rails breaks—were encouraged, where the surprise of taking the familiar into unfamiliar territory turned out—here's that word—*classics*. Rick doesn't get the girl and that's what makes *Casablanca* (1942) so poignant even seventy years later. The big, soapy melodrama that's *Gone with the Wind* (1939) crackles like lightning when Rhett Butler, after chasing Scarlett O'Hara for three hours, gets fed up and tells her to kiss his ass (well, actually he says, "Frankly, my dear, I don't give a damn," but that's what he meant). Not only does astronaut Taylor not escape from the *Planet of the Apes* (1968), but he finds out—in one of the most iconic final shots in American movies—that that's what's left of his nuke-torched home.

The Wild Bunch (1969) learn that with the Old West overrun with civilization, their only option is a form of glorious suicide. *The French Connection*'s (1971) Popeye Doyle busts the biggest heroin ring in U.S. history, but the ringleader escapes, and, in trying to nail him, Doyle winds up accidentally shooting another cop. Private eye J. J. Gittes finds himself at the end of *Chinatown* (1974) with his girlfriend dead, her husband's killer—her incestuous, morally bankrupt father—going free with her daughter in his arms.

Not all classics have to break rules, not all classics need to end tragically. What they typically have in common is an allegiance to their own nature: they go where they *should* go. As long as Hollywood keeps running movies and TV shows through gauntlets like Comic-Con and feels (understandably, I should say, considering the money at stake) compelled to satisfy instead of challenge, the chances of a classic are slim.

An Uneasy Peace: The Disappearing War Film
(posted 5/21/11)

*They shall beat their swords into plowshares
and their spears into pruning hooks;
One nation shall not raise the sword against another,
neither shall they learn war any more.*
Isaiah 2:4

War is a nation's ultimate commitment of blood and treasure. As such, the stories a people tells about its wars—and don't tell—and the ways it remembers its wars—or chooses to forget them—tells us much about the kind of people they consider themselves to be at different times in their history, as well as the kind of people they really were... and are.

For most of the twentieth century, the war film was a Hollywood staple. From one era to the next, war movies documented the nation's conflicts, reflected the national consciousness on particular combats as well as on thinking going far beyond any one, particular war. They've been propagandistic and revisionist, salutary and melancholic, topical and universal, thrilling and ruminative. And, of late, as far as the commercial mainstream is concerned, they've all but disappeared.

Few American movies were turned out about World War I during the course of that war. The U.S. had been neutral for much of the conflict, and had only fielded troops during its last eight months. As well, the motion picture industry was still in a chaotic, nascent state, unable to respond to the war in any uniform or muscular fashion. However, by the 1920s, as the Hollywood studio system took root, movies about The Great War began appearing regularly and continued to be popular until eclipsed by World War II; the war that tragically proved that the World War of 1914-1918 had not been the hoped-for War to End All Wars.

The First World War had been a traumatic experience, the battle in the trenches of the West Front having been an exceptionally horrific exercise in mass bloodletting. The causes of the war had been both confusing and, in retrospect, avoidable, and combat had been conducted with nineteenth century tactical thinking oblivious to the capabilities of the new twentieth century killing technologies, all of which gave the four years a sense of purposeless waste.

Consequently, movies about WWI in the '20s and '30s almost universally tended to be melancholic, rueful paeans to a young generation whose courage and valor had been thrown away in the meat grinder of the battle for the trenches (or the skies) e.g. *The Four Horsemen of the Apocalypse* (1921), *The Big Parade* (1925), *Wings* (1927), *Hell's Angels* (1930), *The Dawn Patrol* (1930, remade in 1938), *All Quiet on the Western Front* (1930), et al.

The experience of World War II was wholly different. The Japanese attack on Pearl Harbor on December 7, 1941, united the nation in the idea that war was not only necessary, but vital to the survival of the country, and established an unimpeachable rightness to the American cause. The Hollywood studio system was now at its peak, and brought its considerable creative muscle to bear in support of the war effort.

Every type of studio entertainment vehicle, from cartoons to A features, shorts to documentaries, the heaviest of dramas to the most flyweight of comedies, was retooled for war. There was hardly a talent on the Hollywood roster who didn't find him/herself, at one time or another, doing battle on-screen against the Axis forces, from A-list stars (at least those that hadn't enlisted) to Daffy Duck and The Three Stooges. By the end of 1942, the country's first full year of war, Hollywood had already pumped out eighty movies that touched on the war in one way or another. By war's end in August of 1945, about thirty percent of the 1,700 features produced 1942-45 had been war-related.

Hollywood could not have maintained such an output on the basis of patriotic duty alone. There was an obvious and understandable appetite among the movie-going public for stories about the war.

The scope of World War II—the way it touched nearly every family in America—is almost unimaginable today. Consider that by 1945, over 15 million men aged seventeen to forty-five had served in the military (as well as tens of thousands of women, and the men of the civilian merchant marine who battled German air and naval forces while transporting vital war supplies across the North Atlantic). In a country of a little over 132 million people, this meant that approximately one in every nine Americans went off to war (and one in thirteen would be a casualty; about one percent of the total U.S. population). It was the rare household that didn't know someone in service.

But the men who, in the parlance of the times, "put on the suit" were not alone in the war effort. Men ineligible for military service were joined by hundreds of thousands of women working in the nation's factories that had been converted to producing war materiel. All families dealt with the rationing of any number of household items, from gasoline to shoes, butter to meat. The citizenry harvested scrap metal, old tires, and cooking grease in scrap drives to provide raw materials for war manufacturing. They grew "victory gardens" in their backyards to supplement their rationed groceries. Everyone, literally, was part of the national effort.

Understandably, then, movies about the war—particularly combat movies—were unabashedly supportive, and sometimes rabidly propagandistic. In *The Purple Heart* (1944), for example, a fictionalized telling of a true-life show trial of downed American pilots by the Japanese, the court officers are portrayed in the broadest Asian racial stereotypes down to buck teeth and owlish glasses. In *Action in the North Atlantic* (1943), the German U-boats preying on American convoys are given all the dignity of a mugger (even though American movies like *Destination Tokyo* [1943] and *Crash Dive* [1943] depict US submariners doing the same thing as the valiant young men of the "Silent Service").

Hollywood movies regularly distorted the facts on the ground for the sake of American morale. The battle for *Wake Island* (1942) neglects to mention the fight actually ended in a surrender rather than the movie's fight-to-the-last-man climax; *A Wing and a Prayer* (1944) makes America's first six months of losses in the Pacific look like part of a master plan to bait the Japanese into a trap at Midway; *Air Force* (1943) explains away the Pearl Harbor disaster as the result of Japanese sabotage and Fifth Columnists rather than American unpreparedness.

Hollywood also tweaked any number of technical details also for the sake of bolstering national confidence. In *A Wing and a Prayer*, the battle at Midway is won by carrier torpedo planes when, in reality, squadrons of torpedo planes had been slaughtered by Japanese fighters without landing a single hit on the enemy; in *Sahara* (1943), tank sergeant Humphrey Bogart delivers a stirring salute to the capabilities of the M3 "Grant" tank while, on the battlefield, the Americans never fielded a tank until the closing months of the war that could go head-to-head with German heavy armor; the B-17 in *Air Force* is as spacious and comfortable as a jumbo jet instead of the cramped, cold, noisy aircraft it truly was.

Yet in other major ways, war movies of the time were admirably honest. Although there were any number of wartime adventure movies like *Flying Tigers* (1942) and *Desperate Journey* (1942), which were heavy on grandstanding heroics and derring-do and showed the American fighting man capable of out-thinking, out-brave-ing and out-fighting any enemy, there were also a steady stream of movies showing that America's heroes were decidedly life-sized. In movies like *Guadalcanal Diary* (1943), *Sahara, The Story of G.I. Joe* (1945), *A Walk in the Sun* (1945), *Objective, Burma!* (1945), *They Were Expendable* (1945), to name just a few, the American soldier was resolutely portrayed as an Everyman, a one-time cabbie or grocery clerk doing what he thought was a dirty job only because it had to be done, and the sooner it was done the sooner he could return to the home and family he longed for. True to life, the G.I. in these films was no over-muscled Rambo, but the schlub next door; no steely-eyed professional warrior, but a guy who wasn't afraid to admit to his fear when the bombs came in. In the often poignant *The Story of G.I. Joe*, a squad leader, having led one too many futile attacks during the Italian campaign, finally cracks after hearing the recorded sound of his unseen son's voice for the first time, while his company commander admits to feeling like "a murderer" as he writes letters home to the relatives of the men he's lost.

Hollywood was also frank about what the painful cost of victory would be, and the simple, brutal fact that not everyone was coming back. One of the moments bringing that idea heartbreakingly home comes in *Objective, Burma!*, as a G.I. looks down on the body of a comrade killed during the night by a Japanese infiltrator, saying, "So much for Mrs. Hollis's nine months of pain and twenty years of hope."

After the war's end, moviemakers no longer felt obligated to be tireless cheerleaders. The war had been won and they could now afford to be more reflective than wartime circumstances had allowed.

While there was never any question the war had needed fighting and winning, moviemakers were now freer to present a more clear-eyed view of the human toll of that victory. To be sure, there would still be any number of action-adventures saluting the triumph of WW II (e.g. *Fighter Squadron* [1948], *The Sands of Iwo Jima* [1949], *An American Guerilla in the Philippines* [1950], *Flying Leathernecks*

[1951]), but another vein of combat movie strove for something more profound and more telling. Movies like *12 O'Clock High* (1949), *Battleground* (1949), *The Cruel Sea* (1952), *Command Decision* (1949), *Halls of Montezuma* (1950), *Breakthrough* (1950), *The Caine Mutiny* (1954) and others showed the war to have been more brutal and emotionally traumatic than the morale-boosting movies of the war years had ever let on. Men had been maimed in body (William Campbell screaming "I got no legs!" in *Breakthrough)* and mind (migraine-afflicted platoon leader Richard Widmark in *Halls of Montezuma)*, and the strain of command had brought down the strongest of men (Gregory Peck's steely group commander ultimately collapses into catatonia in *12 O'Clock High)*. In such films it seemed their makers had taken to heart Hemingway's "Notes on the Next War": "They wrote in the old days that it is sweet and fitting to die for one's country. But in modern war there is nothing sweet nor fitting in your dying. You will die like a dog for no good reason."

War movies took a still darker turn with the outbreak of the Korean War in June of 1950.

It was a confusing war for most Americans. It was the country's first "limited" war, and its first "war of policy"; a war fought for political reasons so abstract to the common man as to seem meaningless.

It was also keenly frustrating. After the victory of WW II, it was unfathomable to many that the greatest military power on earth found itself, after the first six dynamic months of the war, mired in a bloody two-and-a-half year stalemate.

Even more troubling was that so soon after the most momentous conflict in history—a war that had cost some 60 million souls globally—we were at war again. The Great Crusade, it now sadly seemed, had resolved nothing; only traded one great threat for an apparently endless number of smaller ones.

Some Korean War movies propagandized (*One Minute to Zero* [1952], *Retreat, Hell!* [1952], *The Steel Helmet* [1951]), while others saluted the men tasked with fighting an ugly, unwanted war (*The Bridges at Toko Ri* [1954], *Pork Chop Hill* [1959]), but still others tapped into this postwar disillusionment, and none better than *Men in War* (1957).

Men in War is set in Korea, but director Anthony Mann keeps the enemy largely off-screen. Its simple story of platoon leader Robert Ryan's decimated platoon trying to find safe haven is the war story reduced to poetically bleak elementals. Ryan and his men are any unit in any army in any war simply trying to get to the end of the day alive, fighting not for a cause but because, as Ryan says, "we've got no place else to go."

That same disillusionment spilled over into Korean era WWII tales as moviemakers used the majestic stage of the Great Crusade as a platform to illustrate the futility, brutality, and insanity of war—any war, even those fought for the noblest of causes and with the best of intentions, e.g. *Attack!* (1956), *The Young Lions* (1958), *The Bridge on the River Kwai* (1957—ending with medic James MacDonald looking out over the finale's carnage declaring, "Madness! Madness!").

Korea ended in not quite a victory, not quite a defeat, but something unpalatable enough that by the end of the '50s, the country had pretty much pushed the war from the national consciousness. If Korea was doomed to be America's Forgotten War, Vietnam was to be the country's great national trauma; one whose scars can still be found in U.S. foreign policy and military thinking to this day.

In the early '60s, American involvement in Southeast Asia was limited to a few thousand advisors. By 1968, the country had committed over 550,000 men to the effort, always upping its manpower ante on the military's estimate that just a few more troops would bring a win. With each boost in troop levels, victory remained a constantly receding horizon, and Vietnam began to look like a winless war without end. The ongoing war led to protests, social unrest, a sense of broken faith between the people and the country's leadership. The apotheosis of the national agony was the 1970 killing of four Kent State University students by National Guardsmen during a protest over the expansion of the war into Cambodia.

Hollywood (in)famously avoided addressing the major issue of the day, and throughout the duration of the war—from the time combat troops first set foot in Vietnam in 1965 through the collapse of South Vietnam a decade later—there was only one major studio release about the conflict; John Wayne's jingoistic and laughably simple-minded *The Green Berets* (1968).

The movie industry's avoidance was understandable. Making a movie viewed as supporting the war could alienate the generally antiwar young audience so critical to the box office. On the other hand, to make a movie slamming the war might not only alienate older moviegoers, but risk antagonizing the government authorities who regulated and policed the business and media practices of the studios.

This didn't mean Hollywood avoided making war movies. In fact, it seemed to make movies about every war *but* the one in Vietnam—from purely action-adventures (*The Guns of Navarone* [1961], *Von Ryan's Express* [1965]) to melodramas (*The Blue Max* [1965]) to near-surreal black comedies about the absurdities of armed conflict (*Catch-22* [1970], *Castle Keep* [1969], *M*A*S*H* [1970]).

Though Hollywood avoided dealing with Vietnam directly, there were a number of releases over the period which, to some degree or another, alluded to the conflict (as well as to the sad fact that the country was, yet again, at war). *The Sand Pebbles* (1966) found the same moral confusion, naïve idealism, national hubris, and ignorance of native peoples bedeviling the effort in Vietnam in America's "gunboat diplomacy" in 1920s China; *Shenandoah* (1965) was an adamantly antiwar drama set during the American Civil War; *Lost Command* (1966) was a disturbingly prescient look at how Vietnam would play out through the experience of a French combat unit fighting a similar guerilla war in Algeria; the bitter Western *Ulzana's Raid* (1972) was as much about what was going on in 1960s-'70s Southeast Asia as it was about the 1880s Indian wars of the American southwest.

American audiences also found Vietnam resonating in a number of imports. WWII had weakened the global empires of the European powers, and, for decades after, countries like Britain and France found themselves embroiled in wars of empire; conflicts between an outdated colonial mindset and exploding native nationalism. The Europeans proved themselves more frank than Hollywood in dealing with their own Vietnams in movies like *The Guns at Batasi* (1964), *The Battle of Algiers* (1966), the allegorical *Burn!* (1969), and, one of the all-time best combat films, *Zulu* (1964), written and directed by Cy Endfield.

A dramatized version of the 1879 Battle of Rorke's Drift in the British African colony of Natal, *Zulu*, like *Men in War*, seemed to encapsulate larger truths about so many of the conflicts that had followed WWII. The soldiers are in a place they don't want to be, fighting a war against an enemy they don't know, for a purpose they don't understand. "Why us?" one frightened trooper asks. "Because we're here," answers his sergeant, "and no one else."

With the fall of South Vietnam in 1975, American moviemakers began to tentatively test audiences for their receptivity to movies about the war, but initial efforts—*Twilight's Last Gleaming* (1977), *Rolling Thunder* (1977), *Who'll Stop the Rain?* (1978), *Go Tell the Spartans* (1978) and *The Boys in Company C* (1978)—gained very little box office traction. But the success of *Coming Home* and *The Deer Hunter* (both 1978) showed, finally, a growing interest in America's most troubling war, and a desire to understand the country's first major military defeat.

While neither movie holds up particularly well—*Coming Home* now seems a too-neatly structured melodrama, and *The Deer Hunter* often comes off as a hysterical rant—they did open the door for what would be one of the definitive movies of the time as well as a timeless war movie: Francis Ford Coppola's *Apocalypse Now* (1979).

Less a movie about Vietnam than a reworking of the Joseph Conrad novella, *Heart of Darkness*, it is precisely the movie's Conradian core that extends the movie's thematic reach beyond Vietnam to become a darkly poetic portrait of the moral corrosion and infectious insanity of combat.

Apocalypse was the Vietnam genre's first major hit ($79 million domestic—over $200 million in today's dollars), but despite that success, other moviemakers remained hesitant about following suit. There was *The Killing Fields* (1984) about the spillover of the war into Cambodia, but the cultural catharsis didn't come until Oliver Stone's *Platoon* (1986).

Unlike Coppola's film, *Platoon* didn't concern itself with larger philosophical issues, but only in giving a uniquely realistic representation of the grim existence of a U.S. infantryman in Vietnam (Stone himself had served in 1967). The blockbuster success of *Platoon* ($139 million domestic) was enough to open the floodgates, and the late 1980s into the early 1990s would see a torrent of Vietnam combat movies hit the screens.

But with a major difference.

Apocalypse Now and Stanley Kubrick's *Full Metal Jacket* (1987) used Vietnam as the setting for an exploration of larger, existential themes, while *Platoon* placed itself squarely in the mind of a frightened front-line G.I., but all of them had addressed the curiosity of the mass audience regarding how and why the war had gone so badly.

There was, however, a more palatable picture of the war already asserting itself.

These were the years of the Reagan presidency, and Reagan rallied a country emotionally exhausted by the social upheavals of the 1960s-'70s and dispirited by the loss in Vietnam by re-embracing the American myths which had taken such a beating over the previous twenty years: that America was The Good Guy, was always The Good Guy always fighting in a good cause. He recast Vietnam as a noble effort; a source of pride rather than an embarrassment.

Plugging into the new, patriotic national zeitgeist were movies like *Rambo: First Blood, Part II* (1985), *Uncommon Valor* (1983), *Missing in Action* (1984 plus two sequels), *Flight of the Intruder* (1991) and others. These movies re-fought Vietnam, showing it not to be the war we lost, but the war we could have—*should* have—won had it not been for weak-kneed politicians, misguided peaceniks, and soft-headed left-wing intellectuals.

This resurgent patriotic fervor showed up in a range of films about war and the military: *An Officer and a Gentleman* (1982), *Red Dawn* (1984), *Iron Eagle* (1986), *The Delta Force* (1986), *Memphis Belle* (1992), and most spectacularly in *Top Gun* (1986).

Grossing a whopping $177 million domestic (around $350 million in today's dollars), *Top Gun* aped the fervent flag-waving of WWII era war movies even though it was their thematic antithesis. While 1940s war movies made the case for the skills necessary to fight the war—discipline, teamwork, obedience—*Top Gun* struck a chord with young audiences with the generationally appealing fantasy of a cocky, rule-breaking, go-his-own-way young hero so preternaturally skilled he could outfly even the best veteran pilots. Director Tony Scott often interrupted the youth v. grown-ups drama for MTV-style montages set to thumping rock music. Some critics called *Top Gun* the best TV commercial military recruiters ever had.

By the early 1990s, this cycle of war movies was burning itself out, and while the wars the country had successfully weathered since Vietnam had helped revitalize America's self-image, they had been too nebulous—or questionable—in their meaning to add much to the popular culture. The invasion of tiny Grenada in 1983 had provided the basis for the Clint Eastwood starrer *Heartbreak Ridge* (1986), but little else, and the 1989 invasion of Panama passed completely unremembered. Strangely, America's biggest military engagement since the end of Vietnam would make little impression at the movies, even though it had ended with the kind of king-sized decisive victory it seemed a self-doubting nation had been waiting on for fifteen years.

In 1990, the U.S. led a large coalition of countries in pushing the occupying army of Iraqi strongman Saddam Hussein out of the small, oil-rich country of Kuwait. The actual ground combat, which began in February 1991 after weeks of aerial bombardment, lasted only five days, but in that time the U.S.-led forces destroyed much of Hussein's sizable military power and liberated Kuwait at a cost of less than 1,400 killed and wounded.

Perhaps the war had been too quick, or too ambiguous (many wondered why the unstoppable U.S. forces had not gone all the way to Baghdad and toppled the Hussein regime). Cynics thought—particularly in light of the pragmatic constraints on the war, such as leaving Hussein in power—this had been less a fight against oppression than a fight to maintain economic stability in the oil-dependent west. In any case, though the mood in the country was buoyed by the quick win, few major films were inspired by the war: *Courage Under Fire* (1995), a salute as straightforward as its title; and darkly comic, bitterly cynical *Three Kings* (1999), which mocked the soaring rhetoric of the war with the reality on the ground.

Throughout the 1980s and into the late 1990s, of whatever stripe, the war movie had been losing ground. There had been a small handful of major hits *(Rambo: First Blood, Part II, Top Gun, Platoon)*, a few respectable midrange earners *(Heartbreak Ridge, Full Metal Jacket, Born on the Fourth of July* [1989], *Courage Under Fire)*, but, as a genre, it seemed to be fading.

The war movie found new energy not in dealing with the ambiguous wars of the present, but by going back to the moral clarity of a long ago war: WWII. The revitalizing agent was Steven Spielberg's *Saving Private Ryan* (1998).

Saving Private Ryan is such an oft-repeated classic these days, it's hard to appreciate how brave and bold it was at the time. It had been decades since a WWII combat movie had been a major box office success, and the last combat movies of any type to earn big had been the chest-thumping *Top Gun* and the grim *Platoon* twelve years before. Spielberg made no attempt to appease or pander to get an audience in the doors. Instead, he opted for blunt honesty, showing combat with a graphic stomach-turning realism never before seen in a mainstream film. He managed the deft balancing act of saluting the sacrifice of WWII's Greatest Generation without sanctifying them, showing how the desperation of combat can push the most decent of men to acts of callous brutality. *Ryan* demonstrated the thesis Studs Terkel had laid out in his 1984 oral history of the Second World War, *The Good War*: that there was no such thing as a good war.

For all its horrific violence and deglamorization, *Ryan* earned $217 million domestic and won Spielberg an Oscar for Best Director. And, as success usually does in Hollywood, it spawned a host of imitators.

In short order came a gush of WWII actioners, some even aping the jittery camerawork and wrenching violence of Ryan: *The Thin Red Line* (1998), *U-571* (2000), *Pearl Harbor* (2001), *Enemy at the Gates* (2001), *Windtalkers* (2002), *Hart's War* (2002), and director Clint Eastwood's our-side/their-side pairing, *Flags of Our Fathers* and *Letters from Iwo Jima* (both 2006). The patriotic fervor stirred up by Ryan filtered into other war movies as well: *Black Hawk Down* (2001), a heroic portrayal of an ill-fated mission during the U.S.' effort at nation-building in Somalia; the Bosnian bombing campaign provided the basis for *Behind Enemy Lines* (2001); and there was Vietnam-set *We Were Soldiers* (2002). But few compared to Spielberg's creative achievement, and none even came close to matching Ryan's earnings.

Perhaps the problem was that America's mind was on a new war... two of them, in fact.

In response to the 9/11 terrorist attacks on the World Trade Center and the Pentagon, the U.S. invaded Afghanistan in October of 2001, and then Iraq in 2003. In both cases, the period of ground combat was short, and the conventional forces of both countries soundly defeated. It seemed that America was on a roll, militarily, anyway, but the giddiness of two quick victories began to evaporate as both wars stubbornly refused to conclude. Instead, they devolved into grinding, low-intensity conflicts, wars with an often unseen enemy—or, as is the case in these faction-ridden tribalized countries, enemies.

The exuberance over what had, at first, seemed rapid-fire triumphs began to devolve as well, into frustration, puzzlement, and ultimately the sinking Vietnam-like sense that, again, the country was stuck in two endless wars, both of which it seemed we could neither win nor afford to lose. After those opening months, there were no set-piece battles, few firefights. They became steady-state wars of IEDs and drone attacks moved to the inside pages of the newspaper.

As both wars ground stubbornly on, Hollywood turned out a series of movies about America's embroilment in the Middle East. Some were big budget efforts (*Jarhead,* 2005), some intimate art house releases (*In the Valley of Elah,* 2007); some were among the best movies Hollywood could offer (*The Hurt Locker,* 2009), and others not so much (*Lions for Lambs,* 2007). They came in all flavors: espionage thriller (*Syriana,* 2005), political drama (*Lions for Lambs,* 2007), comedy-drama (*Charlie Wilson's War,* 2007), documentary (*Taxi to the Dark Side,* 2007), empty-headed actioner (*The Kingdom,* 2007), even horror movie (*Red Sands,* 2009). But no matter the genre or the quality, they all remarkably shared one similar characteristic:

They didn't perform.

The bigger earners never did better than midrange (*Jarhead, Munich* [2005], *Charlie Wilson's War, The Kingdom*), standing as disappointments when measured against their costs. Even the more intimate-sized films hit a wall early: *In the Valley of Elah*—$6.7 million; *Brothers* (2009)—$28.5 million; *The Hurt Locker*—$17 million.

In fact, going back to the movies that followed the first Gulf War of 1990-91, with the exception of Michael Moore's heavy-handed and inflammatory documentary *Fahrenheit 911* (2004—$119 million domestic), not one American movie dealing with the Middle East has been a major commercial success, and most have been financial failures:

Three Kings (budget: $75 million/U.S. box office: 60.7 million); *Charlie Wilson's War* ($75m/66.7); *Jarhead* ($72m/62.7m); *Courage Under Fire* ($46m/61.7m); *Rules of Engagement* (2000—$60m/61m); *Syriana* ($50m/50.8m); *The Kingdom* ($70m/47.5m); *Munich* (2005—$70m/47.4m); *The Siege* (1998—$70m/40.9m); *Brothers* ($26m/28.5); *Lions for Lambs* ($35m/15m); *Mighty Heart* (2007—$16m/9.2m); *Rendition* (2007—$27.5m/9.2m); *In the Valley of Elah* ($23m/6.8m); *Redacted* (2007—$5m/.065m); *Red Sands* (less than $500,000/na).

Perhaps no movie better defines the wholesale rejection of cinematic consideration of the defining foreign policy issue of the day by the American moviegoer than the fate of *The Hurt Locker.* Despite near-universal critical acclaim culminating in a Best Picture Oscar as well as a Best Director award for Kathryn Bigelow, the movie crawled to a domestic take of $17 million, and barely earned back its spare $15 million budget only after overseas receipts were added in (a movie's breakeven is typically twice its cost; *Locker*'s total worldwide take: $32 million).

It is an unprecedented response. In every decade prior, there can be found some box office reflection of the movie-going public's desire to understand even its country's most problematic conflicts, or at least buy into some myth of same. In fact, every decade prior to the '00s can boast at least a few war movies among the top earners of the period: the '20s had *The Four Horsemen of the Apocalypse, The Big Parade, What Price Glory* (1926) among the box office champs of the decade; the '30s had *All Quiet on the Western Front*; the '40s boasted *For Whom the Bell Tolls* (1943), *The Fighting 69th* (1940), *Sergeant York* (1941), *Thirty Seconds Over Tokyo* (1944), *A Guy Named Joe* (1944) and *Sands of Iwo Jima*; the '50s brought *Battleground, The Bridge on the River Kwai, From Here to Eternity* (1953), *The Caine Mutiny, Mr. Roberts* (1955), *Battle Cry* (1955), *To Hell and Back* (1955); from the '60s, *The Dirty Dozen* (1967), *The Longest Day* (1962), *Lawrence of Arabia* (1962) *The Sand Pebbles* (1967); the '70s had *Patton* (1970), *Tora! Tora! Tora!* (1970), *Apocalypse Now, The Deer Hunter, M*A*S*H*; the '80s—*Top Gun, An Officer and a Gentleman, Platoon,* and *First Blood* and *Rambo: First Blood, Part II*; and from the '90s, *A Few Good Men* (1992) and *Saving Private Ryan*.

But since the century has turned, no war movie since *Black Hawk Down* and *Pearl Harbor* (both released in 2001) has crossed the $100 million mark in domestic earnings except for Quentin Tarantino's comic bookish rewriting of World War II, *Inglourious Basterds* (2009—$121 million). Think of it: a host of movies, some of them quite acclaimed, about one of the most pressing issues of the day go ignored, while only an over-the-top wish-fulfillment fantasy about a long-ago war can pull an audience.

There may be several things at work.

A number of educational and social studies surveys suggest that Gen X/Yers—the same age bracket that has been a box office cornerstone for decades—has limited interest in the issues of the day, though whether that's the product of distraction in a world of infinitely varied electronic entertainment or disillusionment is open to argument. (A personal observation: in a university business class I teach, I asked my class of twenty-two where Libya was when news of the still on-going uprising broke: a few put it on the Suez Canal, some knew it was somewhere on the Mediterranean, but most had no idea at all nor seemed to particularly care.)

Another factor may be the near complete isolation of most of the American public from the military experience. Since WWI and up through Vietnam, U.S. combat forces have largely been made of up draftees. Even in WWII, despite the nation's wholesale commitment to fighting the war, about half of the massive military fielded by the U.S. was made up of draftees. Truly citizen soldiers, they came home after the treaties were signed bringing their experiences back to mainstream America.

But after Vietnam, the U.S. converted to an all-volunteer service, and the overall size of this professional military has remained quite small. Today, about 1.5 million men and women make up the country's active duty forces in the Army, Air Force, Navy and Marines, with another approximately 1.5 million in the reserves: about one in every 100 Americans (compared to one in nine for WWII).

The nature of today's wars has meant a limited number of veterans re-assimilating into the general population. Korea produced 6.8 million veterans against a total population of 151 million (about one in every twenty-one Americans); Vietnam, 2.59 million against a population of 194 million (one in every seventy-five). But for as long as the wars in Afghanistan and Iraq have ground on, their limited scope and reliance on redeployments of the same units over and over has produced just 755,000 veterans—somewhere around one in 400.

The mass public—and particularly the young people historically tasked with fighting most of the country's previous wars—are insulated from the impact of our present-day conflicts. The military man is an alien concept to them, which explains on-screen portrayals that, while popular, are frankly incredible. Consider James Cromwell's camp commander in military mystery *The General's Daughter* (1999—$103 million domestic) willing to accept the gang rape and murder of his serving daughter for the good of the Army; or Jack Nicholson's sociopathic Guantanamo Marine commander in *A Few Good Men* ($141 million), a military courtroom drama about a commander who seems just fine with the accidental murder of one of his own men as part of maintaining discipline; or, in the same movie, Tom Cruise's party-hearty, irreverent Navy lawyer, who comes off less a serving officer than a frat boy in uniform.

Is this important? Does it matter? After all, don't we go to the movies simply to be entertained?

We have always wanted to be entertained by our movies. But sometimes we were entertained because a movie appealed to our interests. We have, in the past, been interested in the experience of the men we have sent out to fight and sometimes die on our behalf, just as, at other times, we have been interested in the threats of nuclear war, racial intolerance, sexual politics, government conduct, police corruption—interested to a level that entertaining movies about such non-fun topics could produce significant coin for moviemakers.

But our interest—at least for many of those who are regular moviegoers—seems to have narrowed to the lightweight, the escapist, the fantasies fulfilled. The real world doesn't interest us much these days, or so it sometimes appears.

During the Vietnam days, young people unhappy with a war they saw as devouring their generation went into the streets to express their dissatisfaction with the direction of the country, while their elders went out into the streets to declare them un-American and tell them to get a haircut.

Today, we are in two equally unpopular wars. Together, the wars in Afghanistan and Iraq have cost us over 5,500 dead and over 35,000 wounded.

No one is in the streets. They've all gone to the movies to watch Iron Man kick terrorist ass.

The Case of the Disappearing Private Eye
(posted 8/10/12)

I looked for him, but he was gone. I checked the boozy dives and the greasy spoons and the street corners where the not-nice girls hang out.

Nothing.

He was gone.

Tall guy, fedora, trench coat. You must've seen him. Usually smoking. He was always hanging around, poking his nose where it didn't belong and usually getting it punched.

A real wisenheimer too. Always cracking wise.

You see him, you call. And if I find out you've been holding back…

If you don't miss that kind of patois, you're either too young to remember it, or you've got a tin ear. God knows, *I* miss it.

Back in May, some of you might remember I interviewed *Road to Perdition* author Max Allan Collins. A lot of the discussion had to do with his connection with one of the giants of private eye fiction, Mickey Spillane.

In the course of the conversation, it was mentioned that Spillane's Mike Hammer novels had hit their commercial peak during the early 1960s. It was only days later it occurred to me why there had been something about that comment that kept it buzzing around in my head. Then, like someone who buys a red car and suddenly notices how many other red cars there are on the road, it came to me: it wasn't just Spillane's Mike Hammer novels that had slipped out of view.

In literature, private eye stories have been moneymakers for at least a century and a half. The names of the authors are as legendary as their characters: Poe, Doyle, Hammett, Chandler, Cain, McDonald, Spillane, Parker…

As soon as the movies learned to talk, the private eye story became a big screen staple as well: *The Maltese Falcon* (1941), *Murder, My Sweet* (1944), *Kiss Me Deadly* (1955), *Harper* (1966)… They ranged from the mass-produced private eyes series of the 1930s—like the Boston Blackie and Charlie Chan flicks—to the grim postwar *noirs* like *Out of the Past* (1947); from flyweight Abbott & Costello and Bowery Boys entries to the transcendence of *Chinatown* (1974).

Then came TV and by the end of the 1950s, the private eye was as much a boob tube regular as cowboys and cops. One studio—Warner

Bros., which took a deep jump into TV production in the '50s—had found a successful formula with *77 Sunset Strip* and was soon pumping out private eyes on a production line. The formula: one somewhat mature but good-looking snoop for dad, a younger, even better looking private investigator for mom, and a still-younger hepcat to bring in the kids. Add a sexy address, stir, and *77 Sunset Strip* begat *Hawaiian Eye*, *Surfside Six* (set in Miami Beach), *Bourbon Street Beat* (set in New Orleans), and *The Roaring Twenties* (set in Prohibition era New York).

They never stopped coming. The 1960s gave us *Mannix*, the '70s had *The Rockford Files*, and *Magnum, P.I.* surfed in on the '80s.

And then...

If I'm not mistaken, there hasn't been a private eye movie from a major studio since Paramount's release of Robert Benton's *Twilight* in 1998. The police procedural seems to have monopolized the crime genre on TV, and even in the world of print, the private eye story has become more of a niche market offering rather than a mainstream regular.

Which raises the obvious question: what happened?

What goes on in the entertainment arena to cause a once enormously popular genre to virtually evaporate all across the media spectrum?

*****

As it happens, I've recently read an advance copy of Ariel S. Winter's bravely ambitious debut novel, *The Twenty-Year Death*, which Titan Books is releasing this month. Audaciously constructed, *The Twenty-Year Death* is actually three stand-alone mystery novels that combine to tell a greater, overarching story of violence and tragedy. Set in three different decades—the 1930s, 1940s, and 1950s—each echoes popular crime fiction from its time: *The Dain Curse*-type mystery for the 1930s, the hard-boiled patter of Sam Spade for the 1940s, and the angst and cynicism of *noir* in the 1950s. Winter's assured command of each suggests a writer at home with much of the private eye canon (unsurprising, I guess, from a long-time bookseller), and a good guy to ask about what happened—and what's happening—to the private eye genre in print...

Q: In print, the private eye story dates at least to Edgar Allan Poe's Auguste Dupin stories in the 1840s. The genre seems to connect with American audiences in a truly American way with writers

like Dashiell Hammett and Raymond Chandler in the first half of the twentieth century. How do you see the evolution of the private eye story? What was it about the genre that engaged you?

A: The evolution of the private eye story proceeds from detectives in the nineteenth and early twentieth centuries like Dupin and Sherlock Holmes who prize deductive reasoning over action, to in-the-thick-of-the-action detectives like Sam Spade and Philip Marlowe in the 1930s and 1940s. The Marlowe model then dominates the next several decades, with the only significant development the introduction of the female private eye like Sara Paretsky's V. I. Warshawski, and Sue Grafton's Kinsey Milhone in the 1980s. These women, however, were still modeled on the hardboiled detectives of the pulp era. All of these detectives follow a strict moral code, whether that moral code coincides with the law or not. Then, in recent years, there's been something of a subversion or appropriation of the private detective in books like *Motherless Brooklyn* by Jonathan Lethem, *Look at Me* by Jenifer Egan, and *Inherent Vice* by Thomas Pynchon where the detective is flawed, and his code of honor is looser.

I would also argue that bounty hunters and superheroes often function like private detectives, so if you're looking at current film, I wouldn't discount the Batman—he is the world's greatest detective after all—or Tarantino's upcoming movie, *Django Unchained*. And, of course, there's the popular BBC show *Sherlock*, the Robert Downey, Jr. Sherlock Holmes movies, and another network Sherlock Holmes show about to start. Obviously, Holmes is a special subset on his own, but he is a private eye.

As to what attracted me to the genre, I'd probably say the attitude. My favorite movie as a child (and possibly still today) was *Who Framed Roger Rabbit?* (1988), which is a gateway movie in that it has the cartoons to draw a kid in, but it is solidly a hardboiled detective movie. Around the same time, I began reading Paretsky and Grafton, and shortly after that I became a diehard comic book fan, especially *Batman*, so the lone, grim detective was something I've always liked. I like their fearlessness, their strong moral code, their steadfast determination.

Q: The glory days for the private eye story, in both print and film, seem to be from the 1930s into the 1960s, maybe 1970s. Would you say that's a fair assessment?

A: I don't know. As I already said, the 1980s saw a pretty major development with the female detective. I'd throw *Murder, She Wrote* in there too, even though she's an amateur detective instead of a true private eye. And comic books have never let the detective go, like *Batman* or *Sin City*, and the 1990s was a banner time for comic books. So, I don't know that I'd cut it off completely in the 1970s, even if there's been some decline.

Q: There's obviously still an audience for the private eye story in print, but it doesn't seem to hold the same kind of stature it once did. What changed in audience sensibilities? What changed in the market?

A: One thing might be the public's relationship to the police. In the early part of the twentieth century, there was a lot more anti-police sentiment across all parts of society. They were seen as tools of the system that was keeping everyone down, and their corruption was taken for granted, so outlaws and people working for a moral code instead of for the state were more acceptable heroes. Even many of the police stories in the pulps have as their protagonist a police officer who doesn't exactly follow orders, operating almost as a private detective within the system. And corruption is still taken for granted and there are segments of society that still hate the police, such as in impoverished urban environments. Overall, the role of the police as protectors and a positive force has come to dominate public opinion, especially post-9/11 when the police were truly heroes. People in real life are more inclined to go to the police with a problem than to a private detective now, so the kinds of cases real private detectives handle have become limited as well. As a result, police drama in literature, television, and film has come to represent much of the detective drama.

My editor, Charles Ardai, also points out that the advancement of forensic science has made it almost impossible for a lone private investigator to run a successful investigation. Crime detection relies heavily on fingerprinting, fiber analysis, DNA testing, and a private investigator just isn't going to have the resources needed to do that kind of forensic work. When Holmes was doing his own forensics, he was the only one doing it, so he could do it alone, but even in the BBC depiction of the character, he relies on the pathologist and other police resources.

Q: When one thinks of the iconic literary private eyes—Hammett's Nick Charles and Sam Spade, Chandler's Philip Marlowe, Mickey Spillane's Mike Hammer, Ross Macdonald's Lew Archer—there doesn't appear to have been a P.I. character with that kind of dramatic weight since. Why do you think that is?

A: Again, I'd really throw Batman out there as the exception to that, even if his first appearance predates all of those characters. His current hold on the public is stronger than most of the other detectives have ever been. But Batman and the continuation of other characters developed in the earlier period withstanding, I, again, would argue that the type hasn't disappeared, just their profession. The same way the hardboiled figure appeared in Westerns before private eye books, and are now usually police officers or superheroes. And perhaps, as people began to have greater trust in the police, the idea of someone who works outside of the law has become more suspect (this contradicts my Batman point, of course). Instead of cheering on or wishing to be Mike Hammer, maybe now we see him as someone who's out of control, a bad element in society.

Q: P.I. stories may be more of a niche genre these days, but they obviously still have their following. What is it about the private eye that still hooks a reader?

A: Mysteries in general are popular because they pose a question with very high stakes, and then give a satisfying answer. They horrify and reassure. So, regardless of who the detective is, whether private or public or military, people are attracted to mysteries. And so, most mystery lovers won't care whether the detective is private or public. So, it might be hard to say whether there are any specifics unique to the private eye that draws people in.

Q: A lot of P.I. fiction being turned out today seems to echo the hardboiled, noirish style of an earlier literary age. Why do you think that is? Is it nostalgia for a certain kind of storytelling? Or is it that hard to find a contemporary voice that works for that kind of fiction?

A: Some of it is definitely nostalgia. Some of it is because people today are often more passive and equivocating than people were in the 1930s and 1940s. A male twenty-five year old in the 1940s didn't question whether he was a man or not, while many male twenty-five-year-olds today don't feel that they are men at all. So, it's much harder to believe that a self-assured man of action could do the things we expect fictional detectives do without a lot of formal training as a police officer, in the military, or in martial arts. That's why so many of the lone vengeance movies are (about) former military trainees.

Q: By and large, people are reading less for entertainment, the big movers are titles of the fantastic and supernatural, which appeal to younger readers. What's the future for the literary private eye?

A: First, from what I understand about the explosion of e-books, not to mention all of the reading that's done online, I'm not sure that people are actually reading less for entertainment. It's true that fantasy sells big, and, as a result, you'll find a lot detective stories written in fantasy worlds, like Jeff VanderMeer's work, so perhaps the future is that kind of genre bending. But just like *Deadwood* brought back the Western in Hollywood, I'm sure there will be a detective story that brings private eyes back as well.

*****

David Breckman's TV resumé goes back to the late 1990s when he was a staff writer for *Saturday Night Live*. Most recently—and one of the reasons I sought him out for this piece—he was one of the producers for USA Network's long-running hit cop show, *Monk*. This series, starring Tony Shalhoub as a detective afflicted with OCD, ran from 2002-2009, was nominated for 16 Emmys over the course of its run, winning seven of them including three for Shalhoub as "Outstanding Lead Actor in a Comedy Series." The mystery community showed *Monk* some love as well with four Edgar Award nominations during its time on the air. When USA renewed the series in 2006, it was, according to them, the "... highest-rated series in cable history," and, indeed, the series' finale pulled an outstanding 9.4 million viewers making it the most-watched scripted drama episode in cable history up to that time.

Breckman is not just a respected industry vet with a braggable credit under his belt. Get him talking and he has the same passion for TV and film as any other media geek. He seems to never have forgotten a movie or TV show he saw, even as a child, and the years since have only allowed him to augment those memories with an insider's insight, and a buff's love of behind-the-scenes arcana...

Q: It seems that almost as soon as TV transitioned from being dominated by live drama and variety programming to filmed programming, the private eye story became almost as much of a TV

staple as Westerns and cop shows with offerings like <u>Peter Gunn</u>, <u>Richard Diamond—Private Detective</u>, and <u>77 Sunset Strip</u> just to name a few. What do you think it was about private eye shows that made them so popular? And continued to keep them popular for the next twenty years or so?

A: To me, the private eye's chief appeal is a certain aspect of knight errantry. The courtly knights of medieval romance (if not always in fact) were brave, noble, pure of heart, steadfast in love, meager of fortune, and committed to wandering the land rescuing fair maidens from the predations of fire-breathing dragons. Classic TV gumshoes like Peter Gunn, Richard Diamond, and (perhaps especially) Mannix all embody this chivalric ideal. They may be swooping to the rescue in a grey Plymouth Valiant instead of on horseback, and slaying the dragon with a snub-nosed .38 instead of a broadsword, but the tradition is the same.

Another attraction: The classic private eye is a lone wolf, not a bureaucrat. He's not a "joiner." He doesn't function well in groups. This quality of rugged individualism used to hold tremendous appeal for many Americans, but, at a certain point, that changed.

But who knows why the genre started being popular... and eventually stopped being popular? We need to put Joe Mannix on the case.

(On a side note, I've always been fascinated by the differences between what a private eye does in real life compared to his fictional counterparts. From the very first appearance of Poe's C. Auguste Dupin in the mid-nineteenth century, fictional private eyes have been responsible for the unraveling of literally *hundreds of thousands* of homicides, but have any real life private detectives ever solved even *one*? I'm curious.)

Q: In your view, what were the best of the crop and what was it about them that still deserves critical respect?

A: Thanks to the digital miracle known as DVD, lately I've been catching up on *Mannix*. Great stuff. As played by the criminally underrated Mike Connors, Joe Mannix was tough but vulnerable (he seems to get bludgeoned unconscious almost every single week; in fact he really shouldn't leave the office without a crash helmet!)... whipsmart but never infallible (often being duped for a good portion of each episode before unraveling the mystery du jour)... self-effacing, fast with a quip, and always ready to put himself on the line for a friend... or a stranger. Mannix was the quintessential urban knight.

Producer Bruce Geller gave these shows a rich, cinematic quality missing from most of the TV of the time, and, thanks to executive producers Ivan Goff and Ben Roberts, the storytelling, particularly from Season Two onward, was superb. Are there a few clunkers in the bunch? Naturally. But in the main, these are smart, violent, beautifully crafted mysteries. Any lover of classic hardboiled storytelling needs to make *Mannix* part of his Netflix queue.

Q: At what point do you think TV became a less hospitable home for the private eye story?

A: Hmm. I guess the genre started petering out around the time *The Rockford Files* (in the 1970s) left the airwaves, and disappeared completely after *Spenser: For Hire* (in the 1980s).

Q: The crime genre has come to be dominated by procedurals like the various members of the CSI and Law & Order franchises, Criminal Minds, and others. These seem more plot-driven than the old private eye stories, which, in my view, hung a lot of their appeal on the central character. Does it seem that way to you? These procedurals almost seem interchangeable; what's the attraction in them vs. the charm of a character-driven series like, say, The Rockford Files?

A: Tastes change. The archetypal "wise-cracking reporter" was the hero of countless A-pictures, B-movies, and radio shows in the 1930s, '40s, and '50s before eventually going the way of the Underwood. In the 1950s, it was the cowboy who dominated prime-time before riding off into the sunset. P.I.s, as you indicated, were big in the 1960s, (it was) maverick cops in the '70s and '80s, but at a certain point in the last twenty years or so, the public seemed to lose its appetite for Lone Wolf heroes in favor of—wait for it—*The Group*.

The Group; captured in ads and posters by a half dozen thin, beautiful, under-40 bureaucrats standing in bowling pin formation with arms folded, looking defiantly at the lens.

The Group; exemplified by a seemingly interchangeable array of forensic teams on *NCIS*, *CSI*, *Criminal Minds*, *Bones*, and *Without a Trace*, and by the cops of *Law & Order*, *Southland*, and *The Wire*.

The Group.

One theory holds that the Lone Wolf hero held particular appeal for male viewers who have since turned their backs on TV in favor of their X-Boxes and laptop screens. So it is now women who make up the majority of the prime time audience, and women, the theory holds, respond strongly to shows about families, both biological and surrogate. Hence the popularity of The Group.

Like I said, it's just a theory. Who the hell knows if it's true? (But it certainly *feels* true.)

Q: There are some cop shows that seem to sneak elements of the private eye tale into their formats. The title character of <u>Castle</u> isn't a cop, for example, although he works with them, and the lead character of <u>The Mentalist</u> is also a "consultant" rather than a member of the force. The same could even be said of your own <u>Monk</u>. Is that some vestige of the private eye genre? Some desire to go outside the straight police procedural?

A: To a degree, but the divergence is largely superficial, because like you say, while *The Mentalist* and *Castle* aren't working for the cops in any "official" capacity, they may as well be. They work *with* the authorities. At the *request* of the authorities. With the *support* and *approval* of the authorities. They are de facto cops, if you will, and definitely part of The Group.

Monk, I grant you, did represent an exception. *Monk* was a conscious throw-back to an era when the colorful "lone wolf detective" was a fixture in prime time.

Q: Do you miss private eye shows? And what do you think the chances are of the genre ever coming back on TV?

A: Of course I miss them! One problem with network (as opposed to pay-TV) crime drama is calcification. When any of the Big Four stumbles upon a formula that seems to work for them, they tend to replicate it *ad nauseum*. Then do it for seven more seasons.

But any genre is only ever one blockbuster away from revival (the sitcom was dead until *The Cosby Show* revived it). So, yes, I think the networks will develop more private eye shows, and maybe even put some on the air. And then it's up to the audience.

All it takes is the report of one loud gunshot to start a landslide. And I hope it comes from a .38.

*****

Sonny Grosso is a garrulous bear of a guy, someone who, by his own admission, loves to talk, and especially loves to talk about cops and movies and, naturally enough, cop movies. Asking him about the evolution of the private eye in movies and on TV pulls a cork that lets spill a flood of stories about Grosso's adventures in the movie and

TV biz, and in his years as a cop. And, they are stories worth hearing (if not always on point).

His name is usually familiar to police buffs and cop movie aficionados. In the early 1960s, as a narcotics detective with the New York City Police Department, Grosso and his partner, Eddie Egan, cracked the famous "French Connection" case; the largest heroin bust in U.S. history up to that time. Writer Robin Moore later turned the case into a book, which producer Philip D'Antoni, director William Friedkin, and screenwriter Ernest Tidyman turned into the Oscar-winning *The French Connection* (1971), starring Gene Hackman as "Popeye" Doyle (a slightly fictionalized version of Egan, which copped Hackman an Oscar), and Roy Scheider (in an equally dramatized rendering of Grosso, which earned him an Oscar nomination). Besides winning a total of five Academy Awards, *The French Connection* went on to become one of the biggest commercial successes of the 1970s as well as one of the acknowledged all-time great cop movies.

Grosso, along with Egan, was a consultant on the film, and that gig led to similar consulting stints on a host of cop and crime movies and TV shows, including *The Godfather* (1972; that's Grosso's pistol Al Pacino uses on Sterling Hayden and Al Lettieri in the memorable restaurant assassination scene), and series like *Kojak*, *The Rockford Files*, and *Wise Guy*. It then seemed natural that when Grosso retired from the force, he moved into film and TV production, kicking off a thirty-year second career. While his producing credits range from *Pee Wee's Playhouse* to Mary Higgins Clark adaptations, his acknowledged strong suit has always been cop stories. To name just a few: *A Question of Honor* (1982), *Trackdown: Finding the Goodbar Killer* (1983), *Kings of South Beach* (2007), penning the story for Phil D'Antoni's big screen feature, *The Seven-Ups* (1973).

I spoke with Grosso by phone, asking him if, during his cop days, he'd dealt with private investigators; what were they *really* like?

"I'm thinking about it and I'd say they came in two categories:

"One: ex-cops.

"Two: wannabes. These were guys who wanted to be cops, but something kept them out. Ya know, in those days, it didn't take much for you to not make it. You had a problem with a knee, you were color blind, you didn't get in. Maybe you think, it's small—So what?—but there was a reason. 'What color were his eyes?' 'I dunno, I can't see color.'"

There was a certain air of ruefulness to the cop-turned-private investigator. Often, they made the change because they thought it would pay better, but they almost always regretted it. "When they were gonna leave I'd try to talk 'em out of it, and they'd go, no, no, I don't wanna work for half-pay anymore, then later, they come back to you and say, 'Remember when you told me not to leave? You were right.'"

It was psychological, says Grosso. "Even if you worked a desk, somebody says to you, 'What do you do?' and you say, 'I'm with the police force,' there's *something* to that you don't get when you say, 'I work in a grocery store.'"

One of the things about P.I.s Grosso says movies and TV never really caught was how symbiotic the relationship is between them and the police. "We used each other," he says. "Every single P.I. I knew had a cop," meaning a contact on the force. "But, it was like a marriage. If it's gonna work, it's gotta work for both sides."

The cops provided P.I.s with information they could never get on their own: running down license plates, access to wire taps, which subjects were still on parole, and so on. "I even gave one guy the information he needed to catch a guy and get a reward!" The P.I.s, on the other hand, could go places and do things the cops—restrained by protocols, regulations, and the law—couldn't, and provide cops with information they might not have been able to get otherwise.

"In a way, we treated each other like informants. We used them for information, and, I guess you'd say they used us the same way. It was like we were each other's stoolies."

P.I.s didn't suffer for stepping over legal lines the way cops did. "We both had to worry about breaking the law, you had to be careful. But if a private eye does something wrong, there's a chance he's gonna go free. Me, I'm gonna lose my job. You see it all the time; a cop might even get exonerated in court, but then he gets tried by The Department and he's out of a job."

Grosso says nothing prepared someone for work as a private investigator better than time on the force. "You learn a lot as a cop: how to get information, how to groom a 'stool.' That's why P.I.s I knew who hadn't been cops often teamed up with an ex-cop. There's just no way to learn that stuff on your own."

Grosso thinks the great popularity for private eye stories in the movies and on TV in the 1950s, '60s, and '70s had a lot to do with the way cops were typically portrayed. "There was a time when it seemed most movie cops were dumbos, stumbling, bumbling assholes. A lot of cops on private detective shows were morons. In their (P.I. series) heyday, no cop could do what (private eyes) did. Not only could he do things cops weren't allowed to do, but he was smarter, too."

Grosso believes that changed with the release of *The French Connection*.

One of the accolades Grosso most treasures came in a recent July piece written by *The Los Angeles Times'* Steven Zeitchik saluting the passing of producer and one-time 20th Century Fox chief Richard Zanuck, the man who brought *The French Connection* into Fox. The story was headlined, "Six Movies That Changed the World," and one of them was *French Connection*.

One might argue about whether or not any of those films actually changed the world, but they certainly had a massive impact on the movies. Grosso thinks *Connection*'s portrait of cops had a lot to do with the fading popularity of TV and movie private eyes thereafter. Hackman and Scheider played two smart, shrewd, forceful cops willing to bend the rules (or tiptoe around them) in ways that had previously been reserved for movie P.I.s. "(*The French Connection*) showed real cops as dazzling." It was an idea reinforced by the movie's true story nature, and the great effort D'Antoni and Friedkin & Co. put into the gritty, realistic feel of the movie. "That movie showed that if you show it the way it happened, (cops) didn't need private investigators."

"This is a copycat business," Grosso says, and the success of *Connection* spawned a flood of movies and TV shows about equally tough and smart cops, from *Baretta* and *Kojak* on the small screen, to Grosso's own *The Seven-Ups*. Cops didn't need private eyes anymore; not in movies and TV shows, and not in the eyes of a now wised-up audience.

One measure of the effect of *Connection*: "I've met guys who told me they became cops because they saw *The French Connection*. I never heard anybody say they became a private eye because of a detective show."

Asked if the genre can come back, Grosso is admirably optimistic, responding with an unhesitating, "Sure!" The catch is getting the right actor and the right creative talent, and remembering that the best P.I. stories were always about creating a character an audience cared about and wanted to spend time with.

His thoughts pinball off to *The Godfather* as an example of the dynamic he's talking about. "The shooting and all that bullshit was window dressing. What you cared about was that family, what Michael (Corleone) did for that family, and what the family did to him, his brother betraying him (in *The Godfather: Part II* [1974]). That's the stuff you cared about.

"Don't get me wrong. You *need* the window dressing! It's great you got the goods in the store, but nobody comes in because you got Bon Ami on the window. You gotta have the shooting and the good-looking guy and tits, but, in the end, does (the audience) want to spend time with this guy? You could do a show about a dog catcher and make it work if you get the right guy.

"It's like the Western," he continues. *"Butch Cassidy and the Sundance Kid* (1969) brought back the Western. The only reason you don't have them now is, who's gonna be John Wayne?"

Grosso's conversation caroms, again, back to a time when he was in Los Angeles in the 1970s and he and his mother had occasion to meet Mike Connors, then star of the long-running CBS hit private eye series, *Mannix*. "My mother *loved* Mike Connors. You figure out why my mother loved Mike Connors, and you can figure out how to bring the private eye back to TV."

*****

Stephen Whitty has been the film critic for *The Star-Ledger*—New Jersey's state paper and one of the largest papers in the New York/New Jersey metropolitan area—for fourteen years. And that follows a 10-year stint at the *San Jose Mercury News*. Having to sit through as many as 300 movies a year over nearly a quarter of a century is bound to give you a sense of the tidal flows of genres and trends over the long haul.

Whitty is more than a discriminating reviewer and a hell of a writer. A graduate of NYU's film program, he still has the young film geek's passion for film history, for the evolution of form and content and of the movie industry itself. My favorite pieces of his are his in-depth Sunday features where he parses a body of work: a genre, a filmmaker's canon, the roles of a particular actor. Those pieces are Whitty at his insightful, analytical best, and qualification enough to invite him to this discussion.

And, if that's not enough, more on point is Whitty's win at the La Jolla Library Raymond Chandler Competition (although one wins by writing *bad* Chandler, so maybe we'll just forget about that one)...

Q: You don't hear much about the private eye movie before the advent of sound, but the genre appears to have detonated in the 1930s. By the end of the decade, most studios had at least one private eye franchise: The Saint, The Falcon, Boston Blackie, etc. Is that an accurate picture? How would you characterize that first generation of cinema private eye movies?

A: I think it's true that the private eye series took off in the '30s, and I think there were a few reasons. First, the pulp magazines, particularly *Black Mask,* that had started out in the '20s had hit a real peak by then. Second, the advent of sound made storytelling easier, particularly for the complicated plots of private eye stories. And third, honestly, so many of the new screenwriters were ex-newspapermen; I think they identified with the character of the private eye; snooping around, not getting paid very much. It struck a chord.

Q: It seems the genre hit some kind of threshold with <u>The Maltese Falcon</u>. It begins to take on a dramatic heft the franchise P.I. series didn't have. Is that how you read the situation?

A: The heft was there, of course, with Hammett's original novel, which added the idea of the private eye as a courageous man with a private moral code that he adhered to; something Hammett came up with independently of Hemingway, but is very similar to his ideas of personal responsibility and "grace under pressure." But it took two versions before John Huston (not coincidentally a very similar character to Hammett and Hemingway) caught the flavor of it with his adaptation of the novel, its third.

Q: The '40s and especially the '50s see a deepening <u>noir</u> sensibility. How did that impact the private eye genre?

A: I think it changed it fundamentally. The classic idea of the private eye is the hero who comes into a briefly disordered society and restores order. But in *noir,* the hero enters an ordered society and uncovers disorder. Even though the Production Code still insisted that evil be punished at the end of every movie, the stories of the private eyes we start to see in the '40s—Philip Marlowe in *Murder, My Sweet* and *The Big Sleep* (1946), and then Mike Hammer in *Kiss Me Deadly* in the '50s—don't end as neatly as they had before. The chief villain may be killed in the end, but he's rarely captured and turned over to the cops in handcuffs, ready for trial. And there's a sense that the crimes he committed go very deep into the society (and very high into the power structure).

Q: I've read where the P.I. genre seemed to be on the wane by the early 1960s, but then Harper comes along and jump starts the form. Is that your take?

A: I think *Harper* was successful for the same reasons that Ross Macdonald, who wrote the novel it was based on, was; he took the feeling, the style of Raymond Chandler, and then updated it to the way L.A. was now. We see that continuing in the (bad) *Marlowe* (1969) update with James Garner, and to a certain extent with *The Long Goodbye* (1973). But I don't think the genre itself really came back to full strength; instead, it seemed to be replaced by cop movies.

Of course, we're talking solely about theatrical motion pictures throughout, here. On TV, private-eye stories seemed to remain firmly popular for decades, from the '50s right into *Magnum, P.I.* (in the '80s).

Q: The private eye movie of the 1960s/1970s seems a wholly different animal from what came before. If you look at movies like The Long Goodbye, Night Moves (1975), The Conversation (1974), and especially Chinatown as symptomatic of the genre's changes, how would you characterize that generation of private eye movie?

A: There's certainly a sexual frankness that wasn't there before; if you look back at Chandler's original novels, the man was a bit of a prude. There's also a willingness, in this Nixon era, to see that corruption stretches to the highest levels of power, that you don't have to be paranoid to see conspiracies around you, and that even our best efforts aren't going to bring people to justice.

Think of the end of *The Conversation*, and especially *Chinatown*; if anything, the people are even worse off because of the hero's involvement. That's something really new for the genre; the private eye, not as white knight, but as impotent bystander.

Q: It almost seems that with Chinatown, the private eye story had reached some sort of creative zenith and it had no place left to go. The genre appears to evaporate after that. What happened?

A: I really think the cop movie took over. Partly that's because of timeliness, I think; private eyes seem more and more like something out of the past, while police officers are characters we see every day in our real lives. But you can't deny the modern movie audience's attention deficit disorder, their very real need for fast cuts and simple stories (or the fact that most Hollywood movies now make most of their money overseas, where English is probably not the audience's first language). Private eye stories have complicated plots that take a while to unfold; they tend to have a good deal of dialogue. These are not things the mass audience has much patience for anymore.

Q: Have the audience and the nature of the business changed too much to ever support a comeback for the genre? Do you see a future for it?

A: I think it will always be with us, but I think it is going to take different forms for a while. I think particularly of the Coen Brothers. In interviews over the years, they told me that they saw *Blood Simple* (1984) as their Hammett film, *The Man Who Wasn't There* (2001) as their James M. Cain film, and *The Big Lebowski* (1998) as their Chandler film. I don't know that many private eye fans from the '40s would see that, but it's true and all of those films work wonderfully on those terms.

There have also been indie films like *Brick* (2005), which moved the private eye genre into the world of high-school, or occasional attempts (like the *Shaft* [2000] remake, or the recent *One For The Money* [2012] flop) to move beyond white male heroes to African-Americans or women.

The classic private eye movie—the guy in the shabby office, with his name painted on the door and a willingness to do anything for "25 dollars a day, plus expenses," isn't something I think we're going to see again outside of period pieces (as *Chinatown* was). But the character of the private detective himself will survive, and I hope in a way that Chandler would recognize; as a man who though he goes down these mean streets "is not himself mean, who is neither tarnished nor afraid... (who is,) to use a rather weathered phrase, a man of honor."

Raising Cain: The Work of James M. Cain
(posted 9/18/12)

Hammett, Chandler, Cain: the modern mystery thriller starts with them. They are the godfathers of that sensibility that would come to be called *noir*, which would, in time, overflow the printed page and onto the stage, the big screen, and eventually even to television. Identified primarily with mysteries, the concept of flawed human beings ethically tripping and stumbling in a moral No Man's Land, equidistant between Right and Wrong, Good and Bad would bleed across genre lines. There would be *noir* Westerns (*Blood on the Moon*, 1948), *noir* war movies (*Attack!*, 1956), *noir* horror (*The Body Snatcher*, 1945), even *noir* melodramas like Cain's own *Mildred Pierce*, adapted for the screen in 1945.

But they all started with what Hammett, Chandler, and Cain did on the page, and each provided an evolutionary step which took what had once been usually dismissed as a flyweight genre dedicated to colorful private investigators and clever puzzles, and turned it into literature's dark star: stories that were less about cleverness than they were about recognizable, identifiable, relatable corruption.

Hammett came first, writing five novels between 1929 and 1934, but it was his third, *The Maltese Falcon*, which arguably had the greatest impact on the thriller genre. *Falcon*'s hero, private eye Sam Spade, redefined the P.I. hero. This was no intellectual superman, like Doyle's Sherlock Holmes, no bit of Agatha Christie whimsy. Spade was working class, a plodding pay-by-the-day dick, a knight errant loyal to a battered code of honor who realized there wasn't always a happy ending, and that justice came with a price... even to the just.

But there was still a touch of the exotic to Spade, and, in fact, much of Hammett's mystery fiction e.g. *The Glass Key*, and *The Thin Man*. Hard-boiled and working class as Spade was, he was still in a world of not exactly run-of-the-mill hoods chasing after a jewel-encrusted statue.

Raymond Chandler introduced us to P.I. Philip Marlowe in the 1939 novel, *The Big Sleep*, and took him through seven more novels including the unfinished *Poodle Springs* in 1959 (Robert B. Parker would complete the novel in 1989). Marlowe was a more evolved Sam Spade: more contemplative, more philosophical, and, for that reason, a bit more world-weary and his battered code of honor even more battered.

But James M. Cain did them both one better.

He published his first thriller—the classic *The Postman Always Rings Twice*—in 1934 and followed it with a hot streak that didn't peter out until 1951; a run that included his two other great works, *Double Indemnity* and *Mildred Pierce*.

There were no jeweled dinguses at stake in Cain's novels, no family curses, and his heroes were not hard-drinking, chain-smoking, P.I.s or dogged cops. Instead, Cain's protagonists were startlingly unremarkable: an insurance salesman and a stifled housewife in *Indemnity*, a drifter and the wife/waitress of a diner owner in *Postman*. They weren't looking for The Big Score, they weren't even particularly criminals. They were people who stood at the edge of the moral abyss and, in a moment of weakness, gave in to that dark impulse to jump in, and almost instantly regretted it.

Our pop culture friends over at Titan Books have uncovered James M. Cain's last, unpublished novel, *The Cocktail Waitress*, released this month. Joan Medford is a typical Cain protagonist: a widow at 21; the accidental death of her alcoholic, abusive husband not quite accidental enough for one overeager cop; left broke; her young son in the custody of her less-than-sympathetic sister-in-law. Without even enough money to keep her house lights on, the unskilled Medford turns to pushing booze as a (if you haven't guessed it) cocktail waitress.

And also, like any Cain protagonist, Joan Medford missteps. Judgment gets clouded by romance, by sex, by her desperation to do right by her son and win him back from her sister-in-law.

For fans of hard-boiled fiction, and particularly for James M. Cain aficionados, it's all here: the tough talk, earthy dames, shady fast-talkers, and a balancing act down the thin moral line with cold-hearted pragmatism on one side, outright greed and deception on the other, and temptation plucking at the wire.

But it should be said that for the non-die-hard fan, *The Cocktail Waitress* can be a disappointment. Though Cain was writing the novel in the mid-1970s and setting the story in 1960, the book feels woefully disconnected from its time. Women still talk about having a pregnancy "taken care of" but won't use the word abortion; people still get their news primarily from the radio. Even Cain's prose feels dusty and archaic. Strip out the few contemporary references, and *Waitress* could easily seem a work from the '40s.

Titan's boss fiction editor, Charles Ardai, generously shared some thoughts with us on James M. Cain, *The Cocktail Waitress*, and how Cain's influence continues to filter through popular entertainment...

Q: Dashiell Hammett, Raymond Chandler, James M. Cain; these are considered the holy trinity of mystery writing, in particular that genre dubbed "hard-boiled fiction." What is it about The Big Three that makes them The Big Three, and what was distinctive about Cain's work?

A: Cain, Chandler and Hammett were the first crime writers to elevate hardboiled or *noir* fiction above the level of simple genre entertainment and make something truly wonderful out of it, something that commented on human struggle and desperation and despair every bit as eloquently as the finest literary novel, while never losing touch with the genre's two-fisted, crowd-pleasing roots.

Chandler and Hammett did it for the detective story, with their invention of Philip Marlowe and Sam Spade, respectively. Cain did it for the non-detective story, the story of people trapped in painful circumstances and committing crimes to get out of them, only to find themselves driven deeper than ever into suffering. All three men wrote novels that remain breathtaking reads more than half a century after being penned. Cain in particular harnessed the dark sexual energy of love affairs gone sour to produce some of the most chilling and visceral portraits ever committed to paper. So discovering a lost book by Cain—a new book, effectively—is truly an important find.

Q: Cain is considered one of the founders of the <u>roman noir</u>, and that sensibility later spilled over into film: <u>film noir</u>. How did what Cain bring to the genre impact on other forms like film and, later, TV? Do you still see traces of it?

A: Cain's impact is still felt in any drama that tackles adultery and the dark ends it sometimes drives lovers to. Any time you see a movie or TV show in which a sweaty couple post-coitally discusses offing the lady's husband, taking the dead man's money, and running away together, that's Cain's voice you're hearing.

And more than that: Cain's there in the atmosphere of so many films where California itself is a character and *femmes fatale* languorously drape themselves over settees, cigarette smoke trailing up toward a lazily turning ceiling fan. Cain's there in the scene in the run-down diner by the side of the highway, where a waitress in a too-tight uniform trades wisecracks with truckers about burning the place down and running away with them, and she's not serious, except maybe she is.

Cain's gift to dialogue writers was the bank shot, the way two people can seem to be talking about something innocuous but really are talking about something else altogether, something that could get them arrested if they talked about it head-on. Cain's influence is very much still there, even when today's writers and directors don't realize who it is they're imitating.

Q: Chandler and his private eye Philip Marlowe may have produced movies' most memorable <u>noir</u> icon—the world-weary gumshoe poking into the dark underside of his clients—but it seems to me that Cain was closer to what <u>noir</u> was really about: impressively average people who make one misstep, then dig themselves deeper into a hole in their effort to get out of it. <u>The Cocktail Waitress</u> seems very much in that vein. Is that what Cain was all about as a writer?

A: Cain was definitely more interested in the people who commit crimes and the consequences it has on their lives than he was in the men who track them down. Even in *Double Indemnity*, where the relentless insurance investigator has a principal role, the focus is on the poor sap who gets lured into committing murder by the woman he hungers for. The police and other investigators are obstacles to be overcome, dangers to be feared, embodiments of retribution; they loom in the shadows and finally come and get you (and, often, kill you). But the "you" here is always an ordinary man or woman facing an extraordinary situation, and doing so without the benefit of a gun or a badge. It's not the only *noir* story worth telling, but it's a hell of a good one, and Cain excelled at telling it.

The only other author who came close was the brilliant Cornell Woolrich (author of *Rear Window* and so many other *noir* classics). Between Cain and Woolrich, you have a catalogue of the way ordinary people's lives can be ruined, with an emphasis on The Man Who Should Have Known Better.

Q: Considering the success—and classic status—of Cain adaptations like <u>The Postman Always Rings Twice</u> (1946) and <u>Double Indemnity</u> (1944), it's surprising to me that more of his novels weren't turned into films. I think <u>Mildred Pierce</u> (1945) was the only

other one of his twenty novels to be turned into a film. Any thoughts on why that might be?

A: Well, the three books you named are his three best—it's not surprising that they've also made the most memorable films. But *The Butterfly* (1982) became a movie starring Stacy Keach and Pia Zadora, the posthumous novel *The Enchanted Isle* was filmed as *Girl in the Cadillac* (1995), the 1956 film *Slightly Scarlet* was inspired by *Love's Lovely Counterfeit*, and also in 1956 *Serenade* was filmed, with Mario Lanza as the opera-singer protagonist and Vincent Price in a supporting role. So there have been other Cain films; they just didn't become famous the way the big three did.

There were also some TV and radio adaptations, and foreign films. And, of course, plenty of *noir*-ish movies that are heavily indebted to Cain, even if they don't credit him as the official source of the material.

Q: For a guy writing hard-boiled fiction, Cain seemed, for his time, extraordinarily sympathetic towards women. Mildred Pierce, and Joan Medford in The Cocktail Waitress ***are women just trying to take care of their families, but forced to extremes by circumstance. Even the*** femmes fatale ***of*** Double Indemnity ***and*** The Postman Always Rings Twice ***have a sympathetic quality to them: women who made a bad decision and now feel trapped into going as far as murder to get out of it. You can't even call Cora in*** Postman ***particularly greedy; the prize for all the conniving and murder is a roadside café. How do Cain's women characters stack up against the*** noir ***standard?***

A: It's true that Cain's women are sympathetic in a way the *femme fatale* types in crime fiction so often are not. That's partly just the touch of a better writer, the sort who can put Shylock in a play but not without giving him the "Hath not a Jew eyes?" speech. Cain's women aren't two-dimensional because he wrote about three-dimensional characters, and that's a big part of the reason (his) books hold up so well after all this time.

But it's true that he seems to have a genuine touch of sympathy in his soul for the hardships of being a woman in the 1930s, '40s, '50s, when marriage could be the only path available, and yet could prove to be more a trap than an opportunity. His women were what they were because their circumstances left them with few or no other options, not because they were the female equivalent of mustache-twirling villains. These aren't comic-book Cruellas toying with men for the sheer pleasure of villainy, or for perverse sexual satisfaction. They're desperate people trapped in dire situations, grasping at a last chance for something better. Unfortunately, the "something better" comes at a terrible price, and turns out to be much, much worse.

Q: Cain often dealt with extremely provocative themes, which had to be tamped down in the film adaptations. In your estimation, how do the film versions of his novels stack up against their source material? Is Bob Rafelson's 1981 adaptation of The Postman Only Rings Twice any closer to the original?

A: Every film adaptation alters the source material; it's inevitable because the media are different, and also because any creative artist wants to put his own stamp on a work rather than just slavishly reproduce another artist's work. So, filmmakers change the books they adapt, sometimes for the better, sometimes not. But that's a matter of artistic choice. The phenomenon you're talking about, of certain themes and incidents being too explicit for the movies back in the day, is a real one, and yes, the 1981 adaptation of *Postman* could go further than the Lana Turner version from 1946 in capturing the book's raw eroticism. Still, is it "closer" to the book?

The erotic element is only one element, and by moving closer along that spectrum it may move farther away along another, such as the economic or philosophical. Cora doesn't take up with Frank in *Postman* just because she's horny and wants to get laid. She *is* horny; she *does* want to get laid. But her desires run deeper, and what drives her to murder is more than an itch in the pants.

Q: In your Afterword to The Cocktail Waitress, you note that Cain's career "... which had risen so meteorically in the 30s and 40s had fallen just as meteorically." What was it about his work that had clicked so well with the reading public early on, and then had stopped working by the early '50s?

A: I think these things just come in cycles. How many authors who were meteorically popular in the 1980s are still a hot number today? If Bret Easton Ellis penned a book in the '80s or '90s, it made headlines; he's still around today, still writing, but the headlines have passed him by.

Cain similarly made a splash in his day, and the ripples kept spreading for a good ten or twenty years, which is nothing to sneeze at. But by the late '50s and '60s, Cain's splash had been a generation back, and the new generation had writers of their own to get excited over.

Then, too, Cain really only published one book in the 1950s, *Galatea*, and it was a weak one, a real misfire. His next book after that didn't come out for nine more years. A decade is a long time to go between books and still keep your name out there, especially in the days before the Internet and social media, when word-of-mouth traveled so much slower and less efficiently.

After publishing a dozen mostly excellent books in the '30s and '40s (and one in 1951, but let's count that as the '40s for our purposes), Cain began a dry spell that lasted the rest of his life: just one book in the '50s, just two in '60s, just two in the '70s, and none of them at the level of his earlier work. It's no surprise than the public's excitement about him waned.

Q: According to your notes in The Cocktail Waitress, Cain wrote that novel in the mid-1970s. The novel seems strangely disconnected from its time. Do you think one of Cain's problems, in the latter part of his career, was that he'd fallen out of step with the times?

A: All old men are out of step with their times. They grew up in an earlier era and still view the present through the lens they ground in the past. Cain may have been writing *The Cocktail Waitress* in the 1970s, but it's so very clearly not a book about a world that contains discos and Olivia Newton-John and Atari and *Star Wars*. Various events in the book date it back to the late '50s/early '60s—basically the *Mad Men* era—but in terms of atmosphere and flavor, it sometimes feels like it takes place in the high *noir* era—the James M. Cain era, if you will—of the 1930s or '40s. Sure, there are passing references to hot pants and joints where the waitresses serve drinks topless... but the world of the book is the world Cain knew, the world of his prime.

During a trip to London in the book, the characters are talking about the wreckage in London left over from the Blitz. This is not a 1970s book. But does that make him out of step with his time? Or does it just make him a period novelist? The book is stronger for not being peppered with 1970s-iana. Reading it today, it's not dated, it's timeless. If it had been more 'in step' with its time when he wrote it, it may well be unreadable today.

Q: It's sometimes said Ross Macdonald took his cue from Chandler. In film and TV, as well as on the page, do you see anyone picking up Cain's torch?

Mcdonald definitely did pick up Chandler's torch, and then Lawrence Block picked up Macdonald's; the Matthew Scudder detective novels are the best and most important since Marlowe and Lew Archer. Who's done that for Cain's situations and themes?

Well, in the '50s and '60s, it was writers like David Goodis and Jim Thompson and Charles Williams and Gil Brewer, though no one of them burned as brightly. And today?

The best *noiriste* working the Cain beat today is probably a woman named Megan Abbott, who has won the Edgar Allan Poe Award, deservedly, and has earned raves for each of her six books. She started out writing period *noir* fiction clearly influenced by Cain, and since has moved on to modern-day novels where the Cain influence is subtler. But it's there, and no other writer working in the genre today quite captures the feverish intensity and the lineaments of desire quite the way Megan does. Her prose makes me breathe faster, the way Cain's does.

That's on the page. On screen? Obviously, what Matthew Weiner has done on *Mad Men* is extraordinary. At the movies, you see *noir* less often than you used to; I guess spandex-clad superheroes and animated, quipping animals rake in the bucks better than homicidal lovers. But every so often you get a good one. I still tell my friends to track down John Dahl's *The Last Seduction* (1994), starring Linda Fiorentino. I think Cain would have been proud to call that one his own.

Max Allan Collins ('Road to Perdition') on carrying on Mickey Spillane's legacy
(posted 5/17/12)

A week before he died in 2006, author Mickey Spillane turned to his wife and said, "When I'm gone, there's going to be a treasure hunt around here. Take everything you find and give it to Max. He'll know what to do."

"Max" is Max Allan Collins. He was, for a number of reasons, an ideal choice to be the keeper of the Spillane flame.

A fan of Spillane's since he'd been a kid, Collins had met the mystery writer at a convention in the early 1980s. The connection developed into both friendship and regular collaboration. But Collins was no junior partner in the duo.

Born in Muscatine, Iowa in 1948, he's been writing mysteries since he was a kid, eventually studying in the Iowa Writers' Workshop at the University of Iowa, one of the most renowned writing programs in the country. By the late 1970s, Collins had published his first novel. Since then, he's published forty-nine more, another seventeen movie- or TV-tie-in novels, and worked in almost every other literary format from comic strips to short stories to graphic novels and even to trading cards. His stature in his field is measured by his unmatched sixteen Private Eye Writers of America Shamus nominations, as well as his regular nods from the Mystery Writers of America Edgar Awards.

Out of that enormous body of work, possibly his most recognized piece is the three-part graphic novel *Road to Perdition* on which he worked with illustrator Richard Piers Rayner, and which served as the basis for the acclaimed 2002 hit film directed by Sam Mendes, adapted by David Self, and starred Tom Hanks.

According to a 2002 interview, Collins's inspiration for *Perdition* was two-fold: "I'd been wanting to do something with the true story of (1930s crime boss) John Looney (the family name was changed to Rooney in the film) and his warped son Connor for a long, long time..." The other reason: "What made it an 'irresistible creative opportunity' was my need for work; I'd just been fired from the *(Dick) Tracy* strip..."

Perdition is moodier, more morally complex, and more melancholic than Spillane's work, yet in it one can still see what made Collins and Spillane such kindred spirits, and Collins such a perfectly matched collaborator. *Perdition*'s Michael Sullivan—a hit man on a relentless crusade for revenge against the man who'd murdered his wife and younger son, and against the father figure who has sheltered the killer who is his own son—is a direct descendant of Spillane's iconic private eye, Mike Hammer, an equally relentless, equally brutal dealer in rough justice (which, in Hammer novels, is often interchangeable with revenge).

Here, Max Allan Collins talks about carrying on Spillane's work, the mystery writer's place in the genre's pantheon of big name talents, and his own *Road to Perdition*.

*****

Q: When you say "Mickey Spillane," what are the characteristics of his work that, to you, are his trademarks? As a brand, what does "Mickey Spillane" mean?

A: Today, Mike Hammer probably personifies the traditional tough private eye. That flows not just from Mickey's books, but from the various Stacy Keach TV shows. In the last century—you know, the twentieth century—Mickey Spillane was the epitome of sex and violence in crime fiction. Mike Hammer novels were "dirty books" in the 1950s and even early '60s.

The actual characteristics of his work are not so simplistic. Hammer is a combat veteran unhappy with the postwar world, a guy who values friendship in the way one G.I. in a foxhole values his buddy. As a hero, he was the first really dark protagonist, a tough, remorseless man who uses the bad guy's methods against the bad guys; the first hero to execute a villain, not turn that villain over to the authorities. Hammer is also the first private eye to sleep around with the lovely, willing women he meets. James Bond is only one of the other characters who would not have happened if Spillane hadn't shown the way.

What gets lost (in talking about his work) is Spillane's storytelling, which can be hypnotic—he is particularly good at arresting openings and shocking, surprising conclusions—and his *noir* poetry (is) a kind of a surrealistic fever dream.

Q: How did you and Mickey Spillane hook up?

A: Spillane was my obsession as an adolescent. I had discovered him and Hammett and Chandler about the same time, loved them all, but was dismayed to learn that Mickey did not share the critical praise heaped on the other two; that, in fact, he was blamed for all kinds of social ills from causing juvenile delinquency to lowering the standards of reading tastes. Before my career got off the ground, and after as well, I was his defender in articles and letters of comment. So, when the 1981 Bouchercon in Milwaukee needed a liaison between the con and Mickey, who was one of their guests of honor, I was asked.

Mickey and I hit it off, and did a memorable two-man panel at the con, which was his first appearance at such an event. He had the mistaken idea that he might not be greeted warmly by mystery fans since a lot of his fellow mystery writers had been vicious in their criticism of him. Anyway, we became friends and I was one of his writer pals since Murrell's Inlet, South Carolina (where Spillane lived) wasn't exactly a writers' commune.

I visited his home once a year or so, and we began doing projects together; co-editing anthologies, creating a comic book, doing a number of movie projects, including my documentary about him, "Mike Hammer's Mickey Spillane," which you can find on the Criterion DVD and Blu-ray of *Kiss Me Deadly*.

Q: How did you come to pick up the baton on the Spillane novels?

A: Mickey asked me to complete *The Goliath Bone* if necessary, which was the book he was working on when he became ill. He asked his wife, Jane, to have me complete the various other unfinished works, and she asked me to, and, of course, I said yes to all of that. Mickey was my hero as a kid, and I was a defender of his in my early career—he was, and is, very controversial—and we'd become friends in the early '80s. We did numerous projects together, anthologies, comic books, films.

Q: Is <u>Lady, Go Die!</u> the first Spillane novel you've completed?

A: There were six substantial Hammer unfinished novel manuscripts. I did *The Goliath Bone, The Big Bang,* and *Kiss Her Goodbye* for Otto Penzler's line at Harcourt. This second round of three novels is being done for Titan, who I feel have a real grasp of popular culture and an unusual sense of history for a publisher.

Q: How incomplete was the manuscript? Any idea why Spillane never finished the book/didn't submit it for publication?

A: This was by far the earliest unfinished manuscript, dating to 1945, and with references in the text that made it clear it was the sequel to the first, hugely famous and popular *I, the Jury* (1947). The next earliest of the unfinished novels was *The Big Bang*, which dated to around 1965. So, this was a major find. But it was the shortest of the substantial manuscripts at around 80 pages. I found a single chapter from a later unfinished book with a similar theme, a similar set of crimes, and was able to use that as well, bringing the Spillane content up to match that of the other novels.

As to why he didn't finish it, I have two theories. One is that *I, the Jury* didn't sell well in hardcover—it didn't become a blockbuster till it hit paperback—and so he decided not to pursue a sequel.

The other is that he may have gone too far (in *Lady, Go Die!*) with the relationship between Mike Hammer and his secretary, Velda, and decided to back off. Spillane always wrestled with the love between Hammer and Velda because readers expected Hammer to be a randy guy bedding all sorts of "dames," but also would resent him if he betrayed the love of his life.

Q: You have your own credits. Is it hard to suppress your own creative voice to pick up Spillane's? Did you ever find yourself being moved to take the story a certain way, but then holding yourself back because you realized that was more Max Allan Collins than Mickey Spillane?

A: I immerse myself in Mickey's work, reading and rereading and marking up the several novels adjacent in time to the manuscript I'm completing. Initially, of course, I am working inside Mickey's manuscript, expanding and extending it, weaving my own stuff in, but staying faithful to the character, the tone, the style. By the time I run out of Spillane material, I'm fully absorbed in the voice of that book and it's really no problem.

Stylistically, I do watch myself in a couple of areas; Mickey's sentences tend to be simpler than mine, unless he's writing a stream-of-conscious passage, and he rarely uses semicolons, and I use a lot of those. Also, our sense of humor is different. Mine is sarcastic, his is more of a macho, Howard Hawks kind of dialogue. So I keep an eye on that.

Q: Your original, *Road to Perdition*, has a brooding melancholy quality, which seems 180 degrees away from the more visceral, hard-boiled quality of Spillane. How much of a reach for you was it, at least initially, to go from something like *Perdition* to pick up Spillane's voice?

A: Every story has its appropriate tone and voice. I just try to do what's appropriate for the story at hand. Moving from one thing to another—say, first-person to third-person—or from one form to another—say, graphic novel to novel—really is a positive thing, keeps me fresh and enthusiastic. So I'd say it's not a reach at all.

Q: When you pick up <u>Lady</u> or any of your other collaborations now, can you see where Spillane ends and Max Collins begins? Or is it a seamless melding?

A: That's for others to say, but, again, I don't pick up where Spillane ends. I collaborate with him. I turn his 100 pages into 200 or more pages before I take over, and sometimes even then I've held back material of his to use later in the book.

In *Lady, Go Die!*, Velda gets kidnapped at the end of Spillane's fourth chapter. I held that back till much, much later in the book. In fact, I think that's another reason he may have put the manuscript aside; he realized he had gotten Velda kidnapped too early. Mike can't go on his rampage at the end of Chapter Four, that doesn't come till around Chapter Eleven.

Q: It's been over a half-century since the peak of the popularity of the Mike Hammer novels, yet people are obviously still reading them. What is it about the books that still engages an audience?

A: The books have enormous energy, and Hammer is one of the great first-person voices in mystery fiction. Only Philip Marlowe and Archie Goodwin (narrator of Rex Stout's Nero Wolfe mysteries) equal him, I think. The emotional content is still surprisingly strong, and, despite a passage of time that includes (the work of) everybody from Sam Peckinpah to John Woo, Spillane's violence is still shocking, really powerful.

Q: Do you think it's a fair appraisal that Spillane was a better storyteller than he was—from a literary point of view—a writer? Or do you think he's been short-changed by the critics?

A: Spillane has consistently been short-changed by critics. He was a born storyteller, but sometimes that term is used as a left-handed compliment.

Mickey was a writer who could do things that even Hammett and Chandler couldn't; his fever-dream prose was his own, and the strong emotional content was something very new to the mystery genre. He could construct better openings and opening sentences than anyone in the field, and his endings were astonishing. The first seven books, written when he was a relatively young man, have a rough-hewn quality—he was notorious for going with his first draft, just lightly edited—but incredible passion and energy. His later books lack some of that, but are much more polished, better-crafted. Early Spillane is primitive genius. Later Spillane is polished professional.

Clearly, he belongs in the top tier of crime writers, certainly one of the big three private eye writers: Hammett, Chandler, Spillane. Ross Macdonald often is given Mickey's spot on that list, but Mcdonald, good as he was, was chiefly a Chandler imitator (and Chandler knew it, and didn't like it). You might need to add Robert B. Parker to the list of major private eye writers. I'm not a huge fan, but, like Mickey, he changed the field and opened a door for the rest of us.

That's the frustrating thing to me. I understand that just because Parker is not my cup of tea that doesn't mean he wasn't a major figure. Those who dislike Mickey's work ignore the obvious impact he had on mystery fiction and popular fiction in general, and really all of popular culture. No James Bond without Mike Hammer, or Shaft or Dirty Harry or Jack Bauer or Spencer's pal Hawk for that matter, and dozens of other tough protagonists who take the law into their own hands and buck the system.

Q: There've been a number of TV and film incarnations of Mike Hammer including one starring Spillane himself. The one that probably gets the most attention is <u>Kiss Me Deadly</u> (1955), although it's my understanding it veers off significantly from the novel. Which do you think did the most justice to the character? Which did Mike Hammer the greatest disservice?

A: *Kiss Me Deadly* is a great movie. Director Robert Aldrich does attempt to deal with right-wing Spillane from a critical left-wing perspective, but nonetheless captures the mood and energy of Spillane's work, and is more faithful to the book than its given credit for. Actually, the screenwriter (A. I. Bezzerides) claimed to have thrown the book out, but the film follows the plot closely, the characters and incidents are largely the same. The major difference is that (in the novel) the mysterious box contains drugs, not atomic material, though both have similar fiery endings.

The worst movie was a TV one, *Come Die With Me (Come Die with Me: A Mickey Spillane's Mike Hammer Mystery,* 1994), with Rob Estes as Hammer and Pamela Anderson as Velda, set in Miami Beach. I never got through it till recently when I had to for a book I've done with Jim Traylor for McFarland called *Mickey Spillane On Screen* (out in September).

The worst traditional Hammer film is *My Gun Is Quick* (1957), but it has its guilty pleasures. The various series' with Stacy Keach benefit from his great performance, but they can be on the campy side. Recently, the wonderful 1958-60 Darren McGavin series *(Mike Hammer)*, all 78 episodes, has been released by A&E, and those are great shows capturing much (of the) Spillane/Hammer flavor. No Velda, though. No time for her in a half-hour show.

Q: What did Spillane think of the film/TV adaptations of his work? I'm especially interested in his reaction to Kiss Me Deadly, and also to The Girl Hunters (1963) where he rather brazenly starred as Mike Hammer.

A: Mickey was generally unhappy with the film versions of his work, which is why he chose to play Hammer himself in *The Girl Hunters* from a screenplay he wrote. He did, in later years, come to appreciate the film of *Kiss Me, Deadly*, which initially he disliked. And, he was fairly positive about both TV versions of his work: the Darren McGavin 1950s series, and the Stacy Keach 1980s-90s series. But it would be fair to say he was more complimentary about McGavin and Keach than he was about the shows. In other words, he thought they were both good Hammers, but that neither series completely conveyed the nature of the novels.

He was pleased with *The Girl Hunters*, but disappointed that it wasn't shot in color. It was intended to be, but budgetary concerns at the last minute made that impossible.

Q: I suspect all authors, when they toy with the idea their work might wind up on the screen, have a vision in their heads of what their story should look like. Then there's a natural adjustment, and often dissatisfaction, with the actual result. But with Road to Perdition, since it wasn't a prose work but a graphic novel, you actually had a concrete visual template for your story and your characters. When Zack Snyder adapted 300 (2006) and Watchmen (2009), he stayed so close to his graphic novel sources he actually recreated certain panels on screen. Sam Mendes didn't do that with Perdition (2002). What did you feel the first time you sat down to watch Perdition, saw that the actors had a physicality and voice different from what you'd envisioned, that the film had its own look and rhythm? Do you write it off thinking, "Oh, that's just what the movies do to your stuff," or do the differences make sense to you?

A: With apologies, I have to disagree with your premise. Mendes and particularly cinematographer Conrad Hall were very influenced by Richard Piers Rayner's art and the storytelling of the graphic novel. The most famous shot in the movie is a recreation of one of Richard's panels; the city of Chicago reflected on the car window that the wide-eyed boy is looking through. I felt the voice was very similar and that the film captured the spirit of the graphic novel beautifully. The first half or more is quite faithful to the graphic novel, and departs only when the graphic novel's episodic nature and length were impossible to contain in a two-hour movie.

My only disappointment was Mendes toning down the violence, which I felt was an important aspect of the father's life, and I'm not wild about what I consider to be a Hollywood ending. But, it's a great film, and I'm proud, and lucky, to have it out there representing my work.

Q: You mentioned, as sort of descendants on the Mike Hammer family tree, characters like James Bond, Dirty Harry, Shaft, yet Mike Hammer never quite connected on the screen the way they did. Any thoughts on why that might be?

A: Two reasons, I think. Hammer was a first-person character who Mickey never described physically to encourage reader identification. A hero as strong as Hammer but who was left to the reader's imagination to picture is impossible to capture on screen. Bond was a third-person character, very exterior, while Hammer is an interior experience.

Also, when Hammer was at his most popular, the movies couldn't probably convey the level of sex and violence that the books did. By the *Dr. No* movie (1962; first theatrical feature in the James Bond series), that kind of sex and violence could be depicted. *I, the Jury* was filmed in 1953. Big difference. *(Note: an* I, the Jury *remake was filmed in 1982 with Armand Assante as Mike Hammer).*

Q: Consider the great literary and film/TV private eyes: Sherlock Holmes, Nick Charles, Sam Spade, Philip Marlowe, Lew Archer, The Rockford Files's Jim Rockford, Chinatown's J.J. Gittes— where does Mike Hammer fit on that spectrum? Is there anything he shares with them? What is it that distinguishes him; that makes Mike Hammer Mike Hammer?

A: That's a great list. Hammer is the toughest, the randiest, and probably the most famous. What all the private eyes share is a rugged individualism, a distrust of the system, and a reliance on rough justice; none rougher than Hammer.

Q: *Are there more Mike Hammers coming? If you ever exhausted Spillane's backlog, would you ever consider writing a Mike Hammer novel from scratch as has been done with the James Bond novels?*

A: There are two more coming from Titan from substantial manuscripts: *Complex 90* and *King of the Weeds*. There are three more significant but shorter works—40-page range—that I will complete if readers are interested. I doubt we'd go past that, but if we do, there are plenty of shorter fragments, including complete opening chapters, from non-Hammer Spillane stories that could be converted into Hammer yarns. There's no need for me to create anything from whole cloth.

This isn't about the market to me. It's about getting Mickey's work out there in a finished form. Mickey only wrote 13 complete Hammer novels in his lifetime. Characters like Nero Wolfe, Hercule Poirot, and Perry Mason were in seventy-five or more. In the 1950s and early '60s, when Mickey was the bestselling mystery writer in the world—a position he held for decades—he had only written seven novels. So, finding Mike Hammer material, unpublished, in his files is a major find. And, for me, a major responsibility. Adding six books to the canon—and as these are cowritten by Mickey and largely plotted by him, they are canon—is a big deal. At least it is to me.

Whatever the Size, Your TV Is Still Just a TV
(posted 11/27/11)

I was looking forward to seeing *Juggernaut* on TCM not too long ago when I saw it show up on the classics channel's schedule. Even in this cable/download/Netflix age of constant program recycling, the movie rarely shows up on TV, maybe because it had been such an instant and complete flop when released theatrically in 1974. Still, this UK-produced film has always been one of my pet favorites, a flick I have long felt died an undeserved death, and I was psyched at the chance to see it again.

In synopsis, I admit the movie doesn't sound like much. Or perhaps I should say it sounds way too familiar. A nutcase has put seven bombs on an ocean liner and threatens to sink the ship unless he's given a ransom of £500,000. The ship is far from land, no other vessels are close enough to render assistance, and the North Atlantic is too stormy for the captain (Omar Sharif) to get his 1,200 passengers safely off in lifeboats. A bomb disposal team led by Richard Harris is airdropped to the ship to try to defuse the bombs while the police back in England (led by a young not-yet-a-star Anthony Hopkins) try to run down the mad bomber (veteran Brit character actor Freddie Jones).

(FYI: the film was loosely inspired by a real-life bomb threat against the *Queen Elizabeth 2* in 1972 in which the British government airdropped a team from the Royal Marines' Special Boat Service to the ship 1000 miles out at sea to find and disarm the explosive. Thankfully, the threat turned out to be a hoax.)

Because of their similarities, *Juggernaut* always brings *Speed* (1994) to my mind. *Juggernaut* has passengers trapped on an ocean liner booby-trapped by a disaffected bomb disposal expert; *Speed* has passengers trapped on a bus booby-trapped by a disaffected bomb disposal expert. But the similarities are all superficial.

Made twenty years apart, the two movies say a lot about how commercial cinema changed over that time. *Speed* generates its suspense from the gimmick of a bus threading through packed freeways, unable to drive slower than 55 mph without setting off its bomb. Its thrills are all visceral, at one point incredulous (getting an antiquated GM bus to jump a fifty-foot gap in an unfinished overpass), and ultimately gratuitous (the bus is driven to the L.A. airport so it can have unlimited running room, yet it still manages to plow into a

747 for no other reason than to provide the movie with a—literally—explosive if meaningless finale). Audiences minded not a bit either the movie's incredulous or gratuitous elements, and the $30 million movie did a monster $121.2 million domestic. In fact, these over-the-top constructs are probably why *Speed* works better on TV than *Juggernaut*. Inarguably, *Speed* has a lot of visceral excitement. In fact, it's got nothing *but*.

Juggernaut doesn't. There's hardly a gut-level thrill to be had. No chases, no shoot-outs. Even the airdrop sequence is a bit on the ho-hum side. But what *Speed* doesn't have that *Juggernaut* does is *intensity*. That's a much harder sensation to create; one that I found, in my disappointing revisiting of the movie on TCM, doesn't always lend itself well to TV. The problem is that in this new age of the home theater, home theaters are more "home" than "theater."

We'll come back to that point in a sec.

Juggernaut is the thinking man's *Speed*. Just look at the cast. Although UA tried to sell *Juggernaut* as an ensemble-style disaster flick, it's anything but. Instead of the usual *The Towering Inferno/Earthquake/Airport 197whatever* mixed bag of big name stars and big name has-beens, backing up Harris and Sharif is a deep bench of high-caliber Brit acting talent. Not a lot of glamour in that rank, but "just" a lot of damned fine acting: besides Hopkins and Freddie Jones are Ian Holm, Shirley Knight, David Hemmings, Cyril Cusack, Michael Hordern, Julian Glover, Jack Watson, the great Roy Kinnear, and slipping past immigration, Yank character actor Clifton James.

And there's Alan Plater's screenplay, which eschews the usual disaster flick melodrama to ground both its plot and its characters as firmly in the real world as possible. There's no Charlton Heston-esque steely-eyed hero here. Richard Harris's Fallon is, at first, a cocksure bit of swagger, but after his close #2 is vaporized by one of the bombs, he collapses with a bottle of the captain's booze into a mix of angry frustration and grief, snarling, "Pay the man his money." Freddie Jones's "Juggernaut" is no ranting madman (à *la Speed*'s scenery-chomping Dennis Hopper), but a worn-out, tossed-aside civil servant whose threat is as much revenge against a system that too soon forgets its heroes as it is about money… maybe more so.

One of my favorite bits of dialogue comes after Jones is arrested, and the silky, slimy government minister who has arm-twisted shipping line exec Ian Holm into not paying the ransom tries to put the conscientious Holm in his place saying, "You would have us negotiate with people like that?"

Holm quickly spits back, "You *make* people like that!"

All of this happens under the guiding hand of director Richard Lester.

I still remember how surprised I was when I saw his name show up in the opening credits. I thought, It can't be *that* Richard Lester!

But it was. Lester was a surprising against-the-grain choice, but it would turn out to be an inspired one (he was actually the third director brought on the project).

Thrillers, to my mind, usually require a certain tightly focused, driving thrust that was hardly Lester's forte. The movies he's most known for have a kind of shambling, deliberately, delightfully unfocused quality to them. He was a master of a certain kind of cinematic marginalia, the film equivalent of those witty little doodles you find around the page borders of *Mad Magazine*. Plot was rarely as strong as all the delicious bits Lester hung on it.

Think of his breakout flick, *A Hard Day's Night* (1964), intended to be a quickie capitalizing on the exploding popularity of The Beatles, but which Lester turned into a sophisticated blend of Brit grit and satirized rock glamour. *Hard Day's Night* presaged both Spinal Tap-type rock mockumentaries, and, with its visually free-flowing, non-linear music sequences, MTV music videos. Lester dumped most of Alun Owen's screenplay and the movie ambles along largely carried by the insouciant charm and improvised, tossed-off, seemingly bottomless wit of the Fab Four.

Or take Lester's biggest commercial success, the more lavish *The Three Musketeers* (1973) and it's de facto sequel *The Four Musketeers* (1974; I say "de facto" because the project was originally intended as one, long epic, but father/son producing team Alexander and Ilya Salkind cut the project in two without consulting cast or director, a move that ignited a raft of lawsuits about who owed what to whom). For my money, Lester's *Musketeers* is the best adaptation of the Dumas adventure classic due to its pitch-perfect blend of tongue-in-cheekiness, visual opulence, impressively choreographed swordplay, and rare fidelity to the source novel. But all around Dumas's solidly plotted swashbuckling orbits Lester-orchestrated anarchy: mumbled one-liners looped in under the main dialogue (as Charlton Heston's Cardinal Richelieu passes down a dungeon corridor, one emaciated caged prisoner politely greets him with, "Good morning, your grace"), bits of business tucked here and there about the frame (Michael York's D'Artagnan confronts Simon Ward's Duke of Buckingham in the rain, then, recognizing him, kneels on the cobblestones, Lester stealing a laugh by adding the splash of York's knee into a puddle even though, in long shot, one can see there's no puddle; a dungeon torturer bakes a potato in the same flame used to heat searing pokers).

Perhaps it was because Lester *wasn't* the typical thriller director he was able to find the kind of grit and heart so many thrillers, including *Speed,* don't have. He junked the original screenplay by Richard Alan Simmons and brought in and worked with Alan Plater to turn out a story that feels credible and life-sized. He filmed his exteriors on an ocean liner he sent on a course through the foulest North Atlantic weather he could find to capture a real world feel.

But the centerpiece of the film is Richard Harris's one-on-one duel with one of Juggernaut's bombs. It's the kind of duel you don't see much of in movies; a battle of *minds;* Fallon's skill at defusing bombs against Juggernaut's skill at designing them. Lester and Plater capture the usually ineffable quality of intellects at work, one trying to decode what the other hath wrought, and here director and his screenplay are aided and abetted in fine form by cinematographer Gerry Fisher and editor Antony Gibbs.

Fallon's is a job of fractions of an inch; simply trying to loosen a single screw is an act pregnant with imminent obliteration as any part of the bomb might be booby-trapped. Fisher gets his lens so close the screw head fills the screen; each micro-move of Fallon's screwdriver without setting off a blast seems a mammoth accomplishment. There is no music in these scenes, no sound except for the whirring of the bomb mechanism, the background thrum of the ship's engines, and Fallon's own, hushed voice describing his actions by radio to his higher ups. Lester, Fisher and Gibbs do their jobs so well that when Fallon is forced to use more muscle and the screw comes loose with a sudden clang of metal, it's hard not to jump in your seat.

And then Fallon has to work in the cramped interior of the bomb; a compressed space jammed with glittering counters, whirring paper tapes, light sensors, trembler switches and, as Fallon says, a dozen triggers. Fisher somehow gets his camera inside that claustrophobic electronic jumble. His most virtuosic display: after one of Fallon's men is killed, Fallon finds the booby-trap: a tripwire no thicker than a hair hidden in a gap between two contacts I would guess to be no more than 1/32 of an inch in width.

But there on TCM, all that sweating intensity I had remembered from the big screen... *evaporated.*

On a forty-foot screen, Fisher's brutal close-ups were just that: brutal. They were close-ups with purpose: Fallon's world is one in which the littlest things—hair-triggers, micro-movements—can have devastating consequences. But that massive screw head wasn't so massive on my big screen TV, and as it diminished, so did the whispery, intimate gravity of Fallon's mental chess match against bomb master Juggernaut.

Now, I grant, my big screen TV isn't one of those mural-sized, wall-hanging monsters, but this isn't just about size. Oh, size, in this case, does matter. But so does *place.*

Movie watching in a theater is a submissive experience. It's a form of hypnosis, really. If you don't think the character of the viewing space changes the experience, go to a church service in a small chapel, and then go to one in a cathedral. The cathedral makes you feel small (as it's supposed to), enhancing the authority of the liturgy and the man in the pulpit delivering it. The experience dominates you rather than the other way around.

Movie-going used to be about that; about giving yourself over to the experience. Everything about it—the large, dark auditorium; your attention focused solely on a screen floating in blackness, big enough to fill your field of vision; the electricity of sharing that experience with hundreds of fellow viewers you sensed in the dark more than saw—took you out of your own reality and into the one on the screen.

That doesn't happen at home. It *can't.* It's your *home.* You *know* you're in your home, and that familiarity works against submission. Even if it didn't, I can't remember ever watching a movie at someone's home where it wasn't a stop-and-start affair: bathroom breaks, snack breaks, walk-the-dog breaks... all of that sure as hell breaks the mood, the trance. You can't get soaked up by that big screen TV because it's never going to be big enough to overwhelm you, to make you forget you're slouched on your sofa with your significant other standing in the doorway wondering aloud, "Why are you watching this crap again?"

I would argue it's even getting harder to have that experience in movie theaters.

For a generation growing up attuned to interactive experiences, willing submissiveness, and the patience required to maintain it for two hours or better, isn't their forte as the little blue glows of texting phones nestled in their laps testify. I find it a little unnerving that theaters need to remind the audience to the fact that they are *not* in their living rooms, and that blabbing on the phone or to each other, bawling babies, intrusive ring tones etc. are—surprise, surprise—not acceptable movie-watching behavior.

But then theaters themselves contribute to the trance-breaking, offering at-your-seat food-and-drink service. I'm not sure how well *Juggernaut* would hold up in today's multiplexes if you had to watch it while the guy behind you chomped and burped his way through his dinner while the lady next to you tried to figure out her tab with the serving staff. *Speed,* on the other hand, could easily survive that, as can—and have—all the actioners since then that have cloned its over-the-top, non-stop, check-your-brain-at-the-door, wall-to-wall action template.

And so I was disappointed when I saw the movie on TCM. Oh, the writing, the acting, the directing—everything—was as good as I remembered. But the intensity wasn't there—*couldn't* be there—in my living room on my big-but-not-big-enough screen TV. It occurred to me, ruefully, that a certain kind of movie-making as well as a certain kind of movie-*watching* might have had its day.

As *Juggernaut*'s closing credits rolled, I remembered Norma Desmond's line from *Sunset Boulevard* (1950): "I *am* big. It's the *pictures* that got small."

The Bullying of 'Bully,' and Other Musings on Screen Violence

(posted 5/24/12)

And so, the war over The Weinstein Company's provocative documentary, *Bully*, ends, to use an exhausted cliché, not with a bang, but with a whimper. Since its release at the end of March, the doc has grossed approximately $3 million; not bad for a reality piece, and, measured against the flick's $1.1 million budget, it means TWC will go home with some money in its pocket. But considering the thundering opening bombardments that accompanied the film's debut, it's hard not to look at that sum as a bit of a disappointment. After all, Disney's warm and cuddly and topically irrelevant doc *Chimpanzee*, released almost three weeks later to a lot less fuss, has earned over $27 million.

Undoubtedly, there are going to be those who think *Bully* was hobbled at the box office by its nasty run-in with the MPAA. But I keep looking at *Bully*'s $3 mil, and *Chimpanzee*'s $27 mil, and I have to wonder if it's that simple.

What happened to *Bully* with the MPAA, and what happened to the doc at the box office raises more questions than the *Bully*-highlighted one about how bad a ratings system the MPAA system is (pretty bad).

But, for those of you who've come late to the party and are wondering how all the furniture wound up in a bonfire in the middle of the living room, let's recap...

*****

Bully, directed by Sundance and Emmy-winner Lee Hirsch, and cowritten by Hirsch with Cynthia Love, follows five young people through a school year in a powerful, compassionate portrait of the psychological wounds and physical damage wrought by bullying. Suicide, paralyzing fear, depression... everything you've ever heard about the emotional cost of bullying is here.

The reviews were overwhelmingly positive. According to Rotten Tomatoes, eighty-seven percent of all critics—and a stellar ninety-seven percent of top critics—praised the film. From *The Denver Post*—"... smart and compassionate..."; "... deeply moving," according to *Newsday*; and, from *Entertainment Weekly*, "... an urgent and moral movie..."

Celebs like Anderson Cooper, Kelly Ripa, and "Dr. Phil" McGraw took up the cause of the doc, declaring it a therapeutic must-see.

The film was prescreened for the American Federation of Teachers and the National Education Association in Washington. Afterward, Randi Weingarten, AFT president, declared *Bully*, "... devastating and compelling and it needs to be seen." Local AFT affiliates around the country held screenings of the film for their members, while other affiliates encouraged members to see it.

The Weinstein Company's Harvey Weinstein was especially keen on getting the movie seen by the young audience the film, in effect, is about. For Weinstein, that meant showing the film in schools. At least, that was his plan.

And then the MPAA slapped the movie with an R.

Now, mind you, there's no nudity or sexual content in the film. There's no gore or graphic violence. What the movie does have are teens using the kind of language teens routinely use. Yeah, we're talking about the F-word. The MPAA didn't like how many times it was getting thrown around.

What movies this year *didn't* get an R? Well, *The Hunger Games*, for one. That just had kids killing kids in a gladiatorial hunt for the entertainment of a TV home audience. But none of the killing or dying kids said, "Aw, fuck, that hurts!" so it was ok. *Games* got a PG-13.

But bullied kids, fully clothed and not shooting anybody, speaking the ways kids in schoolyards across the country speak, in a film about one of the most relevant youth issues of the day, endorsed by the country's two biggest teachers' unions... *That* got an R.

The ever-combative, bombastic, master showman Harvey Weinstein not only found himself with a promotable, ink-generating contest in the MPAA's rating, but a legit cause as well. This was a movie kids needed to see, and the MPAA's R was getting in the way of that. Weinstein appealed the rating... and lost, though, in the process, he managed to get damned near every reviewer in the country writing about his fighting the good fight. Consequently, he chose to release the film unrated, although all that free press didn't help the film much. Many theaters won't touch an unrated film, and others treat it as the equivalent of an R or even NC-17 rating. In limited release, the movie opened unimpressively, and even after it stepped up to a wider distribution platform, quickly plateaued.

Owen Gleiberman, in his *Entertainment Weekly* review of *Bully*, summed up the net result in words which, more or less, were echoed in newspaper and online and magazine stories about *Bully* across the country: "... the very audience that *Bully* was made for still might have a hard time getting near it."

For a few weeks there in March and April, *Bully* and its R was something of a *cause célèbre* in the film community. Reviews became as much indictments of the MPAA as they were about whether or not the film was any good.

And then, as sometimes happens with *cause celebres*, the issue seemed to fizz away. Maybe it was that unimpressive $3 million gross. Maybe it was because everybody preferred talking about *The Avengers*.

Personally—and I know I'm in a minority here—I didn't have a problem with *Bully*'s R. Oh, I didn't think for a moment the film deserved it, and I think the MPAA's rationale for it was as lame as the rationales for their other regularly issued WTF ratings, but I actually thought it wasn't a bad thing for parents and kids to be made to see this doc together. Kids already know what the horror show at school is like; they live it every day. Parents don't. It would've been nice for a mom and dad and their kid to come out of *Bully* with the parents asking, "Anything like this ever happen to you?" Or, better, "If I ever hear you've been treating another kid like that, I'm gonna show you what bullying really is!"

But I digress.

I've got nothing to add to what a lot of writers with more impressive pedigrees than I have already said about the MPAA and that insane R-rating and their whole fucked-up (oops! Sorry, MPAA—*screwed*-up) system since *Bully*'s release. Suffice to say I agree it's a horrible, capricious, often absurd system; I deplore the MPAA's lack of transparency in how it does what it does and why; and I remain completely at a loss to understand its defensive obstinacy in ever acknowledging that maybe—just *maybe*—there's always room in the system for a little improvement; nor do I understand their acting like admitting their system *might* not be the be-all/end-all they want it to be is some kind of crucifiable heresy.

For me, the whole mess raises a larger issue, one even going beyond how you create a ratings system that can serve the contradictory, paradoxical, whimsical, and erratic views of an audience as contradictory, paradoxical, whimsical and erratic one as the American masses. For me, the issue *is* that contradictory, paradoxical, whimsical and erratic mass audience.

But before we get to that, one more digression...

*****

Saying that young people *should* see the movie, and that a lesser rating *could* have made it easier for them to see it, is far from saying they *would* have plunked down money to see *Bully* if it just hadn't been for that obstructing R. I don't think *Bully* would've done any better at the box office if it had been rated G, presented in 3-D, and had a two-burgers-for-the-price-of-one tie-in with McDonald's. The legion of reviewers sharing the opinion that the only thing keeping kids from seeing *Bully* was that nasty R had to have been either painfully optimistic, or unbelievably naïve.

I'm going to go out on what I consider a fairly firm limb and say, I don't think the problem was that R. I'll even crawl out there a little further and say if you were sitting in the audience over the last few months for R-rated fare like *Underworld Awakening* ($62 million domestic gross), *American Reunion* ($56 mil), and *The Cabin in the Woods* ($40.5 mil), and peered into the dark around you, I'm pretty sure you'd find not everybody in the house was seventeen and over.

Parents didn't have any trouble dragging their kids off to watch monkeys snuggle in *Chimpanzee,* but going by the unimpressive earnings of *Bully,* they didn't seem any more moved than their kids to find out what might be going on in their schools, maybe with their own kids.

There's a lot of things young people—and their parents—*should* and *could* do. They should put their Wiis down, get off the couch and go for a walk together, eat more fresh fruits and vegetables, follow the news, not throw gum wrappers on the ground, crack a book every great once in a while and make it one that doesn't involve gushy vampires or zombies and the people who love to kill them.

But they don't.

Kids slept out on sidewalks to get early tickets for *The Hunger Games,* which shows how far they'll go to see what they *want* to see. Short of being hauled off to see *Bully* by their parents—who evidently didn't want to see it either—they weren't going to sit through a shocking, disturbing, and ultimately depressing slice of real life; *their* real life. Harvey Weinstein was right to want to get the movie into schools:

that may have been the only way to get it in front of the kids who most needed to see it.

The Boston Globe's Wesley Morris had written, in his review of *Bully*, that what the movie needed was "... a young audience open to sharing in that shame." That, as it happened, turned out to be a bigger obstacle than the MPAA's R; there was no such willing young audience, at least not in any significant numbers. Maybe it was shame, maybe denial, maybe an understandable unwillingness to revisit that which was already acutely painful, maybe it was disinterest. Possibly, probably, it was a mix of them all. In any case, it was reviewers and Harvey Weinstein squawking about that R; not the kids.

But, as I said, again I digress.

*****

As bad as the MPAA rating system is—and it is—the bigger problem is the constituency it aims to serve. "(What's) fundamentally broken about the MPAA," wrote Owen Gleiberman in his *Entertainment Weekly* piece, "isn't the system so much as the thinking behind the judgments... (They) may be a reflection of 'American values,' but that does not make it right."

The MPAA *does* reflect American values... and that's the problem.

I spent the lion's share of my twenty-seven years with Home Box Office dealing, in one way or another, at one level or another, with the company's subscribers: taking their comments, tracking and breaking them down, strategizing responses. Over the years, we're literally talking about tens of thousands of subscriber comments.

One that still stands out from that mass was a call-in complaint from a polite gentleman telling me how he'd left his twelve-year-old son watching HBO for a moment while he went into the kitchen, then was shocked on his return to see his son watching some naked woman on the service. This, in prime time on a Friday night! Mind you, he pointed out, he was a guy who scrupulously used HBO's content advisories to plan his viewing, and there was nothing in the HBO Program Guide (we still used a printed guide in those days) warning of nudity in the show.

I told him I'd get back to him and started doing some homework. From the time his son was watching, I determined the show he'd seen had been an encore airing of our then hit series, *Tales from the Crypt*, a bit of over-the-top Grand Guignol leavened by heavy doses of camp. The Guide had a number of advisories along the lines of Graphic Violence, Adult Content, etc. But nothing about nudity.

I checked with the Guide department and they told me they listed advisories in accordance with information provided them by Programming. I checked with Programming.

According to Programming, what the boy had seen was, literally, a handful of frames of a woman's breast; less than a half-second of screen time. They hadn't flagged the Guide guys on it because they felt that with warnings about violence and adult content etc., an almost subliminal flash of a woman's breast would be covered. The working assumption—and I agreed—was that because of the gore quotient alone, a supervising parent wouldn't be letting their twelve-year-old spend the evening with *Tales from the Crypt*. At least that was *our* thinking.

When I called the gentleman back to tell him what the story was, our thinking apparently wasn't *his* thinking. He was divorced, a single father, and when his son was with him, it was something of a bonding experience to enjoy the show and its blood-drenched, body-maiming tales of the grotesque together.

In other words, it was OK to watch people get killed in any number of macabre ways (for some reason, I can never forget the episode where Steven Webber has his ear torn off and chomped on like a tasty *hors d'oeuvres* at a ghoul dining party before the gathered ghouls swarm over him for the main course), but a few microseconds of a woman's breast... that was *verboten*.

The Sopranos offered up a parade of similar head-spinning moments throughout its run. Tony Soprano could be a murderer, a thief, a philanderer, a drug abuser, a ruthless schemer, extortionist et al (in fact, one of the most common complaints we received about the show was "Not enough people are getting whacked!"), but did he have to use the Lord's name in vain? Or be racist? The killing and all that wasn't offensive; saying "Goddammit" was.

As Gleiberman writes, the MPAA has always been, for whatever reason, more comfortable with even brutal violence, but not sex, and even more tolerant if the violence comes in a big budget flick by an upscale filmmaker. Anybody remember *Indiana Jones and the Temple of Doom* (1984)? A crazed Indian high priest pulled the living hearts out of his enslaved victims, but it was Steven Spielberg: PG. That same year, the first *The Nightmare on Elm Street* was released... with, natch, an R. That was also the year *The Pope of Greenwich Village* hit theaters; a movie about street level wiseguys. No nudity, the little violence wasn't particularly strong (certainly nothing on the order of some poor panic-stricken slave watching his beating heart yanked out), but the boys did say "Fuck" a lot: R.

George R. R. Martin, author of the *Game of Thrones* novels that have been turned into a hit HBO series, spoke with *Rolling Stone* in a recent interview about the sex v violence double standard:

> *It's a uniquely American prudishness. You can write the most detailed, vivid description of an ax entering a skull, and nobody will say a word in protest. But if you write a similarly detailed description of a penis entering a vagina, you get letters from people saying they'll never read you again. What the hell? Penises entering vaginas bring a lot more joy into the world than axes entering skulls.*

There was probably no clearer demonstration of the screwed-uppedness of the adult American moviegoer (and that's really who the MPAA is designed to appease), then the enthusiastic response to Mel Gibson's 2004 combination cinematic prayer/bloodfest, *The Passion of the Christ*.

Passion sets out in painfully accurate, graphic detail the grisly punishments—flaying, the crown of thorns, etc.—inflicted by the Romans on Jesus leading up to and including his crucifixion. Although the film was rated R, tens of thousands of the devout faithful bought tickets and brought their children along with them too. People who would never have thought of going to other R-rated flicks that year—*Kill Bill: Vol. 2, Dawn of the Dead, Blade: Trinity,* and *Saw*—let alone letting their children see them, had no problem trotting down to the multiplex as a family, sometimes as part of a church group, to watch a human being tortured and murdered in hideous fashion. But, it was ok: see, it was about Jesus.

Stephen King wrote a memorable, heart-tugging piece for *Entertainment Weekly* after witnessing the reaction of an eight-year-old girl brought to the movie by her mother. King overheard the mother tell a friend that the theater manager had warned her that the violence might be too much for her kids (she also had two boys with her younger than their sister). Her response had been "… if it gets too bloody, they can just close their eyes."

King kept glancing over at the little girl throughout the movie:

> *She did okay until the scourging of Christ. Then she did indeed close her eyes, and buried her face against her mother's side. The little body inside the blue dress was all angles, an exclamation mark of horror… (she) hid her face for 15 minutes, but that left another 50 minutes of punishment, torture, cruelty, and death still to go… 50 minutes is a long time to hide your eyes when you're only eight. So after a while, you see, our sweet little girl stopped doing it.*

Passion went on to earn $370.2 million domestic, making it the #3 movie of 2004 behind *Shrek 2* and *Spider-Man 2,* and one of the top-grossing independently produced flicks of all time.

Now compare that to the response to Martin Scorsese's *The Last Temptation of Christ* (1988). The emotional climax of the film comes during Christ's crucifixion (not nearly as blood-drenched as Gibson's version) when he ponders what life might have been like if he had turned his back on his role as Messiah and followed a mortal path including the physical pleasure of loving a woman. But that's the last temptation Christ does not fall for, and he ultimately accepts his role and his death in fulfilling the prophecies of scripture.

For that movie, the church groups also came out—in protest. They marched in front of theaters, they wrote letters and signed petitions, and they did it all over again when the movie appeared on pay-TV a year later.

Evidently, the Christian church's opinion is not only is it OK to watch Jesus tortured and murdered in appalling detail, but, hey, bring the kids; it's as good as going to church. But Jesus fantasizing about sleeping with Mary Magdalene? For that, you go to Hell.

All that in mind, there are times I almost (not quite, but almost) feel sorry for the MPAA. The intent of the system to begin with—as with the Hays office and the studio-era Production Code that were its antecedents—was to keep an easily, often arbitrarily offended public off the industry's back and forestall any public call for government regulation of filmed content (such as the FCC does for broadcast

TV). Owen Gleiberman is right that the MPAA reflects American values, but he's wrong when he says "... that does not make it right."

The MPAA system was not set up to make the "right" calls; those public cohorts who do the most screaming about offensive content don't want the MPAA to make the "right" calls. That was never the MPAA system's job. It was not created to serve filmmakers; it was created to appease those sections of the public that do the kind of yelling and screaming that makes movie studios and exhibitors nervous, and provides blood in the water for public officials looking for a cause to use to troll for votes. The MPAA is expected and designed to do just what it does: make the kind of half-assed, hypocritical, double-standardized judgments it does.

To steal and badly paraphrase a line from Shakespeare, the fault lies not with our ratings systems, but with ourselves.

A Conversation with Reviewer Stephen Whitty
(posted 2/8/11)

At a time of the year that's all about picking the best of the best among movies, it seems singularly appropriate to talk to someone whose year-round profession is assaying the good and the bad up on the big screen.

"I'm one of the few people on the paper who's never had a journalism class, and I'm one of the few people reviewing movies who's actually studied movies, made movies." Stephen Whitty is talking about his job as movie critic for *The Star-Ledger*, the biggest newspaper in New Jersey. Whitty came to *The Ledger* thirteen years ago after a ten-year stint at the *San Jose Mercury News*.

The reference to making movies stems from his time as a student in the film department at New York University, one of the two most respected cinema studies programs in the U.S. (the other being at USC). Whitty hadn't gone into NYU with ambitions of being a movie critic. But, "I didn't like directing. You have to deal with a *lot* of people as a director, and whatever it is somebody has to have in their personality to deal with everybody else's headaches, I didn't have. I found myself gravitating toward the solitary things: editing, writing movies, writing *about* movies..."

Some might think being a movie critic to be a dream job: doing nothing but going to movies every day. But, it requires a certain kind of psychological stamina to sit through the 300 or so pictures Whitty sees each year, most of them not particularly satisfying. "You're sitting there watching Madonna in *Swept Away* (2002) at 10 a.m. and you start wondering, 'Why am I *doing* this?' Then I have to peek at my pay stub to remind myself, 'Oh, *that's* why I'm here!'"

It also requires a boundless enthusiasm for the medium, the kind where even after sitting through a day's worth of the latest Hollywood mind-killers, Whitty can still go home, flip on the TV and "... see what Turner has on tonight."

In the correspondence he receives at work, and sometimes even when he is personally approached, he's had to deal with critiques of his critiques; accusations of snobbery, of a "taste gap" between the critical community and "normal people." He remembers one woman who told him she could always tell she was going to like a movie by the fact Whitty had panned it.

Whitty has an explanation and it has nothing to do with snobbery. "What people don't understand is that I see maybe ten times as many movies as the average moviegoer—and that's only what I see for the job! A typical person who likes going to the movies might go three times a month. A more casual goer; maybe once a month. A lot of people go to the movies only three times a *year* or so. For them, it's like eating out. Maybe they didn't go to a fancy restaurant, and the food wasn't five-star, but they think, 'Well, the veal parmagiana was pretty good, it was ok, the place was nice...' Nothing too special; they had a pleasant night out. For me, it's like going out to eat *every* night, and it's, 'Oh, God, I ate this fifty times *before!*'

"You see so many movies, novelty becomes more important to you. You're hungry to see something even a *little* different. You don't need to see yet *another* shot of Arnold Schwarzenegger—or whoever—running in slow motion toward the screen, jumping for safety as some huge explosion goes off behind him.

"I know that people go to movies for all kinds of reasons. I try to take that into account when I'm reviewing a movie. I'll say, 'Well, *I* didn't like it, but it works if you're looking for a certain thing.' I try to point out *why* I didn't like something, and give it some kind of historical context; how a certain movie, or kind of movie, fits in with a trend, how it compares to movies of the same type that came before.

"If you're going to be useful to people, you need to be consistent in your criticism." He points to the woman who used his pans as a barometer of what she'd like, and laughs. "If you know what you'll like by what I hate, I'm doing my job."

He points out that despite the suspicion of some sort of cultural gulf between movie critics and typical ticket buyers, they're not as far apart as some might think. "I'll tell you, if the average moviegoer looked at my top ten picks from a year, they may not have been everybody's favorites, but I don't think they'd disagree with me. And if they saw my *bottom* five, I doubt *anybody'd* defend them."

The trends in movies from the 1960s to the present, Whitty believes, reflect the evolving conditions of the motion picture business. "In the 1960s, the studios had lost touch with the audience. They were making all these big, gaudy, period musicals and people weren't going. Then you had this explosion of really inventive filmmaking in the 1970s, all these new directors coming into the business: Coppola, Scorsese.... The success of *Easy Rider* (1969) had kicked off a lot of interest in young filmmakers, and that opened the door for young directors most of whom hadn't really done that much. Look at William Friedkin. His big movie prior to *The French Connection* (1971) was *The Night They Raided Minsky's* (1968) and that's it."

Coppola had his *The Godfather* (1972), Spielberg had his *Jaws* (1975), Friedkin had *The French Connection* and *The Exorcist* (1973)...; the tyros of the early 1970s pumped out a string of major commercial hits, which, in an ironic twist, was also their undoing. Their incredible initial successes bought them a creative and financial *carte blanche* from the studios. They were given even more money and latitude with which to indulge their creative visions. As suddenly as the rising class of young directors had all, within a surprisingly short space of time, delivered major successes, they all, just as suddenly and in an equally concentrated period, stumbled. "Scorsese had *New York, New York* (1977), Friedkin had *Sorcerer* (1977), Spielberg had *1941* (1979), Bogdanovich had *They All Laughed* (1981)... all of them had a big, expensive flop. The result was the studios, in the 1980s, they retrenched, they started to rein these directors in. 'We're going to exert more control,' they said. So then scripts would get written, and rewritten, and rewritten the way the studio wanted them. 'We're going to *test* movies.'"

There were other forces at work as well, spawned by the massive success of pictures like *Jaws* and *Star Wars* (1977). "With *Jaws*, (producers Richard) Zanuck and (David) Brown and (director Steven) Spielberg realized you could make a lot of money if you could sell a movie to the same people over and over again." The kind of box office grosses a movie like *Jaws* attains, says Whitty, indicates a lot of repeat business, and repeat ticket buyers are invariably young. The business of turning out blockbuster hits, according to Whitty, has, consequently, become "... very much kid-driven. It has been all the way back to *Jaws.*" The result has been "... these Jerry Bruckheimer kinds of movies that make most of their money off kids. You make a movie that appeals to a twelve-year-old so that he can come back next week and bring his friends."

The box office dynamic of such movies is highly marketing-driven. "Big movies depend on making more and more of their money on their first weekend, with typically huge drop-offs in the second week." Massive marketing campaigns create a sense of awareness and anticipation that can create an opening box office surge for a movie regardless of its quality.

He cites the remake of *Planet of the Apes* (2001) as an example. A familiar title, an extensive, lengthy, studio-mounted ad campaign for the movie prior to its opening, and the result is a tremendous debut weekend ($68.5 million). "By the time the word-of mouth gets around and people realize the movie sucks, the money is already made" *(Planet* earned two-thirds of its domestic take in its first two weeks, ultimately grossing $180 million U.S. when its theatrical run ended twenty-five weeks later).

Other examples: *Mission Impossible* (1996) and *Mission Impossible 2* (2000). "Neither of those movies made much sense," says Whitty. "After they're over, they kind of evaporate." Their releases, however, are textbook examples of how the modern big-budget thriller is packaged and marketed. "You've got a recognizable title, a big star (Tom Cruise), and those pictures had promotional tie-ins everywhere to everything: sunglasses, cars, you couldn't get away from it." That initial box office splash, however short-lived, creates a title awareness among consumers needed to maintain a movie's momentum through ancillary venues. Even if a movie flops in theaters, as long as the title is branded into the consumer's consciousness, there'll be people who will rent it when it comes to home video often out of a curiosity to see what it was that caused the movie to fail. "You now have a situation where most movies make more money on DVD sales and the home video market than they do at the box office."

It's that easily promotable "hook" that has also made the movie "franchise" such a valuable and desired commodity i.e. the *Lethal Weapons*, *Die Hards*, *Batmans*, and so on. The typical flaw with franchises is that once they're established, Whitty observes, the successful elements of the initial success are often flogged lifeless. "I mean, the first *Lethal Weapon* (1987) and *Die Hard* (1988), they were a *bit* over the top, but they were ok. But then they just kept getting bigger and bigger and dumber..." He considers the James Bond series: "They were always over the top, but for me, the best one was *From Russia with Love* (1963). It had the most story, and the big action scene in the movie was just two men fighting in a train compartment." Afterwards, when the series established itself with the hit *Goldfinger* (1964), the Bond pictures became about each succeeding installment outdoing the previous ones in terms of spectacle. The stories, on the other hand, were increasingly reduced to contrivances serving little more purpose than to provide an excuse for a series of overblown action set-pieces.

Another evolutionary change came in industry distribution patterns. Whitty recalls the "road shows" when a movie would premiere only in a limited number of venues. "When I was a kid, a movie would open in New York and a couple of other big cities, then it would move to the smaller theaters, then (still) smaller theaters, eventually to the drive-ins." The change to wide, national releases "... changed everything," he asserts. "I remember (one-time Paramount production chief) Robert Evans saying that when Paramount released *The Godfather,* they opened it on something like 300 screens, and that was the biggest release of any movie to that point. These days, a release is more likely to be ten times that. And, when you have a release that large, buying a quarter-page ad in newspapers isn't going to do it. You have to advertise on TV, and TV spots need to reduce the movie to easily digestible chunks. They're also enormously expensive, so now you have to throw *that* cost on to the cost of production, and that pushes you to look harder for movies you're sure are going to hit big. That answers the question of why anybody would make an expensive movie version of a lousy TV show like *S.W.A.T.* (the movie version was released in 2003). It's highly promotable."

It also answers the question of why the contemporary thriller forms making up most blockbusters have become so dramatically stale as studio production executives crib elements from previous successes hoping to repeat the same box office performance. It's a strategy inevitably leading to creative stagnation. "So many movies I see, twenty minutes in and I'm already thinking, 'Ok, actually he's not *really* dead, they just found someone else's body...,' or, 'Right, ok, turns out she really had this twin sister nobody knew about...' You sit watching a cop thriller and the minute some guy starts talking about how he's almost set to retire and get on his fishing boat, you're saying, 'Ok, he's a dead man.'"

Which brings Whitty to an oft repeated plaint among movie critics that the underlying problem with the current generation of moviemakers is a lack of real-world experience; the dramatic hollowness of their movies is the result of making movies that are really about other movies. "There's some validity to that. Sometimes it's nice to see the familiar, particularly in a genre picture. The girl wakes up in the night, the lights go out, she's walking the dark halls in this long robe, holding up the candle... You expect it, it's comforting to see it. But then *do* something with it. *Pulp Fiction* (1994) is a movie inspired by a lot of other movies, but (Quentin) Tarantino pulled it off so inventively.

"I want to be surprised. *The Usual Suspects* (1995) surprised me. I'm not sure if I saw it again today that the story would actually hold up. It seems like this criminal mastermind went through an awful lot of trouble just to put a bullet through somebody's head, but it kept me interested; you couldn't tell where it was going. *Memento* (2000) was a movie with a gimmick, but it was a gimmick that worked quite nicely for that story.

"Freshness happens in the script. The problem is that the studios have these things rewritten over and over and over. The stars are too involved in that process. Nobody wants to play a bad guy, nobody wants to die in the end, or if they do they want to have a great death scene." Even after the movie is completed, Whitty continues, the process of trying to pre-fabricate success goes on: "They have all these test screenings. They take the picture out to some suburban mall, they grab kids off the street to watch these things. Do you *really* want an army of kids to tell you how to fix a little thriller?"

Under this system, Hollywood pumps out an army of the predictable, the stale, the simplistic, so much so that eventually even critics' standards begin to erode. In Whitty's view, critics have become so benumbed by the inferior that it doesn't take too much to spark some enthusiasm from them, even for a movie that, in an earlier time, might not have fared so well in the press. *Spider-Man* (2002), for example: "This was no classic, but they actually had a credible romance in that picture, you saw characters make some interesting choices. That was enough for that movie to get a lot of good press."

For Whitty, an example of the 1970s antithesis to the current process—and one of the movies regularly cited by many critics as a height from which American cinema has fallen—is *Chinatown* (1974). "It's about a *lot* of things. It's this great, classic, private eye mystery, but it's also about power, corruption, the whole, bizarre history of how Los Angeles lost its water supply, got it back... The movie contains a *ton* of serious issues."

It's that textured storytelling—the careful layering of themes and subplots—Whitty finds distressingly lacking in so many of today's major releases. "I interviewed Larry Cohen. He'd just hit it big with his script for *Phone Booth* (2003), but for much of his career he's worked on low-budget movies and TV. I remember him talking about when he was working as a writer on the old (1960s) TV Western series, *Branded*...."

The series concerned a cavalry officer, played by Chuck Connors, humiliatingly convicted of cowardice. The series' theme song inculcated the character's dilemma in each episode: "What do you do when you're 'branded'... and you know you're a man. Whatever you do for the rest of your life you'll remain... *'branded!'*"

"Cohen told me that when he was writing *Branded*, for him it was really about the McCarthy era. I mean, there was nothing there you could see in the shows that told you this, but that was what he brought to it... that was the subtext. Somehow Connors found out and when he did they fired Cohen right away. But, that subtext (in today's thrillers), that message... that's the first thing they throw out."

He cites the hit *Black Hawk Down* (2001). Though he feels there were some interesting things in the movie, what was more striking was what the movie lacked. "There must've been *some* minorities in that unit that had some strong feelings about what they were doing there in Africa. How did *they* feel?" A lot of military-themed action pictures avoid criticizing the military in order to gain the cooperation of the services so producers can use the personnel, facilities, and equipment on a scale allowing elaborate productions like *Top Gun* (1986), *Black Hawk Down*, and others. "If something goes wrong in one of these movies, it's always, 'It's the politicians' fault,' because that's safe. It's never, 'Was there something wrong with the plan? Did *we* screw up?'" In the process, however, potentially compelling stories become simplistic. It's not just the military moviemakers looking to avoid offending, says Whitty, but there seems to be a terror in contemporary Hollywood of having viewers make decisions and judgments about what's happening on-screen.

He compares the movie *We Were Soldiers* (2002) with the 1993 source book, *We Were Soldiers Once... And Young: Ia Drang: The Battle That Changed the War In Vietnam,* a true account by Lt. Colonel Harold G. Moore (played in the movie by Mel Gibson), who commanded American troops during what would be one of the biggest battles of the Vietnam war, and Joseph L. Galloway. In the book, Whitty says, there were incidents of cowardice, of men who threw down their weapons and ran. The book also pointed out how shabbily soldiers returning to the States from Vietnam had been treated, not just by anti-war protestors but by the Veterans' Administration as well. In the movie, on the other hand, all of the soldiers acquit themselves bravely. "If you make everybody in the movie a hero, then what does it mean to be a hero?"

The Bourne Identity (2002), he felt, tried to recapture some of the moral complexities of 1970s espionage tales. "Basically, they tried to update the spy story for the younger audience. What was interesting about it was it wasn't just the bad guy vs. the good guy, but the bad guy vs. a not-as-bad guy." As a rule, however, the studios seem to prefer their moralities clear and their endings upbeat, even in a pseudo-*noir* like *L.A. Confidential* (1997). For Whitty, a strong, compelling movie came apart in *L.A.*'s tacked on ending. "That was a Hollywood ending," he groans. "It doesn't fit the movie at all. The ending in the (1990) novel (by James Ellroy) is absolutely despairing."

Scripts today, Whitty opines, are not written; they're *built*. "It's Joel Silver telling you, you have to have these 'beats' in a picture, you have to have one in the first ten minutes," and regularly thereafter. Whitty points out how older thrillers didn't have the relentless, forward-pounding pace of today's constructs. "You look back at a picture like the original *The Thing (from Another World)* (1951)..., they'd take a scene to do nothing but establish characters." Characterizations in such a well-crafted piece, he says, are so strong and credible that the nature of the threat is almost irrelevant. "It could've been anything (in *The Thing*). A disease outbreak, a killer on the loose, a fire... It didn't matter, it didn't have to be a monster. You invested in the characters. *Alien* (1979) worked for the same reason. You had time to care about Sigourney Weaver and the other characters."

Even Hitchcock, whose pictures were as meticulously constructed for effect as any in the industry—"He was upfront about the fact that he was building a roller coaster ride"—understood the value of character. "You look at a movie like *Vertigo* (1958) or *Shadow of a Doubt* (1943); they're very character-driven." So, "What you have now is a lot of people making movies they don't believe in. You can only do right by what you believe in."

Movies do surface that echo the interesting product of the past, but they rarely come out of the major studios. "*Narc* (2003) was a throwback. It was gritty, dark, and downbeat. Some of the most interesting scenes in that movie had nothing to do with the plot. There's a scene where Ray Liotta and Jason Patric are called in to look at a murder scene. The scene does very little to move the plot along, but it's a chance to see the characters *be*. Liotta comes in, he sees this medical examiner he knows, 'Hi, how you doing?' there's some back and forth. It's a chance to get to know them. But *Narc* didn't make a lot of money, not the kind of money the studios look for, not like some big, stupid *Die Hard* 5 if they ever get around to making it (which, as it turns out, is scheduled for a 2012 release).

"The supernatural thriller *The Others* (2002) was another one, a throwback to movies like *The Haunting* (1963). No gore, all mood, very clever." Even though *The Others* was a substantial success, Whitty doesn't think it's the kind of movie that changes studio mindsets because "A killer in a hockey mask is still much easier to sell."

Other favorites come from overseas. "Every once in a while Claude Chabrol can still throw something into the mix worth seeing."

Occasionally, the studios do release a similarly exemplary thriller. Whitty points to *Insomnia* (2002), *Road to Perdition* (2002), and *L.A. Confidential*. "Those were all complicated, interesting stories done in interesting fashions, *L.A. Confidential*'s soft-hearted ending notwithstanding." Still, overall, they were good movies with respectable box office grosses. The problem for each of them was their high cost, which Whitty thinks is more a sign of how the studios do business than with the drawing power of the movies themselves. Whitty says the studio excuse is that only big, star-driven vehicles can make big money, but he calls the paradigm self-fulfilling. "They're committed to these aging $20 million per picture stars because they think that guarantees them a return, but once you sign them on your budget balloons and that causes you to try to tailor the movie into something that you think will make $100 million.

"You constantly hear the complaint from some directors that they want to work in the $20-40 million range, and at that range these kinds of movies could work quite well financially. But the studios don't want to hear that. You either have to pitch the movie as being very small, or huge, otherwise they don't want to hear about it. Me, I would rather see ten $16 million movies instead of one $160 million movie, but the studio knows that that $160 million picture can get them a billion." He looks at Paramount's *Changing Lanes* (2002), another movie he considers interesting and well-written and speculates on what it took to get it made. "Would Paramount have made that movie without stupid *The Sum of All Fears* (2002) (which, like *Lanes*, starred Ben Affleck)? I don't think so."

The irony, says Whitty, is that for all their calculations and tailorings, Hollywood's batting average isn't much better than it was back when tyro directors were given their heads and coming back with expensive flops like *Heaven's Gate* (1980). "You can test and do the other things they do and *still* lose."

A critic's year, Whitty sighs, is rife with frustration. "There's an *awful* lot of bad movies out there. You have to be an eternal optimist to get yourself back into a theater every day, hoping you'll see something a little different. In any given year, I could probably only recommend ten to fifteen percent of what I see. I'm not even talking four-star pictures, or even necessarily American movies, but maybe just that ten to fifteen percent." His voice turns hopeful, then: "Still, that means thirty to forty movies worth seeing."

Ask him if he thinks there's any chance of the situation changing and there's a pause. "If people support smart movies, yes. The only thing Hollywood is committed to is making money. But, it's hard to get people to go. I tell them, take a risk on something with subtitles. Try a movie with people in it you don't know. Take a chance once in a while. You might get a nice surprise."

Why Can't an Oscar-Winner Look More Like a Hit?
(posted 2/8/12)

Whether one of the major studios takes the top prize at the Academy Awards or not, they have no squawk this year.

Several years ago, as you might recall, the Big Guys were getting fed up with having their clocks cleaned in the Best Picture category every year by releases from independent companies. The last time one of the majors walked home with Best Picture gold was 2006 when Warners' *The Departed* took the trophy. Before that, you have to go back almost a decade—to 1997—to *Titanic*, split between 20th Century Fox and Paramount.

Over the last decade and a half or so, the indies have usually taken a fair share of the nomination slots and almost always the grand prize. The majors retaliated by pushing for an expansion of the Best Picture category beyond five nominees, feeling the kind of big budget spectacles where they could really strut their stuff—like, say, *The Dark Knight* (2008)—were getting squeezed out by the Academy's infatuation with snooty low-budget indies. (The last big budget Best Picture winners were *The Lord of the Rings: Return of the King* in 2003, and *Gladiator* in 2000, but both came from outside the circle of majors, with *King* from New Line, and *Gladiator* from then independent DreamWorks; the last major studio extravaganza to win was, again, *Titanic*.)

The only shot the Big Boys had at getting one of their spectaculars in the running this year was Warners' *Harry Potter and the Deathly Hallows—Part 2*. It seemed a sentimental shoo-in. An Oscar nod would not only have recognized a film demonstrating big budget effects fests could be done with intelligence and style and taste, but also serve as a deserved salute—as it has often thought the Oscar for *Return of the King* had been—to a series that has maintained an outstanding level of quality over a decade and eight films. Sentiment or not, poor *Harry*, alas, didn't make the cut, but, as I said, the major studios still have no squawk. For the first time in a loooong time, the majors dominate.

Of the nine nominees for this year's Best Picture Oscar, two are from Disney (Spielberg's heart-tugging *War Horse*, and the heart-warming *The Help)*, one from Sony (true sports tale *Moneyball)*, one from Paramount (Scorsese's grand scale fairy tale *Hugo*), and Warner Bros. and Paramount are jointly behind 9/11 drama, *Extremely Loud & Incredibly Close*. If you add in films from the majors' specialty divisions—those small companies within big companies charged with turning out indie-like films—the studios own eight of the nomination slots with Fox Searchlight's brand on Terry Malick's poetic *The Tree of Life*; and Alexander Payne's mix of domestic comedy and domestic drama, *The Descendants*; and Sony Classics behind Woody Allen's late-career box office triumph, *Midnight in Paris*.

(Ironically, the only release from a true independent also happens to be considered the frontrunner for the award: The Weinstein Co.'s *The Artist*.)

You can argue with some of the individual choices, grumble about flicks that didn't make the cut, but let's face it; generally, it's a pretty respectable group. Certainly nothing embarrassing there, and it's a reminder to all concerned that the Big Guys haven't forgotten what it too often seems they've forgotten: how to make a good movie.

What *hasn't* changed is the Best Picture category's persistent lack of big hits. As of this writing, only one nominee has crossed the $100 million mark in domestic box office, with the rest ranging from mid-range to strictly niche performers, and none showing any promise at all of ever breaking through that deliciously round-numbered ribbon of green and gold:

The Help:	$169.6 million domestic box office/budget: $25 million
War Horse:	77.3/66
Moneyball:	75.6/50
The Descendants:	65.5/20
Hugo:	61.9/150
Midnight in Paris:	56.5/17
The Artist:	20.6/15
The Tree of Life:	13.3/32

Looking at those numbers, particularly when measured against costs (rule of thumb is breakeven requires a gross of two-three times cost), may explain why the majors don't make too many of these kinds of movies. While there have been a few heavyweight earners in the Oscar nominee field over the last ten to fifteen years, generally, Oscar contenders don't have the same box office muscle as other releases.

The top earner in this year's group—*The Help*—did terrific numbers, particularly against such a modest budget, and was one of the top money-makers of the year coming in at number thirteen. Yet it only did about half the business of the clanking mess that was *Transformers: Dark of the Moon* (number two for the year). *War Horse, Moneyball, The Descendants, Midnight in Paris,* and *Hugo* (this last easily one of the most acclaimed releases of the year) were outearned by such craptasms as *Alvin and the Chipmunks: Chipwrecked, Green Lantern, Battle: Los Angeles, The Green Hornet,* and—say it ain't so, Joe—*The Smurfs.*

Extremely Loud & Incredibly Close was not nearly as loud at the box office as tired sequels *Final Destination 5* or—shudder—*Spy Kids: All the Time in the World.*

Oscar frontrunner and a tie with *Hugo* as the most praised film of the year, *The Artist,* couldn't get its numbers past bottom-dwelling junk like *Mars Needs Women* and the *Conan the Barbarian* remake.

And *Tree of Life?* Ok, *Tree* is a demanding flick. Even a lot of the art house crowd had trouble getting it down. Still, more people managed to swallow *Judy Moody and the NOT Bummer Summer.*

Among the general public, there's long been a suspicion movie reviewers and bodies like the Academy voters are some other species: "They don't watch movies *normal* people do." Undoubtedly, most of us who like to gather at this site and fancy ourselves somewhat serious in our film interests have had a conversation along the lines of the following at one time or another:

You're at the table for some family dinner, you mention a movie. "I never heard of that," somebody says, and turns to the others at the table. "You ever hear of that?" Blank faces.

Or somebody mentions whatever is riding high at the box office at that moment, and you mention—knowing the second it passes your lips it's a mistake to bring this up—that the reviews have been less than kind.

"What do they know?" someone says.

Someone else chimes in, "I already know I'm gonna like it. You know how I know I'm gonna like it? Because those review guys hate it! (or vice versa)"

And then there's that all-time favorite chat after the Oscar nominations come out. They look to you for some sort of enlightenment because "You know a lot about movies," and they say, "I never heard of half them pictures. I don't even know anybody who's seen any of 'em. Where do they find these things?"

Are these two worlds apart? Are reviewers and awards-givers just a bunch of cinema snobs with their noses so high in the air it's a wonder they don't wind up in neck braces? Does the mainstream viewing audience consist of a bunch of yahoos who wouldn't know good movie-making if a glowing Divine Finger came down from Heaven and pointed to a title on the multiplex marquee to the accompaniment of a herald of angels singing, "This one, morons!"?

Is it so *freaking* impossible to make a movie that's everything good filmmaking should be *and* that's also fun for a lot of people to watch?

Well, these days, kinda, yeah.

Which, in itself, I grant may sound kind of snobby, but it's a question of demographics, and the changing sensibilities of the bulk—pay attention to that; I didn't say "all"; I said "the bulk"—of the movie-going audience. Or, to put it more simply, it's about where the money is. The *big* money.

The movie box office has been primarily driven by young ticket-buyers since the end of World War II, but the sensibility of the young audience has gone through a radical change over the last thirty years or so. How they watch movies—or anything else, for that matter—has been shaped by growing up in households where they can cruise hundreds of cable channels, millions of websites, spend hours playing meth-paced shooter videogames. Thanks to smart phones and other portable electronics, they can, and do, stay connected to that hyperactive digital realm everywhere and anywhere. Providing you can even get that audience into a movie house—and attendance numbers suggest that's getting harder and harder to do—they want a movie that fits in with the rest of their ADD-like time-killing experiences: fast-paced, comic book-simple, and as much over-the-top action as can be packed into two hours. *No Country for Old Men* (2007) or *The Hurt Locker* (2008) or *The Artist* ain't gonna cut it for them.

What cuts it are the kind of movies that ruled the top of the 2011 box office: behind *Harry Potter* and *Transformers*, this means *The Twilight Saga: Breaking Dawn Part 1*, *The Hangover Part 2*, *Pirates of the Caribbean: On Stranger Tides*, *Fast Five*, *Mission Impossible–Ghost Protocol*, *Sherlock Holmes: A Game of Shadows*, *Thor*, *Rise of the Planet of the Apes*, *Captain America: The First Avenger*.

You say, "Good cinema... award-winner... critically acclaimed" to that audience, and it's like telling a kid to eat his broccoli because it's good for him. Well, it may be good for him, but come Friday night he and his friends just want to go out and binge on cinematic Twinkies because that's what kids do, which pushes movie companies interested in big earnings into the cinematic junk food business.

It's easier to *amuse* people than to *engage* them. Good storytelling—whether you're talking about movies, TV, theater, books, whatever—is about trying to land some of your shots on three targets: the gut, the heart, the head. Most of the box office kings tend to shoot low: eye dazzle, easy humor, an occasional glop of manipulative sentimentality to give you the illusion something in the last two hours actually counted for something. Those are typically the easiest targets to hit. Think *Hangover Part 2*.

All nine Oscar nominees, however, to some degree or another, spread their shots out among all three targets. You can almost guarantee that the greatness of a film—its ability to hang with you long after you've left the theater, and maybe even continue to connect with audiences years later—is connected to a filmmaker's ability to strike all three targets in some sublimely deft, or deftly sublime, way. Think *Lawrence of Arabia* (1962).

As for critics and awards-givers being snobs, well, undoubtedly, some are. But part of their sensibility—much of it, actually—comes from the simple fact that this is what they do for a living. Before last year's Oscars, I interviewed Stephen Whitty, reviewer for *The Star-Ledger*, the major newspaper where I live. Whitty hit the situation so squarely on the head then, it still seems the best way to put it:

> *... I see maybe ten times as many movies as the average moviegoer... A typical person who likes going to the movies might go three times a month. A more casual goer, maybe once a month. A lot of people go to the movies only three times a year or so. For them, it's like eating out. Maybe they didn't go to a fancy restaurant, and the food wasn't five-star, but they think, 'Well, the veal parmagiana was pretty good, it was ok, the place was nice...' Nothing too special; they had a pleasant night out. For me, it's like going out to eat every night, and it's, 'Oh, God, I ate this fifty times before!'*

You see that many movies, it's easy—painfully easy—to see when moviemakers are being lazy, derivative, when their only inspiration is that a certain bit got a laugh/gasp/shudder in a dozen other movies. It's not that critics are snobby (well, not necessarily, let's say), but it's like that line Bill Murray has in *Groundhog Day* (1993): "Maybe (God's) not impotent. He's just been around so long he knows everything."

Even the older, mature audience has grown increasingly conservative in its choices. *The Help* is a wonderful, inspiring, touching movie... but it's also rather safe. It's a beautifully rendered, if hardly subtle, feel-good picture of something we all know (or should know) about race in this country. It's not quite as challenging or unfamiliar as some of the other nominees, which may be why *The Help* did blockbuster numbers and the others did not.

I'm not saying the other flicks are all "deep" pieces of cinematic art. Quite the contrary; a number of them, like *The Help*, are just terrific storytelling (*Midnight in Paris, Moneyball, The Artist, War Horse*). But there is an air of *un*familiarity about them, and that doesn't work for mass audiences all that well these days.

As it happens, while I'm writing this, I'm also flicking an eye to my TV where TCM is running *Town Without Pity*, an American/German co-production from 1961. It reminded me there was a time when the mainstream audience didn't have a problem with trans-Atlantic collaborations like *Pity* and *The Train* (1964) and *Is Paris Burning?* (1966) with half their casts dubbed, or with Clint Eastwood and Lee Van Cleef exchanging shots with swarthy dubbed Italians trying to pass as swarthy Mexican *banditos* in spaghetti Westerns. For that matter, we didn't mind TV series like *The Avengers, The Saint,* and *The Prisoner*—produced in the UK for UK audiences—airing on American network TV, in prime time no less. We kind of liked the variety. It strikes me we've gotten a bit more parochial, from that older, supposedly more mature audience on down to the sit-through-*Pirates-of-the-Caribbean*-twice young crowd.

Look at *The Artist*. It's a lovely, charming, sometimes funny, sometimes romantic, sometimes touching tale of Hollywood. If you liked *Singin' in the Rain* (1952) or any of the myriad versions of *A Star Is Born*, if you're looking for a movie that can work for the cineaste as a Valentine to the movies, or just one that'll be a great date movie, it'll work for you. Watching *The Artist* isn't like asking the audience to do *Tree of Life* high hurdles.

The Weinstein Co. release had been doing great art house business. When the award noms started coming in and the adoring critical buzz seemed to be reaching some sort of peak, Weinstein broadened the film's release apparently hoping for a breakout... and the box office stalled. Was it because the movie was in black-and-white? That it was a silent flick? That it was perceived as being a—God forbid!—*foreign* film? Maybe all of them. But *The Artist* hitting the box office wall so abruptly once out of the safe haven of limited distribution says something about the limited tolerances of even the older mainstream audience.

Yeah, yeah, I know: "I just go to the movies to be *entertained!*"

Ya know something? That's *always* been the reason most people have gone and still go to the movies. It's not like anybody, even the snootiest critic, says to him/herself, "Ah, the weekend! I really need to go get myself edified and enlightened at the movies on Saturday!" It's just that what entertains most people seems to be funneling down to a suffocatingly narrow range of stuff.

These two separate worlds of the general movie-going public and picky critics and awards-givers? The sad thing about this is they weren't always so separate.

*****

You'd have to be near-delusional not to know Hollywood has *always* made more crud than cream. Back in the days of the silents, back during the golden years of mogul-run Hollywood, back during the 1960s-1970s era of filmmaking mavericks and renegades, the junk always outnumbered the jewels. And the mass audience was fine with that.

But there *were* jewels, and they came from the same outfits making the junk. The same Hollywood that gave you Ma and Pa Kettle also gave you *The Grapes of Wrath* (1940), and the mass audience was fine with that too.

In the 1930s, the top earners of the decade ranged from wonderfully soapy *Gone with the Wind* (1939) and the all-star melodrama *Grand Hotel* (1932) to the screen adaptation of *David Copperfield* (1935) and Frank Capra's still-frighteningly-relevant acidic comedy about politics, *Mr. Smith Goes to Washington* (1939). The '40s list of top earners includes *The Best Years of Our Lives* (1946; this touching story of returning vets was actually the top grosser of the decade); the then revelatory portrait of alcoholism in *The Lost Weekend* (1945) and classic *noir The Postman Always Rings Twice* (1946); right along with flyweight fun like *Road to Utopia* (1945) and *The Bachelor and the Bobby-Soxer* (1947). The 1950s brought outsized sword-and-sandal epics like *Ben-Hur* (1959; #1 for the decade) and *The Ten Commandments* (1956); but it also brought the bitter damning of war in *The Bridge on the River Kwai* (1957), and Billy Wilder's dark comedy, *The Apartment* (1960).

The list of box office champs from the 1960s/1970s is dizzying in its breadth and sheer number of American classics. Among them: *The Graduate* (1967; #3 for the '60s), *The Godfather* (1972), *Bonnie and Clyde* (1967), *One Flew Over the Cuckoo's Nest* (1975), *2001: A Space Odyssey* (1968), *Apocalypse Now* (1979)... The list goes on. People still wanted to be "just entertained"—*National Lampoon's Animal House* (1978) was the eleventh highest-grossing movie of its decade—but there was room on studio slates, on movie screens, and in the audience's appetite for all of it.

Take a movie like *All the President's Men* (1976). It's the story of the uncovering of the Watergate scandal by *Washington Post* reporters Carl Bernstein and Bob Woodward. Typing and phone calls are about as visceral as the action gets. Yet all the elements of fine film storytelling came together in a way that made it one of the sixty highest-grossing movies of the 1970s; up there on the same list with *Star Wars* (1977) and *Jaws* (1975). Can you imagine how that kind of movie would play today?

Actually, you can. *Shattered Glass* (2003)—another true story, another drama based in the world of journalism—despite a stratospheric ninety-one percent Rotten Tomatoes positive rating and a seventy-seven percent positive from viewers, did less than $3 million... *worldwide*. *All the President's Men* did ten times better than that domestically *without* adjusting for inflation! Movies as good—as *great*—as movies of any other generation are still getting made, it's just fewer people are interested in seeing them.

If there's snobbism at work in the movies today, it's a sort of a reverse snobbism; it's not the critics or the Academy or the Golden Globes or whomever who are elitist, but the average moviegoer who equates popularity with quality, and unfamiliarity with the unnecessary risk of the bloated price of a movie ticket. Saying a movie is good and critics are out of touch, simply because a lot of people go to a particular picture and even enjoy it, is like saying, to go back to our gastronomic allegory, Twinkies are a better dessert then crème brulee because more people eat Twinkies than crème brulee.

As we have nutritionally, cinematically we have also become addicted to junk food and we've developed a sort of cultural obesity as a result; we don't exercise our intellects in a way we once did, we don't try different "foods" as we should, and we ingest too much crap.

The nice thing, the admirable and inspiring thing, is despite this regular run on the Twinkie stand, God bless 'em, there are still cinematic chefs toiling away in their kitchens, blending nutritional value with a refined, discriminating palate to turn out orgasmically divine treats. But once done, garnished and iced to perfection, they put their work on display, and ruefully ruminate, "Now, if I could only get somebody to try it..."

The Artful Roger: A Thank You To Roger Ebert
(posted 3/1/11)

Some of you (hopefully) may have noticed my recent profile on the late, great Robert Mitchum. In the course of researching the piece, I came across the fun tidbit that Mitchum had been a favorite of film critic Roger Ebert.

The mind rarely works in linear fashion, and I suspect mine may even be more chaotic than most. That item pinballed around the ol' noggin, and, somewhere in all that bouncing here and there, triggered a bit of nostalgia. Probably because I was working on the piece during Oscar week, the mention of Ebert reminded me that there had been a time when this would've been the point in the year I'd be looking forward to the annual "If We Gave Out the Oscars" (or something like that) show done by Ebert along with his on-screen partner of nearly two dozen years, fellow film critic Gene Siskel.

That first Ebert/Siskel memory triggered others, and as they bubbled up and percolated a bit, they started to gel together and *bing*: Gestalt light bulb.

Roger Ebert, and the long-lasting TV presence he's had, particularly in association with Siskel, has been such a visible part of the media landscape for so long that he's taken for granted; viewed as an institution with a sense of was-is-and-always-will-be.

Which, as is the case with any institution, is hardly true. There was a time before, and the difference between then and what came after is so stark as... Well, you wouldn't think it, but when Ebert and Siskel hit the air, the changes they wrought on the public face of film criticism, were—dare I say it? Yes, I dare!—nothing less than revolutionary. And if it doesn't seem so today, that only testifies as to how some revolutions, in time, become the new long-standing status quo.

As late as the 1970s, and, arguably, even into the 1980s, the public face of movie criticism—... Well, it didn't have a public face. Not much of one, anyway.

According to Gerald Peary's 2009 documentary, *For the Love of Movies: The Story of American Film Criticism*, in which Ebert is a prominent talking head, up to that period most people didn't know reviewers, not by name, anyway, nor did they much care what they had to say.

Not that there weren't a number of critics out there flexing considerable intellectual muscle. Several were, in fact, among the all-time heavyweight champs of American film criticism, like Pauline Kael at *The New Yorker*, and her rival Andrew Sarris at *The Village Voice*, or Bosley Crowther over at *The New York Times*, to name just a few.

They were more than just reviewers. Their passion went far beyond recommending a good watch for the weekend. They appreciated film *in depth*, in a way extending past what was at the movies that week. They wrote articles and essays and books that seriously contemplated the larger issues—corporate and aesthetic, and that area where they overlapped or bumped into each other—in cinema. When I took my first film study class in high school, Kael's novella-length essay "Raising Kane"—the story behind the making and an appreciation of *Citizen Kane* (1941)—was our text. Later, as a film student in college, Sarris's *The American Cinema* was a much-dog-eared reference work, a landmark as the first aesthetic overview of the body of all significant American directors up to that time compiled outside of the *Cahiers du Cinema* crowd.

They had their notable triumphs too. Kael's support for *Bonnie & Clyde* (1967) is—at least by some—considered the beginning of the commercial turn-around for that ground-breaking piece of 1960s moviemaking. She fired the first volley in a critical cannonade, which turned what had been a sputtering, often panned, release into one of the major commercial hits and artistic highpoints of the decade.

These were serious appreciators as well as serious students of film, writing seriously about—as often as they could—serious films and serious filmmaking. But as such—and *Bonnie & Clyde* notwithstanding—they had little to say to less serious Joe and Joan Average, or at least little Joe and Joan were interested in hearing… or could possibly want to make an effort to understand. Kael, for instance, managed to get herself fired from an early gig at *McCall's* by, according to her editor Robert Stein, "… panning every commercial movie from *Lawrence of Arabia* and *Dr. Zhivago* to *The Pawnbroker* and *A Hard Day's Night.*"

We film students—a rather serious lot too, or so we considered ourselves—knew who many of these critical leading lights were, we read their work, argued about what they had to say, but beyond that… Not a lot of echo out there with all those Joes and Joans who were only looking for a fun movie for date night. Kael and Sarris and that crowd wrote and mused in something of an intellectual bubble, and it was easy to imagine they were really only talking to each other; their true and possibly only peers.

There were a few reviewers who did manage to connect with the general public, and I suspect that some in the critical community at that time wished they hadn't.

Like Rex Reed. Reed, who still writes for *The New York Observer*, was a semi-regular guest on the talk show circuit back in those days. Draped lazily in a chair opposite Johnny or Merv, wallowing in an air of boredom and bare tolerance, he was colorful as hell, and a real-life Waldo Lydecker: a professional snob. He vindicated every suspicion the general public had of film critics as something vastly removed from themselves, coming off, as he did, as effete, arrogant, condescending, and skewering most movies and the general public who enjoyed them with volleys of acid-tipped *bon mots*.

Still more public and recognized was NBC's resident film reviewer, Gene Shalit, who presented as something of a cross between a kiddy party clown and a bad Borscht Belt comic. He wore goggle-sized eyeglasses and garish bowties, had an electro-shocked head of hair with a face-bisecting mustache to match. His one-two minute reviews, delivered with a frozen grin and a tone of malicious delight, were line after line of groan-inducing puns and corny one-liners. I recall times when it seemed Shalit had been *so* committed to being funny, in his groan-inducing corny way, that I hadn't been able to tell if he'd ever actually gotten around to saying if the movie he'd been reviewing had been any good or not.

But that was the thing with Reed and Shalit and others like them. They weren't there to inform or edify as much as entertain. I've always fancied people were more interested in watching them "perform" than in hearing if they had anything of value to say. And the way they entertained was with a flair for a well-honed but gratuitous bitchiness in their reviews, an edge sometimes bordering on a nastiness and cruelty simply for the fun of being nasty and cruel.

And this was, more or less, the lay of the land, at least as I remember it, when, in 1975, a Chicago PBS affiliate teamed up the film critics from the city's two leading newspapers on a movie review show: Roger Ebert—the first and only film critic to win a Pulitzer Prize—from *The Chicago Sun-Times*, and, from the competing *The Chicago Tribune*, Gene Siskel.

The format of what was then called *Sneak Previews* was staggeringly simple. The two men, seated in a mock cinema balcony (remember movie house balconies anyone?), would screen clips of the week's releases, opinionate on each movie and conclude with a recommended/not recommended vote of thumbs-up/down.

It was also staggeringly effective. In 1978, PBS picked the show up for national telecast. Come 1982, the duo would leave PBS for the still-larger audience—and more lucrative paychecks—of syndication with *At the Movies with Gene Siskel and Roger Ebert,* and then later, in 1986, come out with yet another incarnation in *Siskel and Ebert and the Movies*. The show would be nominated seven times for prime time Emmys, and the two critics would become so recognizable they graduated to the tier of talk show-worthy guests. In 2005, Ebert received what must be considered the ultimate recognition of his prominent standing in the movie universe: a star on the Hollywood Walk of Fame. Try to find another film critic there.

Pairing up the critics did something for the public that stand-alone reviews by stand-alone reviewers didn't do: it gave viewers the ability to compare and contrast two sensibilities as the reviewers argued the merits—or lack thereof—of recent releases. It seems simple enough now, but that kind of back-and-forth was unique at the time.

It helped that they were accessible. Ebert and Siskel didn't talk over viewers' heads, but didn't talk down to them either. Their passion for movies was obvious, especially when they found one they liked, and, more particularly one they *both* liked.

Conversely, as much as they might hate a particular title to the point of denouncing it with scalpel-sharp sarcasm, they still lacked the bitchy cruel-for-cruelty's sake of a Reed or Shalit. For Ebert and Siskel, it wasn't about showcasing their wit as much as it was about making a point.

Whether they were arguing or in rare communion, in the back-and-forthing the show also displayed what any successful TV show has: that ephemeral, unpredictable, often accidental, yet essential quality called *chemistry*.

Ebert and Siskel were perfect for each other. They were intellectual peers so it was always a fair fight and, frankly, when the sparks flew was when the show was at its best... well, at least at its most fun. I know some people watched the show waiting for a spat the way some

NASCAR freaks watch races hoping for the excitement of a crash. There were times the dueling duo were so impassioned in their clash of opinions it seemed they were just a hair's breadth from "Jackass!" "Pinhead!" and throwing Milk Duds at each other.

They even looked great together. People who couldn't remember their names still remembered *them*, even if it was by the rather politically incorrect labels of The Skinny One and The Fat One. They were the Stan & Ollie of film criticism; iconic.

Stephen Whitty, film critic for New Jersey's *The Star-Ledger*, understands the nature of the lightning in a bottle Roger and Gene caught. Asked about it, he says they "… did more than anyone to popularize (film) criticism, and show people just what fun arguing about movies could be…."

And, I suppose, that was the thing. They were fun to watch, but they weren't entertainers. They sometimes stumbled when they talked, they weren't always particularly glib; it wasn't about *them*. It was about *movies*. The fun in watching them sometimes go at each other was knowing it came from the absolute cocksure commitment on each of their parts that they thought the other one—on this one, particular occasion—had his head up his ass. I think that honesty was what people connected with, and what they responded to, and why the show, combined with their unique chemistry, was such a success.

I suspect Ebert—and I'm only guessing here—probably had more mainstream fans than Siskel because he approached movie reviewing from a different perspective. Siskel more or less judged movies against an absolute, whereas Ebert understood some movies were, well, they were what they were… and that was ok. It wasn't about an absolute good or absolute bad, but whether or not a movie did what it set out to do. He explained his philosophy in a 2004 review of *Shaolin Soccer*:

> *When you ask a friend if* Hellboy *is any good, you're not asking if it's any good compared to* Mystic River, *you're asking if it's any good compared to* The Punisher. *And my answer would be, on a scale of one to four, if* Superman *is four, then* Hellboy *is three and* The Punisher *is two. In the same way, if* American Beauty *gets four stars, then* The United States of Leland *clocks in at about two.*

As the show grew in popularity and became more entrenched in the media landscape, the two critics used it as a bully pulpit to regularly bring attention to the small, low-profile art house flicks most average moviegoers didn't even know were out there. Better, they tried to make the case for those movies expressly to that average moviegoer; to demystify for Joe and Joan out-of-the-mainstream flicks, and show they could be just as entertaining, if not more so, than the star-filled big releases taking up three and four screens at the multiplex.

They expanded the format of the show to include occasional one-offs, like their annual Oscar show, or focusing on films of a particular actor, genre, etc. A personal favorite I've always remembered was a compare-and-contrast show they did between the films of Woody Allen and Mel Brooks, then the two kings of the movie comedy heap. It was a great layman's lesson in the evolution of two ultimately opposite comedic sensibilities; the kind of opportunity to broaden mass audience sensibilities TV and TV pundits rarely take.

Gene Siskel died in 1999 of complications from surgery for a cancerous brain tumor. Ebert continued on, first with a rotating series of co-hosts before settling on his *Chicago Sun-Times* colleague Richard Roeper. Roeper was—and is—a capable enough critic, but Siskel's absence showed just how much of the show's charm had been about the spark between he and Ebert. One only had to look at their PBS replacements—Neal Gabler and Jeffrey Lyons (Gabler would leave in 1985 and be replaced by Michael Medved)—to see that as easily as the Ebert/Siskel format was to reproduce, the Ebert/Siskel dynamic was one of a kind. The PBS show was finally cancelled in 1996 while Roger and Gene were still a syndication staple.

And if it proved impossible to follow their act, they still opened a door, making talking about movies something of popular interest. As it happens, while working on this piece, I heard an interview with actor Topher Grace on a New York radio station. Grace knew Bosley Crowther; the critic had introduced Grace's parents. Grace unknowingly told me the difference between pre-E&S and today: "There were, like, a billion less critics in those days."

Everything from Robert Osborne's one-on-one chats on TMC to Rotten Tomatoes, Peter Bart and Peter Guber dissecting the current state of Hollywood on AMC to the bazillion websites devoted to movies (including this one) are all branches off the family tree first planted by Roger and Gene on *Sneak Previews*.

Between 2002 and 2006, Roger Ebert underwent several surgeries for cancer in his thyroid, salivary glands, and jaw. Complications from the surgeries robbed him of his voice, his ability to eat and drink forcing him to be nourished through a feeding tube, and left him seriously scarred. He no longer regularly appears on TV. But, as he has said, though he may not be able to speak, he can still write.

It is the paradox of our visually driven age that Roger Ebert is—and will probably always be—known most for his TV presence. But before then, during, and since, he has first and foremost been a journalist, a chronicler of movies and the business of movies. He may be famous for being on TV, but his reviews, essays, and many books are probably his more substantive contribution, and one he amazingly continues despite his travails. He's put out at least a half-dozen books since his first surgery. It's impossible, even for those who question his taste, not to be impressed by Ebert's choice to keep following the passion that so obviously drives him. "I'm still in awe of his work ethic," says Steven Whitty. "The only thing more remarkable than Roger Ebert's influence... is his indomitability. It's not just that he's still at it, after more than forty years and a host of ailments worthy of Job—it's that he works harder and with more enthusiasm than writers half his age. He's an inspiration to everyone."

CGI and the Banality of the Incredible
(posted 1/2/11)

"If it can be written, or thought," said Stanley Kubrick, "it can be filmed." Kubrick could very well have been articulating the credo for every cinematic explorer of the fantastic since Georges Méliès.

Ironically, Kubrick—who was second to none in pushing the limits of filmmaking technology—several times found himself in the position of *not* being able to turn something written or thought into something filmable. On *2001: A Space Odyssey* (1968), his most aesthetically and technologically daring work, Kubrick wanted to create an alien life form for the film's climax but abandoned the idea after several attempts using various techniques, always feeling the results were unacceptable. Twelve years later on *The Shining*, Kubrick was forced to abandon his plan to bring topiary animals in a haunted hotel's gardens to life when, again, he felt it couldn't be done credibly.

Just a few years after having made *The Shining*, Kubrick might easily have managed to pull off both effects and gone on to create even more remarkable images thanks to Computer-Generated Imagery (CGI). Evolving over the course of three decades, CGI has brought movie-making to that Kubrickian ideal; with CGI, the only limitations on what's possible on screen are the time and money available, and the imagination and expertise of the creative personnel involved. CGI does more than make the impossible possible; its photorealistic capabilities make it credible as well, trumping traditional, more transparent effects like miniatures, puppetry, stop-motion animation, superimposition, split screens, and so on. CGI can make the big bigger, the extravagant ever more spectacular, and the apparently precarious eminently safe.

The critical importance of CGI to commercial moviemaking today is declaratively illustrated by Hollywood's 2010 slate. Although final tallies are yet to come in on such late-year releases as *Gulliver's Travels*, *The Chronicles of Narnia: The Dawn Treader*, *Tron Legacy*, and *Yogi Bear*, going into December nearly half of the year's fifty top-earning releases depended, to some degree, on CGI to carry off their storytelling. In fact, it wouldn't be an understatement to say that at least one-third of 2010's top 100 films probably couldn't have even been *made* were it not for CGI.

It was only a few years after *The Shining* when CGI began to appear in any substantial way in features (although usually in brief sequences), first in *Star Trek II: The Wrath of Khan* (1982), and then in the original *Tron* (1982), a movie which, appropriately enough, was set inside a videogame. In 1984, *The Last Starfighter* used CGI more extensively, using the process to create spaceship-v-spaceship battles in its interplanetary adventure tale. The following year came *Young Sherlock Holmes* and the first fully, three-dimensional photo-realistic fantasy character generated by CGI: a human figure from a stained glass window come to life.

Every year or so thereafter, it seemed the CGI process became more sophisticated, its repertoire of photorealistic fantasy more extensive and effective, its use more versatile. In 1991's thriller *Backdraft,* for example, CGI created controllable flames and convincingly put fire chief Kurt Russell on the collapsing roof of a burning building. Similarly, in *The Fugitive* (1993), CGI made possible Harrison Ford's last-minute leap to safety from in front of an onrushing train, while the following year the process credibly inserted Tom Hanks into any number of real-life historical tableaus in *Forrest Gump.* For period saga *Braveheart* (1995), CGI helped director/star Mel Gibson pump up his $53 million budget to epic proportions, multiplying his hundreds of extras into screen-filling thousands for the movie's grand scale battle scenes. In 2000's *Gladiator,* director Ridley Scott's effects crew digitally grafted actor Oliver Reed's face on to another performer's body to finish out Reed's performance after the actor died before shooting was completed. In 2004, writer/director Kerry Conran shot all of his sci-fier *Sky Captain and the World of Tomorrow* in a studio with just his actors and minimal sets, using CGI to create the rest of a retro-styled futureworld hearkening back to 1930s serials like *Flash Gordon.* The following year, co-directors Robert Rodriguez and Frank Miller did likewise on *Sin City,* this time using CGI to recreate the visual flavor of Miller's graphic novel on which the movie was based. In one pointed illustration of the extent to which CGI technology grants filmmakers unprecedented and total control over content, director Robert Zemeckis used CGI in the 1996 sci-fi adventure *Contact* to—among other more spectacular effects—adjust the position of one of actress Jodie Foster's eyebrows.

Any number of the most notable thrillers produced over the last twenty-five years or so (as well as some of the most forgettable) might not have been possible without CGI. CGI made possible the alternately majestic/terrifying leviathans of *Jurassic Park* (1993), the destructive storms of *Twister* (1996), the crushing waves of *The Perfect Storm* (2000), the alien worlds of the second *Star Wars* trilogy, the here-to-horizon besieging armies of fantasy creatures in *The Lord of the Rings* trilogy, as well as the *X-Men, Spider-Man, The Matrix, Pirates of the Caribbean, Batman,* and *Harry Potter* series' to name a few. It's arguable whether or not the commercial ascendance, proliferation, and box office dominance of the blockbuster over the last several decades would even have been possible without CGI technology.

Since the 1980s, thrillers have grown faster and their action and effects more spectacular as they have come to mimic the non-stop, escalating, action-driven constructs of videogames as well as the restless pace of flipping through a hundred-plus cable channels and cruising the boundless, ever-changing terrain of the Internet. CGI allows moviemakers to take the level, pace, and quantity of action beyond what was possible and/or could be credibly portrayed through more traditional, non-digital forms of special effects, with some moviemakers pushing digital technology still further to replicate even the *look* of videogames.

Sword-and-sandal adventure 300 (2006)—a fanciful telling of the Battle of Thermopylae inspired not by history but by the graphic novel by Frank Miller and Lynn Varley—was largely shot on a soundstage with bare bones sets, with CGI providing most of the settings and nearly everything else, from the portentous skies overhead to the whirling, suspended slow-motion spurts of blood as scantily clad, heavily muscled ancient warriors hacked away at each other. Director Zack Snyder's compositions often replicated the illustrations from the Miller/Varley work exactly, while CGI gave 300 a surface texture and color palette so closely resembling videogame imagery some viewers seeing the film's first teasing TV ads wondered if they were, in fact, watching a promo for a new videogame rather than an upcoming movie release.

Director Robert Zemeckis went one step further with *Beowulf* (2007), a liberal interpretation of the sixth century heroic poem shot entirely on a Culver City sound stage. Zemeckis completely replaced not only physical settings but his actors as well with digital replication through "motion-capture" technology. Motion-capture records the movements and even facial expressions of live actors, using that data as a computerized armature over which is built whatever digitally-created form the moviemaker desires. Motion-capture can provide a natural fluidity of movement as well as a sense of heft not always achieved in wholly computer-generated entities. Director Peter Jackson had used actor Andy Serkis to provide the motion-captured movements for the skeletal Gollum in his *Lord of the Rings* series, and, again, as the basis for the movements of the titular great ape in his 2005 remake of *King Kong*, but these were still digital creations inserted into a live-action context. Zemeckis had previously used motion-capture on his Christmas fantasy, *The Polar Express* (2004), to turn out a completely CGI-rendered movie, and did the same for *Beowulf* but with more refined motion-capture technology. Co-screenwriter Neil Gaman, himself a graphic novelist, caught the photorealist-yet-unreal flavor of the movie's CGI visuals when he said, "Watching this thing is like walking around in a graphic novel."

Freed by an escapism-addicted, sensation-seeking young audience from any obligation to be credible or even remotely possible, excess has become the blockbuster's rule-of-thumb, and CGI technology puts infinite excess within easy reach. Said Rob Moore, president of Paramount marketing and worldwide distribution in an article on *Beowulf,* explaining the blockbuster aesthetic, "For a young audience, this is the world they live in."

But despite the increasing amounts of money, time, effort, and digital technology thrown into creating ever-more-spectacular and first-of-a-kind CGI-visuals, there may be a point of diminishing return to all this eye-drowning, mind-blowing, computer-generated razzle-dazzle. When miracles become commonplace, they no longer seem miraculous, and the gift of CGI is also its curse; the ability to produce miracles on demand for a market constantly demanding ever more amazing miracles.

In 1993, audiences gazing on the truly imposing sight of dinosaurs come to life in *Jurassic Park* felt the same sense of jaw-dropping awe displayed by the movie's human characters. Nothing in movie history could compare to what Steven Spielberg and his CGI crew were able to put on the screen: not the herky-jerky stop-motion-animated lizards of 1950s monster-on-the-loose movies like *The Beast from 20,000 Fathoms* (1953), nor the pet store lizards made up to look like supposedly threatening beasts in Irwin Allen's back lot *The*

Lost World (1960), and certainly not a man in a rubber reptile suit rampaging through a miniature Tokyo in the original *Godzilla* (1954). But as impressive a sight as it was, once the novelty of *Jurassic*'s CGI creations wore off, so did some of their appeal.

Jurassic Park earned a whopping $350.5 million domestic gross, and while its sequels were, without question, major box office successes, none had the same attraction as the original with *The Lost World: Jurassic Park* (1997) earning considerably less with $229.1 million, and *Jurassic Park III* (2001) bringing in $181.2 million. In the same vein, the big budget remake of *Godzilla* (1998) brought in $136 million, Peter Jackson's remake of *King Kong* $218.1 million, and an attempted revival of the monster-on-the-loose vehicle in *Cloverfield* (2008) just $78.8 million.

Similarly, after the debut of CGI-created catastrophic weather in *Twister* ($241.7 million domestic gross), similar meteorological terrors seemed a little less engrossing in *The Perfect Storm* ($182.6 million) and *The Day After Tomorrow* (2004, $186.7 million).

The inspired visuals of the $171.4 million-grossing *The Matrix* (1999) had grown stale by the time of the series' third and final installment—*The Matrix Revolutions*—just four years later. With the novelty gone and the series therefore more reliant on its muddled storytelling and emotionally flattened characters, what had once been mind-blowing had become mind-numbing, and *Revolutions*'s U.S. gross topped out at $139.3 million, particularly disappointing in light of the movie's $150 million cost—almost two and a half times that of the original.

The fall-off in the appeal of sword-and-sandal epics trying to capitalize on the success of *The Lord of the Rings* series is even more marked:

	U.S. gross
The Lord of the Rings: The Fellowship of the Ring (2001)	$314.8 million
The Lord of the Rings: The Two Towers (2002)	340.5
The Lord of the Rings: The Return of the King (2003)	377
Troy (2004)	133.2
Alexander (2004)	34.3
Kingdom of Heaven (2005)	47.4
Prince of Persia: The Sands of Time (2010)	90.8

And so the pattern continues to this day with each new innovation or application of CGI. *300* had been a surprise hit. Despite lacking any major stars and being released in the winter/spring lull of early 2007, the videogamey-looking thriller easily overpowered bad reviews on its way to a U.S. gross of $210.6 million. Released later that same year, the similar-looking and better-reviewed *Beowulf*, made for twice the cost, stalled at $82.2 million.

In his book *Which Lie Did I Tell? More Adventures in the Screen Trade* (Pantheon, 2000), two-time Oscar-winning screenwriter William Goldman recalls walking out of a screening of *The Matrix* suitably impressed by the movie's special effects, but also wondering, "How long will they hold? How long before they look just as dated as (the original) *King Kong* seems to us today?"

The box office scores above suggest they don't hold up very long at all. It may be that in how CGI turns the incredible into the commonplace, it robs spectacle of what had previously been its chief draw; its power to *awe*.

The movies have always relied on special effects magic to do what was either physically or financially impractical. There are no twenty-odd feet tall gorillas, and even if there were, it would hardly be prudent to let one go tearing through midtown Manhattan for the sake of making a movie. Instead, producer/director Merian C. Cooper and his co-director, Ernest B. Schoedsack, set effects wizard Willis O'Brien to sending a twenty-four-inch-tall ape marauding through a miniature model of Manhattan one stop-motion frame at a time for *King Kong* (1933).

But, as long ago as D.W. Griffith's *Intolerance* (1916) and its Babylonian sequence with its monumental 100-feet high sets peopled by thousands of costumed extras, there have, conversely, always been occasions when a filmmaker has decided that the best—and sometimes *only*—way to adequately convey something spectacular is to *do* it: build a full-sized set, engineer an extraordinary physical feat. And so, in 1931, director Wesley Ruggles sent 5,000 extras charging in front of his cameras to recreate the Oklahoma land rush in his epic Western, *Cimarron*; exacting producer David O. Selznick brought to life the burning of Atlanta in his Civil War epic *Gone with the Wind* (1939) by sending his stunt people running past sky-filling flames as MGM torched old back lot sets to represent the burning city; in 1949, when director Henry King needed a B-17 to crash-land in his classic WW II tale, *12 O'Clock High*, stunt pilot Paul Mantz provided the spectacle by really crash-landing one of the bombers for the cameras; for his 1959 version of *Ben-Hur*, director William Wyler felt the only way to pull off the movie's all-time classic action centerpiece—a bitterly contested chariot race—was to construct a full-scale arena filled with 15,000 costumed extras, then send his stunt crew (and, occasionally, his stars) roaring around the track; for the ship-sinking thriller *The Last Voyage* (1960), the producers leased the decommissioned *Ile de France* and partially sunk her; in his quest to make the ultimate war movie, producer Darryl F. Zanuck used 23,000 U.S., British, and French soldiers to recreate the storming of the Normandy beaches for *The Longest Day* (1962).

In the face of such staggering physical productions, it was hard not to be *absorbed;* to look at Japanese planes coming across the waters of the real Pearl Harbor as explosive charges detonated around a full-size, moving replica of the battleship *Nevada* in the 1970 WW II epic *Tora! Tora! Tora!,* and think, *This is what it must have looked like!* What viewer could not have felt the same daunting awe that must have been felt by freedom-seeking slaves facing off against the Roman Empire 2,000 years ago as Stanley Kubrick's cameras caught the massive coordinated maneuvering of his 8,500 uniformed extras during the climactic battle of sword-and-sandal epic *Spartacus* (1960)?

These pre-CGI spectaculars never failed to impress at some level. Because of the great effort and, particularly, expense of executing them, their value was always maintained, at least to some degree, by their comparable rarity. Whether the movies were good or bad, the difficulty in producing them meant any pre-CGI movie of extraordinary scale or marked by special effects wonderment was often a singular event.

Even when a big budget spectacle failed as effective drama, it was still hard not to be taken with the sheer physical accomplishment of, say, the recreation of the Roman Forum in one of the largest outdoor sets ever built for *The Fall of the Roman Empire* (1964), or the sixty-acre replica of Peking c. 1900 for *55 Days at Peking* (1963).

When drama and spectacle meshed and fed each other, few sensations in the American movie canon can match them. When stuntman Bud Ekins (masquerading as escaped WW II POW Steve McQueen) makes his sixty-five-foot motorcycle jump over the German/Swiss border in a bid for freedom, it's an emotional as well as visceral peak for *The Great Escape* (1963), so dramatically resonant it remains one of the iconic moments in American popular movies even as more spectacular stunts have come and been forgotten. The original screenplay for *Spartacus* had no on-screen battles, but Kubrick saw the emotional necessity of adding one to the film's third act; a full-scale depiction of the final battle between the slave army and the massive, almost inhuman might of Roman legions. The sense of the waste and misguided priorities of war finds no better reflection than in a troop train following a collapsing full-scale bridge into the Kwai River at the bitter finale of David Lean's WW II epic, *The Bridge on the River Kwai* (1957).

Having to rely on real world replications could sometimes bring a level of unplanned authenticity to the experience not possible in the totally controlled virtual reality of CGI effects. During a scene depicting Japanese planes strafing an American airfield in *Tora! Tora! Tora!*, effects crews lost control of a taxiing plane, sending stunt men literally running for their lives—a scene the makers kept in the film, and which is one of the most memorable in the movie. The movements of locomotives colliding to sabotage a Nazi train filled with looted French art in John Frankenheimer's WW II thriller *The Train* (1964) were so chaotic, the careening engines destroyed several of the cameras set up to capture the crash while still providing Frankenheimer with one of the best shots from the sequence as one engine unpredictably side-slipped directly into one of the cameras. At one point in the classic chase scene from *The French Connection* (1971), star Gene Hackman's car is sideswiped by a car that had somehow slipped past the production's traffic control. During the chariot race sequence from *Ben-Hur*, Charlton Heston's stunt double, Joe Canutt, was nearly thrown from his chariot during a jump—an action director William Wyler thought so exciting he incorporated it into the scene. That these were unscripted events was often patently obvious and only made what was on-screen seem all that more true-to-life (and exciting), much like the way a well-delivered bit of verbal adlibbing can enliven an actor's performance.

CGI has changed all this. The technology has not only put spectacular visuals and effects within the reach of even modest theatrical releases, but effects dazzle has long since become a routine aspect of popular entertainment. CGI effects are pervasive in TV advertising (the GEICO gecko, for example), and appear throughout the TV spectrum, from expensive broadcast network series like *CSI* and *House*, to cable programming like Syfy's monster-of-the-week original movies, and documentary series like The History Channel's *Dogfights* to name just a very few. Produced for a fraction of a blockbuster's costs, these and many other TV programs now offer better special effects than what had previously appeared in most Hollywood effects showcases throughout the six decades before CGI.

Not only has CGI made it easier to turn out spectacles and effects/action-driven movies, but it has also made it possible for those movies to feature as much action as moviemakers demand, amping the action/effects quotient up to what would have been an impossibly extravagant level in the pre-CGI era to satisfy the expectations of a young audience producer Peter Guber once described as "… weaned on videogames." Instead of *Spartacus's* single battle, *Braveheart, Gladiator,* and 300 offer cascades of escalating CGI-enhanced contests; where Steven Spielberg had to shoot around the cantankerousness of his mechanical shark in *Jaws* (1975), Renny Harlin had a squadron of CGI sharks on a ceaseless prowl in *Deep Blue Sea* (1999). Fleets of spaceships, marauding monsters, aliens and mutants, past and future civilizations, specters and mythological beasties can now be produced on demand in any quantity.

But in this, their prevalence, special effects have, inevitably, become less… *special.*

CGI has created a new baseline for effects showcases and spectacles to the point where what would have been amazing as recently as the early 1980s, is only a starting point for today's theatrical action/effects fests. What would, at one time, have instilled an audience with wonder and amazement has, through its near-constancy, become just so much visual chaff. The ability of CGI to inflate even the most banal of stories to epic proportions in turn pushes thriller-makers to even greater heights of improbability.

Which, it appears, matters little to today's thriller audience.

Consider that among such truly engaging CGI-dependent fare as *Inception, Harry Potter and the Deathly Hallows Part 1,* and Martin Scorsese's more life-sized *Shutter Island* where CGI was used to create psychologically-fractured cop Leonardo DiCaprio's hallucinations, 2010's box office chart toppers also include creative disappointments like *Alice in Wonderland,* and wholly disposable efforts like *Clash of the Titans* and *The Last Airbender.*

It's worth considering just how much dramatic impact would Bud Ekins's *The Great Escape* motorcycle jump have had if, before the movie's release, audiences had seen a segment on *Access Hollywood* or published in *Entertainment Weekly* showing how Ekins and his motorcycle had been suspended by wires in front of a green screen, with CGI filling in the background and barrier fence slipping by below while also extending the jump to an impossible one hundred feet or so? Would the jump have been just as thrilling if audiences had known it wasn't really a jump? That Ekins had been perfectly safe inside a sound stage?

Not only is that kind of artifice (and awareness thereof) commonplace in today's blockbusters and the promotional bombardments that accompany them, but, if box office performances like those cited above are any indication, it has also been embraced by both thriller-makers and their audience. The blockbuster thriller audience has no particular requirement for what they see to be plausible or in any way credible, but simply dazzling.

To be sure, there have been enough underperforming (and some flat-out disastrous) big-budget, effects-filled extravaganzas to demonstrate that spectacular visual effects and action hardly guarantee success, e.g. the 1998 remake of *Godzilla*, *The Hulk* (2003), *Superman Returns* (2006), Peter Jackson's *King Kong*, Harry Potter wannabes *The Golden Compass* (2007) and *The Spiderwick Chronicles* (2008), graphic novel-inspired *The League of Extraordinary Gentlemen* (2003), *The Matrix Revolutions*, *Prince of Persia: The Sands of Time*, and so on.

But at the same time, the box office charts have, for some time, been regularly dominated by dramatically anemic spectacles overstuffed with eye-catching effects and improbable action suggesting the mass audience has willingly exchanged drama and character for often empty spectacle. According to Peter Biskind in his book *Down and Dirty Pictures: Miramax, Sundance, and the Rise of Independent Film* (Simon & Schuster, 2004), mainstream commercial cinema has become monotonously immersed in escapism, improbability, and obvious artifice to the point where the "absence of content has actually become a virtue."

Is Motion Capture A Three-Legged Dog? Discuss
(posted 1/29/12)

Back before the dawn of time when I was in college, there was a neighborhood a few blocks off campus of rental duplexes mostly inhabited by college kids. A lot of them had dogs, and the dogs would pal around together, running up and down in a pack between the duplexes. One of those dogs was Sebastian.

Sebastian was a boxer, about knee-high, and even though he had that grumpy, furrow-browed face boxers have, he was actually a sweet-natured, everybody-pet-me thing. Although he was the tallest of the dogs, he always had trouble keeping up with the rest of the pack because poor Sebastian only had three legs, having lost one after being hit by a car (in that politically incorrect way college kids have, we nicknamed him "Tripod"; insensitive, but granted with affection, I assure you).

Sebastian, as his name suggests, was a male, and I don't think you have to be a dog fancier to know that male dogs pee by lifting a rear leg. What non-fanciers may not know is that males tend to always lift the same leg. Sebastian's wont, as I remember, was to stand on his left while he lifted his right. The car accident had cost Sebastian his left rear leg; the one he was used to standing on.

Here's the thing:

Common sense tells us, OK, the dog loses his left leg, why doesn't he just pee out that way and stand on his good leg?

But as watchers of *America's Funniest Home Videos* know, dogs, having a brain the size of a walnut, don't always have a lot of common sense.

Sebastian had been standing on his left and raising his right since he was a pup, and that little walnut brain had managed to program itself to think that's the way it was supposed to be, come hell or high water or missing limb. So, Sebastian learned to balance himself on his two front legs so he could continue to lift the one rear leg he still had and pee out in the same direction he'd always had.

I remember me and some of the other guys often sitting on one of the duplex porches watching Sebastian go into his two-legged stance (this was years before cable—our entertainment threshold was pretty low), and one or another of us would invariably pronounce some variation of, "That's impressive... but stupid."

As I'm looking over the Sound on Sight Twitter debate about whether or not *The Adventures of Tintin* should be considered an animated film or not, I'm reminded of Sebastian as I consider the whole concept of motion capture technology.

It is impressive, and I don't think it's stupid, but I still get stuck on the question of: *Why?*

Don't get me wrong. There have been things done with motion capture I doubt could have been pulled off any other way: Gollum in *The Lord of the Rings* films, say, or Caesar in *Rise of the Planet of the Apes* (2011; Caesar may be the best thing about *Rise*; maybe the only good thing, depending on your tastes). And so on. It does have a unique value.

But when I look at entire films done in motion capture—like *The Polar Express* (2004), *Beowulf* (2007), and now *Tintin*—I'm a little bit at a loss. How much of a difference would there be in these movies if they were completely digitally animated films rather than mostly animated films with motion capture performers in the leads?

I'll give you Gollum and Caesar, but the knock on most motion capture human characters—and I have to go along with this –is they feel neither animated nor human, but a kind of doughy, plasticky hybrid.

In a more high-tech, more sophisticated way, what's being done with motion capture (and I concede the problem may not be the technology but how it's being applied) reminds me of what Ralph Bakshi tried to do with rotoscoping in movies like *Wizards* (1977), *American Pop* (1981), and his attempt at an animated *The Lord of the Rings* (1978).

In its way, rotoscoping was a primitive form of motion capture: animators would shoot live-action footage, than create animated figures over that footage. Bakshi used the technique as a way of producing animation on tight budgets. In *Wizards*, he built fantastic images atop his live-action figures. But in *Lord*, and especially in *American Pop*, Bakshi used rotoscoping to create more "realistic" animation, so real-worldly critics began to wonder why he was bothering to animate the films at all.

That was Bakshi's three-legged dog: trying to make animation as much like real life as possible. It's a bit paradoxical if you think about it—trying to take a medium to the point where you defeat the very magical qualities so unique about it.

And I'm wondering if at least some of the applications of motion capture aren't the same thing. Do you want a real-feeling Tintin in something so clearly unreal as *The Adventures of Tintin*? Might not *Beowulf* have actually been more impressive if the B-man had, indeed, been a live-action man doing battle with Grendel?

Frankly, I don't know. I'm torn between the ideas that maybe we just haven't learned to use motion capture as well as we might... or that it's a three-legged dog.

But looking at how adamantly people were tweeting about *Tintin*, I thought I'd open the question to all of you out there and see what you have to say.

So, gang, what is it? Is motion capture technology the next evolutionary step in animation? Or maybe it's just a new tool in the toolbox, to be applied judiciously? Or is it "Impressive... but stupid?"

When "Great Leaps Forward" Aren't, or, the Art of Looking Bad
(posted 6/11/12)

I recently came across *Washington Post* critic Ann Hornaday writing about a screening several weeks ago at CinemaCon of ten minutes from Peter Jackson's (and Warner Bros.') attempt to extend the *Lord of the Rings* franchise with *The Hobbit: An Unexpected Journey*. The film is currently slated for release in December of this year. Some of what she had to say has me wondering if looking crappy might not be the new cool for the silver screen.

CinemaCon—or, more formally, the Official Convention of the National Association of Theatre Owners—is an annual come-together in Las Vegas of exhibitors and other industry professionals gathered to see what the studios have coming down the pipeline. Exhibitors have been just as hungry as *LOTR* fans to see if Jackson has pulled off his long buzzed-about four-play. After all, the original trilogy grossed a combined theatrical box office total of nearly $3 billion worldwide. If *Hobbit* plays at the same level, that kind of lobby traffic will move an awful lot of popcorn.

Jackson had startled audiences and woken up the movie industry with how far he'd pushed the use of CGI and motion-capture throughout the *LOTR* films. Though they've become routine now, remember how fresh those from-here-to-the-horizon hordes of invaders looked at the time? And no one had, to that point, used motion-capture as deftly as Jackson had with the obsessed, skeletal Gollum. Match Gollum against CGI-created Jar Jar Binks from George Lucas's second *Star Wars* trilogy, and the consensus is Jackson had out-Lucased Lucas.

Exhibitors had reason to be a little drooly about what Jackson might visually have in store with *The Hobbit*, and they weren't the only ones. *LOTR* fans, sci-fi and fantasy geeks, cinema tech heads and movie hounds have all been sitting up, heads cocked, tongues out, their fingers flying around their keyboards as they've blogged away in a lathered frenzy of anticipation because Jackson has been shooting *The Hobbit* in a new 3-D digital format designed to make previous 3-D processes look like your grandpa's GAF Viewmaster in comparison. The new process shoots film at forty-eight frames per second—twice as fast as the since-anyone-can-remember standard of twenty-four—providing an unprecedented clarity of image.

From what Hornaday says, the new process did exactly what it was supposed to do... and, evidently and ironically, that may be the problem.

The images screened at CinemaCon were so clear, so vivid, they looked more like video than film. And while that seems to have given *Hobbit*'s CGI-rendered critters a unique visual pop, it doesn't seem to have done as well by the movie's humans. According to *Variety*'s Josh L. Dickey, "... human actors seemed overlit and amplified in a way that many compared to modern sports broadcasts... and daytime television."

Hornaday also reports, however, that not everyone was put off by the *Good Morning, America*-ish results of the new process. Let me quote from her story:

> *But at least one film-lover in Vegas liked what he saw. The* Hobbit *footage, wrote online film columnist Jeffrey Wells on his Web site,* Hollywood Elsewhere, *was 'like watching super high-def video, or without that filtered, painterly, brushstroke-y, looking-through-a-window feeling that feature films have delivered since forever.' The high frame rate, he continued, 'removed the artistic scrim or membrane that separates the audience from the performers'.*

I thought Wells' was a remarkable statement because I wouldn't normally consider descriptives like "painterly," "brushstroke-y," and "artistic scrim" a bad thing. It's ironic I came across this story during the same week we've been discussing Ridley Scott's *Prometheus* (2012) and *Blade Runner* (1982) here at Sound on Sight. "Painterly"—and correct me if I'm wrong—is what Scott usually *tries* for.

My take on Wells' comment was it was a bit like saying that the 48 fps process had made a dream seem less, well, *dreamy*... and that that was a good thing.

But then the longer I thought about what he'd said, the more it made a kind of unhappy sense to me.

*****

Providing Mr. Wells isn't just some contrarian who likes to stir the pot to get a good argument going, he may be onto a new, developing visual sensibility.

One reason movies have changed over the years is because the sensibility we bring to watching them has changed. The movies, by and large, of the 1940s look substantially different from the movies of the 1960s and 1970s. The standardized briskly paced, master-medium-close-up formula of Old Hollywood gave way to a European-influenced languor in the 1960s: long shots, long takes (think Altman, Coppola, Kubrick), alternating with an Eisensteinian delight in fracturing space and time (Peckinpah); a veering between dense, naturalistic dialogue (Scorsese and, again, Altman), and a dramatic, almost opaque minimalism (Boorman, Pakula). Those were stylistic changes that worked for the young, cinema-attuned audiences of the time.

Come the 1980s, another change for another audience sensibility. Films became faster (more edits, more beats) reflecting a sensibility first cultivated by cruising through the growing cable spectrum, then by videogaming, then by cruising the infinite variety of the Internet.

Jeffrey Wells may have tipped to yet another evolutionary phase in audience sensibility; something being shaped by the interplay of, principally, two media dynamics.

1. Speed Freaks

Videogames, the Net, talking to each other in 140 characters bits on Twitter, texting during every waking moment because five minutes without some kind of stimulation is a form of mini-death have long had their impact on movie storytelling: hyper-accelerated, action/effects-packed movies that may not make much sense because they don't have to, populated with broad-stroked characters because that breakneck pace won't allow for much more. Think Michael Bay (I try not to).

2. The (Un)Real World

The boom in reality programming since the Writer's Guild strike of 1988, both on the broadcast networks and on cable, is cultivating a generation of audience growing attuned to the unsophisticated, unpolished, unapologetically raw quality of unscripted TV.

Each demographic cohort following the Baby Boomers has been watching less TV than the generation before, and, not coincidentally, spending more time on alternate, generally non-narrative media (online, videogaming, texting, tweeting, etc.). When those younger generations do tune in to TV, they're just as likely to head for cable's more sensational unscripted offerings as for the broadcast nets.

It's primarily a young audience fueling cable successes like MTV's *Teen Mom* (the series' 2009 premiere was MTV's highest-rated launch in over a year) , Comedy Central's *Tosh.0* (which outdraws both *The Daily Show* and *The Colbert Report),* Bravo's various *The Real Housewives of Wherever,* and MTV's ratings monster, *The Jersey Shore* (drawing approximately nine million viewers at its peak putting it on par with a number of broadcast network hits and ahead of shows like *Glee, House,* and *Law & Order: SVU*).

Throw that in with how much time young users spend on YouTube (which accounts for forty-three percent of the online video market and is the third most visited website behind Google and Facebook) watching amateur video, and it's not a hard stretch to conceive of a generation of video viewer for whom the badly lit, badly framed footage produced by non-professionals has become a new standard.

That might—and I emphasize *might* since this is nothing more than an instinctive guess—account for the popularity of "found footage" flicks like the *Paranormal Activity* series (three installments so far with a fourth due in October), *Cloverfield* (2008 with a sequel in the works), *The Last Exorcism* (2010), *The Devil Inside, Chronicle, Project X* (all 2012), and the flick given credit for kicking off the found footage craze, *The Blair Witch Project* (1999).

You mix those two ingredients together and you get an intriguing paradox: an appetite for a more "honest" look, something devoid of the usual studio veneer and artifice, something visually pure and true... in service—at least in the case of *The Hobbit*—of a story that's pure artifice. It's like saying, I want a fairy tale that looks like a hidden camera documentary.

Say *what?*

Why?

*****

If it turns out, in time, Wells is onto something, there's no "why" to it—it's an almost natural by-product of those two cultivating influences. And, to be fair, there's not a "good" or "bad" to it anymore than there was a good or bad to the change in how movies looked from the 1940s to the 1960s. The eye learns to look anew at a new way of looking.

Wells may like the unvarnished quality of this new 3-D, but we've been through this kind of thing before: the Mumblecore movement of the early 2000s, and before that, Lars von Trier and his Dogme 95 disciples, each looking for something more natural, more real, something *honest*.

Which it never really is, particularly—as is the case with a number of Mumblecore and Dogme 95 films—when it's in service of stories that are, in their own, *faux* naturalistic way, as contrived and manipulated as an old-fashioned, high-gloss studio "meller." *Dancer in the Dark* (2000) isn't any more life-like than *Tyler Perry's Good Deeds* (2012). It just does a better job of *looking* more life-like.

Being enthused about how Gandalf *won't* look like a carefully crafted, studio-polished, CGI-enhanced envisioning, but, instead, like somebody being quizzed by Matt Lauer isn't something I can quite plug into. There's a part of me that, intellectually, gets what Wells is saying. But there's another part of me that keeps saying, "Dude, ya know the guy's a *wizard*, right?"

*****

Every step forward usually requires leaving something behind, and if this is, indeed, the direction the crowd is taking, I'm going to miss that painterly and—God forbid!—artistic look.

When I was a film student a few million years ago, I remember a discussion about comparing film to other forms. Yeah, you sat in a theater and watched the action play out in the proscenium of the screen, but it wasn't like theater. Stories played out often like novels, but it couldn't go interior the way novels could; nope, it wasn't quite like a novel.

The closest we could approximate was a movie was like a dream.

Like dreams, movies range from the brutally real to the utterly fantastic, but always have their own, consistent (when done well) logic. In the hands of a good director, a movie *feels* real although it's intangible. In fact, it's that very intangibility—its unreal-ness—that fosters the illusion of reality. Wells is right; there has always been a separation between the audience and the performance in movies, but it's that inability by the audience to reach beyond that "artistic scrim" and disrupt the dream that keeps the dream intact and makes it real.

You stare at a painting, you get lost in the painting. But then you stand too close, close enough to see the blots and brushstrokes, and the illusion dies. Wells seems to think that's a good thing... or believes it won't kill the illusion.

Even at their most earnest, movies have only ever given a creative impression of reality. The shadowy *noirs* of the 1950s were more emotionally honest than the glossy melodramas of the 1930s, but, in their own way, they were just as stylized; just as the milestone flicks of the 1960s were stylized in a different way, but with the same intention of reflecting something of the complexity and ambiguity of the real world.

The second a director—even a documentary director—decides what goes in the frame, that he grants a figure power with an up-angle, mystery by cloaking it in shadow, or fakes authenticity with a handheld camera, he or she has manipulated reality, and any talk of visual purity after that is pointless. The magic of movies, just as with any magic trick, has been in convincing us that what couldn't possibly be real *is* real. Once we see it's just a trick, it's not magic anymore.

Will The Hobbit's New Tech Be Enough to Satisfy Audiences?
(posted 8/2/12)

As a rule, I don't revisit a subject (well, not often), but a recent *USA Today* story by Brian Truitt spurred me to go back to a piece I wrote last month triggered by a *Washington Post* story about Peter Jackson's screening of ten minutes of his upcoming *The Hobbit: An Unexpected Journey* at CinemaCon.

Jackson is shooting *Hobbit* in a new digital forty-eight frames-per-second format, which gives the image a startling clarity—according to the *Post*'s Ann Hornaday, maybe a bit *too* much clarity for some eyes.

Jackson is still pushing the 48 fps format not just because of how it enhances *Hobbit*, or even as the next big technological advance in filmmaking, but as a matter of industry survival. Let me quote from Truitt's story:

> ... Jackson predicts that by the time <u>The Hobbit</u> is released, there will be several tent-pole movies that will be using the technology. If not, he says, the industry might as well throw in the towel.
>
> "While audiences are dwindling, while kids don't come to the movies anymore because they're happy to watch films on their iPads, do we all sit back and celebrate the technology of 1927 and say, 'Wow, let's not do anything with it because that's the look of cinema?' Or do we try to get all these audiences to come back to the movies by saying, 'You know what, this is really cool?' It's going to be like you're really there."

If anybody knows how to push technology to entrance an audience, it's Jackson, even more so than that great pioneering cinematic technocrat, George Lucas. In his *Lord of the Rings* trilogy, Jackson pushed CGI effects to the limit with his horizon-filling battles, his it's-alive! rendering of Gollum—all of it credible, believable, and backed with heart and drama in a way few tech savvy filmmakers have managed. I'd argue that even in his disappointing *King Kong* (2005), Jackson's demonstration of turning the most incredible ideas into credible CGI-generated imagery is impressive.

And that's why I think—unless he's just dishing out prerelease hype for his film—Jackson should know better.

Screenwriter William Goldman once told the story of coming out of a screening of *The Matrix* (1999) amazed at the film's effects, but also wondering how long it would take before what at first seemed fresh, novel, and dazzling, became routine. The answer: by *The Matrix Revolutions* just four years later. What had seemed equally dazzling in Jackson's *LOTR* trilogy was almost immediately beaten lifeless through overuse by the host of sword-and-sandal epics that tried to capitalize on Jackson's successes (e.g. *Alexander* [2004], *Troy* [2004], *Kingdom of Heaven* [2005]). It only took a few years for what Jackson had managed to create to acquire a tired been-there-done-that feel.

The capper is despite *LOTR*'s phenomenal box office success, neither the trilogy nor its technological advances did much to stem sliding attendance numbers; a slide that has, with an upward bump here and there, been ongoing since 2003.

In fact, technology has a pretty lousy record in Hollywood as a cure for attendance ills. The 1950s saw the industry pulling everything out of its magic tech hat but a rabbit: wide screen, stereo sound, broader use of color, 3-D, and such off-the-wall gimmicks as Smell-O-Vision and Emergo-Vision, and the like to stem an attendance bleed dating to 1945. OK, they weren't all great ideas (or even particularly good ones; Smell-O-Vision?), but wide screen, color, stereo were popular enough to become industry standards, yet attendance *still* dropped and didn't bottom out until the early 1970s.

Even the recent reintroduction of 3-D (at least the third go-around for the format by my count) hasn't done much for attendance. Oh, 3-D surcharges have boosted revenues, but once the initial oh-wow novelty response passed, it hasn't done much to put more tushes in theater seats. That leads me to wonder why Jackson thinks the 48 fps format will play out any differently. I think—as did the 3-D proponents of just a few years ago—he's missing the central issue entirely.

Ironically, the filmmaker inadvertently put his finger square on the problem: "... kids don't come to the movies anymore because they're happy to watch films on their iPads..." That young, dwindling audience Jackson is trying to lure back with technological muscle is already opting to watch movies on a small screen (one would argue the smallest screen outside of smart phones) and hear sound through either a dinky, tinny speaker or through earphones. This isn't about providing that audience with a visually impressive offering; this is about a fundamental change in the movie-watching sensibility: in my lap over the theater, on my schedule not the theater's, at my pace pausing when I want for as long as I want, giving it as much or as little attention as I want. Jackson's treasured 48 fps—as stunning as it might be (initially)—doesn't address any of that.

According to Truitt, Jackson says, "The entire industry is in some respect waiting to see what happens with *The Hobbit*," and I think he's right. For going on a decade, the industry has been hoping and praying for some sort of magic bullet to stem the ebbing attendance tide. Improved CGI didn't do it, motion-capture didn't do it, 3-D didn't do it, and now they're hoping, according to the filmmaker, 48 fps will do it.

And, it's entirely possible that, for a little while, it may. But it doesn't take long in this tech-saturated environment with its dizzying evolutionary clip for the new to grow old, for dazzle to dull. Peter Jackson could turn out a prequel the qualitative equal of his *LOTR* films, but in a form even more visually arresting… only to find that the audience he chased at the rate of 48 fps prefers to wait until they can download it onto their laptops.

We Live In A 3-D World—Or Do We?
(posted 12/29/12)

"We live in a three-dimensional world," James Cameron admonished Hollywood a few weeks ago on the opening of *Life of Pi*. Calling Ang Lee's film some of the best use of 3-D since his own *Avatar* (2009). Cameron was trying to push the movie industry—as he has been for some time—toward a more full-bore commitment to 3-D filmmaking. The approximately forty 3-D titles slated for release in 2013, evidently, still represents only a chicken-hearted effort in Cameron's eyes.

What Cameron has been hoping for with *Pi* is that the movie shows 3-D to be more than a gimmick for action flicks like *The Avengers*; that 3-D can be used eloquently in movies that aren't about pyrotechnics and superheroes sailing through the air, that it isn't just for making the fanboys chuckle with glee as they duck 3-D ejecta. *Pi*, in Lee's more than capable hands, uses 3-D to draw people deeper into a reflective, even spiritual movie, and Hollywood is wearing blinders if they don't see the greater dramatic possibilities for applying the process.

Well, that's his thesis. It's doubtful *Pi* is going to clinch that argument. If anything, *Pi* may be the pistol Cameron shoots himself and his case in the foot with.

It's a question of math. *Pi* cost about $120 million. The rule of thumb is that a film needs to gross two-three times its budget to reach breakeven, which puts the level at which 20th Century Fox's accountants can breathe easy on *Pi* at somewhere between $240-360 million.

Life of Pi's domestic gross after five weeks of release is a hair over $76 million.

To be fair, it's done quite well overseas, with its total worldwide take now standing at $235.8 million. That, however, doesn't take into account overseas marketing costs. Still, the movie has held remarkably steady in the marketplace with its week-to-week falloff on the domestic scene averaging just thirty-six percent (want a comparison? *The Hobbit: An Unexpected Journey* dropped almost fifty-seven percent from week one to week two, while *The Twilight Saga: Breaking Dawn Part 2* has averaged a week-to-week drop of fifty-four percent).

But, as I say, it's a question of math, and the math says that while *Pi* will probably hit breakeven—well, crawl to it, actually—it's hardly shown itself to be a home run.

Here's some more math: Lee himself estimates that about a quarter of the budget was due to the added costs of shooting in 3-D. Without it, breakeven could have been as low as $180 million meaning that, by now, a non-3-D *Pi* would've been in the black.

Yeah, Bill, but would that many people have come if the movie hadn't been in 3-D?

Good question.

The track record for 3-D is a checkered one. It's sure as hell boosted the bottom line on movies like *The Avengers, Brave, The Amazing Spider-Man*. It doesn't look like it helped clunkers like *Underworld: Awakening, Ghost Rider: Spirit of Vengeance, Dredd, Abraham Lincoln: Vampire Hunter*, or *Piranha 3DD* whose domestic gross didn't even break $400,000 (that's right: four hundred thousand bucks).

Probably most telling, despite universally glowing reviews, 3-D couldn't get people in to see the Tim Burton animated delight, *Frankenweenie*, while the generally panned 3-D toon *Hotel Transylvania* has already got Sony talking sequel.

Conclusion: if people're gonna go, they're gonna go, and if they ain't gonna go, they ain't gonna go, 3-D be 3-damned.

Funny thing: Cameron's already been burned once trying to make this case. Let's flashback to last year and see if you remember this scenario:

A 3-D feature based on an acclaimed literary work, a master filmmaker at the helm, universal critical acclaim and a bucketful of Oscar nods to boot, and there's Cameron calling the flick—I kid you not—the best use of 3-D since his own *Avatar*. Remember it?

It was Martin Scorsese's *Hugo*, an adaptation of Brian Selznick's *The Invention of Hugo Cabret*. The movie's worldwide gross was $185.8 million. The production tab was $156 million (putting breakeven north of $300 million at a minimum) meaning that even after you roll in DVD and Netflix sales, TV rights, etc., Paramount still comes up a loser.

Pi may offer an improvement on that but not a definitive rebuke.

But this leads to a bigger question.

Here's Cameron, yet again, beating the drums for 3-D. At the same time, there's Peter Jackson calling his forty-eight frames-per-second 3-D he used in *The Hobbit* the salvation of the movie business. And if you don't want to see these comin'-at-ya flicks in the theater, you can get yourself a sixty-inch flat screen TV and watch them in all their head-ducking, stereophonic, multi-dimensional glory at home.

Meanwhile, there's a growing young audience spending most of their viewing time in front of dinky screens with dinkier speakers, and it gets me wondering if the hi-tech boys aren't running a helluva race flat-out but in the wrong direction?

*****

Laptops are getting smaller, phone video screens are getting bigger, and Amazon's Kindle Fire tablet—with an 8.9 inch screen—is aimed at eating into the movie-streaming market that used to belong to the laptop.

So the question I ask is: what's the point of adding twenty, thirty, forty million to your production budget to make your movie visually spectacular in a state-of-the-visual-arts way just so somebody can watch it on his/her four-inch iPhone screen while they're waiting for the bus?

The visual sensibility may be changing in a way that state-of-the-art big screen moviemaking doesn't address. And it's not the first time.

Back in the late 1970s and early 1980s, two technologies were battling it out for supremacy in the new home video market: Betamax and VHS. Beta provided the better picture, but you could cram more stuff on a VHS tape (two hours vs. Beta's sixty minutes). If you were willing to record at the slowest of VHS's three rates and tolerate the crappy video and audio quality that went with it, you could get six hours of programming on a single tape.

That was the choice: better picture and sound, or six ugly hours of movies cribbed off HBO.

The market went to the six ugly hours.

And don't even get me started on what happened to the poor LaserDisc that provided signal and audio quality superior to both… but you couldn't record at all.

"The best" is not always what people want, otherwise more people would be eating French pastry with their coffee instead of Dunkin' Donuts.

I don't pretend to know where this is going. The multi-platform arena is nothing short of chaotic. New devices cannonball into the market with bewildering frequency, offering an ever-expanding range of apps for a market that seems to have an insatiable appetite for the next new thing, eager to toss away yesterday's gizmo for today's, even before they know whether it offers any practical advantage over what they just tossed. One evolutionary phase has barely begun before it gets steamrollered over by another.

The sensibility that gizmo-makers are chasing seems, to an old pre-millennial like me, to be just as chaotic, just as ever-changing as it gloms on to each new thing. Traditional TV and movie programming don't have the same hold on the attention of the new generation of audience as they did on that of their parents.

James Cameron is easily one of Hollywood's great tech geeks, second to none in his belief in the value of what the new can bring to the movies. But just in the fact that he's still talking in terms of movies, I'm wondering if Cameron the tech pioneer isn't something of a dinosaur himself.

The World's First Screenwriter: Aristotle
(posted 12/8/10)

Measured against the guidelines for creating good drama as articulated by Aristotle in his *Poetics* a few millennia ago—the earliest surviving treatise on literary theory—many of the big-budget studio releases of the last twenty to thirty years stand pretty feebly. While some might understandably wonder whether anything *anybody* said about good stage drama nearly 2,400 years ago has any relevance to movies today, Michael Tierno, a one-time story analyst for Miramax Pictures, says, firmly, *yes!* Taking it a step further, Tierno maintains the Greek philosopher's tenets of dramaturgy have held first playwrights, then screen scenarists and TV writers in good stead for centuries. Tierno set that credo down in his book, *Aristotle's Poetics for Screenwriters: Storytelling Secrets from the Greatest Mind in Western Civilization* (Hyperion, 2002), applying the ancient Greek's primordial how-to concepts to such contemporary fare as *The Godfather* (1972), *Rocky* (1976), and even the hyperkinetic, chronological juggling act of *Pulp Fiction* (1994).

Tierno's assessment of so much of what is on screen today is that the typical big-budget action-fest elevates to the fore the element of dramatic storytelling Aristotle considered to be "... the *least* important": spectacle.

The Greek philosopher divided drama into six component parts. In order of importance, they're:

Plot
Character
Character thought
Dialogue
Music
Spectacle

The Aristotelian concept of spectacle in drama is different from what we think of in using the word today. Aristotle did not mean epic scope or eye-dazzling production values. By spectacle, he meant the substance of the medium itself; elements Tierno identifies in film as cinematography, editing, production design, and the other physical makings. His interpretation of Aristotle's prioritizing of spectacle is that the dramatic storyteller become not so steeped in the mechanism that he/she forgets the human dynamic of the story. "But that's what film schools emphasize," he says. "Tell the story *visually*, they keep saying, so these young filmmakers ignore things like dialogue and character."

Tierno speaks with a table-banging passion about the necessity of character, and how little of what passes for such in modern-day films really is character. "Character is not this contemporary idea of funny quirks and traits," he says. "Character is the moral choices that reveal who the character is." He refers to the concept of the "mental object," which might be most easily transposed to the idea of *story* v. *plot*. *Plot* is generally perceived as the sequence of events we see unfold, while *story* is something deeper and more abstract; it is very much a part of the drama in front of us without actually being seen.

As an example, Tierno cites the restaurant assassination scene from *The Godfather*. Al Pacino, playing the son of crime lord Marlon Brando, meets with corrupt police captain Sterling Hayden and ambitious narcotics peddler Al Lettieri, ostensibly to discuss a gang war truce, but actually to kill them both to avenge their attempted murder of his father. The incident is pivotal not just in terms of the plot, but in its impact on the emotional and psychological subtext of the movie.

Pacino's killing of the two men pushes him from his law-abiding arm's-length relationship with his father's occupation into a morally corroding slide, which will leave him steeped, by the end of the movie, in self-rationalized evil. "That's what I mean by a 'mental object'," says Tierno. "The mental object of that scene is not just what Michael Corleone (Pacino) is going into that restaurant to do; it's about what the act will cost him." This, Tierno explains, is what Aristotle meant by the concept of "character thought"; not what we *see*, but what we *understand* to be in the character's head.

If today's big budget movies come up short on story and character, Tierno fails them equally on the matter of plot, despite their often non-stop action. "Aristotle says that your plot should be so strong that if you related it to somebody, they should be as moved as if they had actually seen it." In a world of fifteen-minute pitch meetings and thirty-second TV promotional spots, the opportunity to develop those kinds of plots are rare at the major studio level. Tierno sees the current studio mentality as being, "We're gonna *spend* a lotta money to *make* a lotta money" i.e. spectacle. And, unfortunately for

Aristotle and his aesthetic disciples, audiences for these kinds of films "... interpret that expenditure as value."

Tierno, whose own passion found its put-up-or-shut-up moment in writing and directing his self-financed feature, *Auditions* (1999), looks at what pours into multiplexes each summer and shakes his head. "You need to make the film *you* want to see. Trying to guess what the audience wants produces empty films. There is no soul there."

Taxman and the Box Office
(posted 4/16/11)

It's tax time, so what better time to talk money.

Sky-high budgets, costly marketing blitzes, revenues siphoned off by profit participants—it's never been harder for a studio to make back its ever-increasing outlays. Even with sharp increases in ticket prices, recoupment for a studio is anything but assured. In 1990, the average movie's production cost ($18.1 million) stood at more than four million times the price of the average admission ticket ($4.11); just ten years later, the proportion grew almost three-fold, to better than 11 million times, despite an approximate thirteen percent hike in the average ticket price ($52.7 million/$4.69). This, in turn, has forced a drastic evolution not only in how studios attempt recoupment, but the financial dynamic that occurs in every multiplex and its direct impact on the consumer.

More simply: we're going to answer the question of why you need a second mortgage to buy a king-sized Coke and a bucket of popcorn.

The transformation of exhibition from a circuit of primarily single-screen auditoriums to today's multiplex-dominated environment was a move on the part of exhibitors to build themselves a cushion against weak-performing flicks. Multi-screen theaters had been around since the 1930s, but the concept flourished in the 1980s, piggy-backing on the explosive growth of suburban shopping malls and plazas that often incorporated a movie theater.

The concept was always very simple. A plex theater's fortunes didn't live or die week-to-week with the strength/weakness of the feature on any one screen. Multiple screens meant a dud on one screen could be offset by a hit on another. Advances in automated projection technology eliminated the need for projectionists and made multiplex operations highly cost-efficient (it is also, however, the reason that finding a plex staffer who can fix a projection problem has turned into such a monumental task for patrons; back in The Day, a simple disgruntled yell of, "Focus!" aimed at the projection booth used to suffice).

As Hollywood became more addicted to the outsized box office possibilities of big budget blockbuster flicks, multiplex operators saw an opportunity to maximize their gate by ironically offering *fewer* choices and running heavily hyped major releases on multiple screens, particularly during the first weeks of release.

The payoff in doing so, however, wasn't in the money earned at the box office which—even with monster hits—isn't what you'd think it might be.

Ever since the 1948 decrees separating studios from their theater chains, box office receipts have been split between exhibitor and distributor. Typically, approximately forty-five percent of a venue's box office goes to the exhibitor. For blockbusters, though, the studios have—by necessity—imposed a harsh change in the formula, one based on a sliding scale in which, during the early part of the run, the overwhelming bulk of the box office goes to the distributor, with the percentage gradually swinging toward the exhibitor with each passing week.

As recently as the 1990s, studios had been demanding extended minimum-run commitments from exhibitors on major releases. George Lucas, for example, exacted twelve-week guarantees from exhibitors wanting to screen *Star Wars: Episode 1—The Phantom Menace* (1999). What made such a demand digestible to exhibitors was the belief that the movie would continue to perform well enough weeks into its run to provide the theater with an eventual pay-off for its commitment.

In most cases, however, today's foreshortened box office arcs have distributors asking for as much as 100% (yeah, you read that right) of gross ticket revenue during the biggest-earning opening week with the percentage not swinging toward the exhibitor's favor until a movie's drawing power is well—and quickly—on the wane (major releases typically earn as much as fifty to seventy-five percent of their total take by their third weekend in release, with receipts dropping by approximately a half or better week-to-week). As one studio executive put it, "When you know that there's another blockbuster a week behind you, you want to earn as much as you can as quickly as you can." With such one-sided box office splits, the exhibitor usually operates his blockbuster-dedicated auditorium at a loss, with only a slim chance the picture will still be throwing off enough revenue after the box office split turns in his favor to be profitable for the venue.

The most obvious and predictable effect of this dynamic at the exhibition level has been a boost in ticket prices well above the rate of inflation. In 1963, the average ticket price was $.83; twenty years later, it stood at $3.15; in 2007, $6.74; today, somewhere around $7.50, and typically over $10 in theaters charging extra for 3-D screenings. In some major urban markets, like New York City for example, base ticket prices have been over $10.00 for several years. Still, even as ticket prices continue to climb, with an exhibitor turning over the bulk of the gate to the distributor, the theater-retained percentage is still only enough, at best, to moderate an exhibitor's loss rather than generate a significant profit.

Unsurprisingly, then, theater managers have turned to a variety of tactics to augment their revenues. Strategies include offering auditoriums for meeting rentals, hosting children's birthday parties, and, most visibly, providing a venue for advertising. As part of their film program, as well as appearing on-screen between scheduled features, multiplexes are turning over increasing amounts of screen time to local and national advertising. One newspaper account of multiplex advertising in New Jersey venues clocked five to six minutes of advertising as a typical part of the feature program on top of the interstitial time given over to slide ads. While many moviegoers may rankle at being a captive audience for multiplex advertising, "The majority of theaters," says one small theater chain operator in New Jersey, "are doing it because it does help defray costs." According to the National Association of Theater Owners, on-screen advertising is a necessary tool for theaters to "... keep ticket prices affordable..." (although as ticket prices continue to climb, one wonders about NATO's idea of "affordable"). By the middle of the first decade of the 2000s, movie house advertising had become a $300 million a year business, with two-thirds of the U.S.' 36,000 screens showing ads. By 2009, the theater take from ads was up to $584 million.

The biggest revenue-generator for exhibitors, however, is not the box office nor its on-screen advertising business, but the area of concessions. In effect, as big-budget blockbusters have steered studios from the movie-making business into the event-hyping business, the studios' lopsided box office splits have steered movie theaters from the movie exhibiting business into the snack food vending trade.

Profits earned by a theater's concession stand belong wholly to the theater. In fact, during the early part of a blockbuster's run where the lion's share of the box office is dedicated to the distributor, cash from the snack bar may be the only profit the theater sees. This explains not only the stratospheric mark-up on snack bar items (a story in *Playboy* put the markup on a bucket of popcorn around 1,300% making it bite-for-bite as expensive as filet mignon) and aggressive "upselling" (pushing "supersize" portions and special "combo" offerings), but the expansion of snack bar menus far beyond the traditional offerings of soft drinks, candy, and popcorn. A tour of several multiplexes in Manhattan and suburban New Jersey finds concession stands offering, along with the usual sodas, candy, etc.: hot dogs, nachos and hot cheese, French fries, chicken fingers, "personal-sized" pan pizzas, popcorn shrimp, and cappuccino/espresso bars complete with muffins, scones, and cakes.

Some theaters have gone one step further, turning a visit to the multiplex into an exercise in (sometimes) fine dining as well... with prices to match. AMC Theatres has rolled out their Cinema Suite concept at a few locations in Kansas, Texas, and New Jersey. Your $30 admission (that's right; *thirty* bucks... *apiece*) gets you a non-refundable $20 food coupon with your ticket, an auditorium with reclining leather seats, and attendants serving you everything from a traditional popcorn-and-soda movie nosh to a full dinner from the house menu. Other exhibitors—the Academy Theater in Portland, Oregon; the Alamo Drafthouse with locations in Texas and Virginia; the Theatres at Canal Place in New Orleans—offer similar evolutionary leaps in the concessionary arts with offerings ranging from cocktails and local microbrews (the Academy) to a Mediterranean-flavored menu put together by a gourmet chef (the Theatres at Canal Place). In most cases, combining dinner and a movie into a one-stop event including $8.75 Tanqueray gin and Cointreau cocktails (Seattle's The Big Picture) and $18.50 *churrasco* steaks (Miami's Cinebistro) can easily run up the tab for a couple's movie night close to three digits. The price of a family night out? Bring some collateral with you.

At the risk of seeming curmudgeonly nostalgic, it does seem there was a time when people went to the movies to see a movie. Snacks were, well, just that: *snacks*. Something to hold you over until the movie was over.

But, in an era of declining attendance and one-sided receipts splits, exhibitors seem to be turning the movie part of going to the movies into an afterthought.

"Your drinks, madam, sir."

"Oh, why thank you. Mmm, these are quite good!"

"Thank you. Your dinner will be out in a moment. The movie starts in five minutes."

"Oh, we get a movie, too? Fancy that! What'll they think of next?"

The Piracy Wars: No White Hats Here
(posted 3/13/12)

It's strange how the mind works; the odd connections it can sometimes make. I've been reading a few articles recently that have brought to mind the 2003 Errol Morris documentary, *The Fog of War: Eleven Lessons from the Life of Robert S. McNamara,* an extended self-critical analysis by the Kennedy/Johnson Secretary of Defense often considered the architect of the policies that went oh-so-wrong in Vietnam. Four of his eleven lessons in particular lit up for me:

> **Empathize with your enemy,** meaning see the world through their eyes; understand their values, goals, what is important to them, what they see as a threat and why;
> **There's something beyond one's self**, which I take to mean to avoid judging other parties by your own values;
> **Get the data,** which seems self-explanatory;
> And **be prepared to reexamine your reasoning,** which is a diplomatic way of saying never take off the table the possibility that you're—at least in part and maybe *en toto*—really *really* wrong.

The odd connection at work here is that what brought these savvy tips to mind wasn't the latest flap in the current extraordinarily vicious political campaign, or some foreign policy Quran-burning gaffe or anything like that. Rather, it was several articles on content piracy (yeah, I know; it seems a reach, but I did say minds work in strange ways, at least mine does).

The reason I made these connections to McNamara's tenets was that after reading them, it finally occurred to me the piracy debate isn't about legal and/or moral rights, although it's often positioned that way. No, it's a culture war; a combat between two opposing worldviews, neither of which, I fear, quite understands the other, neither of which can—or is willing to—get past its own inflexible standards of what should and shouldn't be, neither of which seems to have any clear idea of the possible impact their stands can have on the media terrain years down the road.

Or, to put it simply and bluntly, both sides are doing an awful lot of talkin' but not a hell of a lot of listenin'… or, for that matter, much clear thinkin'.

*****

A few weeks ago, a student in one of my university classes emailed me a link to a February 3 article on Forbes.com: "You Will Never Kill Piracy and Piracy Will Never Kill You." The author is a bright twenty-something gentleman named Paul Tassi. According to Tassi's bio, he is the editor-in-chief of Unreality, a film/TV/gaming site he founded, and is also the movie news editor at JoBlo.com. He typically contributes to Forbes.com on the videogame industry, and prides himself on being "... part of the first generation of journalists to skip print media entirely."

Tassi puts forward a couple of theses about video piracy in the article that tripped the McNamara warnings for me. For one thing, he doesn't consider video piracy to really be piracy: "Piracy is not raiding and plundering Best Buys and FYEs, smashing the windows and running out with the loot... when you take a copy of (a) movie, another one materializes in its place, so you're not actually taking anything..." ergo "The movie and music industries' claim that each (pirated) download is a lost sale is absurd."

Tassi also suggests that content controllers—the movie studios, in this case—kinda/sorta bring it on themselves: "The primary problem movie studios have to realize is that *everything* they charge for is *massively* overpriced" and that they have also "... failed to realize that people want things to be easy." The effort of going to the movies is demanding enough, says Tassi, but particularly onerous at current outrageous ticket prices and ditto for buying DVDs.

Tassi's bottom line is that the studios will never gain a step on pirates. Pirating technology, he asserts, will always be ahead of protective technologies. As for the controls content providers advocate—like the defeated SOPA and PIPA bills—those are a form of censorship of the Internet for the purpose of "... studio and label executives (adding) a few more millions onto their already enormous money pile." Their best anti-piracy strategy, says Tassi, is to provide content at the low prices and with the easy access Internet users want.

In a follow up article less than a week later ("Lies, Damned Lies and Piracy"), Tassi went even further positing that the entertainment industry's Chicken Little run-in-circles-scream-and-shout attitude about content piracy is "... way more smoke than fire, and if you were to actually look at the numbers, the entertainment industry isn't suffering the way they claim they are at the hands of file-sharers."

Tassi's comments jibe with a post that recently came up in Sound on Sight's Tumblr account from Paralegal.net: "How Hollywood Is Using Piracy Against Us." Paralegal looks at the 120-odd year history of the motion picture in America to call the movie industry's current anti-piracy stance hypocritical, and also that Hollywood's own numbers don't justify its assertion that piracy is a dagger held against the industry's financial jugular.

As it happens, about the same time I was mulling over these pieces, the issue spilled over into the mainstream press with a 2/19/12 Associated Press story by Martha Irvine. According to Irvine, piracy—at least at a certain generational level—is so rife as to be some kind of norm. She cites a recent Columbia University survey that found "… that 70% of 18- to 29-year-olds said they had bought, copied or downloaded unauthorized music, TV shows or movies, compared with 46% of all adults who'd done the same." Irvine reports there is a view among users that their piracy isn't the problem. "The real problem," according to a quoted Drexel University law student, "is… a failure to innovate on the part of content providers."

Going to my point that this is less about who deserves to get what and for how much than it is about two mindsets trying to decide how to define the alternate media universe, Irvine quotes Joe Karaganis, vice president of the American Assembly, a public policy institute at Columbia University, as describing the anti-anti-piracy voice as signifying "… the emergence of a real *social movement* around these issues" *(italics mine)*.

This isn't a business issue. This isn't a copyright issue. *This* is *war!*

And caught in the crossfire between the content users and the content providers, unheard when not simply ignored, suffering, as they usually do, the collateral damage from the bombs being dropped by both sides, are the content *creators*.

But when did anybody ever care about them?

*****

If you want to put forth the proposition the studios and TV networks and record labels are run by a bunch of money-grubbing robber barons, you won't get much argument from me. Or from talent, or craft unions, or anybody else who doesn't sit in the executive suites, hold a desk at the banks providing them with their credit lines, or own a share of stock. Just don't expect me to be terribly surprised or shocked and appalled—*shocked* and *appalled,* I say!—at the news. Telling me these companies are driven by greed is like telling me Al Capone was only in business for the money. No kidding.

Without disagreeing with content users who do seem—God knows why—shocked and appalled by this, I would only point out that outfits like 20th Century Fox and Warner Music and Disney and all the rest of the media empires are not PBS. They were never set up with the intention of being only modestly profitable enterprises. Charlie Chaplin didn't make movies for scale, so none of this is exactly news.

Nor is it any great revelation that Hollywood—or much of the rest of the traditional entertainment business—is behind the curve on effectively adapting to the Internet. Hollywood, for one, has a long, sorry history of being a late adapter, and only then of making belated changes out of desperation. The movies didn't want the expense of converting to sound; they were doing quite well without it, thank you. But a struggling Warner Bros. needed a gimmick to stay afloat and sound was their Hail Mary pass. Wide screen, color, stereophonic sound; more woefully late advances to beat back TV after Hollywood had already underestimated both the staying power and popularity of the upstart medium. Cable, the home VCR; the same initial denial, then panic, and then a shamefully tardy recognition that, "Hey, ya know, we can actually make money with this!"

About the only time I can recall the movie business getting the jump on a new technology was with the introduction of the DVD. Hollywood had always felt burned about how the VHS business had played out. The high prices set at first-issue for VHS releases had meant few individual consumers bought tapes; most were purchased by video stores and used as rentals. Hollywood looked at all that rental revenue in which it didn't share, and never forgave itself for mis-designing its business model and missing out on those piles of dough. Instead, DVD was priced as a sell-through product, and the proportion of private purchases to rentals reversed itself. It was one, shining, and sadly singular moment of industry smarts and foresight.

I spent twenty-seven years at Home Box Office. I don't want to come off that I was privy to the inner, upper level councils of the company because I wasn't. But I saw enough of how the company worked to think of them as one of the shrewdest, savviest, just plain damned smartest TV companies in the business. Through them, I got a peek at the thinking in other media companies as well. From that viewpoint, I'm thinking here's where Tassi et al don't know their enemy. Traditional media organizations may be greedy, but they're not stupid. It's not like they don't see the impact the Internet is having—and is going to have—on their business. Tassi writes, "They have failed to realize that people want things to be easy."

Tassi's wrong. They *know* that. That was the founding principle behind HBO and all the other pay-TV services, just as it was the driving idea behind home video. Hell, it was the idea behind commercial TV in the late 1940s. That "they" Tassi likes to regularly lambaste knows people want things easy, and they want them cheap.

That's the problem.

*****

Both the Tassi and Paralegal pieces throw around a lot of revenue numbers to make the case that Hollywood hand-wringing over piracy is like Ebenezer Scrooge boo-hooing over the pocket change he's lost in his sofa.

True, piracy isn't driving anybody out of business, nobody's going home poor and having to break the heart-breaking news, "Honey! Kids! There'll be no villa on Lake Como this summer thanks to those nasty, copyright-violating movie pirates!"

But the movie business does have its health problems, and these stories take a very un-analytical, carelessly superficial view of revenue numbers.

Paralegal, for example, looks at the monumental worldwide grosses of the "Most Pirated Movies of All-Time" to make the point "Despite Hollywood's claim that piracy will deal a huge blow to ticket sales, Hollywood is still continuing to break box office records." Paralegal picks ten titles—two of them the top-grossing movies of their release years, and none coming in lower than number six—including *Avatar* (2009; $2.5 billion worldwide), *The Dark Knight* (2008; $1 billion), *Pirates of the Caribbean* (2003; $960 million), *Inception* (2010; $832 million), and *Transformers* 2007; $709 million).

Those are some pretty staggering sums, granted. But the year *Avatar* became one of the biggest-earning movies of all time, eighty-two percent of the 521 movies released that year grossed less than $30 million domestic. In fact, of the combined 2,800 films released in the five years cited above, a little over 2,300—a hair over eighty-three percent—didn't make $30 million domestic. The worst batting average was in 2007—the year the first *Transformers* was released—when eighty-six percent of the year's 631 releases fell below the $30 million domestic mark. What that means is that nearly nine out of every ten movies hitting screens that year was probably a money-loser in theatrical release.

How do I figure that?

The Motion Picture Association of America stopped disclosing average production and marketing costs in 2009 (maybe because the numbers always made people blanche—outsiders at how profligate it made studios look; studio people because of how profligate it made them look to outsiders). But as of 2007, the last year stats were disclosed, on average it cost $106.6 million to make and market a studio feature, and there's no reason to suspect the price tag has gone down since then. The rule of thumb is that since not every dollar at the box office goes back to the studio, a movie needs to gross two-three times its cost to reach breakeven (or more depending on how much revenue is siphoned off by profit participants), which means the theatrical side of the movie business is a Harvard MBA's nightmare in terms of Return on Investment.

Granted, in any given year, the tally of low-grossers includes a fair number of low-budget art house indies and foreign language flicks, all of which have extremely low breakevens. But the bottom line is that most theatrical releases flop. In fact, most releases from any given studio flop.

More than half of Hollywood's revenue comes from overseas distribution, but in terms of the ROI on individual titles, overseas money is no panacea for domestic box office weakness. While one often hears about movies that stiffed here at home but made a killing overseas, that's not a rule. More often, movies that flop here flop overseas. Look at the 2011 $90 million remake of *Conan the Barbarian*. It died almost immediately on release, grossing just $21.2 million domestic. Despite being the kind of empty-headed actioner that is supposed to travel well overseas, it didn't play much better anywhere else pulling in just $27.5 million from all out-of-country markets combined.

And then there are the movies that are hits here, but the success doesn't travel well. Oscar-contender *The Help* (2011) did a huge $167.7 million domestic, but its situations were too specifically American for the overseas audience where it pulled in just $37 million.

Nor is any of that foreign revenue free money. It comes with additional marketing and distribution expenses for each language-specific market.

The typical major studio might release twenty or better titles in a year. It hopes two or three will be breakout hits—blockbusters. It hopes another few will earn some good midrange coin. And then it prays the combined revenues from those winners will outweigh the great proportion of losers.

Paralegal wants to talk about *Avatar?* That same year, 20th Century Fox, which distributed the James Cameron sci-fi epic, released twenty-three other titles. It was a good year for Fox. They had some other major hits (including *Alvin and the Chipmunks: The Squeakquel, Ice Age: Dawn of the Dinosaurs, X-Men Origins: Wolverine)*, and some nice art house-caliber moneymakers (among them: *Crazy Heart* and *(500) Days of Summer)*. But, using a 2:1 ratio to calculate breakeven, and not including marketing costs, fourteen didn't make their money back during theatrical release, even *after* including overseas revenue. Overall, the studio had a good year pulling in about $2.9 billion against total production costs of $793.7 million. Even after figuring in marketing costs, Fox still ended 2009 well into the black ink on its theatricals.

But the breakdown demonstrates that moviemaking is a crap-shoot, and the plan in releasing so many flicks is based on not knowing which ones are going to hit (and for how much), which are going to miss (and by how much), and praying the winners win enough to pay for the losers.

Nor does the wealth get spread evenly around. Fox may have had a good year in 2009, but the average domestic take for each of the 521 movies released that year—and mind you, this was a year when the top twenty releases pulled in almost $8 *billion* domestic out of a total US box office of $10.8 billion—was just a hair under *$21 million*. And studios are nothing if not inconsistent. The year of *Avatar*, Fox had five other films in the domestic top twenty. In 2010: zero. In 2011, four, but all in the bottom half of the top twenty.

Another aspect of box office revenue neither Tassi nor Paralegal touch on is just how shaky the theatrical business is once you get past the impressive size of the numbers. Last year's domestic tally was down 3.5% from 2010, and the only thing keeping the decline from being sharper was rising ticket prices and 3-D surcharges. In fact, ticket price inflation has been puffing up box office numbers for several years. The measure of the vitality of the theatrical business is attendance, and it's not a great measure. Attendance for 2011 was down 5.2% from 2010, which was down 6% from 2009. Generally, attendance has been heading south since 2003, with last year's stats representing the lowest attendance in sixteen years. In other words, despite those fat-looking revenue numbers, the theatrical business is eroding, and has been for quite some time.

To boil all that down, the commonly held industry view is theatrical release is, more or less, a breakeven business. Some years you'll do better than others (and vice versa), but theatrical's primary value for all but a handful of breakout titles is to create enough visibility for a title to carry it through its ancillary markets: commercial and pay-TV, on-demand, DVD, downloads, etc.

The aftermarkets: that's where the gravy is.

*****

The impact of movie piracy on theatrical is, I'm guessing, modest. With so many aftermarkets, both legit and otherwise, the only reason to go to the movies is either because you're one of those I-gotta-see-it-first obsessives, or you're in that shrinking audience that still enjoys going to the movies and/or seeing a flick on the big screen. Pirated copies can't replace that experience.

But DVDs? Legal downloads? Television broadcasts? That's a different story, and since that's the revenue flow keeping Hollywood afloat and studio execs in their Bel Air mansions, that's why the studios get all foamy at the mouth about piracy.

Tassi claims because a physical object isn't being stolen—that illegal downloads can never cause a shortage of supply—that it's not really/not quite stealing.

But content piracy is about degrading the *value* of content, not about diminishing its quantity. Or, put it another way: only saps shell out for the cow when everyone else is drinking pirated milk for free. And we're not just talking about other consumers here. The Columbia survey limits prevalent piracy to a young demographic, but do some forward projection to where that cohort ages into being the foundation of the consumer universe. If more people are pirating than not, what's the value of movies to pay-TV? To commercial television?

Tassi's generation is too young to remember, but as late as the 1970s, the then three broadcast networks had theatrical movies on in prime time every night of the week. Pay-TV channels like HBO, and then home video, devalued movies for the nets to the point of—... Well, how many movies do you see on network TV these days? It is not inconceivable that both legal and illegal downloads could devalue theatricals to the point where premium and basic cable channels pay less and less for telecast rights.

One aftermarket that is already bleeding is the DVD business. Once one of the crown jewels in the ancillary market crown, DVD sales have been sliding since 2007 and there's no sign they've bottomed out. Tassi's right: people prefer downloading rentals—it's easier, it's cheaper. Then why, writes Tassi, are the Hollywood powers-that-be threatening "... to put Netflix out of business by charging them *huge* amounts of money to have access to their content"?

Because, at the moment, online delivery hasn't shown it's going to generate the same kind of revenue DVD sales did and still do. Downloads and streaming have grown, but not nearly enough to offset the overall decline resulting from the fading appeal of DVD purchase, and it's an open question at this point whether or not they ever can.

I suspect any number of studio and TV execs look at these stats and are haunted by what they saw happen to the music business. Yeah, music company execs still get to drive around in stretch limos, rock stars still trash hotel rooms, but in terms of revenue generation, the music industry is a shell of what it was just a little more than a decade ago. Downloads haven't even come close to making up for what's been lost in CD sales: From 1999 to 2008, worldwide music sales dropped twenty-five percent; in the US over the same period, by almost twenty-nine percent. Financial analysts see the numbers continuing their southward march for the foreseeable future. That in mind, Tassi & Co.'s demand for cheap, easy access doesn't exactly set the studios drooling.

So, on the one hand, you have content providers trying to protect a fading revenue model and digging in their heels with efforts like SOPA to forestall what I'm sure they see as an inevitable eventual reconfiguration of how home entertainment works; and, on the other end, content users who want cheap, liberal access to that content.

Ok, so that's the money end. What about this "culture war" I've been talking about?

Well, in my view, that's where it gets *really* ugly.

*****

There's a certain Power-To-The-People/Death-To-All-Tyrants/Robin-Hoody flavor to this anti-anti-piracy view, from Tassi's and Paralegal's pieces down to the attitude of that Drexel law student quoted by Martha Irvine. The title of the Paralegal post—"How Hollywood Is Using Piracy Against Us"—hints at some nefarious scheme to deprive all Americans of their inalienable rights.

Let's be clear about what this fight is over. There's a lot of militant blather going back-and-forth about First Amendment and censorship and freedom of information and blah blah blah. I won't deny there's legitimate spillover into those issues, but at heart, what's driving this fight only collaterally has anything to do with those more noble-sounding, comparatively abstract ideas.

Right now, you can go on the Internet and find out whatever you need to know to self-diagnose your suspected cancer, do your taxes and learn how your Federal, state, and local governments are wasting them, discover the skeletons in any big-mouthed politician's closet, find out the "truth" behind every conspiracy from the Lincoln assassination to what the Air Force *really* has tucked away in Hangar 18. From porn to foreign policy details, it's all available to you for the price of Internet service. Other than that, it doesn't cost you a damned dime, and it's all (well, mostly) provided to you legally. Whatever your appetite is for pictures of naked celebrities or for the Face on Mars or for trying to track how many times Mitt Romney has flip-flopped on the pivotal issues of our time, there are no inhibitions on your ability to access this stuff.

This fight is about the ability to get movies cheaply at home. That's it. Don't let anybody fool you, but that's the bottom line, the endgame, the Big Enchilada everybody's grabbing at in the middle of the table.

The anti-anti-piracy gang takes an NRA slippery-slope tack—"Let them take away your Teflon bullets and the next thing you know they're kicking down your door and taking away your God-given right to defend yourself!"—suggesting controlling entertainment content might be just the first step in controlling the free-flowing stream of info on the Internet. But the dialogue is almost strictly based on entertainment content, which, let's face it, has all the practical value of Kleenex; it's nice to have but your well-being hardly depends on it. This is a fight over what seems to be an assumed inalienable right to be amused in your home at consumer-friendly prices. Yup, that's what the boys suffered for at Valley Forge to win for you.

I'm in strong agreement with Tassi and his peers that the entertainment industry is driven by a bunch of overpaid execs turning out empty-headed entertainment in wasteful fashion and then offering it to the public at ungodly prices. I practically have to take out a second mortgage to take my family to the movies, particularly if it's in 3-D. But I've solved this problem in simple fashion: I don't go. I don't find that this gives me less fit air to breathe (well, as fit as air in New Jersey gets), less potable water to drink (ditto), or starves me or my kids (we do have some great pizza in this state).

Call me old-fashioned, but I still think if it's your property, you can do any stupid, selfish, short-sighted and ultimately self-destructive thing with it you want; it's yours. You want to spend $200 million to turn some comic book nutbar in tights and a cape into an action figure/videogame/Happy Meal-shilling franchise, and then spend another fortune hyping the hell out of it to get the ComicCon geeks to shell out way too much of their hard-earned stock-boy-at-WalMart pay to see it? Well, that's American enterprise for you. I think it's a waste of your time and money and theirs, but that's just me. And, if I don't like it—either because the movie is crappy and/or it just costs too damned much—I don't go.

Tassi, Paralegal, the law student (which I find terrifically ironic; what the hell kind of law are they teaching at Drexel these days?) in the Irvine story, blames piracy on content providers. "If you made it cheaper, people would stop stealing it," which is as prized a bit of self-serving sophistry as I've heard in a long time.

Besides, I don't know that that's true. Hollywood can never lower the price enough to beat "free." But I take their point. And I interpret that point as being, "If a Lexus didn't cost so much, I wouldn't have to steal one." That's not some oppressed group railing about the exploitative policies of some power elite; that's just a brawl between two different kinds of greed.

(Or maybe three kinds. Aggregators—like YouTube, The Huffington Post, and so on—make their living, to some extent, by attracting audiences through content produced by others. Ya gotta love the irony of New Media living and dying by its ability to freely use Old Media content.)

What you're dealing with, I think (Alert! This here's the culture war bit) is a changed generational worldview on proprietorship, and—in my highly, highly, *highly* subjective, retrograde, atavistic, and undoubtedly stone-aged view—it extends well beyond the issue of paying or stealing to watch junk like *Transformers: Dark of the Moon* (2011) at home. The fallout from the Internet's greatest asset—free-flowing data and communication—has been an erosion of traditional concepts of boundaries, both personal and professional.

You see it in the epidemic of plagiarism on college campuses. It doesn't happen because students are lazy (although you'll probably get some argument from some instructors) or because they're malicious. By the time they're college-aged, they are so used to accessing information without any sense of it "belonging" to someone, the traditional concepts of attribution and proprietorship seem antiquated if not downright irrelevant.

People post online the kind of personal information they used to reserve for their bartender after a couple of tall scotches, and then, having posted it on a universally accessible platform, seem shocked there's any kind of blowback. Here in New Jersey, we're witnessing a trial in which the defendant—a young college student—allegedly thought it was OK to spycam his gay roommate during a date, and then tweet to his followers to view a second show. (The prosecution alleges the resultant embarrassment pushed the gay roommate to suicide.) The personal has become public, the private the communal. And this social movement Joe Karaganis referred to regarding entertainment content—"If it's there, I should be able to get it, and get it cheap!"—seems (to me) to fit right into that sensibility.

Throw that up against Hollywood's corporate sensibility—"Our goal is to squeeze every last penny out of every last bit of content!"—and you wind up with a brutal war between two, unforgiving, all-or-nothing views of how media is supposed to work.

Somewhere in between, with everything to lose—and they probably will—are the content *creators*.

*****

When people like Tassi write about Hollywood corporate greed, I have to laugh. Oh, I don't disagree with them, but they tend to take a very simplistic view of the industry. It's like judging the financial health of the average American by what Warren Buffet makes. What Tassi doesn't see nor the studios overly care about is that the matter of aftermarkets, particularly residuals, and trying to protect that revenue stream, is a bread-and-butter issue for an awful lot of people in movies and TV.

Tassi may rail against the "A-list actors (who) do not need multi-multi-million dollar salaries," but the erosion of residual value of films and TV shows—either through legit lower-value online downloading and streaming, and/or piracy—isn't going to hurt *them*. After all, they have those multi-multi-million dollar salaries. But the average annual pay for a member of the Screen Actors Guild as of March 2012 is $40,000. For Hollywood-based actors, the average is $13,000. Considering that in any given year, most of the membership doesn't work, and those multi-multi-million dollar salaries are pulling the average *up* to $40,000, it means most of the membership at any given time is living on air. When they do get a residual-paying gig, that's gold.

Or take screenwriters. They're not all Akiva Goldsman. Most screenwriters, providing they ever do get traction in the business, do not have extended careers nor do all that much better than scale. Most screenwriters are like the rank-and-file players in pro football: with luck, you'll have a few hot years, but then it's selling used cars for the rest of your life. In any given year, somewhere around half of the members of the Writers' Guild of America don't work, and the average annual income for a WGA writer is about $40,000.

Talent has a long, appalling history of being exploited by studios and producers. Shady (but somehow legal) bookkeeping, one-sided contracts, etc. are as much a part of Hollywood history as sprocket holes. No news there. But if piracy—and here I agree with Tassi et al—is survivable by Hollywood, at least to some degree, simply because the entertainment industry makes so damned much money, not so the talent at the rank-and-file level. Tassi may think this conflict is just Old Media execs defending their ability to "... add a few more millions onto their already enormous money pile," and he's not completely wrong about that, but below those execs are people who will take a hit (if they haven't already) by this new paradigm that eats away at aftermarket value.

But, as I said earlier, when did anybody ever care about them? They're just as invisible to the Tassis as they are to the industry that's always exploited their talent. The sad irony here is that without them, there'd be nothing to exploit or steal.

*****

Tassi's prediction the online terrain is going to change for Hollywood whether Hollywood goes along with it or not is probably true. I'd be surprised if the sharper execs in the business didn't feel the same. And for any of those with dim foresight, YouTube is providing a glimpse of the future rolling out nearly 100 channels of original programming. It'll be TV… and it won't. It'll favor short form, it'll be accessible at the user's convenience instead of based around an anchored schedule, and it will feature niche-oriented content to try to grab that advertiser-coveted eighteen to thirty-four demo. It'll be TV tailored to the tastes and impatient, insatiable viewing habits of a totally wired, constantly stimulated new generation of entertainment consumer.

The movie-going audience will continue to shrink, and those ancillary markets that are not already downtrending may take a hit as a more Internet-focused, Internet-weaned breed of consumer takes the keystone position in entertainment spending. The movie business will try to prop up revenues by bumping prices, but that'll hit a point of diminishing returns (if it hasn't already), and overall revenues will decline.

Tassi and his peers will not weep for a Hollywood that winds up contracting along the lines of the music industry. Tassi thinks "Projects with bloated budgets and massively overpaid talent might start to fade away, but that can only be a good thing creatively for all the industries."

He's probably right about the former—or at least there'll be less of it—but I doubt it's going to kick off an explosion of better, more moderately budgeted fare. There's plenty of writing here at Sound on Sight about how many small, terrific movies, including Oscar-winners, go ignored by the general public. I sincerely doubt not having *Ghost Rider: Spirit of Vengeance* or *John Carter* around would have driven more people to *The Artist*. Besides, Hollywood doesn't need big budgets to make crappy movies; the industry already makes plenty of crappy cheap movies.

Box office for the year so far is up twenty-four percent over the same period 2011 (though still behind 2009 and 2010), and admissions up twenty-five percent. It's still too early to tell if this signals 2012 as a turnaround year or just an uptick. A recent *Entertainment Weekly* story looking at the hot start to the year attributed it to the strong performances of movies like *The Vow, Safe House, Journey 2:*

The Mysterious Island, Dr. Seuss's The Lorax, Contraband, The Devil Inside, Underworld Awakening, Chronicle, Act of Valor, and *Project X*. That's the good news.

The bad news—at least for anybody who, as Tassi seems to, likes a good flick—is that most of these movies range, by critical consensus, from weak to downright suckiness. Only found-footage sci-fier *Chronicle* received good reviews (an impressive eighty-four percent positive on Rotten Tomatoes). Every one of the other titles was rated "Rotten," with all but two not even breaking the fifty percent positive mark. Among the bottom-crawlers, combat movie *Act of Valor* (twenty-nine percent positive; $51 million worldwide gross so far against a $12 million budget); teen-party-out-of-control found-footage flick *Project X* (twenty-six percent positive; $32.6 million and still earning against $12 million); horror franchise sequel *Underworld Awakening* (thirty percent positive; $152.5 million against $70 million); and the box office story of the year, the brilliantly marketed but monumentally awful *The Devil Inside* (the year's record-holder so far with a microscopic seven percent positive; $77.5 million worldwide against a cost of just $1 million).

So, I agree with Tassi to the extent we may get less big budget crap... but we won't be getting less crap.

If Tassi's right about how the scenario will play out, however, Hollywood may very well cure its piracy problem though inadvertently. Tassi may not think much of those big, overpriced, air-headed blockbusters, but according to Paralegal's chart, they're driving piracy just as much as they're driving the legit box office. The only movie remotely resembling a drama on Paralegal's "Most Pirated Movies of All-Time" list is crime flick *The Departed* (2006). The rest of the list looks pretty much like any year's box office toppers with movies like *Avatar, Transformers,* and *The Hangover* (2009). In other words, the numbers suggest movie pirates don't want a more cost-effective Hollywood turning out higher quality films they can make available at lower prices. What they want is the same crap everybody else wants; just cheaper. Changing economics could push Hollywood toward following Tassi's prescription; curing piracy by no longer being able to make the kinds of things most people want to steal.

*****

I honestly don't know how much of this is probable, but a lot of it does seem possible. The currents—unwanted or no—seem plain, and

Tassi and Paralegal and that Drexel kid seem to be on the side of history, however one judges the morality of their view. As an occasional content creator, their casual attitude about proprietary rights does bother me, and I'm even more bothered by how I see it reflected in the attitude of many of the students I teach, but maybe that's just old fartdom at play.

One thing I'm sure of: there are no Good Guys in this fight. This isn't about competing needs, but competing wants. The final irony I'll cite is that list a few paragraphs up about the movies currently energizing the box office. I look at them and think, "Hardly seems worth the fight."

So Long, Luce: A Mother and Son at the Movies
(posted 4/16/12)

Somehow we'd fallen into calling her "Luce the Moose." No one even remembers why. After that, I used to buy her some kind of moose—a stuffed doll, a carving, anything—every Christmas. Her given name was Lucy Sylvia Mesce. Lucia, actually, but other than her immigrant parents, I don't think anybody ever called her that.

She passed away from a sudden cardiac arrest on Monday, April 2, sometime around 5:30 p.m., at the age of eighty-one.

She was my mother.

We are, each of us, at any given instant, the sum total of our lives. Everything that we have seen and heard, the people that we have known and the experiences we have had shape us, influence us, nudge and shove us this way and that. And all of it—even that which we have forgotten or thought we had completely ignored or considered so minor as to be irrelevant—leaves some trace, even if microscopic. We are, in the end, like glaciers, moving on our way and constantly picking up something from every inch of the path over which we travel.

I'm hardly venturing into new psychological terrain when I say that for most of us there is no influence more powerful than that of our parents. For good or for ill, they form the basis on which everything else that becomes "us" is built. And for me—since my father died in 1970 when I was fourteen—much of that influence came from my mom. The Moose.

I'm sharing this with you because she's much of the reason I've been writing here at Sound on Sight for the last twenty months. And since this work has, personally, come to mean so much to me, I thought I owed her the tribute. I hope you won't mind too much. And if you do—as The Moose used to say with a certain Newark-bred bluntness—you can go scratch.

*****

I was lucky, growing up in the tail end of that period when families still, at least on occasion, went to the movies together. That's how it had been in the old studio days. Theaters offered a package of entertainment changing every week with enough of a spread to cover every member of the clan: two films (maybe a weeper for mom, a shoot-'em-up for dad), a cartoon and a serial episode for the kids, a newsreel. Even though the movies had changed, and the cartoons and serials and newsreels had gone the way of the dinosaurs, my parents still had that everybody-in-the-car-we're-going-to-the-movies habit.

We didn't manage it often. My dad, a bricklayer, often worked a second job at night, sometimes squeezed in some freelance work on weekends. Even when he was around, he was often exhausted. That made the few times we all went out together all that more memorable, and I remember them still, even to specific titles. Like when we went to see the Cary Grant/Audrey Hepburn light-hearted thriller *Charade* (1963). To this day, I still don't know how my three-year-old brother was the only one of the four of us to figure out who the killer was... and pull that rabbit out of his beanie in the first half-hour.

In those days, movies weren't released on the waves of hype that carry them into the multiplex today, and they weren't released nationally. A movie started off in the major cities, then wandered around the country's movie houses for months. You often didn't even know what was playing in the neighborhood. Somebody felt in the mood for a night out, you picked up the newspaper for the movie listings. "Oh, hey, there's this picture with Cary Grant in it. You like him, right?" And maybe that's all it took.

You walked through the movie house doors a blank, promised and hoping for a surprise.

Looking back, I have to give my mom and dad credit. For people of their generation, they were commendably open. Movies were getting more brazen, tougher, and Mom and Dad were still willing to go along for the ride. In *The Scalphunters* (1968), I heard the n-word in a movie for the first time and tried to show my great maturity in front of them by not being shocked. I saw my first glimpse of a woman's breast in *The Professionals* (1966), and of a bare posterior in *The President's Analyst* (1967), and tried to save us all some embarrassment by acting like I hadn't noticed so my parents wouldn't notice that I *had* noticed and feel obligated to "discuss" it with me. I suspect *they* were pretending not to notice I'd noticed for the same reason.

Even though he was often either working or sacked out, my dad did manage to carve out a little daddy/son time. We went to see the Japanese monster pic *Mothra* (1961) together. I got the creeps when the ooky zombie-like natives from Mothra's home island started coming out of the bushes to jump a scientific expedition and we had to go out in the lobby. I still remember my father trying not to let me see him smile over how I was getting spooked by such ripe cheese. "Are you ready to go back in?"

I'd peek through the auditorium doors. "Not yet."

But the best time with Dad was when he took me and my brother to see *2001: A Space Odyssey* (1968). We were all home with the Asian flu and running fevers, so of course it made perfect sense to take us to a matinee on a slushy, winter afternoon. It was playing at the Clairidge.

The Clairidge was one of those huge caverns of a place built during the days when theaters looked like a mix between a palace and a cathedral. I remember getting giddy from looking up into the grand, graceful dome that capped the place. Not too many years before *2001* had come out, the Clairidge had installed a massive, curved Cinerama screen, the only one in New Jersey, I think. The dwarfing auditorium, stereo sound, that enormous screen, and Kubrick—*2001* washed over us and took us like a fever dream.

2001 is a hard enough movie to get your adult head around, but try being a naïve thirteen *and* delirious with the flu. God only knows what my seven-year-old brother made of it. I don't know; at seven, maybe it makes sense... *particularly* with a fever. Then it was over, the lights came up and we sat there for a few seconds, a little overwhelmed I guess. We started filing out with the crowd.

"What was it *about*, Dad?"

He just shook his poor, befuddled head. "I dunno. Something about God, I think."

The other thing I remember about my father was he didn't care for war movies. He'd been in WW II, from 1942 until the end, serving in North Africa and Europe. We know he was in the Ardennes during the Battle of the Bulge, but we don't know what he saw. But he saw *something*; my mom told me he was still having nightmares when they married... in 1953.

The only clue of what he carried inside was when I came home after an uncle had taken me to see *The Battle of the Bulge* (1965), an epic-sized, comic book version of the biggest battle on the western front during the war. My ten-year-old head was still filled with rather naïve ideas about war mostly stoked by old flag-waving war movies still running on TV and Sergeant Rock comic books. I had been bothered by scenes early in the movie when overrun American troops break and run.

"I can't believe they ran away," I said to my father, telling him about the movie.

"Billy," he said matter-of-factly, "we *all* ran."

There was one war movie I remember him watching whenever it ran: Robert Aldrich's bitter *Attack!* (1956). The thing about Aldrich's movie is it's less about fighting the enemy then about the wars men on the same side fight among themselves: courage and cowardice, moral integrity and moral corruption. As I've gotten older, I think of my dad, I think of what there might have been about that movie that brought him back time and again, and I wish he'd been around long enough for me to ask, "What happened?" Because he never told us.

*****

But I came here to talk about The Moose. I spent more time with her, even when Dad was alive.

Mom and her four sisters were like a pack. When one of them had a child, it was that it-takes-a-village-to-raise-a-child thing, because you belonged to all of them. Looking back, it seems to me none of them ever went anywhere alone. They took vacations down the shore together, went to Bingo together, gathered at one or another's house for a night of cards and coffee and cake, the kids carried along with them.

And going to the movies was a regular part of that. Sometimes, we'd load up a couple of cars and trek out to the drive-in at Totowa or the one in Troy Hills. It was as much a picnic as anything else. One of the drive-ins had a small playground under the screen where we could kill time until it got dark enough to start the movie. Some people would bring folding beach chairs and make themselves comfortable around the cars.

In theaters, I can still remember the snug feeling sitting between my mom and one of her sisters (most of whom tended toward being a bit... "cushy," thus the snugness). I remember the heavy feeling in my chest when members of *The Magnificent Seven* (1960) died off, flinching as Kirk Douglas ferociously badgered poor, frail Christine Kaufmann in *Town Without Pity* (1961) (although I had no idea all the badgering and flinching was over rape since I didn't know what rape was), and dimly recognizing that Anthony Quinn and Lana Turner were making a lot of bad choices in *Portrait in Black* (1960).

But where Moose made her big contribution toward turning her oldest boy into a serious cineaste was in the summers while we were still living in Newark. Almost every Saturday—and Sunday if she was a bit financially flush and I was particularly irritating—to get me out of her hair for the afternoon, she'd give me a dollar and say, "Here, go to the movies." And then I'd hook up with four, five, six other kids whose mothers wanted them out of the house too, and off we'd traipse to the Elwood.

The Elwood Theater was only three blocks from my house. Built in the 1930s, I remember it had a distinct angled entrance diagonal to the corner of the block. It was a big house, 800-900 seats, and the dark, high-ceilinged, carpeted lobby ran the whole width, with wide stairs leading upstairs to the balcony. Inside, the left-hand third of the auditorium was separated by a low partition of corrugated plastic: the smoking loge.

For that buck you got your ticket and then a soda, (my preferences) a box of Raisinettes or Milk Duds (Raisinettes had the edge because you could make a horn out of the box), and then something cold like a Dixie Cup or a frozen Milky Way bar. Man, a half-dozen of us trying to gnaw our way through frozen Milky Ways sounded like a pack of wolves working on soup bones. If you marshaled your funds properly, you even had enough money left over to stop off at Bernie's Confectionary on the way home and get a comic book.

We never knew what was playing, but there was a different double bill there every weekend and we saw damned near all of them. Adult dramas like air disaster flick *Fate Is the Hunter* (1964), all the Frankie Avalon/Annette Funicello beach movies (we all learned how to do the Eric Von Zipper snap-clap-point move), the Cliff Robertson I-don't-wanna-be-a-gigolo-no-more soap *Love Has Many Faces* (1965), all of Roger Corman's Edgar Allan Poe flicks watched through half-closed eyes thinking we could shut them faster that way if something gross happened, *It's a Mad, Mad, Mad, Mad World* (1963) starring every funny guy in the whole mad world, resurrected low budget junk like *The Four Skulls of Jonathan Drake* (1959) and *The Monolith Monsters* (1957), *The Great Escape* (1963)... and on and on and on, weekend after weekend, summer after summer.

And in those days, theater managements didn't clear the auditorium after the show, at least not at the matinees. I remember sitting through *The Great Escape* twice back-to-back—six hours of King of Cool Steve McQueen—and then coming back on Sunday to see it twice more.

Out of those hours in the dark at the Elwood, somewhere along the line I morphed from someone who loved going to the movies to someone who loved the movies. Years later, when The Moose fretted about whether or not I was wasting my time studying film in college, I'd throw it back at her: "Well, it's your fault, ya know."

"*My* fault?"

"Hey! Who was the one who sent me off to the movies every weekend!"

Eventually, we moved out to the suburbs, but by then the habit was dug in deep. I was paying for it myself, now, with money I earned at a pizzeria. This time, it was the Park Theater. Nobody played double bills any more, and a buck didn't even buy you a smile at the box office, but I went to nearly everything, anything. When the Park converted to a classics/foreign film house, I kept going. I went to the foreign flicks because I thought they'd be dirty, but the classics were movies I'd heard about for years but never seen. And they gave me and my mom something to talk about, although we were coming at movies from two different perspectives. I was getting more serious about film, and The Moose... well...

Like when I'd finally seen *On the Waterfront* (1954). It's still one of the most atmospheric location shoots in movies, and that authenticity hit me even as a young teen. And there was Brando.

He was already past his peak, and his resurrection with *The Godfather* (1972) was still years away, so I'd never understood what all the hushed tones about Marlon Brando were about. Until I saw *On the Waterfront*. The scene between he and Eva Marie Saint in Hudson Park, with Brando futzing around with her fallen glove, is as real as the ash can fires in the park and the crowded Hoboken tenements. I wasn't old enough to drive, yet, but I now knew what was so special about Brando.

"What'd you see tonight?"

"They had *On the Waterfront* up at the Park."

"Oh, I *love* that picture."

"Ya know, I never got what it was everybody was always saying about Marlon Brando—"

"*Man*, he was gorgeous, wasn't he?"

"Yeah, he was pretty good looking. But his *acting*—"

"He was *beautiful* in those days!"

"It didn't seem like acting! He's got this scene with a glove—"

"He looked like one of those Greek statues! *Gorgeous!*"

And so on.

Years later, when I was studying film at the University of South Carolina, we were still talking about movies. She called me long distance one night when one of the networks was running 2001. Remembering my post-viewing conversation with my father at the Clairidge seven-eight years earlier, it was hard not to laugh when she asked, "So what's this movie about?"

*****

The Park Theater burned down in the 1970s. Some said it was arson. The Elwood was killed off by the 1967 Newark riots. The Clairidge is still there, but carved up into a half-dozen little boxes. Jersey—the birth place of the drive-in—saw its last outdoor screen close in 1991.

And The Moose is gone.

She lived long enough to see that while I never became any big thing, I did get just enough done to show her my passion for film had not been totally misplaced. Over her last years, the question she most asked me was, "Are you happy?" And one of the things that made me happy was the writing I've done here, and I told her so.

For that, I owe my colleagues here at Sound on Sight, and I also owe you out there who occasionally drop by to see what I have to say. So, from me and The Moose to all of you… thanks.

REFERENCES

Along with the articles and other publications cited by name in the text, I'd be remiss if I did not give credit to the additional works listed below which have long provided me with invaluable background information on the motion picture industry and the art of the motion picture.

Bach, Steven. *Final Cut: Dreams and Disaster in the Making of Heaven's Gate*. NY: Plume, 1985.

Badger, Steve. "Mann Movies: A Guide to the Films of Anthony Mann." www.playwinningpoker.com, March 17, 2003.

--. "Remembering John Sturges: A Guide to the Films of John Sturges." www.playwinningpoker.com, Feb. 11, 2013.

Balio, Tino, ed. *The American Film Industry*. Madison, WI: University of Wisconsin, 1976.

Barnouw, Erik. *Tube of Plenty: The Evolution of American Television*. 2nd ed. NY: Oxford University Press, 1990.

Bart, Peter. *The Gross: The Hits, the Flops – The Summer That Ate Hollywood*. NY: St. Martin's, 1999.

Baxter, John. *Science Fiction in the Cinema*. 2nd Printing. NY: Warner Books, 1974.

--. *Sixty Years of Hollywood*. Cranbury, NJ: A.S. Barnes & Co., 1973.

Biskind, Peter. *Down and Dirty Pictures: Miramax, Sundance, and the Rise of Independent Film*. NY: Simon & Schuster, 2004.

--. "*Easy Riders, Raging Bulls: How the Sex-and-Drugs-and-Rock-'n'-Roll Generation Saved Hollywood*. NY: Touchstone, 1998.

Donovan, Hedley., ed. *Life Goes to the Movies*. NY: Time/Life Books, 1975.

Douglas, Kirk. *The Ragman's Son: An Autobiography*. NY: Simon & Schuster, 1988.

Dunne, John Gregory. *Monster: Living Off the Big Screen*. NY: Random House, 1997.

Ehrenstein, David. *The Scorsese Picture: The Art & Life of Martin Scorsese*. NY: Birch Lane Press, 1992.

Emery, Robert J. (p/d/w). *The Directors*. "George Romero." Media Entertainment Inc., for Encore (2003).

--. *The Directors*. "Oliver Stone." Media Entertainment Inc., for Encore (2001).

Evans, Robert. *The Kid Stays in the Picture*. NY: Hyperion, 1994.

Everson, William K. *The Bad Guys: A Pictorial History of the Movie Villain*. NY: Citadel Press, 1964.

--. *A Pictorial History of the Western Film*. Secaucus, NJ: Citadel Press, 1969.
Fine, Marshall. *Bloody Sam: The Life and Films of Sam Peckinpah*. NY: Donald I. Fine, 1991.
Finler, Joel W. *The Hollywood Story*. NY: Crown, 1988.
--. *The Movie Director's Story*. NY: Crescent, 1985.
Folsom, James, ed. *The Western: A Collection of Critical Essays*. Englewood Cliffs, NJ: Prentice-Hall, 1979.
French, Philip. *Westerns: Aspects of a Movie Genre*. Cinema One. NY: Viking, 1974.
Froug, William,, ed. *The Screenwriter Looks at the Screenwriter*. Los Angeles: Silman-James Press, 1991.
Gianetti, Louis D. *Understanding Movies*. 2nd ed. Englewood Cliffs, NJ: Prentice-Hall, 1976.
Gifford, Denis. *A Pictorial History of Horror Movies*. NY: Hamlyn, 1973.
Goldman, William. *Adventures in the Screen Trade: A Personal View of Hollywood and Screenwriting*. NY: Warner, 1983.
--. *The Big Picture: Who Killed Hollywood? and Other Essays*. NY: Applause, 2001.
Gordon, David. "Why the Movie Majors Are Major." *Sight and Sound* #42 (Autumn 1973): 194-196. Rptd. in *The American Film Industry*. Ed. Tino Balio. Madison, WI: University of Wisconsin Press, 1976: 458-467.
Greenberg, James. "Western Canvas, Palette of Blood." *The New York Times*. (Feb. 26, 1995): 19+.
Guback, Thomas H. "Hollywood's International Market." *The American Film Industry*. Ed. Tino Balio. Madison, WI: University of Wisconsin Press, 1976: 387-409.
Harlan, Jan. (d). *Stanley Kubrick: A Life in Pictures*. Warner Bros.: 2001.
Higham, Charles, and Joel Greenberg. *The Celluloid Muse: Hollywood Directors Speak*. NY: Signet, 1972.
"Is the Original Screenplay Dead?" CNN.com. Feb. 17, 2005.
Jennings, Gary. *The Movie Book*. NY: Dial, 1963.
Jensen, Jeff. "Videogame Nation." *Entertainment Weekly* (Dec. 6, 2002): 20+.
"Jerry Bruckheimer." www.askmen.com, Feb. 4, 2004.
Johnson, William, ed. *Focus On: The Science Fiction Film*. Englewood Cliffs, NJ: Prentice-Hall, 1972.
Jones, Ken D., and Arthur F. McClure. *Hollywood at War: The American Motion Picture and World War II*. Cranbury, NJ: A.S. Barnes, 1973.

Kearney, Jill. "What's Wrong with Today's Films?" *American Film* (May 1986): 53+.

Kemp, Philip. "The Story of All Wars." *Film Comment*. (July-August, 1996): 50+.

Kirschling, Gregory. "Rise of the Merchandise." *Entertainment Weekly* (May 30, 2003).

Knauer, Kelly, ed. *TIME: American Legends – Our Nation's Most Fascinating Heroes, Icons, and Leaders*. Special Edition. NY: Time Books, 2001.

Lester, Will. "We're Hooked on High Tech." Associated Press. Rptd. in *The Star-Ledger* (Dec. 22, 2005): 42.

Linson, Art. *What Just Happened? Bitter Hollywood Tales from the Front Line*. NY: Bloomsbury, 2002.

Lyman, Rick. "Fewer Soldiers March Onscreen." *The New York Times* (Oct. 16, 2001): E-1+.

Manvell, Roger. *Films and the Second World War*. Cranbury, NJ: A.S. Barnes, 1974.

McGee, Henry, President, HBO Video, NY. Interview, Nov. 14, 2003.

Munn, Michael. *Gene Hackman*. London: Hale, 1997.

Parkinson, Michael, and Clyde Jeavons. *A Pictorial History of Westerns*. London: Hamlyn Publishing, 1973.

Peel, Eva. "Plotting 401." Hollywoodlitsales News, www.Hollywoodlitsales.com, Newsletter Vol. 4 #19: Oct. 7, 2003.

Rose, Charlie. *Charlie Rose*. "Peter Bart." Jan. 1, 2004.

Sarris, Andrew. *The American Cinema: Directors and Directions 1929 – 1968*. NY: Dutton, 1968.

Scanlon, Paul. "The Force Behind George Lucas." *Rolling Stone* (Aug. 25, 1977): Rptd. in *The Rolling Stone Reader: The Best Film Writing from Rolling Stone Magazine.* NY: Pocket, 1966: 118-130.

Scherman, David E., ed. *Life Goes to the Movies*. 2nd Printing. NY: Time-Life Books, 1975.

Schickel, Richard. "The Arts: 100 Years of Attitude." *Time* (Dec. 31, 1999): 135-137.

Scott, A.O. "The Invasion of the Midsize Movie." *The New York Times* (Jan. 21, 2005): E-1+.

--. "It's a Joy Ride, and the Kids Are Driving." *The New York Times* (Aug. 11, 2002): E-11+.

--. "Kicking Up Cosmic Dust." *The New York Times* (May 10, 2002): E-1+.

Server, Lee. "The Man in the Steel Helmet." *Film Comment* (May-June, 1994): 64+.

--. *Robert Mitchum: "Baby, I Don't Care."* NY: St. Martin's Griffin, 2002.

Seydor, Paul. *Peckinpah: The Western Films*. Urbana, IL: University of Illinois Press, 1980.

Siegel, Don. *A Siegel Film*. London: Faber and Faber, 1993.

Sklar, Robert. *Movie-Made America: A Cultural History of American Movies*. NY: Vintage, 1975.

Smith, Roger. "Five Things That Matter More in Hollywood." *Film Comment* (March-April 2001): 48.

--. "Why Studio Movies Don't Make (Much) Money." *Film Comment* (March-April 2002): 60-61.

Smith, Sean. "Periscope: Westerns – Riding Into the Sunset." *Newsweek* (March 22, 2004): 14.

Snider, Mike, and Andre Montgomery. "New Generation of Video Games Grows Up Fast." *USA Today* (May 19, 2003): 5D.

Spielberg, Steven. *The American Film Institute Seminar with Steven Spielberg*. Center for Advanced Film Studies, Beverly Hills, CA: May 24, 1978.

Svetkey, Benjamin, et. al. "Who Killed the Hollywood Screenplay?" *Entertainment Weekly* (Oct. 4, 1996): 32+.

--. "They Shoot R-Rated Movies, Don't They?" *Entertainment Weekly* (May 9, 2003): 10-11.

"Symposium on Violence: Rites of Collective Ignorance." *Osceola* (Feb. 7, 1975): 8-9.

Terrill, Marshall. *Steve McQueen: Portrait of an American Rebel*. NY: Donald Fine, 1993.

Thomas, Bob. *King Cohn: The Life and Times of Hollywood Mogul Harry Cohn (Revised and Updated)*. Beverly Hills, CA: New Millenium, 2000.

Thomson, David. "The Real Crisis in American Films." *American Film* (June 1981): 41+.

--. "The Decade When Movies Mattered." *Movieline* (Aug. 1993): 43+.

Thurman, Tom (p/d). Tom Marksbury (w). *Sam Peckinpah's West: Legacy of a Hollywood Renegade*. Starz/Encore Entertainment: 2004.

"Time for Popcorn." *The Star-Ledger* (Dec. 1, 2003): 19.

Ury, Allen. "A (Set) Piece-of-the-Action." *Fade In*. E-zine. FADEINMAGE@aol.com, March 5, 2003.

"Using Generational Marketing to Build Arts Audiences." Arts & Business Council of Chicago, 2002.

Von Gunden, Kenneth, and Stuart H. Stock. *Twenty All-Time Great Science Fiction Films*. NY: Arlington House, 1992.

Webb, Michael, ed. *Hollywood: Legend and Reality*. Boston: Little, Brown, 1986.

Weber, Bruce. "Fewer Noses Stuck in Books in America, Survey Finds." *The New York Times* (July 8, 2004): E-1+.

Weddle, David. "Dead Man's Clothes: The Making of *The Wild Bunch*." *Film Comment* (May-June 1994): 44+.

Whitty, Stephen. "Getting Our Money's Worth for the Price of a Movie Ticket." *The Sunday Star-Ledger*. Section 4 (Oct. 17, 1999): 8.

--. "Memo to Hollywood: It's the Movies, Stupid." Section 4 *The Star-Ledger* (Sept. 4, 2005): 1+.

--. "Underserved Audiences at Cross-Purposes with Critics." *The Star-Ledger* (March 20, 2005): 15.

Wright, Will. *Six Guns & Society: A Structural Study of the Western*. Berkley and Los Angeles: University of California Press, 1975.

"Young Male Audience 24% Lower in Summer 2005 than Summer 2003; Movies Now Battle Digital Entertainment Options to Attract Critical Demographic." PRNewswire, Oct. 10, 2005. Rptd. www.prnewswire.com, Dec. 5, 2005.

Research Assistance:
Steve & Madeline D'Alessio.
Ron & Carol Kochel.
Christina Krauss, Grosso/Jacobson Productions, NY.
Bill Maass.

And a special salute to the wizards at the Internet Movie Data Base, Box Office Mojo, and Rotten Tomatoes, all of whom have made their sites indispensible to anyone and everyone who writes about movies and the movie business.

INDEX

*Batteries Not Included (1987) 85
A. I.: Artificial Intelligence (2001); 116-117; "Supertoys Last All Summer Long" (1969 short story) 116
Abbey, Edward (writer) 51
Abby (1974) 129
Abraham Lincoln: Vampire Killer (2012) 348
Abrams, J. J. (producer/director) 218
The Absent-Minded Professor (1961) 1
Ace Ventura: Pet Detective (1994) 175
Across 110th Street (1972) 128
Act of Valor (2012) 373
Action in the North Atlantic (1943) 238
Adam, Ken (production designer) 29-30, 31
The Adventures of Tintin: The Secret of the Unicorn (2011) 107, 336, 337
Affleck, Ben (actor/director) 91, 123-124, 202, 308
After Hours (1985) 197
The Age of Innocence (1993) 192, 194, 195
Air America (1990) 89
Air Force (1943) 16, 238-239
Akins, Claude (actor) 19
Albee, Josh (actor) 51
Aldrich, Robert (director) 34, 98, 280
Alexander (2004) , 329, 345
Alice Doesn't Live Here Anymore (1974) 82, 194
Alice in Wonderland (2010) 94, 104, 333
Alien (1979) 101, 122, 306
All Men Are Beasts (2001) 180
All the President's Men (1976) 81, 82, 99, 316
All Quiet on the Western Front (1930) 237, 248
Allen, Irwin (producer/director) 328-329
Allen, Woody (actor/screenwriter/director) 193, 310, 323
Alonzo, John (cinematographer) 83
Altman, Robert (director) 34, 98, 340
Alvin and the Chipmunks: The Squeakquel (2009) 365
Alvin and the Chipmunks: Chipwrecked (2011) 311
Always (1989) 115
The Amazing Spider-Man (2012) 233, 234, 348
Amblin Entertainment (production company) 85, 109, 114, 118
American Beauty (1999) 109, 118
The American Cinema (1968 book) 319
American Gangster (2007) 122
American Gigolo (1980) 98

American Graffiti (1973) 83, 110, 111, 150
An American Guerilla in the Philippines (1950) 239
American Ninja franchise 154
American Pie franchise 160; American Reunion (2012) 291
American Pop (1981) 336
American Reunion (2012) 291
The Americanization of Emily (1964) 80
Amiel, Jon (director) 124
Amistad (1997) 116
The Amityville Horror (1979) 101
The Andromeda Strain (1971) 7
Anhalt, Edward (screenwriter) 50, 54-55
Aniston, Jennifer (actress) 219
The Apartment (1960) 315
Apocalypse Now (1979) 83, 84, 99, 209, 243, 248, 316
The Appaloosa (1966) 120
Arachnaphobia (1990) 85-86
Ardai, Charles (publisher/editor) 254, 269-274
Armageddon (1998) 91, 93, 124
Arnold, Jack (director) 9-10
Aristotle's Poetics for Screenwriters: Storytelling Secrets from the Greatest Mind in Western Civilization (2002 book) 351
The Artist (2011) 310, 311, 312, 314, 315, 372
The Asphalt Jungle (1950) 27
The Assassination of Jesse James by the Coward Robert Ford (2007) 106
Assassins (1995) 87
At Long Last Love (1975) 84
Attack! (1956) 214, 241, 267, 378
Auditions (1999) 353
Avary, Roger (screenwriter) 196
Avatar (2009) 107, 195, 347, 348, 363, 365
The Avengers (2012) 291, 348
The Aviator (2004) 190, 194, 195
Babes in Toyland (1934) 213
Bacall, Lauren (actress) 26-27
The Bachelor and the Bobby-Soxer (1947) 316
Back to the Future franchise 109; Back to the Future (1985) 85
Backdraft (1991) 326
Bad Boys (1995) 90, 91, 93, 123, 124
Bad Boys II (2003) 207
Badlands (1973) 62, 99, 114
Baker, Joe Don (actor) 129-130
Bakshi, Ralph (animator)
The Ballad of Cable Hogue (1970) 69
The Ballad of Josie (1967) 50

Bambi (1942) 1
Band of Brothers (2001 TV miniseries) 118
Barancik, Steve (screenwriter) 182
Barnes, George (producer) 175-181
Barry, John (composer) 29
Barry Lyndon (1975) 80, 81
Bart, Peter (production executive/film writer/commentator) 104, 106, 124
Basic Instinct (1992) 89
Bassey, Shirley (singer) 29, 30
"Batman" franchise 4, 29, 252, 254, 255, 302; *Batman Begins* (2005) 206; *The Dark Knight* (2008) 234, 309, 363; use of CGI 327
Battle Cry (1955) 248
Battle: Los Angeles (2011) 311
The Battle of Algiers (1966) 242
The Battle of the Bulge (1965) 377
Battleground (1949) 240
Bay, Michael (director) 93, 123-126, 188, 342
The Beast from 20,000 Fathoms (1953) 8, 327
A Beautiful Mind (2001) 205
Becket (1964) 54
Beginning of the End (1957) 6, 7
Behind Enemy Lines (2001) 246
Being There (1979) 62
Ben (1972) 132
Ben-Hur (1959) 209, 211, 316, 330-331, 332
Benton, Robert (screenwriter/director) 99, 252
Beowulf (2007) 336, 327-328, 330
Bergman, Ingrid (actress) 209
Berkeley, Xander (actor) 150
Berry, Halle (actress) 88
Bertolucci, Bernardo (director) 60-61
The Best Years of Our Lives (1946) 315
Beverly Hills Cop (1984) 90, 91
Bezzerides, A. I. (screenwriter) 280
Big (1988) 205
The Big Bang (2010 novel) 277
The Big Country (1958) 13
The Big Lebowski (1998) 266
The Big Parade (1925) 237, 248
The Big Sleep (1939 novel) 257
The Big Sleep (1946) 7, 264
The Big Steal (1949) 7
Big Top Beach 137
The Big Trail (1930) 12
Bigelow, Kathryn (director) 247
Billy Jack (1971) 129
Binder, Maurice (credits designer) 30
Biskind, Peter (film writer) 196, 198, 216, 334
Bissell, Whit (actor) 23
Bisset, Jacqueline (actress) 28

Black Caesar (1973) 129
Black Godfather (1974) 129
Black Hawk Down (2001) 90, 91, 92, 246, 248, 305
Black Mama, White Mama (1972) 129
The Black Oak Conspiracy (1977) 129
Black Rain (1989) 122
Blackenstein (1973) 129
Blacula (1972) 129
Blade Runner (1982) 117, 211, 339
Blade: Trinity (2004) 296
The Blair Witch Project (1999) 341
blaxplotation movies 128-129
The Blob (1958) 127
Blockbuster Video (home video chain) 142, 164, 224; bankruptcy 163
Blood Feast (1963) 130
Blood on the Moon (1948) 7, 267
Blood Simple (1984) 266
Blow Out (1981) 121
The Blue Max (1966) 83, 242
Boardwalk Empire (2010-present TV series) 191
Bob & Carol & Ted & Alice (1969) 59
Body Double (1984) 121,
Body Heat (1981) 110, 184
The Body Snatcher (1945) 7, 267
Boetticher, Budd (director) 18-19, 20, 23, 24
Bogart, Humphrey (actor) 44, 209, 216, 217, 238
Bogdanovich, Peter (director) 84, 99, 169, 301
Bolton, Delle (actress) 51
Bonnie and Clyde (1967) 37, 38, 62, 98, 100, 316, 319
Boone, Richard (actor) 19
Boorman, John (director) 69, 98, 115, 340
Borgnine, Ernest (actor) 37
Born on the Fourth of July (1989) 245
The Boston Strangler (1968) 54
Bottoms, Timothy (actor) 169
The Bounty Hunter (2011) 219
The Bourne Identity (2002) 306
Boxcar Bertha (1972) 141, 196
The Boys in Company C (1978) 243
Bozzufi, Marcel (actor) 47
Branded (1965-1966 TV series) 305
Brando, Marlon (actor) 60-61, 217, 380-381
Brave (2012) 348
Braveheart (1995) 326, 332
Breaker! Breaker! (1977) 129
Breaking Bad (2008-2013 TV series) 219, 232
Breaklthrough (1950) 240
Breckman, David (producer/screenwriter) 256-259

Brewer, Gil (writer) 274
Brick (2005) 266
Bridesmaids (2011) 217
The Bridge on the River Kwai (1957) 215, 241, 315, 332
The Bridges at Toko Ri (1954) 240
The Bridges of Madison County (1995) 109
Bring It On (2000) 160
Bring Me the Head of Alfredo Garcia (1974) 78, 100
The Brinks Job (1978) 48
Brokeback Mountain (2005) 208
Broken Arrow (1950) 17
Bronson, Charles (actor) 21, 22-23, 83
Brooks, Mel (screenwriter/director) 323
Brothers (2009) 247
The Brothers Grimm (2005) 207
Brown, David (producer) 114, 301
Brown, Walter (screenwriter) 22
Bruckheimer, Jerry (producer) 85, 90-93, 123, 144, 301
Brynner, Yul (actor) 25
Buchanan Rides Alone (1958) 18
bubba market 129
Bucholz, Horst (actor) 25
The Bullfighter and the Lady (1950) 18
Bullitt (1968) 45, 47, 83, 98, 99, 189
Bully (2012) 290-294
Bunker, Robert (writer) 55
Burn! (1969) 242
Burton, Tim (director) 209, 348
Busting (1974) 120
Butch Cassidy and the Sundance Kid (1969) 33, 56, 82, 263
The Butterfly (1982) 271
CGI (Computer-Generate Imagery) 105, 195, 325-334; 342, 344, 346; history of CGI in film 325-326
Cabin Fever (2002) 161
The Cabin in the Woods (2012) 291
Cage, Nicolas (actor) 91-92, 123, 184
Caged Heat (1974) 130, 141
Cagney, James (actor) 44
Cain, James M. (writer) 251, 266, 267-274
The Caine Mutiny (1954) 240, 248
Caligula (1979) 59
Callaghan, Duke (cinematographer) 57
Calley, John (producer/studio executive) 41, 80-81, 82, 96
Cameron, James (screenwriter/director) 89, 195, ,347, 348, 349, 350, 365
The Campaign (2012) 232
The Cannonball Run (1981) 101-102

Cannon Films (production company) 154, 156, 179
Cape Fear (1962) 194
Cape Fear (1991) 194, 197
Capital Arts (production company) 144
Capitol (1982-1987 TV soap opera) 374
Capote (2005) 186, 208
Capra, Frank (director) 48, 49, 315
Capricorn One (1978) 120
Captain America: The First Avenger (2011) 94, 102, 312
Carlito's Way (1993) 121
Carnosaur 2 (1995) 165, 169
Carolco (production company) 88-89, 91
Caroline at Midnight (1994 DTV feature) 147-151
Carpenter, Camilla (TV executive) 158
Carrey, Jim (actor) 176
Carrie (1976) 99, 121
Cars 2 (2011) 102
Casablanca (1942) 79, 96, 209, 217, 221, 228, 229, 230, 234
Casino (1995) 195
Casino Jack (2010) 167
Casper (1996) 86
Casper: A Spirited Beginning (1997 DTV feature)
Cast Away (2002) 109, 118
Castle (2009-present TV series) 259
Castle Keep (1969) 57, 99, 242
Castle, William (producer/director) 127
Casualties of War (1989) 121
Catch Me If You Can (2002) 194
Catch-22 (1970) 242
The Cave of Forgotten Dreams (2011) 221
Chandler, Raymond (writer) 251, 252, 255, 265, 266, 267, 269, 270, 274, 276, 279, 280
Changing Lanes (2002) 307-308
Chaplin (1992) 89
Charade (1963) 376
Charlie and the Chocolate Factory (2005) 206
Charlie Wilson's War (2007) 247
Cheyenne Autumn (1964) 15
Chimpanzee (2012) 290, 291
The China Syndrome (1979) 99
Chinatown (1974) 62, 82, 83, 98, 99, 209, 234, 251, 265, 266, 282, 304
The Chinatown Kid (1978) 130
Chinese Connection (1973) 130
Chisum (1970) 33
chop-socky movies 128, 130, 131, 196
Christie, Julie (actress) 28
Chronicle (2012) , 341, 373

The Chronicles of Narnia: The Lion, the Witch and the Wardrobe (2005) 208
The Chronicles of Narnia: The Voyage of the Dawn Treader (2010) 104, 325
The Cider House Rules (1999) 206
Cimarron (1931) 330
Cimino, Michael (director) 84
The Cincinnati Kid (1965) 68, 80
Cinderella Man (2005) 168, 202-208
Circle of Iron (1979) 130
Citizen Kane (1941) 7, 221, 228, 229, 319
Clark, Matt (actor) 52
Clash of the Titans (2010) 104, 333
Class of Nuke 'Em High (1986) 156
Cleopatra (1963) 215
Cleopatra Jones (1973) 129
Cliffhanger (1993) 89
A Clockwork Orange (1971) 39, 41-43, 62, 80, 81, 99, 189
Close Encounters of the Third Kind (1977) 101, 108, 108, 112, 113, 115, 116
Cloverfield (2008) 329, 341
Coburn, James (actor) 19, 21, 23, 83
The Cocktail Waitress (2012 novel) 268-270, 273
Coen Brothers (screenwriters/directors) 78, 266
Coffy (1973) 129
Cohen, John (screenwriter) 117
Cohen, Larry (screenwriter) 305
Cohn, Harry (studio executive) 79
Cold Comfort see *The Heat of Passion II: Unfaithful*
Collateral (2004) 118
Collins, Max Allan (writer) 251, 275-283
The Color of Money (1986) 197
The Color Purple (1982 novel) 115
The Color Purple (1985) 115
Columbia Pictures (movie studio) 79
Comanche Station (1960) 18
Come Die with Me: A Mickey Spillane's Mike Hammer Mystery (1994 TV movie) 280
Comic-Con (convention) 231-235
Coming Home (1978) 243
Command Decision (1949) 240
Commando (1985)
Con Air (1997) 90, 91, 92
Conan the Barbarian (1982) 54
Conan the Barbarian (2011) 102, 311, 364
Concorde New Horizons (production company) 135-145, 148, 149, 151, 153; changing distribution model 142-143
Connery, Sean (actor) 28, 91
Connors, Chuck (actor) 305
Connors, Mike (actor) 257, 263
Conran, Kerry (screenwriter/director) 326
Conspiracy Theory (1997) 87, 88
The Constant Gardner (2005) 208
Contact (1996) 326
Contraband (2012) 373
Convoy (1977) 129
The Core (1998) 124
The Contender (2000) 77
The Conversation (1974) 62, 83, 84, 99, 121, 189, 229, 265
Cooper, Merian C. (producer/director) 330
Coppola, Francis Ford (director) 33, 82, 83, 84, 98, 141, 143, 182, 217, 229, 243, 300, 340
Corman, Roger (producer/director) 82, 134-145, 146, 148, 149, 151, 153, 161, 165, 196, 379
Cotton Comes to Harlem (1970) 128
Courage Under Fire (1995) 245
Cowboy (1958) 17
Cowboys & Aliens (2011) 102
Coyote, Peter (actor) 174
Craig, Daniel (actor) 28
Crash (2005) 208
Crash Dive (1943) 238
The Crawling Eye (1951) 214
Crazy Heart (2009) 365
Creature Feature 213
Crimson Tide (1995) 90, 92
Cromwell, James (actor) 249
Crow Killer (1958 book) 55
Crowe, Russell (actor) 206, 207
The Cruel Sea (1952) 240
Cruise, Tom (actor) 91, 117, 249, 302
Cruz, Elvis (producer) 180
Cruising (1980) 47-48
Cusack, Cyril (actor) 285
Cutthroat Island (1995) 89, 90
Cyran, Catherine (director) 152
DTV (direct-to-video) 135, 140, 142, 143, 157, 158, 163, 173, 181; DTV films on pay-TV 158; collapse of DTV market 158-159, 169, 174-175; DVD rental business 161, 163
DTDVD (direct-to-DVD) 160, 163-164, 181; distribution 160
DVD 159, 186, 257, 360, 362, 367; theatrical release to DVD 218
D'Antoni, Phil (producer/director) 46, 47, 48, 260
Dahl, John (screenwriter/director) 182-189, 221, 274
Daisy Miller (1974) 84
Dante, Joe (director) 114
Daly, Tim (actor) 149, 150
Damon, Matt (actor) 195

Dancer in the Dark (2000) 342
Dark Water (2005) 207
Daves, Delmer (director) 17, 18, 19, 20
David Copperfield (1935) 315
The Dawn Patrol (1930) 237
The Dawn Patrol (1938) 237
The Day After Tomorrow (2004) 329
The Day the Earth Stood Still (1951) 7
Day the World Ended (1955) 6, 7
Days of Thunder (1990) 90, 123
De Bont, Jan (director) 122
De Sica, Vittorio (director) 191
Dead End (1937) 209
Deadlock aka *Wedlock* (1991 DTV feature) 166
The Deadly Companions (1961) 34, 68
The Deadly Mantis (1957) 6
Deadly Rivals (1993) 175
Dean, James (actor) 217
Death Proof see *Grindhouse*
Death Race 2000 (1975) 143
Death Wish franchise 154
Decision at Sundown (1957) 18, 19
Dee Blue Sea (1999) 333
Deep Impact (1998) 87, 118
The Deer Hunter (1978) 84, 243, 248
Deliverance (1972) 59, 62, 68, 69, 81
Delta Force franchise 154; *The Delta Force* (1986) 244
The Delta Force (1986) 244
Dementia 13 (1963) 141
Demme, Jonathan (director) 141
Demolition Man (1993) 87, 88
DeNiro, Robert (actor) 83, 194
DePalma, Brian (director) 99, 120-121, 190, 217
The Departed (2006) 190, 191, 195,309, 373
Depp, Johnny (actor) 91-92
The Descendants (2011) 310, 311
Desperate Journey (1942) 239
Destination Moon (1950) 9
Destination Tokyo (1943) 238
The Detective (1968) 8
Deterrence (1999) 77
The Devil Inside (2012) , 341, 373
The Devil's Rejects (2005) 161, 207
Devine, Andy (actor) 15
Devlin, Dean (producer) 89
DiCaprio, Leonardo (actor) 194, 333
Dick, Philip K. (writer) 117
Dickinson, Angie (actress) 37
Die Hard franchise 87, 88, 302, 307; *Die Hard* (1988) 302; *Die Hard 2* (1990) 39
Dillinger (1973) 120
Dinosaur Babes (1996 DTV feature) 177-178

The Dirty Dozen (1967) 37, 98, 100, 248
Dirty Harry (1971) 7, 80, 81, 83, 98, 99, 280, 282
Dirty Mary, Crazy Larry (1974) 129
Disney see The Walt Disney Company
Django Unchained (2012) 199, 232, 252
Dmytryk, Edward (director) 13
Doc (1971) 50
Dr. Black, Mr. Hyde (1976) 129
Dr. Seuss's The Lorax (2012) 373
Dr. Strangelove or: How I Learned to Stop Worrying and Love the Bomb (1964) 41, 62, 99, 209
Dr. Zhivago (1965) 319
Dog Day Afternoon (1975) 62, 99
Dolemite (1975) 129
Donaldson, Roger (director) 78
Donavan's Reef (1963) 13
Donnie Brasco (1997) 92
Don't Bother to Knock (1952) 27
Don't Look Now (1973) 98
Double Indemnity (1943 novel) 268, 270, 271
Double Indemnity (1944) 183, 189, 209, 221, 270
Douglas, Gordon (director) 8-9
Douglas, Kirk (actor) 21, 22, 25, 216, 377
Downey, Jr., Robert (actor)252
Doyle, Sir Arthur Conan (writer) 88, 267
Dragnet (1948-1957 radio/1951-1959/1967-1970 TV series) 45
Dreamer: Inspired by a True Story (2005) 202
DreamWorks SKG (production company) 85, 109, 118, 124, 309
Dredd (2012) 348
Dressed to Kill (1980) 121
Dreyfuss, Richard (actor) 83, 115
The Driller Killer (1979) 130
drive-ins 223-227
The Driver (1978) 120
Duel (1971 TV movie) 113
The Duelists (1977) 122
The Dukes of Hazard (2005) 160, 207
The Dukes of Hazzard: The Beginning (2007 DTDVD feature) 160
Dumas, Alexander (writer) 286
Dunlap, Dr. Benjamin (film instructor) 221
Duvall, Robert (actor) 83
E. T.: The Extra-Terrestrial (1982) 86, 102, 115, 116
Earthquake (1974) 285
Eastwood, Clint (actor/director) 7, 54, 83, 244, 245
Easy Rider (1969) 300-301
Eat My Dust (1976) 129

Ebert, Roger (film critic) 183-184, 207, 318, 320-324
Ed Wood (1994) 92
Egan, Eddie (police officer) 45, 260
Egan, Jenifer (writer) 252
Einhorn, Stephen (producer) 144
El Dorado (1966) 16, 33
Elliott, Mike (production executive) 135-145, 146, 148-152, 153
Emergo (special effect) 127, 345
Emmerich, Rolamd (screenwriter/director) 89
Empire of the Sun (1987) 115
Enemy at the Gates (2001) 246
Enemy of the State (1998) 90, 228-229
Endfield, Cy (director) 242
Enter the Dragon (1973) 130
Escape from Alcatraz (1979) 7
Escape from Fort Bravo (1953) 21, 22, 24, 25
Essex, Harry (screenwriter) 45
Evans, Robert (studio executive) 80, 81, 82, 303
Executive Decision (1996) 87
The Exorcist (1973) 81, 84, 301
Extreme Prejudice (1987) 120
Extremely Loud & Incredibly Close (2011) 310, 311
Eyes Wide Shut (1999) 81
Fahrenheit 911 (2004) 247
Fail-Safe (1964) 98, 209
The Fall of the Roman Empire (1964) 331
The Fan (1996) 122
Fantastic Four (2005) 206, 208
The Far Country (1955) 20
Farewell to the King (1989) 120
Farrow, Mia (actress) 28
Fast 5 (2011) 95, 218, 312
Faster, Pussycat! Kill! Kill! (1965) 130
Fat Guy Goes Nutzoid (1986) 156
Fate Is the Hunter (1964) 379
Femme Fatale (2002) 120
Fernandez, Emilio (actor) 37
Ferrell, Will (actor) 219, 232
A Few Good Men (1992) 150, 248, 249
Fielding, Jerry (composer) 35, 36
55 Days at Peking (1963) 331
Fighter Squadron (1948) 239
The Fighting 69th (1940) 248
Fillion, Nathan (actor) 232
film noir 119-120, 182, 183, 184-185, 200, 252, 255, 264, 267, 269, 270, 271, 273, 274, 276
Final Destination 5 (2011) 95, 102, 311, 316
Fincher, David (director) 202
Finding Nemo (2003) 207
Fine, Marshall (writer) 69-70

Fink, Harry Julian 35
Fiorentino, Linda (actress) 274
Firefly (2002-2003 TV series) 232, 233 see also *Serenity* (2005)
First Blood (1992) 89, 102, 248
Fisher, Gerry (cinematographer) 287, 288
Fist of Fear, Touch of Death (1980) 130
Fists of Fury (1980) 130
(500) Days of Summer (2009) 365
Flags of Our Fathers (2006) 86, 118, 248
Flashdance (1983) 91
Flight of the Intruder (1991) 54, 244
The Flight of the Phoenix (1965) 100
Flightplan (2005) 208
The Flintstones (1994) 86
Flying Leathernecks (1951) 239-240
Flying Tigers (1942) 239
Fonda, Henry (actor) 209
Fonda, Peter (actor) 177
The Fog of War: Eleven Lessons from the Life of Robert S. McNamara (2003) 359
For the Love of Movies: The Story of American Criticism (2009) 318
For Whom the Bell Tolls (1943) 248
Forbidden Planet (1956) 214
Ford, Glenn (actor) 17
Ford, Harrison (actor) 326
Ford, John (director) 13-16, 17, 18, 20, 21, 24, 35, 51, 191, 216, 221
Forrest Gump (1994) 326
Forster, Robert (actor) 177
Forsythe, John (actor) 22, 24
Fort Apache (1948) 24
48 Hours (1982) 102
Foster, Jodie (actress) 326
The Four Horsemen of the Apocalypse (1921) 237, 248
The Four Musketeers (1974) 286
The Four Skulls of Jonathan Drake (1959) 379
1492: Conquest of Paradise (1992) 122
Foxy Brown (1974) 129
Fraker, William (cinematographer) 45, 83
Frank, Scott (screenwriter) 117
Frankenheimer, John (director) 33, 98, 332
Frankenstein (1910) 6
Frankenweenie (2012) 348
The French Connection (1969 book) 44, 260
The French Connection (1971) 44-47, 49, 82, 83, 84, 98, 99, 120, 128, 188, 229, 235, 260, 263, 301, 332
The French Connection 30th Anniversary Special 47
Fresh Prince of Bell-Air (1990-1996 TV series) 91

Friday Foster (1975) 129
Friday Night Lights (2004) 202
Friday the 13th franchise 39
Friedkin, William (director) 45-47, 48, 98, 217, 260, 301
The Friends of Eddie Coyle (1973) 99
Fright Night (2011) 102, 103
From Here to Eternity (1953) 248
From the Earth to the Moon (1904) 6
The Fugitive (1993) 326
Full Metal Jacket (1987) 80, 243, 248
Fuller, Sam (director) 191
Furie, Sidney J. (director) 120
The Fury (1979) 121
Funicello, Annette (actress) 379
G. I. Jane (1997) 122
Gable, Clark (actor) 79
Galatea (1953 novel) 273
Galaxy Quest (1999) 86
Galifianakis, Zach (actor) 232
Galligan, Zach (actor) 150
Gaman, Neil (screenwriter) 328
The Gambler (1974) 99
Gambling with Souls (1936) 127
Gangs of New York (2002) 192, 194, 195
Garfield, Andrew (actor) 234
Garland, Judy (actress) 79
Garner, James (actor) 265
Geer, Will (actor) 51
Geffen, David (producer) 85
Geller, Bruce (producer) 258
The General's Daughter (1999) 249
Gentlemen Prefer Blondes (1953) 27
George A. Romero's Dawn of the Dead (2005) 206, 296
George Harrison: Living in the Material World (2011) 191
George, Susan (actress) 70
The Getaway (1972) 78, 114
The Getaway (1994) 78
Ghost Rider: Spirit of Vengeance (2012) 348, 372
Ghost Ship (2002) 87, 88
Giamatti, Paul (actor) 208
Gianetti, Louis (film writer) 119
The Giant Gila Monster (1959) 127
Gibbs, Antony (editor) 287
Gibson, Mel (actor/director) 87, 88, 89, 296, 305, 326
Gierasch, Stefan (actor) 51
Gilbert, Lewis (director) 30-31
The Girl Hunters (1963) 281
Girl in the Cadillac (1995) 271
Gladiator (2000) 86, 109, 206, 309, 326, 333

Gleason, Joanna (actress) 174
Globus, Yoram (producer) 154
Glover, Julian (actor) 285
Go Tell the Spartans (1978) 243
The Godfather franchise 83; *The Godfather* (1972) 47, 62, 81, 82, 98, 99, 100, 120, 260, 263, 301, 316, 351, 352, 380; *The Godfather: Part II* (1974) 81, 84, 99, 120, 263
Godzilla (1954) 229, 329
Godzilla (1998) 8, 229, 329, 334
Goff, Ivan (producer) 258
Goldberg, Whoopi (actress) 88
Golan, Menahem (producer/director) 154
Golden Harvest (production company) 130, 196
Goldman, William (novelist/film writer/screenwriter) 82, 185, 330, 344
Goldsmith, Jerry (composer) 83
The Golden Compass (2007) 334
Gone in 60 Seconds (2000) 91, 92
Gone with the Wind (1939) 79, 96, 210, 211, 212, 215, 218, 234, 315, 330
Good Night, Good Luck (2005) 208
The Good War (1984 book) 246
Goodbye Columbus (1969) 81
Goodfellas (1990) 191, 193, 195, 197
Goodman, David Zelag (screenwriter) 70
The Goonies (1985) 85
Gordon, Abraham (production executive) 164-169, 204-205
Gordon's War (1973) 129
Gothika (2003) 87, 88
Gould, Elliott (actor) 83
Grable, Betty (actress) 26-27
Grace, Topher (actor) 323
The Graduate (1967) 99, 316
Grand Hotel (1932) 315
Grand Theft Auto (1977) 141
Grant, Cary (actor) 209, 376
The Grapes of Wrath (1940) 315
Greaser's Palace (1972) 50
The Great Escape (1963) 331-332, 333-334, 379
The Great Raid (2005) 182
The Great Smokey Roadblock (1976) 129
The Great Train Robbery (1903) 12
The Great Waldo Pepper (1875) 56
The Green Berets (1968) 241
The Green Hornet (2011) 95, 134, 311
Green Lantern (2011) 95, 102, 311
Green, Walon (screenwriter) 35, 38
Gremlins (1984) 86, 114, 150
Griffith, D. W. (screenwriter/director) 330
Grindhouse (2007) 134, 198, 199

grindhouses 131-134, 154, 161
Grosbard, Ulu (director) 98
The Gross: The Hits, the Flops – The Summer That Ate Hollywood (1999 book) 124
Grosso, Sonny (producer) 44-49, 260-263
Groundhog Day (1993) 314
Grown Ups (2011) 94
Grusin, Dave (composer) 83
Guadalcanal Diary (1943) 239
Guess Who's Coming to Dinner? (1967) 128
Gulliver's Travels (2011) 325
The Guns at Batasi (1964) 242
The Guns of Navarone (1961) 242
A Guy Named Joe (1943) 115, 248
The Gunfight at the OK Corral (1957) 20, 21, 22, 24-25
The Gunfighter (1950) 12
HBO (pay-TV channel) 154, 163, 166, 218, 224, 294-295, 296, 362-363, 367; Cinemax 158
Hackman, Gene (actor) 45, 46, 47, 83, 260, 332
Haim, Corey (actor) 173
Hall, Conrad (cinematographer) 83, 282
The Hallelujah Trail (1965) 50
Halls of Montezuma (1950) 240
Hallstrom, Lasse (director) 206
Hamlet (1990) 89
Hammer (1972) 129
Hammett, Dashiell (writer) 251, 252, 255, 264, 266, 267, 269, 276, 279, 280
The Hangover (2010) 94, 373
The Hangover Part II (2011) 102, 312, 313
Hanks, Tom (actor) 275, 326
Hannah and Her Sisters (1986) 193
Hannibal (2001) 122, 134
The Happy Hooker Goes to Washington (1977) 226
Hard Choices (1985) 167, 171-172, 173
A Hard Day's Night (1964) 286, 319
Hard Times (1975) 100
Hardcore (1974) 100
Harlin, Renny (director) 89, 333
Harper (1966) 251, 265
Harris, Richard (actor) 284, 285, 287
Harry and the Hendersons (1987) 85
Harry Potter franchise 107, 108, 312; *Harry Potter & the Deathly Hollows Part 1* (2010) 94, 333; *Harry Potter & the Deathly Hollows Part 2* (2011) 95, 102, 309; use of CGI 327
Harryhausen, Ray (special effects artist) 8
Hart's War (2002) 246
Haskin, Byron (director) 9
Hatari! (1962) 16

Hathaway, Henry (director) 33
The Haunting (1963) 86, 307
The Haunting (1999) 86, 87
Havana (1990) 175
Have Gun Will Travel (1957-1963 TV series) 34
Hawaiian Eye (1959-1963 TV series) 252
Hawks, Howard (producer/director) 7, 16-17, 18, 20, 21, 22, 23, 24, 25, 33, 190, 201, 278
Hawn, Goldie (actress) 28
Hayden, Sterling (actor) 260
He Walked by Night (1948) 44-45
Heartbreak Ridge (1986) 244, 248
Hearts of Darkness: A Filmmaker's Apocalypse (1991) 167
The Heat of Passion II: Unfaithful (1994 DTV feature) 152
Heaven's Gate (1980) 84-85, 308
Heflin, Van (actor) 17-18
Hell Up in Harlem (1973) 129
Hell's Angels (1930) 237
Hellboy (2004) 322
The Help (2011) 309, 310, 311, 314, 364
Hemingway, Margaux (actress) 177
Hemingway, Mariel (actress) 174
Hemmings, David (actor) 285
Henney, Del (actor) 71
Henrick, Richard P. (screenwriter) 92
Hensleigh, Jonathan (screenwriter) 124
Hepburn, Audrey (actress) 376
Hercules and the Women of Atlantis (1961) 214
Herzog, Werner (director) 221
Heston, Charlton (actor) 35, 286-287
Hickenlooper, George (director) 167
Hidalgo (2004) 202
High Noon (1952) 12, 17
Higgins, John C. (screenwriter) 45
High Ballin' (1978) 129
High Plains Drifter (1973) 50
Hill, George Roy (director) 33, 56
Hill, Walter (director) 120
Hirsch, Lee (screenwriter/director) 290
His Girl Friday (1940) 7, 209
A History of Violence (2005) 2008
Hitchcock, Alfred (director) 189, 196, 221, 306
Hoffman, Dustin (actor) 71, 83
Hogan, Hulk (wrestler/actor) 175
Holden, William (actor) 21, 22, 24, 35, 36, 37
Hollingshead, Richard (entrepreneur) 223
Hollingsworth, Cliff (screenwriter) 169, 202-208
Holm, Ian (actor) 285-286
Hombre (1967) 50
Home Box Office see HBO

Hook (1991) 115
Hooper (1978) 81
Hope and Glory (1987) 115
Hopkins, Anthony (actor) 39
Hordern, Michael (actor) 285
Hopper, Dennis (actor) 174
The Horse Soldiers (1959) 15
Hostel (2005) 161, 162
Hotel Transylvania (2012) 348
Hour of the Gun (1967) 25, 50
House of a 1000 Corpses (2003) 161
House of Sand and Fog (2003) 86, 109
The House on Haunted Hill (1959) 127
House on Haunted Hill (1999) 87
"How Hollywood Is Using Piracy Against Us" (online article) 361, 368
How to Marry a Millionaire (1953) 26-27
Howard, Ron (producer/director) 141, 206, 207
Howard the Duck (1986) 110
Hud (1963) 98
Hugo (2012) 190, 191, 192, 194, 310, 311, 348
The Hulk (2003) 207, 334
The Hunger Games (2012) 291
Hunter, Jeffrey (actor) 14
The Hurt Locker (2009) 247, 312
Hurt, William (actor) 116
Huston, John (screenwriter/director) 264
Hutchison, Ken (actor) 73
Hyams, Peter (director) 120
I Married a Monster from Outer Space (1958) 127
I, the Jury (1953) 282
I, the Jury (1982)
I Wanna Hold Your Hand (1978) 114
I Was a Teenage Werewolf (1957) 127
Ice Age: Dawn of the Dinosaurs (2009) 365
Iliff, W. Peter (screenwriter) 172, 173
Ilsa, She Wolf of the SS (1975) 130, 161
In Cold Blood (1967) 189
In the Heat of Passion (1992 DTV feature) 152
In the Heat of the Night (1967) 82, 99, 128, 209
In the Valley of Elah (2007) 106, 247
Inception (2010) 32, 94, , 333, 363
The Incredible Shrinking Man (1957) 10
Independence Day (1996) 210
"Indiana Jones" franchise 108, 109, 110, 111; *Raiders of the Lost Ark* (1981) 86, 102, 110, 115 *Indiana Jones and the Temple of Doom* (1984) 295
The Informer (1935) 13
Inglourious Basterds (2009) 197, 198-199, 248
Inherent Vice (2009 novel) 252
Innerspace (1987) 85

Insomnia (2002) 307
Intolerance (1916) 330
Invaders from Mars (1953) 6, 7, 214
Invasion of the Body Snatchers (1956) 7
Invasion of the Saucer Men (1957) 127
Invasion U.S.A. (1985) 154
The Invention of Hugo Cabret (2007 novel) 348
Invincible (2006) 202
Iron Eagle (1986) 244
Iron Man 2 (2010) 94, 104
Ironside, Michael (actor) 39
Is Paris Burning? (1966) 314
The Island (2005) 93, 124, 206
It Came from Outer Space (1953) 10
It's a Mad, Mad, Mad, Mad World (1963) 212, 379
It's a Wonderful Life (1946) 222
Jackass 3-D (2010) 202
Jackie Brown (1997) 197, 198, 199
Jackson County Jail (1976) 129
Jackson, Peter (screenwriter/director) 233, 328, 329, 334, 338, 344-345, 346, 349
"James Bond" franchise 28-32, 276, 280, 282, 283, 302-303; *Dr. No* (1962) 28, 29, 30, 28; *From Russia with Love* (1963) 29, 30, 302; *Goldfinger* (1964) 29-30, 302; *You Only Live Twice* (1967) 30-31
James, Clifton (actor) 285
Jaws (1975) 85, 99, 100-101, 102, 108, 112, 114, 115, 118, 209, 229, 301, 316, 333; Benchley, Peter (writer) 100, 112
Jarhead (2005) 247
Jeremiah Johnson (1972) 33, 50-58, 81, 99
Jewison, Norman (director) 68
Joe (1970) 62, 99
John Carter (2012) 372
Jones, Freddie (actor) 285
Jones, L. Q. (actor) 19, 37
Journey 2: The Mysterious Island (2012) 372-373
Joy Ride (2001) 182
Jubal (1955) 17
Judy Moody and the NOT Bummer Summer (2011) 311
Juggernaut (1974) 284-289
Jumpin' Jack Flash (1986) 87, 88
Jurassic Park franchise 118; *Jurassic Park* (1993) 108, 115, 327, 328, 329; *The Lost World: Jurassic Park II* (1997) 116, 329; *Jurassic Park III* (2001) 329
Kael, Pauline (film critic) 319
Kagemusha (1980) 110
Kaminski, Janusz (cinematographer) 117

Kangaroo Jack (2003) 90, 91
The Karate Kid (2010) 94
Karlson, Phil (director) 129
Kasdan, Lawrence (screenwriter/director) 110, 184
Kassar, Mario (producer) 85, 88
Katzenberg, Jeffrey (producer) 85
Kaufmann, Christine (actress) 377
Kazan, Elia (director) 54
Keach, Stacy (actor) 271
Kennedy, Arthur (actor) 20
Kennedy, Burt (director/screenwriter) 18, 33
Kill Bill franchise 197, 198, 199, 200; *Kill Bill Vol. 1* (2003) 190; *Kill Bill Vol. 2* (2004) 190, 296; *Kill Bill Vol. 3* 199
Kill Me Again (1989) 182, 183
The Killer Shrews (1959) 6, 7
The Killers (1964) 37
The Killing Fields (1984) 243
The Killing of Sister George (1968) 59, 62
Killing Time (1987) 172
Kind Hearts and Coronets (1949) 222
King Arthur (2004) 91, 92
King, Henry (director) 330
King Kong (1933) 213, 330
King Kong (2005) 208, 328, 329, 334, 344
King of Comedy (1983) 197, 198
King of the Weeds (2014 novel) 283
King, Rick (screenwriter/producer/director) 167, 169-175
King, Steven (writer) 296-297
The King's Speech (2010) 94, 161
The Kingdom (2007) 106, 247
Kingdom of Heaven (2005) 329, 345
Kings of South Beach (2007 TV movie) 260
Kingsley, Ben (actor) 192
Kinnear, Roy (actor) 285
Kirshner, Irvin (director) 110
Kiss Her Goodbye (2011 novel) 277
Kiss Me, Deadly (1952 novel) 280
Kiss Me Deadly (1955) 251, 264, 277, 280, 281
Klute (1971) 83, 100
Knight, Shirley (actress) 285
Kracauer, Siegfried (film writer) 221
Krakatoa, East of Java (1969) 132
Kramer vs. Kramer (1979) 99
Kubrick, Stanley (screenwriter/director) 1, 39, 41-43, 80-81, 98, 116, 243, 325, 331, 332, 340, 376
Kundun (1997) 192
Kung Fu Panda (2011) 102
Kurosawa, Akira 22, 38, 110
L. A. Confidential (1990 novel); differences with movie 306

L.A. Confidential (1997) 306, 307
L. A. Story (1991) 89
Lady and the Tramp (1955) 1
Lady, Go Die! (2013 novel) 277, 279
Lancaster, Burt (actor) 21, 22, 209, 216
Land of the Pharaohs (1955) 191
The Land Unknown (1957) 6
The Land Before Time (1988) 111, 160
The Land Before Time franchise 160
Land of the Lost (2009) 219
Landham, Sonny (actor) 88
Lanza, Mario (singer/actor) 271
The Last Airbender (2010) 104, 333
The Last Boy Scout (1991) 87
The Last Castle (2001) 77
The Last Detail (1973) 82
The Last Exorcism (2012) 341
The Last House on the Left (1972) 162
The Last Picture Show (1971) 99, 169
The Last Seduction (1994) 182, 184, 185, 221, 274
The Last Starfighter (1984) 326
Last Tango in Paris (1972) 59-61, 62, 99
The Last Temptation of Christ (1988) 192, 194, 297
Last Train from Gun Hill (1959) 20, 22, 24, 25
The Last Voyage (1960) 331
The Last Waltz (1978) 194, 198
Laura (1944) 222
The Law and Jake Wade (1958) 21, 22, 23
Lawrence, Martin (actor) 91
Lawrence of Arabia (1962) 211, 218, 248, 313, 319
Le Mat, Paul (actor) 150
Leacock, Richard (director) 169
Lean, David (director) 332
The League of Extraordinary Gentlemen (2003) 334
A League of Their Own (1992) 205
Leaving Las Vegas (1995) 92
Lederer, Mimi (director) 118
The Left-Handed Gun (1958) 13
Legend (1985) 91, 122
Leigh, Janet (actress) 37
Leone, Sergio (director) 190
Lester, Richard (director) 286-287
Lethal Weapon franchise 87, 123, 302; *Lethal Weapon 3* (1992) 88; *Lethal Weapon 4* (1998) 88; *Lethal Weapon* (1987) 302
Lethem, Jonathan (writer) 252
A Letter to Elia (2010) 191
Letters from Iwo Jima (2006) 86, 118, 246
Lettieri, Al (actor) 260
Levinson, Barry (director) 114

"Lew Archer" 255, 274, 282
Lewis, Herschel Gordon (director) 196
"Lies, Damned Lies and Piracy" (2012 online article) 360
The Life of Pi (2012) 347, 348
Linson, Art (producer) 90
The Lion King (1997 stage play) 188
Lions for Lambs (2007) 247
Lionsgate (production company) 145
Liotta, Ray (actor) 307
Little Big Man (1970) 33, 50, 62, 99
Little Fockers (2010) 94
Living Dead franchise 39
Lolita (1962) 41
Lombardo, Lou (editor) 38, 83
London, Julie (actor) 20
The Long Goodbye (1973) 265
The Long Riders (1980) 120
The Longest Day (1962) 211, 248, 331
The Longest Yard (2005) 202, 206
Lord of the Rings (1978) 336
Lord of the Rings franchise 107, 336, 338, 344, 345, 346; *Lord of the Rings: Return of the King* (2003) 309, 329; *The Hobbit: An Unexpected Journey* (2012) 233, 338, 339, 341, 347, 344, 346, 349; use of CGI 327, 328, 329; *The Lord of the Rings: The Fellowship of the Ring* (2001) 329; *The Lord of the Rings: The Two Towers* (2002) 329
Lost Command (1966) 242
The Lost Weekend (1945) 315
The Lost World (1925) 6
The Lost World (1960) 328-329
Lourie, Eugene (director) 8
Love, Cynthia (screenwriter) 290
Love Has Many Faces (1965) 379
Love Story (1970) 81, 100
Lovers and Other Strangers (1970) 70
Lucas, George (producer/director) 1-2, 86, 91, 99, 101, 107-112, 113, 114, 115, 118, 121, 182, 217, 338, 344
Lumet, Sidney (director) 33, 98
Lundgren, Dolph (actor) 89
Lurie, Rod (critic/screenwriter/director) 63, 76-78
M*A*S*H (1972) 62, 82, 98, 242, 248
MGM (Metro-Goldwyn-Mayer)(motion picture studio) 79, 128, 330
MTV (Music Television)(cable channel) 175, 188, 244, 341
MacDonald, James (actor) 241
Macdonald, Ross (writer) 251, 255, 265, 274, 280
MacGraw, Ali (actress) 28

MacMurray, Fred (actor) 183
The Mack (1973) 129
Macon County Line (1974) 129
Madsen, Virginia (actress) 150
The Magnificent Ambersons (1942) 7
The Magnificent Seven (1960) 21, 22, 23, 24, 25, 377
Major Dundee (1965) 35, 68-69, 74, 78
major motion picture studios: 186-187; studio system 79; audience falloff 79, 127-128; cannibalization by TV 79, 95-96, 128; collapse of the studio system 79-80, 95-96; Motion Picture Association of America (MPAA) rating system 105, 290, 291-292, 294-298; changes in distribution patterns 131-132, 133, 210-212, 217-219, 303, 354-355, 365; licensing to TV 132, 212-215, 218-219, 366-367; development process 152-153; video exploitation of backlist 157; home video distribution 159; DTDVD strategy 159-160; marketing 184, 185-186; re-releasing 211-212; pre-WWI 236; WWII 237; changing movie-going demographic 312; changing film aesthetic 340; average production budget 354; box office split with exhibitor 355; in-theater advertising 356; concession expansion 356-357; wide screen 345, 362; color 345, 362; stereo sound 345, 362; attendance slide 345, 365
Malick, Terry (director) 99, 310
The Maltese Falcon (1930 novel) 264, 267
The Maltese Falcon (1941) 209, 251, 264
The Man from Laramie (1955) 19-20
Man in the Wilderness (1971) 120
Man of Steel (2013) 232-233
Man of the West (1958) 20, 21
The Man Who Had Power Over Women (1970) 63
The Man Who Shot Liberty Valance (1962) 15-16
The Man Who Wasn't There (2001) 266
The Manchurian Candidate (1962) 98
Maniac (1980) 130
Mann, Anthony (director) 19, 21, 23, 24, 45
Mannix (1967-1975 TV series) 252, 257, 263
Marathon Man (1976) 83
Margulies, Juliann (actress) 88
Marlowe (1969) 265
Mars Needs Women (2011) 311
Marshall, Penny (actress/director) 205
Martin, Dean (actor) 16
Martin, George R. R. (writer) 296
Martin, Steve (actor) 89
Martin, Strother (actor) 37

Martinez, Joaquin (actor) 52
Marvin, Lee (actor) 15, 19, 37, 83
The Mask of Zorro (1998) 86
Master and Commander: The Far Side of the World (2003) 206
Master of the Flying Guillotine (1975) 130
Matchstick Men (2003) 122-123
Matheson, Richard (screenwriter) 10
The Matrix franchise 87, 88; *The Matrix* (1999) 329, 330, 345; *The Matrix Reloaded* (2003) 207; *The Matrix Revolutions* (2003) 329, 334, 345; use of CGI 327
Mayer, Louis (studio executive) 79
McCabe & Mrs. Miller (1971) 34, 81, 99
McCrea, Joel (actor) 34-35
McDowell, Malcolm (actor) 42
McG (director) 122
McGavin, Darren (actor) 281
McGinnis, Scott (actor/director) 149, 150
McGlynn, Jim (screenwriter) 172
McIntire, Tim (actor/singer) 52-53, 57
McLaglen, Andrew V. (director) 33
McLerie, Allyn Ann (actress) 51
McNally, Stephen (actor) 20
McQueen, Steve (actor) 21, 25, 83-84, 379
Mean Streets (1973) 81, 82, 99, 190, 191, 192, 193, 194, 195, 196, 200
Melies, Georges (director) 6, 192, 325
Melnick, Daniel (producer) 69
Memento (2000) 304
Men in Black (1997) 86
Men in War (1957) 240-241
Mendes, Sam (director) 118, 275, 282
Memphis Belle (1992) 244
Michael Clayton (2007) 106
Mickelson, Robert (producer) 171-172, 173
Midnight Cowboy (1969) 39, 59, 62, 98, 100, 131
Midnight in Paris (2011) 310, 311, 314
Mighty Heart (2007) 247
"Mike Hammer" 29, 251, 255, 264, 276, 277, 278, 279, 280, 281, 282, 283; *Mike Hammer* (158-1960 TV series) 281
Mildred Pierce (1945) 267,268, 270
Miles, Vera (actress) 14, 15-16
Milius, John (screenwriter/director) 50, 54, 120
Miller, Frank (writer/screenwriter/director) 200, 326
Minelli, Liza (actress) 194
minor studios 154-155; distribution pattern 156
Minority Report (2002) 116, 117
Miramax (production company) 206, 351

The Misfits (1961) 27
Missing in Action franchise 154; *Missing in Action* (1984) 244
Mission: Impossible (1996) 121, 302
Mission: Impossible 2 (2000) 302
Mission: Impossible - Ghost Protocol (2011) 312
Mr. and Mrs. Smith (2005) 206
Mr. Nanny aka *Rough Stuff* (1993) 175
Mr. Roberts (1955) 248
Mr. Smith Goes to Washington (1939) 315
Mitchum, Robert (actor) 318
Moder, Mike (second unit director) 57
Moneyball (2011) 309, 310, 311, 314
Monk (2002-2009 TV series) 256, 259
Monroe, Marilyn (actress) 20-28
Monte Walsh (1970) 70
Monterey Pop (1966) 169
The Monolith Monsters (1957) 379
Moonstruck (1987) 92
Moore, Michael (director) 247
Moore, Robin (writer) 44, 260
Morris, Errol (director) 359
Morrison, Toni (writer) 115
"Most Pirated Movies of All-Time" (online chart) 363, 373
Mothra (1961) 376
Motion Picture Association of America (MPAA) rating system see major motion picture studios
Mulligan, Robert (director) 98
Munich (2005) 118, 208, 194, 247
Murch, Walter (sound designer) 83
Murder, My Sweet (1944) 251, 264
Music Box (1989) 89
Murray, Bill (actor) 314
My Gun Is Quick (1957) 281
Mystic River (2003) 322
The Naked Runner (1967) 120
Narc (2003) 306-307
National Lampoon's Animal House (1978) 316
National Treasure (2004) 90, 92
Natural Born Killers (1994) 196
Nelson, Ricky (actor) 16
Network (1976) 62
New York, New York (1977) 84, 301
Neeson, Liam (actor) 115
Nelson, Judd (actor) 148
Netflix 163, 164, 222
Network (1972) 209
New Line (production company) 309
New York, New York (1977) 194, 197, 198
Newman, Paul (actor) 83
Nicholson, Jack (actor) 83, 249

Nicol, Alex (actor) 20
Night Moves (1975) 99, 265
Night of the Living Dead (1968) 68
Night People (1954) 29
The Night They Raided Minsky's (1968) 301
The Nightmare on Elm Street (1984) 295-296
1941 (1979) 108, 301
No Country for Old Men (2007) 312
noir see *film noir*
Nolan, Christopher (director) 32, 93, 234
Noon Wine (1985 TV movie) 69
Norris, Chuck (actor) 154
Nothing but the Truth (2007) 77
O'Brien, Willis (special effects artist) 6, 330
O'Connor, Frances (actress) 116
Objective, Burma! (1945) 239
The Odd Couple (1968) 81
Off the Wall (1977) 169-170, 173
Office Space (1999) 145
An Officer and a Gentleman (1982) 244, 248
Officer and a Movie 219
Oklahoma Crude (1973) 50
The Omen (1976) 101
One Flew Over the Cuckoo's Nest (1975) 62, 316
On the Waterfront (1954) 209, 217, 380
One from the Heart (1982) 84
One for the Money (2012) 266
One Minute to Zero (1952) 240
Only Angels Have Wings (1939) 16
Ophuls, Marcel (director) 194, 195
Osment, Haley Joel (actor) 116
The Others (2002) 307
Out of Africa (1985) 56, 57
Out of the Darkness (1985 TV movie) 44
Out of the Past (1947) 229, 251
Owun Alun (screenwriter) 286
The Ox-Bow Incident (1943) 12
PM Entertainment (production company) 157, 173-175, 175
Pacino, Al (actor) 260
Pakula, Alan J. (producer/director) 340
Pal, George (producer) 9, 118
Pan Am Pictures 179
Panic in the Streets (1950) 54
The Parallax View (1974) 83, 99
Paramount Pictures (motion picture studio) 63, 79, 80, 81, 96, 252, 307-308, 309, 310, 348; Gulf + Western 79, 96
Paranormal Activity franchise 341; *Paranormal Activity 2* (2010) 202
Paretsky, Sara (writer) 252
Parker, Robert B. (writer) 251, 267, 280
Parks, Gordon (director) 128

The Passion of the Christ (2004) 107, 296
Pat Garrett & Billy the Kid (1973), 78, 99-100
Patric, Jason (actor) 307
Patton (1970) 82, 83, 209, 248
The Pawnbroker (1964) 319
Payne, Alexander (screenwriter/director) 310
Paxton, Bill (producer/actor) 172
The Peacemaker (1997) 118
Pearl Harbor (2001) 90, 91, 92, 93, 123-124, 246, 248
Peary, Gerald (director) 318
Peckinpah, Sam 34-40, 51, 54, 62, 68-76, 77, 78, 98, 120, 279, 340
Penn, Arthur (director) 13, 33, 38-39, 40, 98
The Perfect Storm (2000) 327, 329
Persky, Bill (screenwriter/producer/director) 215-216
"Philip Marlowe" 252, 255, 264, 267-268, 269, 270, 274, 279, 282
Pickup on South Street (1953) 29
Pinocchio (1940) 1
Piper, Brett (screenwriter/director) 177-178
Piranha 3DD (2012) 348
Pirates of the Caribbean franchise 90, 91, 92, 107, 122, 314; *Pirates of the Caribbean: The Curse of the Black Pearl* (2003) 90-91; *Pirates of the Caribbean: On Stranger Tides* (2011) 95, 102, 218, 312; use of CGI 327
Pitt, Brad (actor) 205
Pixar (production company) 207
Planet of the Apes franchise 132: *Battle for the Planet of the Apes* (1973) 132; *Planet of the Apes* (1968) 82, 83, 98; *Rise of the Planet of the Apes* (2011) 95, 102, 312
Planet Terror see *Grindhouse*
Plater, Alan (screenwriter) 285, 287
Platoon (1986) 243, 245, 248
Poetics 351
Poison Ivy 2 (1996 DTV feature)
Point Blank (1967) 37, 62, 98, 99, 120
Point Break (1991) 172
Polanski, Roman (director) 33, 98
The Polar Express (2004) 327, 336
Pollack, Sydney (director) 33, 34, 50, 54, 56-57, 98
Poltergeist (1982) 85, 86, 102, 113
The Pope of Greenwich Village (1984) 296
Pork Chop Hill (1959) 240
The Postman Always Rings Twice (1946) 270, 272
The Postman Always Rings Twice (1981) 184, 272
Powaqqatsi (1988) 110
Powell, Michael (screenwriter/director) 191

Prayer of the Rollerboys (1991) 173
Predator (1987) 87, 88
The President's Analyst (1967) 376
Price, Vincent (actor) 271
Priest (2011) 95, 102
Prince of Persia: The Sands of Time (2010) 104, 329, 334
The Princess Bride (1987) 145
The Professionals (1966) 50, 376
Project X (2012), 341, 373
Promark Entertainment (distribution company) 166
Prometheus (2012) 338
The Proposal (2010) 94
Psycho (1960) 37, 222
Public Speaking (2010) 191
Pulp Fiction (1994) 196, 197, 198, 199-200, 304, 351
The Punisher (2004) 322
Puppet Master (1989 DTV feature) 158
The Purple Heart (1944) 238
A Question of Honor (1982 TV movie) 44, 260
Quinn, Anthony (actor) 25, 377
RKO (motion picture studio) 7, 79, 213
Raft, George (actor) 228
The Radioland Murders (1994) 110-111
Rafelson, Bob (director) 272
Raging Bull (1980) 62, 83, 191, 194-195, 197, 198
Raimi, Sam (director) 233
"Rambo" franchise 89; *First Blood* (1992) 89, 102, 248; *Rambo: First Blood, Part 2* (1985) 89, 244, 245, 248; *Rambo III* (1988) 89
Rayfiel, David (screenwriter) 54
Rayner, Richard Piers (illustrator) 275, 282
Reagan, Ronald (politician/actor) 228, 244
Rear Window (1954) 229
Red (2010) 202
Red Dawn (1984) 54, 120, 244
Red Eye (2005) 207
Red Heat (1988) 89
Red River (1948) 7
Red Rock West (1992) 182, 183, 184
Red Sands (2009) 247
The Red Shoes (1948) 191
Redacted (2007) 247
Redford, Robert (actor) 51, 54, 56-57, 83
Reed, Oliver (actor) 326
Reed, Rex (film critic) 320
Reefer Madness see *Tell Your Children*
Reeves, Keanu (actor) 87-88, 172
Reflections in a Golden Eye (1968) 59, 62
Reisz, Karel (director) 98
Remember the Titans (2000) 91
Remsen, Bert (actor) 174

Rendition (2007) 106, 247
Renoir, Jean (director) 8
Reservoir Dogs (1992) 190, 191, 196-197, 198, 199-200
Retreat, Hell! (1952) 240
Return of the Dragon (1973) 130
Ride Lonesome (1959) 18
Ride the High Country (1962) 34, 68
The Rifleman (1958-1963 TV series) 34
Rio Bravo (1959) 16, 201
Rio Lobo (1970) 16, 201
Riot in Cell Block 11 (1954) 7
The Rise and Fall of Legs Diamond (1960) 18
Risky Business (1983) 91
Ritt, Martin (director) 98
Roach, Hal (producer) 8
Road Ends (1997) 173-174, 175
Road to Perdition (1998 graphic novel) 251, 276, 279, 281-282
Road to Perdition (2002) 109, 118, 276, 281-282, 307
The Road to Ruin (1934)
Robbins, Lance (production company executive) 148, 152
Roberts, Ben (producer) 258
Roberts, Julia (actress) 88
Roberts, Pernell (actor) 19
Roberts, William (screenwriter) 22
Robertson, Cliff (actor) 379
Robin Hood (2010) 104, 122
Robinson, Edward G. (actor) 44
The Rock (1996) 91, 92, 123, 188
The Rockford Files (1974-1980 TV series) 49, 252, 258, 260, 282
Rocky (1976) 101, 202
Rocky Balboa (2006) 202
Rodriguez, Robert (screenwriter/director) 133, 198-198, 200, 326
Roeg, Nicholas (director) 98
Rohner, Clayton (actor) 148
Roizman, Owen (cinematographer) 45, 83
Rolling Thunder (1977) 243
Romeo and Juliet (1968) 81
Romero, George (director) 162
Rosemary's Baby (1968) 81
Rough Stuff aka *Mr. Nanny* (1993) 175
Rounders (1998) 182, 183
Roundtree, Richard (actor) 175
Rules of Engagement (2000) 247
Russell, Jane (actress) 26-27
Russell, Ken (director) 193
Russell, Kurt (actor) 326
Rothrock, Cynthia (actress) 158
Ruggles, Wesley (director) 330

Russo, Renee (actress) 88
Ryan, Robert (actor) 240-241
S.W.A.T. (2003) 207, 303
Saban Entertainment (production company) 148, 152
Safe House (2012) 372
Sahara (1943) 238, 239
Saint, Eva Marie (actress) 380
Salkind, Alexander (producer) 286
Salkind, Ilya (producer) 286
"Sam Spade" 267, 269
Sanchez, Jaime (actor) 36
The Sand Pebbles (1966) 7, 82, 242, 248
The Sands of Iwo Jima (1949) 239, 248
Sanford, Isabel (actress) 177
Sapan, Josh (TV network executive) 220
Sara, Mia (actress) 148
Sarafian, Richard C. (director) 120
Sarandon, Chris (producer/actor) 174
The Satan Bug (1965) 54
Saul, Oscar (screenwriter) 35
Saving Private Ryan (1998) 85, 87, 116, 194, 245-246, 248
Saw (2004) 161, 162, 296
Sayles, John (screenwriter/director) 199
The Scalphunters (1968) 34, 376
Scarecrow (1973) 100
Scarface (1983) 121
Schaffner, Franklin J. (director) 82, 98
Scheider, Roy (actor) 45, 83, 260
Schiffer, Michael (screenwriter) 92
Schifrin, Lalo (composer) 83
Schindler's List (1993) 87, 115-116, 194
Schlesinger, John (director) 98
Schneider, Maria (actress) 59-61
Schoesdack, Ernest B. (director) 330
Schoonmaker, Thelma (editor) 83
Schrader, Paul (screenwriter/director) 99, 217
Schwarzenegger, Arnold (actor) 87, 89
Scorsese, Martin (director) 33, 82, 84, 93, 99, 141, 182, 190-195, 196, 197, 198, 199, 200, 201, 217, 297, 299, 300, 301, 309, 333, 340, 348
Scott, Randolph (actor) 18, 19
Scott, Ridley (director) 122-123, 326, 339
Scott, Tony (director) 93, 122, 123, 196, 244
Scream 4 (2011) 95, 217
The Searchers (1956) 14
Seabiscuit (2003) 202, 207
Secretariat (2010) 202
Self, David (screenwriter) 275
Selznick, Brian (writer) 348
Selznick, David O. (producer) 330
Serenade (1956) 271
Serenity (2005) 233 see also *Firefly*

The Sergeant (1968) 59
Sgt. Kabukiman N.Y.P.D. (1991) 156
Sergeant Rutledge (1960) 15
Sergeant York (1941) 248
Serkis, Andy (actor) 328
Serling, Rod (screenwriter) 112
Seven Men from Now (1956) 18
Seven Days in May (1964) 83
The Seven Samurai (1954) 22, 38
The Seven-Ups (1973) 48, 260, 262
Sex and the City 2 (2010) 94
sexploitation movies 128, 130
Shaft (1971) 128, 131; John Shaft character 280, 282
Shaft (2000) 266
The Shaggy Dog (1959) 1
Shaloub, Tony (actor) 256
Shadow of a Doubt (1943) 306
Shalit, Gene (film critic) 320
Shane (1953) 13
Sharif, Omar (actor) 284, 285
Shaoline Soccer (2004) 322
Shattered Glass (2003) 316
Shaw Brothers, The (producers) 130, 196
Shaw, Robert (actor) 115
She Wore a Yellow Ribbon (1949) 216
Shelley, Mary (writer) 6
Shelton, Ron (screenwriter/director) 122
Shenandoah (1965) 242
Sheridan, Ann (actress) 228
Sherlock Holmes franchise 252; *Sherlock Holmes* (2009) 88; *Sherlock Holmes: A Game of Shadows* (2011) 312
Shine the Light (2008) 191
The Shining (1980) 80, 325, 326
shockumentaries 133
Showgirls (1995) 90
Showtime (pay-TV channel) 161, 163, 218
Shrek franchise 109; *Shrek 2* (2004) 297
Shutter Island (2010) 191, 333
The Siege (1998) 247
Sickner, Roy N. (screenwriter) 35
The Siege at Trencher's Farm (1969 novel) 63, 64-68, 70, 72, 73-74, 75, 76, 77
Siegel, Don (director) 7-8, 98
Silliphant, Sterling (screenwriter) 82
Silva, Henry (actor) 177
Silver, Joel (producer) 85, 87-88, 91
Simmons, Richard Alan (screenwriter) 287
Sin City (2005) 200, 326
Six Degrees of Separation (1993) 91
Skin Game (1971) 50
The Silence of the Lambs (1991) 39
Silva, Henry (actor) 19

Silver, Joel (producer) 85, 306
Simpson, Don (producer) 90, 123
Sinatra, Frank (actor) 8
Sinatra, Nancy (singer) 30
Siskel, Gene (film critic) 318, 320-324
Sky Captain and the World of Tomorrow (2004) 326
Slaughter (1972) 129
Slightly Scarlet (1956) 271
Small, Michael (composer) 83
Small Soldiers (1998) 86
A Small Town in Texas (1976) 129
Smell-O-Vision (special effect) 345
Smith, Will (actor) 91
Smokey and the Bandit (1977) 101, 129
Smokey Bites the Dust (1981) 129
The Smurfs (2011) 311
Snakes on a Plane (2006) 184, 186
Sneak Previews (1975-1989 TV series) 321, 324; see also *At the Movies with Gene Siskel and Roger Ebert* (1982-1986 TV series) 321; *Siskel and Ebert At the Movies* (1986-2010 TV series) 321
Snow White and the Seven Dwarfs (1937) 1
Snipes, Wesley (actor) 88
Snyder, Zack (director) 233, 281, 327
The Social Network (2010) 202
Some Like It Hot (1959) 27, 222
Son of Kong (1933) 213
The Sons of Katie Elder (1965) 33
Sony (motion picture studio) 309, 310
Sorcerer (1977) 84, 301
Sorkin, Aaron (screenwriter) 202
The Sound of Music (1965) 82
South Beach (1992) 177, 181
Spartacus (1960) 41, 209, 218, 331, 332, 333
Spectacor (production company) 157, 165-169, 203
Speed (1995) 229, 284-285, 287
Spider-Man franchise 107, 233-234; *The Amazing Spider-Man* (2012) 233, 234, 348; *Spider-Man* (2002) 233; *Spider-Man 2* (2004) 297; use of CGI 327
Spielberg, Steven (producer/director) 1, 85, 87, 88, 91, 99, 107-109, 112-118, 182, 193-194, 209, 217, 218, 245, 246, 295, 301, 309, 328, 333
Spillane, Mickey (writer) 29, 251, 255, 275-283
splatter movies 128, 130, 131, 157-158, 161
Spy Kids 4: All the Time in the World (2011) 95, 311
Stallone, Sylvester (actor) 88, 89, 102
Stanwyck, Barbara (actress) 209
The Star Chamber (1983) 120

Star Trek franchise 102; 1966-1969 TV series 86; *Star Trek II: The Wrath of Khan* (1982) 326
Star Wars franchise 108, 109, 110, 111, 163, 338; *The Empire Strikes Back* (1980) 101, 110, 111; *Return of the Jedi* aka *Star Wars: Episode VI – Return of the Jedi* (1983) 101, 111; *Star Wars* aka *Star Wars: Episode IV – A New Hope* (1977) 1, 80, 85, 99, 108, 110, 112, 114, 118, 121, 123, 209, 316; *Star Wars: Episode I – The Phantom Menace* (1999) 108, 111; exhibitor commitment 355; *Star Wars: Episode III – Revenge of the Sith* (2005) 108-110, 206, 208; *Star Wars: Episode II – Attack of the Clones* (2002) 111; *Star Wars: The Clone Wars* (TV series) 111-112; use of CGI 327
The Steel Helmet (1951) 240
Stevens, George (director) 13
Stevens, Stella (actress) 177
Stewart, James (actor) 15-16, 19, 20
The Sting (1973) 56
Stone, Emma (actress) 234
Stone, Jr. N.B. (screenwriter) 34
Stone, Oliver (director) 106, 196, 243
The Story of G. I. Joe (1945) 239
Stout, Rex (writer) 279
Straight Time (1978) 98
Straw Dogs (1971) 59, 62-63, 69-78, 99
The Street Fighter (1974) 130
Sturges, John (director) 20-25
The Sugarland Express (1974) 85, 113-114, 114-115
The Sum of All Fears (2002) 308
Sunset Boulevard (1950) 183, 289
Super 8 (2011) 102, 104, 218
Super Fly (1972) 128
Superman Returns (2006) 334
Superman: The Movie (1978) 80, 101
Susskind, David (producer) 49, 69
Sutton, Phoef (screenwriter) 122
Swayze, Patrick (actor) 172
Sweet Sweetback's Baadasssss Song (1971) 128
Swept Away (2002) 299
Swick, King (screenwriter) 169
Swick, Marly (screenwriter) 169
Swordfish (2001) 87
Syriana (2005) 208, 247
THX 1138 (1971) 81, 99, 109-110
Take 2 Productions (production company) 175, 177-180
The Tall T (1957) 18, 19
Tarantino, Quentin (screenwriter/director) 92, 133, 190-191, 195, 232, 252, 304

Tassi, Paul (media journalist) 360, 363, 365, 366, 367, 368, 369, 370-371, 372, 373, 374
Taxi Driver (1976) 62, 100, 194, 195
Taxi to the Dark Side (2007) 247
Taylor, Robert (actor) 21, 22, 23
Taylor, Rod (actor) 63
Tell Your Children (1936) aka *Reefer Madness* 127
The Ten Commandments (1956) 210-211
The Terminal (2003) 118, 194
Terminator franchise 89; *Terminator 2: Judgment Day* (1991) 89; *Terminator: Salvation* (2009) 122
The Texas Chain Saw Massacre franchise 154; *The Texas Chain Saw Massacre* (1975) 162; *The Texas Chainsaw Massacre 2* (1986) 154
Them! (1954) 8-9
Thelma & Louise (1991) 122
They Shoot Horses, Don't They? (1969) 96
They Were Expendable (1945) 13, 216, 239
Thieves Like Us (1974) 114
The Thin Red Line (1998) 246
The Thing from Another World (1951) 7, 306
The Third Man (1949) 229
Thir13een Ghosts (2001) 87
Thirty Seconds Over Tokyo (1944) 248
This Gun For Hire (1942) 209
The Thomas Crown Affair (1968) 229
The Thomas Crown Affair (1999) 229
Thor (2011) 95, 102, 218, 312
Thorn/EMI 159
Thorne, Geoffrey (actor) 174
Thornton, Billy Bob (actor) 206
3-D 108, 195, 338-339, 345, 346, 347-350; ticket surcharges 356, 365
Three Days of the Condor (1975) 56, 83
300 (2006) 281, 327, 329-330, 333
Three Kings (1999) 245
The Three Musketeers (1973) 286
3:10 to Yuma (1957) 17-18, 21
3:10 to Yuma (2007) 106
Three the Hard Way (1974) 129
Thunder and Lightning (1977) 129
Thunderball (1965) 30
Thurman, Uma (actress) 198
Tidyman, Ernest (screenwriter) 45, 47, 128, 260
Tierno, Michael (script analyst/film writer) 351-353
The Time Machine (1960) 86
The Time Machine (2002) 86, 87
The Tingler (1959) 127
Titanic (1997) 107, 210, 309

To Hell and Back (1955) 248
To Kill a Mockingbird (1962) 98
Top Gun (1986) 90, 91, 92, 123, 244, 245, 248, 305
Tora! Tora! Tora! (1970) 124, 248, 331, 332
Total Recall (1991) 39, 89
The Towering Inferno (1974) 80, 285
The Town (2010) 202
Town Without Pity (1961) 314
Towne, Robert (screenwriter) 82, 92
The Toxic Avenger (1984) 154, 156
Trackdown: Finding the Goodbar Killer (1983 TV movie) 44, 260
The Train (1964) 314, 332
Transformers franchise 312; *Transformers* (2007) 86, 124; *Transformers: Dark of the Moon* (2011) 95, 102, 103, 311; *Transformers: Revenge of the Fallen* (2009) 124
Truffaut, Francois (film writer/screenwriter/director) 196
The Treasure of the Sierra Madre (1948) 189, 216, 221
The Tree of Life (2011) 310, 311
Troma Entertainment (production company) 155-156, 158-159, 161
Tron (1982) 326
Tron Legacy (2010) 104, 325
Trouble Man (1972) 129
Troy (2004) 329, 345
Truck Turner (1974) 129
True Grit (1969) 33, 78
True Grit (2010) 78
True Romance (1993) 196
Truitt, Brian (journalist) 344, 346
Turner, Lana (actress) 272, 277
20,000 Leagues Under the Sea (1954) 1
The Twenty-Year Death (2012 novel) 252
20th Century Fox 4, 44, 46, 49, 79, 80, 81-82, 101, 114, 164-165; CBS/Fox video distribution 159, 172, 262, 309, 310, 347, 362, 365
12 O'Clock High (1949) 240, 330
Twice Upon a Time (1983) 111
Twilight (1998) 252
The Twilight Saga: Breaking Dawn – Part 1 (2011) 312
The Twilight Saga: Breaking Dawn – Part 2 (2012) 231, 347
The Twilight Saga: Eclipse (2010) 94, 104
Twilight Zone: The Movie (1983) 108
Twilight's Last Gleaming (1977) 243
Twister (1996) 86, 87, 122, 327, 329
2 Fast 2 Furious (2003) 207
Two Rode Together (1961) 14-15

2001: A Space Odyssey (1968) 41, 62, 98, 99, 209, 229, 315, 325
Tycoon (1947) 214
Tyler, Liv (actress) 91
Tyler Perry's Good Deeds (2012) 342
U-571 (2000) 246
Ulzana's Raid (1972) 34, 50, 242
Uncommon Valor (1983) 244
The Undefeated (1969) 33
Understanding Movies (1972 book) 119
Underworld Awakening (2012) 291, 348, 373
United Artists (motion picture studio) 79
Universal Pictures (motion picture studio) 9, 100, 114, 203, 205, 206, 207; DVD strategy 160
Universal Soldier (1992) 89
Unforgettable (1996) 182
Unstoppable (2010) 122
Used Cars (1980) 114
The Usual Suspects (1995) 204
VCR 154, 156, 158, 224, 362
Vajna, Andy (producer) 85, 88
Valley of Gwangi (1969) 50
Van Cleef, Lee (actor) 19
Van Damm, Jean-Claude (actor) 89
VanderMer, Jeff (writer) 256
Vanishing Point (1971) 120
Vaughn, Robert (actor) 23
Ventura, Jesse (actor) 88
Vera Cruz (1954) 216
Verbinski, Gore (director) 122
Verhoeven, Paul (director) 89
Verne, Jules (writer) 6
Vernon, John (actor) 37
Vertigo (1958) 206
video rental business 156-157
video stores 156-157
videocassette recorder see VCR
Vigilante Fever (1976) 129
The Vikings (1958) 216
The Virginian (1929) 12
von Trier, Lars (screenwriter/director) 342
The Vow (2012) 372
Wahlberg, Mark (actor) 172
Wake Island (1942) 238
A Walk in the Sun (1945) 129
Walk the Line (2005) 208
Walking Tall (1973) 129-130
Wallach, Eli (actor) 23
The Walt Disney Company 188, 310, 362; Walt Disney's World of Color 1; Disney, Walt 1-5; Disney World 2-4; Disneyland 2-3
War Horse (2011) 108, 309, 311
War Hunt (1960) 56

The War of the Worlds (1953) 6, 9, 209
War of the Worlds (2005) 118, 206, 208
The War Wagon (1967) 33
Ward, Simon (actor) 287
Warfield, David W. (screenwriter) 182
Warlock (1959) 13
Warner Bros. (motion picture studio) 4, 7, 41-42, 54, 79, 80-81, 96, 163, 206, 310; Warner Communications 4; Warner, Jack (studio executive) 79; Kinney National Service 79, 96; DVD strategy 160, 181; Warner Premiere 160, 181; TV production 251-252; introduction of sound 362
Warner, David (actor) 73
Watchmen (2009) 134, 281
Watermelon Man (1970) 128
Watson, Ian (screenwriter) 116
Watson, Jack (actor) 285
The Way We Were (1973) 56
Wayne, John (actor/director) 14, 15, 16, 33, 216, 217, 241, 263
We Are Marshall (2006) 202
We Own the Night (2007) 106
We Were Soldiers (2002) 246, 305-306; differences with *We Were Soldiers Once... And Young: Ia Drang: The Battle that Changed the War in Vietnam* (1992 book) 305-306
Weathers, Carl (actor) 88
Weaver, Dennis (actor) 113
Webb, Jack (actor/producer/director) 44-45
Webb, Mark (director) 233
Webber, Steven (actor) 295
Wedlock aka *Deadlock* (1991 DTV feature) 166
Weiner, Matthew (producer/screenwriter/director) 274
The Weinstein Company (production company) 134, 181, 290, 291; Weinstein, Harvey (producer) 206, 291
Welles, Halsted (screenwriter) 17
Welles, Orson (screenwriter/producer/director) 119
Werker, Alfred L. (director) 45
West Side Story (1961) 7, 216
Westbound (1959) 18
The Westerner (1960 TV series) 34
Wexler, Haskell (cinematographer) 83
What Happened? Bitter Hollywood Tales from the Front Line (2002 book) 90
What Price Glory? (1926) 248
What's Eating Gilbert Grape? (1993) 92
When Worlds Collide (1951) 9, 118

Which Lie Did I Tell? More Adventures in the Screen Trade (2002 book) 330
White Lightning (1973) 129
White Line Fever (1975) 129
Whitty, Stephen (film critic) 122, 214, 215, 219, 220, 222, 263-266, 313, 322, 324
Who Framed Roger Rabbit? (1988) 86, 109, 252
Who'll Stop the Rain? (1978) 243
Who's That Knocking on My Door? (1967) 196
Wibur, Crane (screenwriter) 45
Widmark, Richard (actor) 23
Wild at Heart (1990) 92
The Wild Bunch (1969) 34, 35-40, 63, 74, 78, 83, 98, 99, 100, 120, 209, 218, 235
Wilder, Billy (director) 183, 189, 221
Willard (1971) 131
Williams, Charles (writer) 274
Williams, Gordon (writer) 63-68, 78
Williams, Grant (actor) 10
Williams, Robin (actor) 115
Williamson, Fred (actor/producer) 177
Willis, Bruce (actor) 39, 49, 87, 88, 91
Willow (1988) 110
Wilson, Tom (actor) 150
Winchester '73 (1950) 20
The Wind and the Lion (1975) 54
Windtalkers (2002) 246
A Wing and a Prayer (1944) 238
Wings (1927) 237
Winter, Ariel S. (writer) 252-256
Wise, Robert (director) 7
Wives Beware (1932) 223
The Wizard of Oz (1939) 79
Wizards (1977) 336
Woo, John (director) 279
Wood, Natalie (actress) 14
Wyler, William (director) 13, 330, 332
X: The Man with the X-Ray Eyes (1963) 143
X-Men franchise: *X-Men: First Class* (2011) 95, 102; *X2: X-Men United* (2003) 207; use of CGI 327
Yates, Peter (director) 33, 45, 98
Yogi Bear (2010) 161, 325
York, Michael (actor) 287
"You Will Never Kill Piracy and Piracy Will Never Kill You" (2012 online article) 360
York, Susannah (actress) 28
The Young Lions (1958) 54, 241
Young Sherlock Holmes (1985) 114, 326
Zachariah (1971) 50
Zadora, Pia (actress) 271
Zaillian, Steve (screenwriter) 93, 115
Zane Grey Theater (1956-1961 TV series) 34

Zanuck, Darryl (studio executive) 81, 331
Zanuck, Richard (producer/studio executive) 46, 80, 81-82, 114, 115, 262
Zemeckis, Robert (director) 114, 118, 326, 327-328
Zulu (1964) 242

www.ingramcontent.com/pod-product-compliance
Lightning Source LLC
Chambersburg PA
CBHW071943220426
43662CB00009B/976